The Amish
and the State

Amishmen leaving prison for refusing to send their children to public high schools in the early fifties. Lancaster New Era *photo by* Ed Sachs

The
Amish
and
the State

Edited by
Donald B. Kraybill

The Johns Hopkins University Press
Baltimore and London

Published in cooperation with the Center for American Places,
Harrisonburg, Virginia.

© 1993 The Johns Hopkins University Press
All rights reserved
Printed in the United States of America on acid-free paper

The Johns Hopkins University Press
2715 North Charles Street
Baltimore, Maryland 21218-4319
The Johns Hopkins Press Ltd., London

Library of Congress Cataloging-in-Publication Data

The Amish and the state / edited by Donald B. Kraybill.
       p. cm.
    Includes bibliographical references and index.
    ISBN 0-8018-4468-1 (alk. paper).—ISBN 0-8018-4469-X (pbk. : alk. paper)
    1. Amish—History—20th century.   2. Church and state—United States—
History—20th century.   3. Church and state—Canada—History—20th century.
4. Freedom of religion—United States—History—20th century.   5. Freedom of
religion—Canada—History—20th century.   I. Kraybill, Donald B.
BX8129.A6A45   1993
322'.1'088287—dc20   92-31568

A catalog record for this book is available from the British Library.

For *John A. Hostetler,*
champion of religious liberty

Contents

Preface and Acknowledgments

"Congress shall make no law respecting an establishment of religion, or prohibiting the free exercise thereof." So begins the First Amendment to the Bill of Rights. A small religious minority in a nation exceeding 250 million people, the Old Order Amish have stirred a remarkable array of controversies with the state in the twentieth century. Seeking to practice their religious convictions faithfully, they have tested the legal fabric of a democratic society. The Amish have pressed the limits and definitions of religious pluralism. Does the free exercise of religion stretch to the cultural margins and afford liberty even to those who refuse to become modern?

Progeny of the Radical Reformation in sixteenth-century Europe, the Amish and their Anabaptist forebears faced severe persecution, even death, for practicing their religious beliefs. Indeed, the opportunity to practice their faith, "unmolested and undisturbed," was one of the factors that enticed them to the New World in the years following 1727. Conflict with the U.S. government in the eighteenth and nineteenth centuries was primarily confined to Amish objections to participation in American wars. Clashes between the state and the Amish spiraled, however, in the twentieth century as the regulatory power of government grew, accompanied by the ever-increasing efficiency and power of enforcement. Apart from European persecution in the early days, the middle half of the twentieth century (1925–75) has generated more conflict with government than any other period in the three hundred years (1693–1993) of Amish history.

Although conflict has strained goodwill on both sides, the trail of Amish-state controversies in North America testifies to two enduring virtues. On the one hand, the conflicts underscore the tenacity of the Amish as they continue to practice their religious convictions regardless of legal consequence or political expediency—a scarce virtue in a time of polite and spineless religious piety. On the other hand, the clash of convictions has fulfilled the high vision of the nation's founders, who hoped to safeguard the liberty of religious minorities. But despite repeated skirmishes with the state, the Amish have enjoyed a remarkable freedom to practice their faith, even though refusing to fight in America's wars. Some have been imprisoned and others have been fined; but none have been tortured or killed, and few have been forced to migrate on account of their religious convictions. In the face of many confrontations, the American character has been rather benevolent and hospitable to these stubborn folks who refuse to embrace modern ways. All things considered, these descendants of the Radical Reformation have fared well at the hands of the American Caesar.

The outcomes of the controversies charted in this volume have preserved the freedom of the Amish to practice their religious faith unmolested by the state; but, just as important, the legal decisions have safeguarded the rights of other American citizens to exercise their faith according to conviction. Although Amish devotion raises unusual and sometimes odd legal questions, these issues have contributed to a richer and expanded understanding of religious liberty. In all of these ways, we are indebted both to the Amish and to the judicial interpreters of the First Amendment—the guardians of religious freedom in the twentieth century.

The contributors to this volume were invited to prepare original essays in their fields of expertise. They conducted research and crafted essays that elucidate the major and significant arenas of contention between the Amish and the state in the twentieth century. Chapter 1 provides an introduction to the Old Order Amish of North America as well as a conceptual framework for interpreting the confrontations ensuing between the Amish and the state. Following a synopsis of the Amish view of the state in Chapter 2, chapters 3–10 focus on substantive areas of conflict as well as on some organizational responses. Chapter 11 assesses the role and influence of sympathetic outsiders in many of the legal battles with the state. Amish interaction with the Canadian government is charted in Chapter 12. Chapter 13, the final chapter, evaluates the meaning of significant Amish legal cases for First Amendment issues and for the future of religious liberty in the United States.

It is a pleasure to dedicate this book to John A. Hostetler, whose scholarship and counsel have aided many of the authors as they conducted research and prepared their chapters for *The Amish and the State*. A long-time student of Amish society, Hostetler has worked tirelessly for the preservation of religious liberty for the

Amish and other religious minorities. An active participant in the National Committee for Amish Religious Freedom, he served as an expert witness when the U.S. Supreme Court decided the landmark *Wisconsin v. Yoder* case. Hostetler's *Amish Society,* now in its fourth edition, has long served as the definitive ethnography of Amish life. Thus, it is fitting to celebrate John A. Hostetler's productive scholarship and advocacy of religious freedom with the publication of this volume.

The authors of the various chapters have graciously consented to my efforts to streamline their essays in order to orchestrate them into a coherent whole. Each contributor necessarily contributed much time and effort, as well as incurring related expenses; for all this, I am grateful. It was a delight to work with George F. Thompson, president of the Center for American Places, who served as the sponsoring editor for this book. He provided counsel, encouragement, and support for the project from inception to fruition. In addition to preparing Chapter 10, Elizabeth Place undertook the detailed work of annotating the listing of legal cases and preparing their proper citations. I am especially indebted to David Luthy, director of the Heritage Historical Library in Aylmer, Ontario, who painstakingly read all the chapters and offered many pages of constructive criticism. Luthy's generous labor of love has greatly enhanced the accuracy and clarity of the entire collection. I also thank Nancy L. Gaines for granting unlimited access to her private collection of source materials.

It was a pleasure to work with Johns Hopkins University Press manuscript editor Carol Ehrlich; her editorial counsel and care greatly enhanced these pages. Anne E. Weidner provided able and substantial editorial assistance throughout the project and organized both the References and the Index. Brenda Troutman in her always cheerful and efficient manner performed the many rounds of word processing and coordinated other aspects of the work as well. Elizabethtown College provided ample support through a faculty research grant and through the auspices of the Young Center for the Study of Anabaptist and Pietist Groups. I am deeply grateful to all these and others who have contributed to the preservation of religious liberty through their assistance with this endeavor.

A Note on Sources

Single source citations appear in the text in author/date format. Multiple source citations appear in appropriate endnotes in author/date format. Materials such as interviews, press reports, correspondence, and informal newsletters appear in endnotes. Author/date references in the text and endnotes are keyed to the References at the end of the book. The full title of a legal case is given in the text with its date the first time it is cited in a chapter. Subsequent references to a case within a chapter employ a key word in the title—for example, *Yoder*. An annotated listing of the significant legal cases mentioned in the text, with proper legal citations, is provided in the Appendix.

The Amish
and the State

An Amish bishop urges a Pennsylvania Senate committee in 1990 to support a bill that would recognize lay midwives. Wide World Photos

CHAPTER ONE

Negotiating with Caesar

Donald B. Kraybill

In this overview, Donald B. Kraybill identifies the salient cultural values and patterns of social organization of the Amish of North America. He suggests that conflicts between the Amish and the state can be interpreted within the theoretical framework of bargaining and negotiating. The state, the foremost agent of modernity, and traditional Amish society are engaged in a process of cultural negotiation on a variety of issues that straddle the border between modern and traditional ways.

In 1938, an Amish leader disturbed by compulsory education laws wrote to Supreme Court Justice Hugo L. Black, "Is there any clause whereby we can live a Christian faith and still be law abiding people?"[1]

These aspirations of the Amish heart—to *practice* their Christian faith without infringement and to *abide* by the laws of the land—undergird their relations with the state. The compatibility of these twin hopes began to strain in the twentieth century as the laws of the land soared in number and scope and as modern expressions of religion veered away from Amish ways. Trying to reconcile these hopes, the Amish found themselves negotiating with Caesar over a host of issues. And despite the irritation and the energy required for bargaining, the Amish were negotiating—albeit sometimes from prison—but they were not burning at the stake or losing their heads to the executioner's sword as their forebears had done in Europe.

The tentacles of government have grown dramatically in the twentieth century along two dimensions: regulatory controls and social welfare functions, formerly provided by private organizations or left undone. The regulatory apparatus of government—designed to protect the rights of individuals as well as the common good—soon stretched from cradle to grave. Regulations touched abortion and embalming as well as seatbelt use, product labels, workplace safety, sanitation, environmental pollution, and thousands of other concerns. The welfare functions, gradually assumed by the state, created an enormous appetite for new revenues and hence a proliferation of taxes—income, Social Security, real estate, sales, workers' compensation, unemployment insurance, school, and a variety of voluntary use taxes.

Ironically, the state's desire to protect the rights of citizens as well as the corporate welfare threatened the prerogative of some minorities to exercise their religion freely as safeguarded in the First Amendment to the Bill of Rights. Conflicts between the Amish and government agencies proliferated as the state's regulatory power, usually based on noble ideals, intruded into terrain that the Amish considered religious. The wide-ranging conflicts with civil authorities included vaccinations, zoning, compulsory education, Social Security, stabling horses in towns, sanitation facilities, manure pollution, and slow-moving vehicle codes, to name but a few.[2]

Government efforts to protect both individual rights and the public welfare created problems for the Amish. To protect infants, certain states required certification of midwives, thus infringing on some Amish families who preferred home deliveries aided by unlicensed assistants. To promote safety on the highway, many states required the installation of slow-moving vehicle emblems on Amish carriages—violating the religious convictions of certain Amish groups. Rising levels of compulsory education threatened to unravel the very core of Amish life. To protect workers at construction sites, federal regulations required the use of hard hats. This ruling obstructed the wearing of traditional hats by Amishmen, a practice which over the years had signaled Amish identity.

These and similar conflicts marked the growing encroachment of Caesar into sacred Amish terrain. The essays in this book chronicle the negotiations that ensued between Caesar and the Amish as they struggled over the contested terrain, stranded between the ever-changing lines of church and state. However, before we explore these negotiations, a word about the Amish. From where do they originate? How are they organized, and what do they believe?

The Amish Story

The year 1993 celebrates the tricentennial of Amish life. Extinct in their European homeland, they live today in more than two hundred settlements across North America.[3] Their story stretches back to the Protestant Reformation in sixteenth-century Europe. Youthful reformers in Zurich, Switzerland, outraged religious authorities by rebaptizing one another in January of 1525. The rebaptism of adults was punishable by death. Previously baptized as infants in the Catholic church, the radicals were soon dubbed "Anabaptists," or rebaptizers, by their opponents. Baptism, in the Anabaptist view, was only meaningful and valid after adults made a voluntary confession of faith. The dissidents insisted that the teaching of the New Testament superseded the Zurich City Council's authority over religious matters such as baptism.[4] The Anabaptists thus argued for a separation of church and state, which would rend the fabric of sixteenth-century society.

Civil and religious authorities were threatened by the rapid spread of Anabaptist groups, and Anabaptist hunters soon stalked the land. The first martyr was drowned in 1527. Over the next few decades, thousands of Anabaptists burned at the stake, drowned in rivers, starved in prisons, or lost their heads to the executioner's sword. A twelve-hundred-page *Martyrs Mirror*, first published in Dutch in 1660 and later in German and English, records the carnage of the bloody theater (Braght 1968).

The Anabaptists sought to follow Jesus in daily life—loving enemies, forgiving insults, and turning the other cheek. Some Anabaptist groups resorted to violence, but many repudiated force and resolved to live peaceably, even with adversaries. The flames of execution tested their simple faith in the power of suffering love. Some recanted, but many died for their faith. Obedient to the words of Jesus, they yielded themselves to God's will, even in the face of torture. The historic themes of submission and obedience, lodged in the martyr stories, undergird Amish values even today.

Harsh persecution pushed many Anabaptists underground and into rural hideaways, and it etched a sharp cleavage between the church and the larger society in Anabaptist minds. The kingdoms of this world, anchored on coercion, clashed with the peaceable kingdom of God. This dichotomy between church and world, reinforced by biblical images, has filled the deep recesses of the Anabaptist soul over the generations.

Hutterites, Mennonites, and Amish, each with their own internal subgroupings, trace their roots back to the Anabaptists. Breaking off from the Swiss Anabaptists, the Amish emerged as a separate group in 1693 when Jacob Ammann, an elder of the church, sought to revitalize it. He proposed holding communion twice a year rather than once—the typical Swiss practice. Following the

Dutch Anabaptists, he argued that Christians, in obedience to Christ, should wash each other's feet at the communion service. To promote doctrinal purity and spiritual discipline, Ammann forbade beard trimming and fashionable dress. He administered a strict discipline in his congregations. Appealing to New Testament teaching and the practice of Dutch Anabaptists, Ammann advocated shunning excommunicated members. This issue drove the decisive wedge between Ammann and other Anabaptist leaders. The brewing theological differences as well as personal entanglements erupted into a breach beyond repair.

Ammann's followers, eventually called Amish, soon became another of the many tribes in the Anabaptist family. Many of the other Anabaptists adopted the name Mennonite after Menno Simons, a prominent Dutch Anabaptist leader. Religious cousins, the Amish and Mennonites share a common Anabaptist heritage. Since 1693 they have remained distinctive communities, but as they arrived in North America they often settled in similar geographical areas. The Old Order Amish and the Old Order Mennonites share many practices and cooperate in projects such as parochial schools.

Searching for political stability and religious freedom, the Amish came to North America in two waves—in the mid-1700s and again in the first half of the 1800s. The "Old Order" label evolved in the latter part of the nineteenth century. At the turn of the twentieth century, the Old Order Amish numbered about 5,000. Now scattered across twenty-two states and into Ontario, they exceed 130,000 children and adults. Nearly three-quarters live in Ohio, Pennsylvania, and Indiana. Numerous settlements are also located in Michigan (24), Missouri (15), New York (14), and Wisconsin (23). New communities have recently formed in Kentucky, among other states. A loose federation of some 900 Amish congregations functions without a national office or an annual convention. Local church districts—congregations of twenty-five to thirty-five families—shape the heart of Amish life. The more than 900 church districts across the nation are organized into different affiliations based on religious practices.[5]

Amish interactions with the state are complicated and unpredictable for several reasons. Regulations and enforcement patterns governing midwife licensing, teacher certification, and slow-moving vehicle codes, to name only a few issues, vary by state. With Amish residing in twenty-two different states, both confrontation and cooperation fluctuate from region to region. Moreover, with Amish people scattered in some two hundred geographical settlements, they face hundreds of local officials and a plethora of regulations in various townships dealing with zoning, land use, sanitation, pollution, and road damage by horses, among many other issues.

Amish-state interactions are also complicated because the Amish have no national headquarters, national polity, or national official to represent them. Amish church polity is supremely congregational. Thus, state and federal officials must often deal with the above-mentioned loose federation of some 900 different church districts. The emergence of the National Amish Steering Committee (Chapter 4) in recent years has partially alleviated this problem.

The church districts within an Amish affiliation will typically take similar stances on an issue, but not always. Additional confusion arises because affiliations may straddle several states. Some of the more conservative affiliations have opposed the use of slow-moving vehicle signs, while members of other Amish affiliations within the same state or county have no difficulty accepting the signs. The various levels of state jurisdiction and the diversity of Amish convictions make the patterns of interaction with the state difficult to generalize and to predict.

Despite considerable diversity between the various districts and affiliations, several badges of identity unite the Old Order Amish across North America: horse and buggy transportation, the use of horses and mules for field work, plain dress in many variations, a beard and shaven upper lip for men, a prayer cap for women, the Pennsylvania German dialect, worship in homes, an eighth-grade education in one-room schools, the rejection of public electricity, and the selective use of technology. These symbols of solidarity circumscribe the Amish world and mark it off from the larger society.

Patterns of Community Life

The *immediate family*, the *extended family*, and the *church district* form the building blocks of Amish society. Amish parents typically raise about seven children, but ten or more are not uncommon. About 50 percent of the population is under eighteen years of age. Amish people are rarely alone, but are usually embedded in a caring community in time of need and disaster. The elderly retire at home—not in geriatric centers away from family. From cradle to grave, kinship and community provide a hammock of social support.[6]

The church district forms the basic social and religious unit beyond the family. Members participate in the district that encircles their home. Church services, held every other Sunday, rotate among the homes. As districts expand, they divide. A bishop, two preachers, and a deacon, without formal pay or seminary education, share leadership responsibilities in each district. The bishop, as spiritual elder, officiates at baptisms, weddings, communions, funerals, ordinations, and membership meetings. The church district—the hub of Amish life—functions as church, club, family, and precinct all wrapped up in a neighborhood parish. Periodic meetings of ordained leaders link the districts of a settlement into a loose federation.

The social architecture of Amish society exhibits distinctive features. It is *local*. Leisure, work, education, play, worship, and friendship revolve around the immediate neighborhood. Amish babies in some settlements are born in hospitals, but many of them greet this world at home or in local birthing centers. Weddings and funerals occur at home. There are frequent trips to other settlements or even out of state to visit relatives and friends. But for the most part the Amish world pivots on local turf. From home-canned food to homemade haircuts, things are likely to be done at or near home.

Social relationships are *multibonded*. The same people frequently work, play, and worship together. Unlike the fragmented networks of modern life, Amish ties have many layers of overlap. Family, friends, and neighbors interact throughout the life cycle. The segments of social life are integrated into a common fabric. In a few settlements, some Amish males work in rural factories, and others work on mobile construction crews; but in most communities work revolves around the homestead, where children apprentice with their parents. Even in the growing cottage industries, work remains relatively close to home. Amish parents govern their own schools. A child may have the same teacher for all eight grades. Grandparents work and play with their grandchildren in the normal flow of life. All things considered, the various sectors of social life cohere more closely than those in modern society.

Amish society is remarkably *informal*. The tentacles of bureaucracy are sparse. A central office, a symbolic figurehead, and institutional headquarters are absent. Apart from schools, a publishing operation, and regional historical libraries, formal institutions do not exist. A loosely organized National Steering Committee handles government relations for many of the settlements. Regional committees funnel the flow of Amish life for schools, mutual aid, and historical concerns, but bureaucracy, as we know it in the modern world, is simply absent. From egos to organizational units Amish society embodies the *small-scale* spirit of humility. Meeting in homes for worship limits the size of congregations. Farms, shops, and schools are relatively small. Small units increase informality and participation and also prevent power from accumulating in the lap of one person. Small-scale commitments assure each person an emotional niche in a network of social support.

The conventional marks of social status—education, income, occupation, and material goods—are missing. Amish society is relatively *homogeneous*. The agrarian heritage placed everyone on a common footing in the past. Today the rise of cottage industries in some settlements and factory work in others threatens to disturb the social equality of bygone years. But the range of occupations and social differences remains relatively small. Common costume, horse and buggy travel, an eighth-grade education, and equal-size tombstones embody the virtues of social equality.

Mutual aid also distinguishes Amish society. Although the Amish own private property, they have long emphasized mutual aid as a Christian duty in the face of disaster and special need. Mutual aid exceeds romanticized barn raisings. Harvesting, quilting, births, weddings, and funerals require the help of many hands. The habits of care encompass responses to all sorts of disasters—drought, disease, death, injury, bankruptcy, and medical emergency. The community springs into action in these moments of despair—articulating the deepest sentiments of Amish life. Shunning government assistance and commercial insurance, the Amish system of mutual aid marks their independence as well as their profound commitment to a humane system of social security at every turn.

Religious Rhythms

At first glance the Amish appear quite religious. Yet a deeper inspection reveals no church buildings, sacred symbols, or formal religious education, even in Amish schools. Unlike modern religion, relegated to an hour or so of services on Sunday morning, religious meanings pervade Amish life. Silent prayers before and after meals embroider each day with reverence. Religion is practiced, not debated. The Amish way of living and being requires neither heady talk nor formal theology. Religious understandings are woven into the fabric of living, not written in systematic theologies. Amish spirituality is deeply communal and filled with modesty. In the spirit of humility, the Amish are slow to make pronouncements about eternal outcomes, but yield to the wisdom of divine providence.

The *Ordnung*—religious blueprint for expected behavior—regulates private, public, and ceremonial behavior. Consisting of the rules for community living, the Ordnung passes on by oral tradition in most settlements. A body of "understandings," the discipline defines Amish ways—wearing a beard without a mustache, using a buggy, speaking the dialect. The Ordnung also specifies taboos—filing a lawsuit, owning a television, wearing jewelry, owning a car, attending college. The understandings, evolving over the years, are updated periodically as the church faces new issues—embryo transplants in cattle, computers and facsimile machines, and factory work. Core understandings—wearing a beard and not owning cars—span all Old Order Amish settlements, but the finer points of the Ordnung vary considerably by settlement, affiliation, and church district. The Ordnung, an informal policy, regulates Amish life by selectively preserving tradition while also permitting change. It defines the Amish world and infuses its texture with religious meanings.

Children learn the ways of the Ordnung by observing adults. The Ordnung defines reality—"the way things are"—in the child's mind. Teenagers, free from the supervision of the church, sometimes flirt with worldly ways and flout the Ordnung. At baptism, however, young adults declare their Christian faith and vow to uphold the Ordnung for the rest of their life. Those who break their promise face excommunication and shunning. Those choosing not to be baptized may gradually drift away from the community but are welcome to return to their families without the stigma of shunning. Rooted in the Anabaptist tradition, baptism symbolizes the ultimate pledge to surrender one's life to the community of faith.

The drama of worship rehearsed in Amish homes reaffirms the essence of the Ordnung. Church districts hold services every other Sunday. A group of two hundred or more, including neighbors and relatives who have an "off Sunday," gather for worship. They meet in a farmhouse, the basement of a newer home, or a shed or barn—underscoring the integration of worship with daily life. A fellowship meal and informal visiting follow the three-hour service.

Baptism and worship are sacred rites that revitalize and preserve the Ordnung. But the Amish, like other humans, forget, rebel, experiment, and stray into deviance. Major transgressions are confessed publicly in a "members' meeting" following the worship service. Violations of the Ordnung—using a tractor in the field, posing for a television camera, flying on a commercial airline, serving on a jury, joining a political organization, or opening a questionable business—are confessed publicly. Public confession diminishes self-will, reminds members of the supreme value of submission, restores the wayward into the community of faith, and underscores the lines of faithfulness that encircle the community.

The headstrong who spurn the advice of elders and refuse to confess their sin face a six-week probation. If their stubbornness does not mellow into repentance, they face excommunication. Exiles also face the *Meidung,* or shunning—a cultural equivalent of solitary confinement. Members terminate social interaction and financial transactions with the excommunicated. A bishop compared shunning to "the last dose of medicine that you give a sinner. It either works for life or death . . . but if love is lost, God's lost, too." For the unrepentant, social avoidance becomes a lifetime quarantine. An excommunicated member noted, "It works a little bit like an electric fence around a pasture."

The Meidung, a silent deterrent, encourages those who think about breaking their baptismal vows to think twice. The firm measures are taken to preserve the purity of the church and encourage repentance. Excommunicated members, even years later, can be restored into membership upon public confession of their sins.

Separation from the World

A cardinal value of Amish society is separation from the world. Galvanized by European persecution and sanctioned by Scripture, the Amish divide the social world into two pathways: the straight and narrow way to life, and the broad, easy road to destruction. Amish life embodies the narrow way of self-denial. The larger social world represents the broad road of vanity and vice. The term *world,* in Amish thinking, refers to the outside society—its values, vices, practices, and institutions. Media reports of greed, fraud, scandal, drugs, violence, divorce, and abuse confirm, in Amish minds, a world teeming with abomination.

The gulf between church and world, imprinted in Amish consciousness by decades of persecution, guides practical decisions.

The separatist impulse infuses Amish thinking and steers both personal and collective decision making. Products and practices that might undermine community life—high school, cars, cameras, television, and self-propelled farm machinery—are tagged *worldly*. Many new products don't receive the label; only those that threaten community values. Definitions of worldliness vary within and between Amish settlements, yielding a complicated maze of practices. Baffling to the outsider, these lines of faithfulness maintain intergroup boundaries and also preserve the purity of the church. Despite their collective commitment to remain separate from the world, some Amish persons develop congenial friendships with neighbors and outsiders.

Amish separation from the world can be conceptualized along four dimensions: *cultural, social, technological,* and *legal.* At the cultural level, Amish values, beliefs, and convictions differ widely from those of the larger society. Social patterns of interaction—marriage, education, commerce, and occupations—also diverge from modern ways. The Amish utilize technology but accept it selectively. Their rejection of electricity from public power lines, of automobiles, and of tractors for field work symbolizes their technological separation from the world. The Amish rejection of force and coercion draws the line of legal separation from the larger society in the use of the law and relations with the state. The Amish readily pay all of their taxes, except Social Security, and use the counsel of lawyers for executing wills, real estate transactions, deeds, and business contracts, but they draw the line of legal separation in their reluctance to engage in litigation and to use force to protect their interests.

Gelassenheit

The value structure of Amish life pivots on *Gelassenheit* (pronounced Ge-las-en-hite)—the cornerstone of Amish values. Roughly translated, the German word means submission—yielding to a higher authority. It entails self-surrender, resignation to God's will, yielding to others, self-denial, contentment, and a quiet spirit. For early Anabaptists, Gelassenheit meant forsaking all ambition and yielding fully to God's will—even unto death. Christ called them to abandon self and follow his example of humility, service, and suffering. The religious meaning of Gelassenheit expresses itself in a quiet and reserved personality and places the needs of others above self. Gelassenheit nurtures a subdued self—gentle handshakes, lower voices, slower strides—a life etched with modesty and reserve.

This way of thinking—yielding to God and others—permeates Amish culture. It undergirds values, personality, symbols, rituals, and social patterns. A favorite Amish saying notes that "JOY" means Jesus first, Yourself last, and Others in between. Amish teachers sometimes remind students that the middle letter of pride is I. As the cornerstone of Amish culture, Gelassenheit collides with the bold, assertive individualism of modern life that seeks and rewards personal achievement, self-fulfillment, and individual recognition at every turn.

The meek spirit of Gelassenheit, modeled after the suffering Jesus who refused to resist his adversaries, clashes with the cultural assumption that individuals have a legitimate right to exercise force to protect their rights and interests. Embracing the stance of Gelassenheit, the Amish avoid using the law to protect their rights as well as to force others to comply with contractual obligations. Holding political office, which might require the use of force, is also taboo, as is serving on a jury and using the law to collect unpaid debts. There are many occasions when the Amish have chosen to suffer abuse rather than exert their rights. A rejection of the use of force, of course, means that the Amish cannot participate in military service.

The spirit of Gelassenheit expresses itself in *obedience, humility,* and *simplicity.* To Amish thinking, obedience to the will of God is the cardinal religious value. Disobedience is dangerous. Unconfessed, it leads to eternal separation. Submission to authority at all levels creates an orderly community. Obedience to divine and human authority regulates social relationships from the youngest child to the oldest bishop, who in turn obeys the Lord. When civil and divine authority conflict, the Amish, following the biblical admonition, prefer to "obey God rather than man."

Humility is coupled with obedience in Amish life. Pride, a religious term for unbridled individualism, threatens the welfare of an orderly community. Proud individuals display the spirit of arrogance, not Gelassenheit. What moderns consider proper credit for one's achievements the Amish view as the hankerings of a vain spirit. Proud individuals tack their name on everything, promote personal accomplishments, draw attention to themselves, seek recognition in the press, hang personal portraits, and take credit for everything. The humble person freely gives of self in the service of community without seeking recognition.

Simplicity is also esteemed in Amish life. Fancy and gaudy

decorations lead to pride. Simplicity in clothing, household decor, architecture, and worship nurtures equality and orderliness. Sacrifice signals a yielded self; luxury and convenience cultivate vanity. Pretentious display reflects the haughty spirit of the outside world. The tools of self-adornment—makeup, jewelry, wrist watches, and wedding rings—are taboo. These cosmetic props, signs of pride, encourage pushy selves to show off "Number One." Modern dress accents individual expression and social status. Amish dress, by contrast, signals submission to the collective order. Common garb symbolizes a yielded self and promotes order and equality.

A Posture of Subjection

The Amish posture toward the state differs considerably from the stance of their non-Amish neighbors. Transposed into the political realm, Gelassenheit yields a position of *subjection* rather than *citizenship.* Unlike citizens who cultivate a sense of civic obligation and responsibility and who also clamor to protect their rights, Amish relationships with the state parallel those of subjects to a king. The posture of subjection flows from biblical injunctions to respect and pray for rulers ordained by God. This stance is also a natural expression of the attitudes entwined in Gelassenheit.

Reacting to a Pennsylvania law that hiked the compulsory school age, Amish leaders sent a petition to their state legislators. Addressed "To Our Men in Authority," it articulated the stance and mood of subjection. "We, your *humble subjects* . . . hereby give you part of our confession of faith and of our misdoings." After explaining why they objected to the new law, the petitioners concluded, "We . . . do not blame our men of authority for bringing all this over us, to undermine the church, not at all, we admit, we ourselves are the fault of it. We confess before God and man that . . . we are too much devoted to worldly things and our Lord has brought this over us, through our men of authority, to chastise us. . . . We beg your pardon for bringing all this before you, and worrying you, and bringing you a serious problem."[7]

In another petition to members of a state legislature, Amish leaders concluded, "We pray you to allow us to live inoffensively and quietly. Let us, *unhindered,* live to our calling. We respect your right; respect our mode. We ask nothing of you, but that which the Word of God entitles us."[8]

Such a posture of subjection diverges from modern assumptions of individualism, civic responsibility, the rights of citizenship, and the accountability of elected officials. An attitude of deference and homage characterizes this stance, rather than modern expectations of accountability, performance, and responsibility, and the commensurate obligations, duties, and rights that accompany citizenship. Modern citizens are obligated to accept a modicum of responsibility for the welfare of the larger social order. By contrast, the Amish are supremely oriented toward internal obligations within their own religious community.

The Amish rarely evoke the "rights" language of modern citizenship, but they do occasionally remind their "men of authority" that certain regulations "interfere with the religious rights and liberties which were promised to our forefathers when they came to America and which are granted to us by the constitution of our state and of our nation."[9]

Although the posture of subjection presents a docile image of obedience and dutiful respect, it nevertheless pivots on cardinal religious convictions that are stubborn to the core. Reluctant to demand rights and privileges, the Amish will not, however, acquiesce on deeply held beliefs but will respectfully take a stand, even if it brings fines, imprisonment, prosecution, or migration.

The cluster of beliefs undergirding the Amish stance of subjection toward the state flows from many tributaries: the legacy of European persecution, biblical admonitions to live a nonresistant life, the emphasis on separation from the world, the embodiment of Gelassenheit, the rejection of individualism, the supremacy of internal obligations to the religious community, and the enduring belief that heaven is their ultimate home. All of these factors forge an apolitical stance in Amish life—a courteous disregard for the affairs of state. And although they respect rulers and pay their taxes, the state is always a foreign entity in the Amish mind. While this stance generally leads to nonparticipation in the political order, Amish persons have on a few occasions held public office at the local level.[10]

A Clash of Cultures

Amish conflicts with the state ostensibly appear as issues of religious liberty. The legal confrontations, however, often reflect the collision of two different social orders. The process of modernization in the twentieth century has spawned, among other things, a high level of functional and structural specialization in industrial societies. Social specialization prodded by technology sharply differentiated sectors of social life that were formerly integrated: the economy, work, family, leisure, education, and religion. Modern societies cohere around the functional interdependence of economic ties and specialized roles. Bureaucracies with their specialized roles, lines of authority, rationalized goals, and performance evaluations are the structural embodiment of modernity. The state, in essence, functions as the supreme agent of modernity—expressing itself in bureaucratic forms with technical, legal, and rational underpinnings, all accompanied by the legitimate authority to use coercion when necessary. Indeed, Weber (1958, 78) has argued that the state claims a "monopoly of the legitimate use of force . . . and the 'right' to use violence." It is precisely at this point that Amish ways diverge from the ways of the state.

The social order of Amish society stands in stark contrast to modern societies. The Amish community is wedded by common values, beliefs, and sentiments; it exhibits minimal specialization, rationalization, centralization, bureaucratization, and formality. Instead of impersonal secondary relationships, Amish life revolves around primary, face-to-face social ties. Basic social activities— birth, play, education, work, worship, and death—remain tethered near home. Traditional patterns of authority and oral communication supersede the legal and formal arrangements of modernity.[11]

The scant specialization and rationalization in Amish life means that religion itself is not viewed as a separate entity to be studied or taught in school or in any other setting. Typical of more primitive societies, religion permeates all levels and dimensions of Amish culture. It is never taught in a formal fashion. In the words of one Amishman, "Our religion is inseparable with a day's work, a night's rest, a meal, or any other practice."[12] By contrast, modern religion is often relegated to special hours, facilities, objects, and officials. Unlike modern society, the sacred canopy of Amish life stretches over their entire way of life. The scientific world-view, largely taken for granted in modern life, is missing here. Amish society is a cultural island of traditional structures, patterns, and values within the ocean of modernity.

The encompassing Amish view of religion raises questions about the stereotypical boundaries dividing sacred and secular. A cross and a Bible are obviously religious symbols. But what about a hat, a photograph, or a slow-moving vehicle sign? The religious significance of these objects, as well as many other practices outside the typical borders of devotion, calls into question modern definitions of the religious and the profane. For after all, much of the legal wrangling over the freedom to exercise religion hinges on the symbolic lines dividing the divine and the mundane. Church and state conflicts—particularly the Amish ones—involve drawing, erasing, and redrawing the symbolic lines of separation.

Some of the Amish face-offs with the state threaten the very core of their culture. To require Amish children to attend public schools beyond the elementary years would not only expose them to contaminating cultural beliefs and foster friendships with outsiders, it would also erode historic Amish values and challenge traditional Amish authority. Forced participation in the Social Security System would cut the cords of economic dependency within Amish society. To require participation in military service would mock the bedrock value of their culture—Gelassenheit. These and other areas of conflict not only are religious controversies but threaten the very character, even the survival, of Amish society.

Thus, discussions of contested issues in Amish-state controversies are not mere games of religious semantics; they often reflect a cultural clash between incongruent social orders. The Amish embody the virtues of a small, highly disciplined community where social control rests on informal sanctions meted out in a dense network of kinship ties. The commitment to order and discipline within this highly regulated society means the Amish have little need for external forms of social control—police, courts, prisons. The high level of compliance with traditional Amish values—obedience, hard work, honesty, responsibility, and integrity—means that Amish persons rarely sit in prison for crimes of theft, vandalism, fraud, robbery, or homicide. Indeed, the withering of such traditional values in mass society has, in part, fostered the need for formal and institutional modes of social control. When the Amish do sit in jail, they are probably there for resisting new statutes that hinder their free exercise of religion.

In sum, many of the feuds between the Amish and the state involve fundamental clashes between diverse social orders. Anchored on opposing values and differing social structures, these duels are essentially face-offs between the Goliath of modernity and shepherds from traditional pastures. These conflicts of conviction, ostensibly religious in nature, mark a collision of cultures—an encounter between the forces of modernity and the sentiments of tradition. Negotiating with Caesar is, in essence, negotiating with modernity.

The Negotiation Model

Interactions between the Amish and the state can be seen as negotiations replete with the vocabulary of negotiators, arbiters, brokers, all employing the concepts of bargaining, compromise, concession, acquiescence, and nonnegotiable issues. Viewed in this fashion, negotiations embody exchanges between the vested interests of a traditional religious minority and the official desires of the state. Bargaining occurs in a direct manner when representatives from both sides literally sit down to work out a solution to a problem at hand. A state official described a conflict with Amish leaders over a proposed bicycle path on an abandoned railroad line in Arthur, Illinois: "The two worlds have to meet sometimes. . . . Hopefully we'll be able to negotiate with all parties and come up with a solution."[13] Negotiation also transpires in an indirect fashion when either side, cognizant of the concerns of the other, acknowledges them by making conciliatory moves that reduce conflict.[14]

Theoretically, negotiations between the Amish and modernity emerge in *legal, social,* and *cultural* domains. The essays in this book focus primarily on legal negotiations. The rise of the National Amish Steering Committee to coordinate church-state relations illustrates a concession by the Amish in the social domain. The formation of this quasi-bureaucratic committee at the national level was an unprecedented development in Amish history prompted by the need to cope with the ever-widening scope of state-related legal issues. The gradual movement of a few Amish business persons ever closer to using the law in threatening ways to collect outstanding debts underscores a cultural compromise— a tendency to accept beliefs and values that historically were unthinkable.

The outcomes of the legal exchanges between the Amish and the state can be analyzed and categorized in traditional bargaining language. Results vary considerably by township, county, and state. But in each instance we can ask, What concessions have been made by and to the Amish? What compromises have been struck? What does either party consider nonnegotiable?

What concessions have been made by the Amish? Most Amish affiliations have agreed to use slow-moving vehicle signs and install flashing lights on their carriages when required by state law. When pressed by public health considerations, even the more conservative groups have been willing to submit to vaccinations. In most municipalities, Amish have conceded to zoning, sanitation, pollution, and land use regulations. What has the state conceded to the Amish? The most notable concession has been the 1972 Supreme Court decision permitting Amish youth to leave school after the eighth grade. Congressional legislation exempting the Amish from the Social Security program represents another favorable outcome for them. Exempting Amish members from the hard-hat regulation as well as the paucity of statutes requiring licensing or taxing of horse-drawn carriages illustrate other acknowledgments of Amish ways. Some states have exempted Amish employers from paying unemployment insurance. Plans for a major highway in one Amish community were scuttled in the face of public outcry that it would slice up Amish farmland. All of these outcomes tilted in favor of Amish sentiments.

What areas have resulted in compromises? The farm program developed for Amish youth in alternative service required those without farm deferments to leave their homes and contribute to the national welfare. But it permitted them to do it in the context of an Amish-supervised rural setting. This arrangement, as described in chapters 3 and 4, was directly negotiated with General Lewis B. Hershey, head of the Selective Service System, in the sixties. The vocational educational program developed in some states in the fifties was also a compromise of sorts. State officials could say that Amish youth were continuing in school beyond the eighth grade, but in reality they were working at home and attending three hours of school a week in an Amish setting.

Many zoning decisions in local townships also reflect compromises with the Amish community. County officials in one state urged local townships to write zoning ordinances that would control haphazard growth while bending to accommodate Amish cottage industries on farms. Upset about the filming of *Witness* in Lancaster County, Amish leaders struck a compromise agreement with the state. Officials promised not to solicit a production company for a similar film, but neither did they promise to prevent a repeat. Both sides were pleased "with what they got" (Kraybill 1989, 223-27).

Nonnegotiables? For the Amish, participation in military service has remained off the bargaining table in the twentieth century. For the state, public health and public safety have been compelling concerns that rarely yield to Amish convictions.

The negotiation model assumes a dynamic, ever-changing matrix of social actors, conflicting values, economic interests, and legal considerations that make outcomes unpredictable. In addition to cultural values and religious convictions, sympathetic outsiders, public opinion, media coverage, and the political consequence of decisions sometimes become factors on the bargaining table as well. The relative political and economic power exerted by either side, of course, shapes outcomes in significant ways. The Amish have gained considerable political clout in communities where they wield economic power by their ability to attract tourists. In such regions of the country, their power to negotiate exemptions and to shape new regulations has grown in recent years. The negotiation model views Amish-state relations in a dynamic process of give and take, compromise and concession, that continually redraws the symbolic lines between church and state.

In any event, negotiations with the state at various levels seek to balance the twin hopes of the Amish heart by enabling the Amish to practice their faith conscientiously while abiding by the laws of the land. They will negotiate with Caesar and they will make concessions, but most of all they desire to live their calling, unhindered. As the Amish are granted freedom to reconcile their twin hopes, the religious liberty of their fellow citizens is also safeguarded and preserved in new ways.

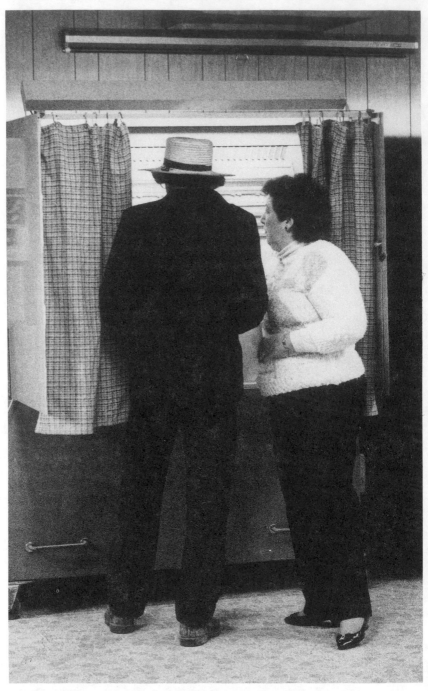

Although they rarely hold public office, Amish persons do occasionally vote when local issues concern them. Dennis L. Hughes

CHAPTER TWO

The Amish View of the State

Paton Yoder

Long-time student of Amish history Paton Yoder describes the historical roots of Amish attitudes toward the state. Yoder explains the Amish understanding of conflict between the political kingdoms of this world, which are based on force, and the spiritual Kingdom of God, which is anchored on suffering love. He traces the emergence of this view in Reformation times and shows how it was galvanized by the severe persecution of Anabaptist groups.

The Amish view of the state has its origins in Reformation times with the nonresistant Anabaptists of the sixteenth century. The Amish rely heavily on the traditions handed down from the early leaders of this movement and readily accept their pronouncements. In particular, the writings of Menno Simons (1496–1561) and Dirk Philips (1504–68) are highly regarded. The Amish view of the state was forged by frequent conflicts between the Anabaptists and civil authorities.

In addition to the writings of early Anabaptists, the Amish lean heavily on later Anabaptist documents, which reflect their view of government. The *Dordrecht Confession of Faith*, drawn up in 1632 after years of consultation among Anabaptist groups, remains the definitive Amish statement on matters of faith and conduct. Article XIII of the confession deals with "Civil Government." This text, to which members subscribe before baptism, heavily influences the Amish view of the state.

We also believe and confess that God instituted civil government for the punishment of evil and the protection of the good as well as to govern the world and to provide good regulations and policies in cities and countries. Therefore, we may not resist, despise, or condemn the state. We should recognize it as a minister of God. Further, we ought to honor and obey it and be ready to perform good works in its behalf insofar as it is not in conflict with God's law and commandment. Also, we should be faithful in the payment of taxes and excises, giving what is due to the state as the Son of God taught, practiced, and commanded his disciples to do. Besides, we should constantly and earnestly pray for the state and the welfare of the country that under its protection we may lead a quiet and peaceful life in all godliness and honesty. (Horst 1988, 32–33)

The *Martyrs Mirror*, an Anabaptist publication first appearing in 1660, shapes the Amish version of church history. Filled with etchings of torture, this large book in its many editions portrays the persecution of nonresistant Christians in the sixteenth and seventeenth centuries by the governments of their day. One Amishman said, "We have an almost non-verbal understanding of the separation of church and state. Centuries of persecution have resulted in an almost instinctive distrust of government. . . . It is passed from generation to generation. We know that the hand which feeds you also controls you. . . . The *Martyrs Mirror* accounts are read and we get our view of governments through 16th century eyes."[1] Thus, the story of martyrdom rooted in their history greatly affects the Amish view of the state even today.

The Amish hymnal, the *Ausbund*, first published in 1564 under another title, contains many songs recounting persecution stories of the Anabaptists.[2] Finally there are the prayer books—the *Christliche Glaubens Bekantnus* [*Bekentnus* in some editions] and the *Ernsthafte Christenpflicht*. Since the Amish are tradition-minded, these historic documents shape the way twentieth-century Amish leaders articulate their view of the state.[3] They often paraphrase the documents of previous centuries with little deviation and are satisfied to apply centuries-old principles to new circumstances. Consequently, any discussion of the Amish view of the state must attend to these pronouncements of past centuries.

Nowhere have the Amish defined the state in the language of the political scientist. Neither did their spiritual progenitors, including the Anabaptists of the sixteenth century. Other than linking the state to the exercise of force—the use of the sword by the police and the army—they have no definition of the state. The Amish recognize that government, as the tangible expression of the state, by definition engages in capital punishment and other forms of physical coercion, and of course has recourse to war.

Relating the state so fundamentally to coercion is not distinctively Amish; it has strong support from both political scientists and theologians.[4] But the Amish, in affirming this relationship, identify government with that aspect of political behavior—coercion—which most contradicts their own world-view. What the Amish find so foreign to their gentle lifestyle in the *modus operandi* of government, in the words of Kraybill (1989, 216), is that "when push comes to shove, governments engage in warfare and use capital punishment and raw coercion to impose their will."

The words that the Amish employ to describe the government's use of force are biblical terms: *vengeance, punishment,* and *restraint.* They use these terms almost interchangeably. The proper function of government is to restrain evil people by punishment or the threat of it. Even when the word *vengeance* is used, its purpose is not revenge for its own sake but as a means of protecting good people. In a simile used by an early Anabaptist, government is comparable to a fence that the owner of a garden sets up to keep the wild animals from his good fruits (Hillerbrand 1958b, 87). Although the Amish think that God instituted government to restrain evil, they believe that as citizens of a heavenly kingdom they cannot participate in the coercive measures employed by governments.

The Doctrine of the Two Kingdoms

The Amish view of the state is based on the early Anabaptist doctrine of the two kingdoms. Medieval in origin, this doctrine was reinterpreted in Reformation times by both Martin Luther and John Calvin. Each interpreted it to bolster his rejection of Catholic authority and to elucidate his own view of the relationship between church and state. Although both of these reformers modified the medieval concept of the *Corpus Christianum* (the union—or partnership—of church and state), neither of them supported the modern view of the separation of church and state (Hillerbrand 1958b, 108–9).

There were vocal minorities, however, who did not acquiesce in what they considered a compromise with the medieval partnership of church and state. They argued that the state churches that Luther and Calvin established were not based on New Testament principles. These small groups of Anabaptists—the religious forebears of Mennonites and Amish in Switzerland, South Germany, and the Netherlands—protested against the continued union of church and state.[5] They also objected to practices emerging from the unholy union between church and government. These included the swearing of oaths as well as the participation of Christians and the Christian church in the wars of the state. Anabaptist

Pilgram Marpeck protested the use of secular power by the church
(ca. 1533) in his "Exposure of the Babylonian Whore."[6] Secular
government and Christ's kingdom, although in juxtaposition,
were two disparate entities, two different kingdoms. The kingdom
of Christ—the church—was a spiritual entity, and the kingdom of
this world was temporal.

The Anabaptist contemporaries of Luther and Calvin seized
upon the doctrine of the two kingdoms and gave it a radical interpretation.[7] In emphasizing the differences between the two kingdoms, the Anabaptists, in contrast to the reformers, reduced the
role of the state and elevated the status ascribed to the church.
While the two-kingdom idea appears early in the writings of Anabaptist leaders, it was fully developed and given singular attention in a treatise written in 1575 by Hans Schnell.[8]

For Schnell (1710, 9), the kingdom of this world and the kingdom of Christ were not only distinct realms, they were antithetical—separated by a great chasm. He said that "neither can have
part of communion with the other." The kingdom of this world is
based on vengeance; the kingdom of Christ is based on love. The
magistrate who, as an agent of the worldly government, metes out
vengeance puts himself outside Christ's kingdom.

The Anabaptist version of the two kingdoms emerged in the sixteenth century when radical reformers were severely persecuted
throughout Europe. Thus, it is not surprising that when they
gained respite from persecution they were extremely grateful to
their benefactors. This gratefulness, embodied in their statements
about tolerant magistrates, sometimes even collides with the two-
kingdom doctrine. In 1578 Hans de Ries, an Anabaptist on trial in
the Netherlands, declared that magistrates who "rule well and
please God shall *receive from Him a golden reward* [emphasis
added]" (Dyck 1962, 153). In 1632, as persecution in the Netherlands abated, the framers of the *Dordrecht Confession of Faith*
(Horst 1988) responded to this friendlier government stance. They
hoped that the Lord might "be pleased to reward them [the magistrates of the Netherlands] here and in eternity" for their policy of
toleration (Horst 1988, 33).

In 1660, Thieleman J. van Braght included a "Prayer for the Secular Power" in the first edition of the *Martyrs Mirror*. Little of
Schnell's harsh analysis of secular government remains in the
prayer. Its format—a broadside with large print symmetrically
arranged on a full page—suggests a special emphasis and an attempt to attract the attention of the magistrates. It begins with a
plea that God intercede so that the sins of the rulers in those coun-

tries that continue to persecute "not be laid to their charge in Thy great day of judgment." Rather, may they be "brought to the right . . . [and] become true followers of Thy church." God is implored to extend abundant grace to the magistrates in the Netherlands who no longer persecute dissenters, so that "they may all be kept and eternally saved."[9] In parts of Europe, however, persecution of Anabaptists would continue for nearly two centuries.

THE AMISH AND THE TWO-KINGDOM DOCTRINE

It was not coincidental that the doctrine of the two kingdoms surfaced again in the latter part of the nineteenth century as the central motif in two essays written by Amishmen. At that time, Amish participation in voting and local office holding was increasing. This alarmed some Amish leaders, and they wrote to protest this trend. In 1874, S. D. Mast wrote an article for the *Herold der Wahrheit*, a paper widely read by both Amish and Mennonites, in which he opposed participation in political elections. Mast justified his position with the Anabaptist view of the two kingdoms.[10] In 1898, Bishop David A. Troyer published a similar tract on "worldly [secular] government."[11] Although written in the context of the Amish church in the nineteenth century, these essays are little more than compressed paraphrases of Schnell's treatise of 1575. Both of these essays, reprinted in the twentieth century, heavily influenced later statements. Some of the later documents use the phrase "Kingdom of God" in place of "Christ's Kingdom."[12]

The differences between the two kingdoms are accented by Amish usage. They refer to secular government as *die weltliche Obrigkeit*, "the worldly magistracy." Although some might translate *weltlich* as *secular*, the Amish disagree. The word must be *worldly*. For them, *world* and *worldly* are religious terms. These words refer not to the globe but rather to "the entire social system outside Amish society," including secular government.[13] Much in the same way that automobiles and glamorous clothing are worldly, so is government.[14] It is sometimes called *fleshly* by Amish writers in their attempt to contrast it with Christ's spiritual kingdom.[15]

As already noted, the worldly magistracy may and does resort to physical coercion. In contrast, Christ came into this world as the Prince of Peace to establish a spiritual kingdom. He stands in extreme contrast with worldly magistrates, who, in biblical terms, "exercise lordship" over their subjects (Luke 22:25). Christ, in the Amish view, "became the perfect model of humility and self-effacement, who not only descended from the throne of God in humiliation and agony, but also openly withdrew from the thrones and kingdoms of this world. [He was] a king who fled when men caught him and wanted to make him king and who on the contrary willingly allowed himself to be seized when men wanted to mock him and spit on him" ("Mein Reich" 1918, 515). He rules his spiritual kingdom through the exercise of love, compassion, and forgiveness. Moreover, he asks his members to follow his example. The people of his kingdom "are a chosen generation, a royal priesthood, a holy nation, a peculiar people" (I Peter 2:9).

Amish writers go to great lengths in contrasting secular government with Christ's heavenly kingdom. They are as different as day and night, light and darkness (Schnell 1710, 11, 14). Government is associated with the "Kingdom of Darkness" (L. R. Troyer 1977; 1978, 3). People of the light do not participate in the affairs of the kingdom of darkness. If secular government is of this world, then the Apostle Paul's admonition to "come out from among them" and to "touch not the unclean thing" (II Corinthians 6:17) applies to the state as well.

When Christ was taken before Pilate, the Roman magistrate, he said, "My kingdom is not of this world" (John 18:36).[16] To the Amish, Christ's statement implies an absolute; the two kingdoms have nothing in common. Most Amish would probably agree with Hans Schnell: "Christ made these two kingdoms at variance with each other and separated. There will therefore be no peace between them. They will fight against each other to the end of the world. . . . In the end, however, Christ with his power and eternal kingdom will crush and destroy all the other kingdoms."[17]

The Role of Government in God's Economy

The Amish also agree with Schnell that God instituted the state after the worldwide flood recorded in Genesis 6–8. It was God's response to sin. In describing the historic Anabaptist view of the state, twentieth-century Anabaptist historian Hans Hillerbrand (1958b, 85–86) has in large measure echoed Schnell's position. The state, he says,

> is an indication of God's punishment and shows his divine wrath. But it also expresses God's love, as it shows that God does not wish to leave man to the ultimate consequences of sin, but wants order and peace even among a rebellious and sinful mankind. The very existence of the office of government therefore points to that time

when sin shall be no more—[at the time of] Christ's second coming and the Last Judgment. . . . God's grace and wrath are integral aspects of the office of government.

Biblicists that they are, the Amish accept the pronouncement of the Apostle Paul in Romans 13: "The powers that be are ordained of God." Paul maintained in the same discourse that "there is no power but of God." The apostle did not flinch, even though he probably wrote these words when Nero was emperor of Rome. In earlier times did God not call Nebuchadnezzar, the wicked king of Babylon, his "servant?"[18] It makes no difference that some regimes are ruthless and that communist governments are atheistic.[19] Thus, although government in the Amish mind is worldly, it is nevertheless instituted by the power of God. Said one Amishman, "We feel that the concept of government is ordained by God but God allows bad governments to come into power but does not will them into power, as God cannot will evil."[20]

God's role in the affairs of nations is not passive. According to Amish convictions, He sets up rulers but then determines the boundaries of their power. He established the Pharaoh of Egypt in great power and then humbled him with the ten plagues "in order to show" his power (Exodus 9:16). After He had used King Nebuchadnezzar to accomplish His purposes He cast him aside, warning him, according to Daniel 4:32, "that the most high ruleth in the kingdom of men, and giveth it to whomsoever He will" (Stoltzfus 1982, 245). Daniel himself understood this and took the several changes in government that occurred in Mesopotamia during his captivity there quite "matter-of-factly as though nothing had happened" ("President" 1963, 471).

Romans 13:1–7 shapes the Amish view of the state; but, in the words of one Amishman, "Matthew 22:21 is what we quote most often to support our belief in the separation of church and state: 'Render unto Caesar the things that are Caesar's, and unto God the things that are God's.'" Already noted is the Amish contention that governments are of God. Therefore, the corollary follows that everyone should obey the government. For, according to Romans 13:2, "Whosoever resisteth the power [the government], resisteth the ordinance of God, for they that resist shall receive to themselves damnation." The Apostle Paul became quite specific: one should pay taxes levied by the government. Referring primarily to magistrates, he concluded, "Render therefore to all their dues, tribute to whom tribute is due, custom to whom custom, fear to whom fear, honor to whom honor" (Romans 13:7).

The Amish do note that many early leaders of the Christian church defied the government. When ordered not to preach, the apostles contended they should obey God rather than the authorities (Acts 4:19, 5:29).[21] And that revered book, the *Martyrs Mirror,* contains innumerable accounts of faithful Anabaptists who suffered martyrdom because they disobeyed the magistrates. Rooted in these traditions, even today the Amish are willing to disobey a law that requires them to violate their beliefs.

The basic stance of the Amish toward government, however, is obedience and submission—*Gelassenheit.* Some modern scholars studying Amish society have used this term to identify the core of Amish culture.[22] The concept includes more than obedience and submission. Other words that capture its meaning are powerlessness and yieldedness. Significantly, the more self-effacing words *untertänig* (translated as submissive, even servile) and *Untertänigkeit* (submissiveness, subservience) appear in twentieth-century Amish religious literature more frequently than Gelassenheit.[23]

They practice the virtue of submissiveness, not only toward the laws they are prepared to obey, but also with respect to the legal consequences that flow from civil disobedience. The Amish, however, have been involved in too many clashes with the government for them to be considered docile. If laws that clash with God's higher law must be broken, even then they are stubbornly passive. In the words of one Amishman, "We are taught to mind our own business and obey the government, but when the chips are down and the government interferes with our way of living, we can balk like a stubborn mule!"

Bold defiance or rebellion, however, are unthinkable. Like the martyrs in *Martyrs Mirror,* one should pray for persecutors and try to bring them to repentance.[24] The story of the fugitive Anabaptist Dirk Willems illustrates the virtuous response to persecution. Willems rescued his pursuer after the latter fell through the river's ice (Braght 1968, 741). Did not Jesus "willingly allow himself to be seized when men wanted to mock him and spit on him?"[25]

In short, the Amish believe that Christians should respect their government, pray for those in power, pay required taxes, and obey the laws of the land, *except* when they conflict with God's laws (E. Stoll February 1989, 12). It matters not that the government uses tax money for armaments or other immoral purposes. Most Amish would agree that "when a tax is paid, it is no longer our money, and it is not our responsibility to dictate how it is to be used" ("Government" 1972, 226). Similarly, the Christian should not tell the government when it may use the sword.[26] This virtual abnegation of political responsibility has been labeled a "strategy of withdrawal" (J. H. Yoder 1964, 89).

By emphasizing submission to government, the Amish reflect the teachings of the defenseless early Anabaptists. Some Anabaptist leaders were less servile, however, than the contemporary Amish church. In Menno Simons's (1956, 193–94) "Exhortation to the Magistrates," he warned magistrates that they are made of the same stuff as "we poor, common people." Menno called upon magistrates to restrict themselves to their God-given task of maintaining order by restraining the wicked. Thus they would "enlarge, help, and protect the kingdom of God." Magistrates, Simons said, are "to chastise and punish in the fear of God with fairness and Christian discretion, manifest criminals, such as thieves, murderers, Sodomites, adulterers, seducers, sorcerers, the violent, highwaymen, robbers, etc." (193). The introductory essay ("*Vorrede*") in the *Ausbund* (1991,iv–v) warns magistrates that they, like Pilate's servants, "will in no way be innocent on that [Judgment] Day before God" if they overstep their appointed role.

In emphasizing that governments are worldly, but nevertheless insisting that they are instituted by God, the Amish introduce a paradox. This was evident already in Martin Luther's statements on the two kingdoms. The problem became even greater for the Anabaptists because they made a sharper distinction between the two kingdoms than had Luther.[27] For example, Luther maintains that magistrates, and even constables, soldiers, and "hangmen," can be good Christians.[28] In contrast, the Amish follow the Anabaptist tradition that Christians may not participate in a system that uses force. When confronted with this seeming contradiction, the Amish respond as their spiritual forebears did: the two kingdoms are firmly rooted in the Scriptures, and if a paradox is involved, so be it (Hillerbrand 1958b, 100–101).

Maintaining Distance from the State

The Amish try to minimize their participation in affairs of state and prefer to keep their distance from government. Nevertheless, they are willing to cooperate as long as accommodation doesn't violate their religious conscience. They pay their taxes, even those imposed by the welfare state, from which they receive little benefit. They obey school attendance laws, although they have persuaded the governments of many states to modify the statutes to accommodate Amish religious scruples. These are but two examples of areas in which they cooperate with government.

To most Amish writers, the questions of whether a Christian should vote or hold public office are of one cloth. The answer to both is negative, and the reasons are the same. As might be expected, the Amish apply the strategy of withdrawal to both voting and holding public office. Accepting jury duty is given the same treatment.

In the context of Amish history, the question of political participation is relatively recent. In the Reformation era, the Anabaptists were largely speaking to Lutherans, Calvinists, Catholics, and some fellow militant Anabaptists when they objected to Christian participation in government. To the Anabaptists, such cooperation signaled participation in the unholy alliance of church and state.[29]

Before the emergence of democratic states in the nineteenth century, the question of participation in government was irrelevant. Prior to that time, the Amish (and other Anabaptists) were rarely able to own land and certainly could not hold public office or even vote in public elections. But when common folks in America and elsewhere became *citizens* rather than *subjects,* voting and holding public office became salient issues. The doctrine of the two kingdoms now had to be applied and interpreted in the light of this new form of government.

As the nineteenth century advanced in America, the Amish accepted much that the youthful democracy offered. They took advantage of their newfound privileges with few misgivings. Conscription into the armed services seemed to belong to a bygone age. Some became relatively affluent. Voting and even local office holding in such a benevolent country seemed quite innocent.[30] In an unusual case in the 1850s, a very wealthy Amishman, Isaac Kaufman, of Somerset County, Pennsylvania, became active in the Whig party. Later he became a director of the local bank in Johnstown and eventually left the Old Order Amish church ("Obituary" 1886, 1).

The Civil War changed all this, but slowly. The Amish and the Mennonites were caught poorly prepared for the challenge that the war brought to their nonresistant faith. In the annual Amish ministers' meeting of 1863, the propriety of serving in local public office, especially in time of war, was raised. No mention was made of voting. But two years later, at the close of the war, Bishop Jacob Swartzendruber included voting in his plea to remain aloof from politics: "Our people should all keep themselves apart from all party matters in political things where brother votes against brother and father against son. What a poverty this is throughout our congregations that we want to help to rule the world, we who are chosen out of the world by God" (H. S. Bender 1946, 225).

The war also prompted Amishman S. D. Mast to write a lengthy article in the *Herold der Wahrheit*.[31] He observed that for the last one hundred years his forebears and other nonresistant people in the United States "have participated in worldly elections," yet all this voting did not prevent a bloody Civil War. Mast's arguments against voting and office holding are well reasoned. His article has been reprinted twice in the twentieth century.[32] Mast posed the question formally: "Can we be true followers of Jesus Christ, observers of his commandments, and true spiritual citizens in his spiritual and heavenly kingdom, and at the same time be citizens in the earthly and worldly kingdom, and take part in worldly rule or government, helping to direct and administer it?" Mast answered his own question with an unequivocal no, as have other Amish writers ever since.

In supporting their policy of nonparticipation in politics, the Amish continue to lean heavily on Schnell's and Mast's version of the two-kingdom doctrine. However, the worldly kingdom envisioned in that doctrine has become, in twentieth-century America, a relatively benevolent democracy. Since in a democracy the people rule, Christians become a part of the collective sovereign. Simply by virtue of their birth or parentage, Christians become citizens with the right to vote and to hold office as they reach adulthood. They are, willy-nilly, citizens and magistrates in an earthly, worldly kingdom. This poses a problem for Amish theologians, for, in the language of the New Testament, Christians have their citizenship in heaven.

Amish writers agree that since Americans live in a democracy, the day-to-day friction between the two kingdoms is often reduced. Said Bishop Troyer in 1898, "We cannot thank God enough that we have such a praiseworthy government as we have."[33] But this circumstance only slightly diminishes the inherent tension between the kingdoms; the separation must be maintained. The Amish perpetuate the separation by not assuming their rights as citizens, by not exercising their part in a shared sovereignty. Nonparticipation absolves them of any responsibility for the exercise of force by the state. If they do not help to elect government officials, the latter are then not their deputies or representatives. It follows that nonvoters are not responsible for the acts of officials they do not help to elect.[34]

In this secular world, Christians are merely "strangers and

pilgrims" (I Peter 2:11) or "strangers and foreigners" (Ephesians 2:19). Using another metaphor drawn from the New Testament, Amish leaders insist that as "ambassadors for Christ" (II Corinthians 5:20) they may not participate in the politics of the nation. In the words of Amishman Eli Garber (1960, 412), "We are not residents but transients."

In accord with Bishop Swartzendruber's denunciation of hiring substitutes in wartime, Amish writers assert that voting is like hiring others to do what we ourselves would not do because it is wrong. Elected officials have recourse directly or indirectly to coercion and are expected to use it if necessary. By participating in their election, one partakes in un-Christlike activities.

Twentieth-century Amish writers have moved beyond narrow doctrinal boundaries to slightly more pragmatically oriented reasons for nonparticipation in the affairs of government. Voting, they suggest, is taking God's role. God sets up anyone he wants to, even a Pharaoh, a Nebuchadnezzar, or a Nero. And who is to divine the mind of God? One Amishman asked, almost derisively, whether God lost the election of 1960 when John Kennedy, a Catholic, won despite the votes of many "Christian" citizens.[35]

The Amish note that the problem of choosing among candidates is compounded by campaign propaganda and the impossibility of knowing them personally. For example, the critics of John Kennedy failed to note that, of all the American colonies, only Catholic-controlled Maryland allowed a full measure of religious liberty. And what of Richard Nixon, who, as Kennedy's opponent, was hailed as the *good* candidate? Obviously, Amish confusion about the qualification of candidates applies to other sectors of the electorate as well. Among the Amish, however, there is corporate agreement that these are reasons why they should not vote.[36]

Because the views and qualities of candidates are blurred, members of the same family, the same community, and the same church frequently vote for opposing candidates. The control of government shifts from party to party. Amishman S. D. Mast (1874, 117) compared these circumstances to the construction of a building where "one party expends every effort to tear down what the other constructs." Amish writers have also accepted the logic of their critics who say that those who do not perform the duty of fighting for their country have no right to vote or to hold public office.[37] Ergo, a nonresistant Christian should not vote.

The very essence of a political campaign repulses conscientious Amish. Gelassenheit is replaced by self-adulation. Exaltation of the candidate approaches idolatry. Ostentatious parades violate the spirit of simplicity and humility. Instead of "preferring one another in honor" (Romans 12:10), the candidates engage in self-glorification and make spectacles of themselves as they harangue the crowd "with a big mouth."[38]

What of local elections, where the candidates are well known and elected officials rarely rely on coercion, if at all? Many Amish writers suggest that citizens in Christ's kingdom should not participate in the affairs of the kingdom of this world in any way.[39] In the words of Elmo Stoll (February 1989, 11): "If we begin to take part in politics, even on a local level, we will soon become confused about our values and our identity. We may even begin to think and act somewhat like politicians."

Some Amish writers propose that, instead of voting, a Christian should pray for those in authority that God's will be accomplished at election time. "A half hour on the knees in a locked closet," wrote Daniel Stutzman, "is worth more than if we had the right to cast a thousand votes. For the Lord does what the God-fearing request."[40]

One example of the Amish attitude toward participation in the political life of the nation comes from the Amish of Holmes County, Ohio. A Christian should not "help to elect or participate in the official functions of government, neither by lobbying nor protesting" (*Truth* 1983, 50). Recently the National Amish Steering Committee (Steering 1981–86, 76), a body outside the traditional polity of the Amish church but in accord with its doctrines, has discouraged both voting and jury duty.

Judging by the Amish writers who oppose voting and other forms of political participation, one might expect total abstention, but such is not the case. Many bishops and congregations have permitted members to vote. The amount of voting varies from settlement to settlement and by the relevance of local issues. The voters follow almost two centuries of practice and their local church discipline rather than attending to their writers. The Amish church has no formal restrictions on voting in either local or national elections. Amish reluctance to vote is shaped more by their belief in the futility of political action than by any formal religious taboos.

This attitude also explains why they are more likely to participate in local than national elections. Said one Amishman, "Some Amish vote in local elections when they feel that their vote can make a difference. Others never vote, no matter what."[41] When elections focus on school consolidation, special education for handicapped children, land use, taxes for the construction of a gymnasium, or other issues directly affecting the Amish, many are quite ready to vote.[42] In fact, in a township election in the late 1980s involving land use issues, one Amishman talked of "the Amish vote."

On the matter of holding public office and serving on juries, church writers find greater accord with church practices. But even with respect to office holding, the proscription has not always been airtight. Rarely, but at times in some localities, Amish persons have served as school directors and road supervisors.[43] The rule against serving on juries is less equivocal. Church disciplines of the nineteenth century strictly forbade it, and the restriction remains intact today. Thus, Amish separation from government sharpens over jury duty and office holding but weakens in regard to voting.

The Amish and Courts of Law

The Anabaptists, whom the Amish consider their spiritual forebears, were, in the words of John Oyer (1985, 5), "unalterably opposed to instituting suits at law." Revenge and retaliation were unacceptable forms of Christian conduct. For the Anabaptists, use of the law clashed with the teachings of Christ as much as personal reprisal.

The Amish have never questioned the taboo on lawsuits. Christ's Sermon on the Mount was very clear on this point. He said, "If any man will sue you at the law, and take away thy coat, let him have thy cloak also" (Matthew 5:40). Moreover, Jesus admonished, "Of him that taketh away thy goods ask them not again" (Luke 6:30). When suing, the retaliator takes on one of God's prerogatives, for the Lord said, "Vengeance is mine; I will repay" (Romans 12:19; Hebrews 10:30). Such self-assertion is out of harmony with the spirit of Gelassenheit. The highly revered *Martyrs Mirror* provides additional support against initiating lawsuits. It explicitly says, "Christians are forbidden to sue for their rights at law" (Hochstetler 1972, 15).

Relinquishing the right to initiate lawsuits became increasingly difficult for the Amish after the mid-nineteenth century. As they began to accumulate personal property and real estate, property owners occasionally used the law. That such violations of church discipline were both new and growing is evinced by the repeated protests of Bishop David Beiler (1888, 115ff.) in his *Wahre Christenthum*, completed in 1857. At the end of the century, Bishop David A. Troyer (Treyer 1898) opined that there was no clearer teaching in the New Testament than that against using the law to recover property. The Amish ministers' meeting of 1868 debated with unusual vigor the question of whether it is right, "if something is stolen from us . . . to pursue the thief and let the government throw him into prison and punish him." The assembled ministers agreed that to do so for the sake of vengeance or the recovery of property was not right. On the question of reporting a thief in the interests of law and order and not for personal reasons, the ministers could not agree (*Verhandlungen* 1868, 6ff.).

Recent decades have put the restriction on lawsuits to the test. As Amish people have become entrepreneurs in a variety of businesses, the temptation to use the law to protect their financial interests has increased. Although Hostetler (1993, 256) asserts that "the Amish do not resort to courts of law to settle disputes among themselves or with outsiders," they have come perilously close to doing so on occasion. They have used the threat of lawsuits and other devices to avoid the formal designation of plaintiff.[44] Some Amish buy types of insurance in which it is assumed that the insurance company will sue to recover damages (Hochstetler 1972, 15).

To be sued is not as culpable as suing, for the defendant may be completely innocent. In any case, he is not the invoker of the law. Nevertheless, the Amish believe that they should avoid such involvement as much as possible and try to "live peaceably with all men" (Romans 12:18). Normally, if the judgment of the court is against the defendant, he should obey the law as interpreted by the court. However, according to Hostetler (1993, 256), if obeying implies a kind of reprehensible guilt as well as legal liability, then noncompliance may be justified on occasion.

Liability suits have been of particular concern to Amish business persons. In the 1960s, some of them began to take out liability insurance with commercial companies. Such companies invoke the law at will, contrary to Amish principles. Thus, the Amish in Lancaster County, Pennsylvania, began their own "Liability Aid" program. Some writers, however, decry this concern for material possessions. Such assets are of "secondary" value. Liability lawsuits cannot take away one's "hope of heaven . . . good conscience . . . [and] peace of mind" (E. Stoll 1984, 8–11).

Sam D. Yoder (1977, 281), a New Order Amishman, reflects the general feeling of the Amish toward lawsuits by observing that (1) they are contrary to the Spirit of God, (2) they are unnecessary, (3) they always cause bitter feelings, and (4) as a rule both sides are losers.

Disputes in which both parties are members of Amish congregations may not be submitted to the courts. For these they have their own time-honored *Prozess*, or congregational court. David Beiler's (1928, 9) description of such a court as it functioned in the nineteenth century shows that its practice was similar to that of today. He described the procedure in the case of an insolvent member of the congregation thus:

> It was unanimously decided that if one comes so far behind that he can no longer meet his [financial] obligations, then he should give an account of his debts, I think before the congregation. . . . Then the deacon and a trusted brother in the congregation shall take over his property and make a distribution which would be fair and brotherly. And if it was done in this manner, then patience was to be extended to him if it [the proceeds] did not reach [cover his debts].

What John A. Hostetler (1993, 355–58) has called rowdyism has produced another kind of legal problem. In some Amish communities, particularly the larger ones, Amish youth who have not yet joined the church sometimes engage in illegal activities. These include consumption of alcoholic beverages, disturbing the peace, and vandalism.[45] Most of this misconduct occurs within the Amish community. As may be anticipated, law enforcement officials are rarely called upon to intervene on such occasions. However, if the rowdyism violates the public peace or safety, officers of the law will arrest Amish youth.

Sometimes adult conduct violates both the standards of the church and the criminal code of the state. Typical of almost any religious body, cases of statutory rape and incest are occasionally discovered among the Amish. Usually such cases are dealt with according to accepted Amish church discipline and do not come to the attention of the courts. This concerns some Amish who feel that such procedure violates the Amish position of submission to government. "If we are willing to suffer imprisonment when we are *innocent* of any crime," says Amishman Stoll (1988, 8), "surely we should be willing when we are guilty."

Related to the Amish position on the use and nonuse of law courts is the Anabaptist rejection of the legal oath.[46] Christ could not have been more direct. "Swear not at all," he said, "not by heaven, the earth, or by Jerusalem. And do not swear by your head," he continued, "for you cannot make one hair white or black." Any expression more emphatic than merely "Yes, yes," and "No, no . . . cometh of evil" (paraphrase of Matthew 5:34–37). Rejecting the legal oath in the sixteenth century was not a simple rejection of a formal court ritual. The oath was "viewed as a basic foundational element for social order, the glue that held society

together."[47] If one swore to the God of the universe in the sixteenth century, committing perjury could bring eternal damnation
to one's soul. The oath made God the guarantor of the integrity of
the legal system.

In today's secular society, the oath no longer commands such
awesome respect. Consequently, it is difficult to comprehend how
revolutionary the Anabaptist refusal of the oath appeared to governments of that day. Nevertheless, the Amish—biblicists rooted
in tradition—are careful to obey Christ's injunction to refrain from
using the legal oath. The modern view of the legal oath, as contrasted with that of the Reformation era, is reflected in a doctrinal
statement drawn up by the Amish of Holmes County, Ohio: "Because Christians always have a high regard for the truth, they do
not accept the worldly system which has a time of being 'especially truthful' (under oath). For the greatest oath is too weak to
make an untruth true" (Truth 1983, 51).

A Paradoxical Stance

The Amish believe that governments are worldly, just as theater
and organized sports are worldly. And they believe that the state
and the church have nothing of consequence in common. If this
relationship were illustrated graphically by two circles, they
would hardly touch. Indeed, they would be separated by considerable space. Nevertheless the Amish do believe that governments
are instituted by God. This ambivalence, or paradox, permeates
the Amish view of the state. They inherited this problem from the
early Anabaptists, and to the present time have neither resolved
nor discarded it. Anabaptist scholar John Oyer (1985, 9) describes
the paradox:

> The state is bad but does a good and necessary task. It is evil to
> the point of being our, the true Christian's, enemy. But it uses a
> necessary physical force to perform its own type of good, some-
> thing that is strictly forbidden to the Christian or that will damage
> the Christian morally. We Christians . . . are vastly different from
> the magistracy: the Christian should let the state be the state, and
> not trouble himself overmuch about how it carries out its evil
> means for its particular type of moral purpose.

The Amish do not want to be involved in the affairs of government in any manner, and they want the state to remain far removed from them in all matters of faith and practice. Nevertheless,

according to Elmo Stoll (February 1989, 12), Amish Christians should (1) honor the magistracy, (2) pray for those in authority, (3) pay their taxes, and (4) obey the laws of the land, except those that conflict with Amish faith and practice. These are the all-inclusive obligations of the Christian to the state.

Without hesitation the Amish agree that government in America is relatively benign. In the United States and Canada they enjoy unusual liberties, and they are highly appreciative of these circumstances. Nevertheless, in their minds, the underlying historic incompatibility of church and state cannot change. With a tinge of sarcasm, one Amish writer responded to a plea by a Mennonite that Amish church members could "serve both God and man" by taking positions in government. "Just think," the Amishman said, "of the grand opportunity Jesus had to serve both God and man, had he accepted the kingship they tried to force on him. He fed the multitude with a few loaves; could he not at least have administered their social welfare department?"[48]

General Lewis B. Hershey, director of Selective Service, discusses alternatives to military service with an Amish leader in 1941. Two Old Order Mennonites listen to the discussion. Richard K. Reinhold

CHAPTER THREE

Military Service and Conscription

Albert N. Keim

 The Amish are widely known for their pacifist convictions and their objection to military service, principles that rest on the most fundamental Amish understandings of religious faith. Expectations for military service constitute a basic threat to Amish religion. Historian Albert Keim charts the variety of negotiated agreements that have developed between the Amish and the state since the Revolutionary War. Primary attention is given to World War II and Amish participation in Civilian Public Service.

David Wagler arrived at Civilian Public Service Camp 20 at Sideling Hill, Pennsylvania, late on the night of 6 November 1942, eleven months after Pearl Harbor. The United States was at war. Wagler, a young Amishman from Daviess County, Indiana, had just been drafted. A conscientious objector (CO), he was sent to a Civilian Public Service (CPS) camp rather than to a military site. Sideling Hill was the first of three CPS camps where he was interned as a CO for the duration of the war. Wagler was finally released in February 1946.[1]

Sideling Hill was one of more than 150 CPS camps created as an alternative to military service for COs during World War II. At Sideling Hill, David Wagler joined Mennonite young men employed by the Soil Conservation Service. The men prepared fields in the area for contour farming by clearing fence lines and constructing new fences. Many of the CPSers also worked on landscape and erosion control projects for the Pennsylvania Turnpike.

American wars have always created serious problems for the Amish. The religious center of their community revolves around *wehrlosigkeit*—nonresistance. Nonresistant convictions are woven into the fabric of the basic Amish belief, nonconformity. To refuse to conform to the outside world, at the most pragmatic level, means to have as little to do with it as possible. The Amish seek to create an alternative community guided by their own set of standards, with only limited and necessary contact with the larger world. For the Amish, war best illustrates a sinful world acting in violation of God's fundamental will and purpose. War is sin. The Amish are biblical literalists: they believe that Jesus' words to enjoin love and nonviolence are to be practiced. This is the fundamental ground of their position. When Jesus said, "Turn the other cheek," that is exactly what he meant—leaving no room for litigation or self-defense. From such a vantage point, participation in war is simply impossible.

The Revolutionary War

The first test of Amish nonresistance in America came during the Revolutionary War. The Amish hoped to remain aloof from the conflict. Hans Lantz, a Pennsylvania Amishman, reflected this when he argued that Christians should "give all just obedience . . . faithfulness, love, honor and taxes, [and] benevolence" to the king; they should pray for him and "live in harmony" (MacMaster 1985, 274). To rebel against the king was unthinkable. The typical Amish response to repressive government for over two hundred years was to flee into exile. It was one of the reasons they had left Europe and were living in Pennsylvania in 1776.

In 1777 Pennsylvania, Maryland, Virginia, and North Carolina passed stringent legislation pertaining to participation in the militia and hiked the fines for those who refused to drill or to hire substitutes. These fines were added to the special tax COs already paid as nonassociators. The penalty money was collected by the county sheriff. Sparse evidence suggests that few if any Amish served in the militia. For example, Richard MacMaster (1985, 254) discovered that in Earl Township, Lancaster County, of nine eligible Amishmen none served.

The evidence suggests that the Amish did pay war taxes and other assessments. Lancaster Amish assured a Lancaster County militia committee that their members were "willing to contribute money to assist the Common Cause otherwise than by taking up arms." In Earl Township many Amish gave to a general fund, ostensibly for poor families and refugees; but the money actually went for military purposes (MacMaster 1985).

There is evidence of real persecution. Amishman Isaac Kauffman, a farmer in Berks County, Pennsylvania, got in trouble when he told soldiers demanding his horse, "You are rebels and I will not give a horse to such bloodthirsty persons." He was jailed for his outburst (MacMaster 1985, 259).

The Revolutionary War tested Amish convictions. In the heat of war they had to take stands on issues such as substitutes, nonmilitary support for the war effort, and war taxes. Richard MacMaster (1985, 276) observes: "Mennonites and Amish came to the American Revolution with their commitment to nonresistance intact. Only a small percentage compromised their faith by taking an active part with either side."

The Civil War

The Amish experience in the Civil War paralleled the Mennonite response: a few enlisted, but most refused the draft. In Ohio, Governor Tod was advised that he should avoid trying to draft the Amish in Holmes County because of their stubbornness in refusing to enlist. Not only that, if drafted they would not fight. Better, his advisers told him, to let them find substitutes. Indiana, Ohio, and Pennsylvania allowed their Amish citizens to pay commutation fees to hire substitutes (Schlabach 1988, 185).

With the national draft of 1863, conscientious objectors could simply pay a three hundred-dollar commutation fee. Most Amish avoided enlistment that way. In several Pennsylvania counties, they chose a more time-honored way—migration. Some moved to Iowa (Schlabach 1988, 188). The Civil War experience of the Amish was not one of their finest hours. Some went to war, and others paid a commutation fee in lieu of military service. The first modern draft encountered by the Amish did not produce any creative ways of dealing with conscription.

World War I

By World War I, the distinctions between the Mennonites and the Amish had grown more explicit. The Amish *Ordnung* expressed specific boundaries of their community through sumptuary regulations on dress and technology. Amish farm technology, for example, was frozen at a turn-of-the-century level. Thus, the distinctions between the Amish and the outside world were more obvious than in the nineteenth century. By World War I, the Amish had developed a cultural and social isolation from American society. This sheltered them from the war hysteria that enveloped so much of the nation in 1917 and 1918.

Most of the Amish young men who were drafted in World War I became COs. One young Amishman went to war. John Bontrager, son of Bishop Eli Bontrager, much to his father's regret, enlisted and worked in a machine shop south of Paris as a mechanic. In his memoirs Eli comments on John's decision: "When this country entered World War No. I in 1917 and conscription started, he was a resident of Montana, and as such he realized that they would get him sooner or later for the army. Not knowing how objectors to war would be dealt with, and possibly not having been indoctrinated with the doctrine of nonresistance as he should have been, he enlisted for service in the armed forces of the nation" (E. Bontrager 1956, 27). After his return from the army, John married a Mennonite and joined the Mennonite church.

During World War I, the War Department, under Secretary of War Newton D. Baker, played a cat-and-mouse game with COs. The draft law recognized conscientious objection but left the deployment of COs to the president and the War Department. As a result, COs were drafted into the army and posted to military camps with the hope that they would enter noncombatant service.

After Secretary of War Baker inspected a group of COs at Camp Meade in Maryland, he told President Wilson that he had ordered the segregation of COs from their fellow soldiers. Baker hoped that the feeling of rejection would force their cooperation and that only a hard core of Amish and Quakers would be left (Beaver 1966, 33). Baker's experiment failed. Few COs changed their minds.

Young COs at the army bases struggled with how much to cooperate with the camp authorities. Should they work in the canteen? What about weeding flower beds? Should they wear a uniform but refuse to carry a rifle? Whatever the decision, it rarely satisfied the officers in charge, who were often short-tempered with the troublesome "conchies." As a result the COs often suffered shortened rations, solitary confinement, physical abuse, and court-martial.

Henry H. Miller was a young Amishman drafted in the fall of 1917. After a few weeks at Fort Dodge near Des Moines, Iowa, he was shipped to Fort Cody, New Mexico. Upon arrival he was asked to pick up a gun and to drill. When he refused, his clothes were taken from him; with some reluctance, he finally put on the uniform left in his cell. Several weeks later, apparently having convinced the authorities that he was incorrigible, he was allowed to wear his civilian clothes again (*Herold*, 1 January 1918, 21).

Mose Miller, from Holmes County, Ohio, was interned at Camp Sherman in southern Ohio. In a letter he reported that about forty COs were living in the hallway of a barracks. Their only duty was to keep things tidy and be present for roll call (*Herold*, 1 April 1918, 166).

A poignant scene, reflecting the trauma of an Amishman caught in the military machine, is described in a letter from young Menno Brenneman. Bewildered and frightened, he was marched from a train to nearby Camp Taylor, Kentucky. As they entered the camp, he looked up; to his immense delight, he spotted an Amish friend, Jacob Mast, sitting in an upstairs barracks window. As his troop marched by Jacob yelled to Brenneman, "Macht's Gut!" ("Good Luck!"). Never, wrote Brenneman, had those commonplace words meant so much to him. He needed reassurance, for in the same letter he reported that one Amishman was already in the brig, and he would soon be there too, since he was refusing to cooperate with his sergeant (*Herold*, 15 July 1918, 338).

All COs were sent directly to army camps, without a clear word from the War Department about their disposition. Officials hoped that being young and malleable, they might succumb to the peer pressure of the drill field. Thus the real burden of deciding how to respond fell on the shoulders of the young COs. The plaintive complaint from a Church of the Brethren CO at Camp Funston captures the dilemma faced by many young men: "We don't know how far to go because our church hasn't defined our privilege yet."[2] This was not so for the Amish. The editor of the *Herold der Wahrheit*, an Amish paper, laid out the Amish position with clarity: "We can't have anything to do with the war machine whatsoever."[3]

Earlier in 1918, the editor noted that just as millions of young men are called upon to fight and give their lives for the victory of their countries, Amish youth must see their refusal to cooperate with the military as a way to achieve eternal life (victory) for themselves and the church. "The church depends on you," the editor continued, "for you are the church of the future. Don't accept any work which is under the military, because if you do you will be part of the war machine whose purpose it is to destroy people and property" (*Herold*, 15 May 1918, 222).

An Amish committee had participated in a Mennonite conference on the military draft on 29 August 1917 and helped to fashion a two-point statement to guide Amish draftees: (1) "We advise our brethren to state their position on the church, creed, and principles to Army officers at mobilization camps." (2) "We again encourage our brethren not to accept any service, either combatant or non-combatant, under the military arm of the government in violation of their conscience and the creed of the church" (*Herold*, 15 September 1917, 351).

Amish ministers, concerned about their young men, frequently visited the camps. The young men also received free copies of *Herold der Wahrheit*. A minister visiting young Noah Gingerich at Fort Dodge discovered that Gingerich was not getting the *Herold*. His suspicions aroused, he accosted the captain, who admitted he had not been forwarding it. "Why?" asked the minister. Replied the captain: "It's in German, and military regulations require it to be translated before I can let Noah have it" (*Herold*, 21 July 1918, 294).

On 16 March 1918, Congress passed the Farm Furlough Bill, ostensibly releasing soldiers needed in agriculture. In fact, however, the new law offered a means of moving absolutist COs out of army camps and onto farms for the duration of the war. Unfortunately, bureaucratic red tape and the preoccupation with the war slowed down the process. Eventually some of the COs were furloughed to farms, though not without public protest from the communities where the men were employed. The COs were paid at the rate of a private, though some men refused payment.

The number of Amishmen actually drafted was likely less than one hundred. One reason for the small number was that Pennsylvania draft boards readily gave farm deferments. James Juhnke (1989, 237) quotes Congressman William Griest, Lancaster County representative, as saying that as many as 95 percent of Mennonites and Amish were deferred on vocational grounds. World War I was a traumatic event for the Amish. Nothing suggests this more strongly than the extraordinary step that they took in sending an Amish delegation to visit Secretary of War Baker in August 1917 (Hartzler 1921, 66). The visit did not change the secretary's strategy, but he must have been impressed by their concern and sincerity.

The War Department was surely not prepared for the tenacity of Amish and other peace church objectors. The Amish, committed to sectarian separation from American culture, had to depend on the steadfastness of their young men. The naive sincerity of the young Amishmen is perhaps the most inspiring aspect of what was, in many ways, a sad encounter between the Amish and the warring state.

World War II

Conventional pacifism typically waxes between wars and wanes during them. Except for a small coterie of the devoted, pacifism has not withstood the winds of patriotic fervor generated by twentieth-century wars. For the Amish, the cycle is just the opposite: pacifist convictions emerge primarily when the warring state requires conscriptive service. American wars have always threatened the Amish community and its values. Behind the protective cover of nonconformity to the world, the Amish resist societal pressures in wartime far better than their more principled pacifist comrades.

World War II presented a particular challenge to pacifists. Studs Terkel has called it "The Good War," a clear case of good versus evil, freedom versus tyranny. On what possible basis could one choose not to fight against Hitler and his minions? It was a hard call for most pacifists, and most elected to join the war effort.

Of 34 million men registered for the draft during World War II, only 72,354 applied for CO status. Among the COs, 25,000 accepted noncombatant service in the army. Another 27,000 failed the physical health examination or were deferred for other reasons. Some 6,000 were jailed for refusing to do service of any kind. Just 12,000 chose the only other option: work of "national importance" under the CPS program. Among the 12,000 CPSers were 441 Amish (Keim 1990, 8). The number of Amish might have been much higher, but by 1944 many Pennsylvania draft boards readily gave farm deferments to the Amish. This was not true everywhere, however: some counties in Iowa gave almost no deferments.

Mennonites, Brethren, and Quakers—known as "historic peace churches"—held bad memories of their CO experience in World War I. Determined to repair the mistakes of the past in this new war, they proposed a new plan. They tried to forge a program called "alternative service," which would, in the words of Quaker Clarence Pickett, be a "moral equivalent to war" (Pickett 1953, 309). This would provide humanitarian work for COs in lieu of serving in the army or going to jail.

By strenuous lobbying efforts, the historic peace churches succeeded in writing an alternative service clause into the 1940 Draft Act, signed by the president on 16 September. It officially recognized a class of COs who would not do any military service whatsoever. Instead, they would perform work of "national importance under civilian direction" as established by the president.

During the fall of 1940, the historic peace churches designed the CPS program through delicate negotiations with the new Selective

Service bureaucrats. It became the alternative service program for COs who chose not to go to jail or to enter noncombatant service.

Civilian Public Service resulted from an unusual collaboration between the United States government and the historic peace churches. The men were housed in former Civilian Conservation Corps camps. Their work was managed by government agencies such as the National Park Service, the Soil Conservation Service, and the Forest Service. These agencies provided the tools and materials for the projects. The historic peace churches funded all the expenses for the men, including food, administrative costs, and a tiny monthly stipend of two dollars and fifty cents. Selective Service paid travel costs for the men.

The program was jointly administered by Selective Service and a church agency called the National Service Board for Religious Objectors. The CPS camps were managed by different church groups. For example, the Mennonites operated camps primarily for Mennonite men; the Brethren and the Quakers did the same for their own adherents. About half of all the CPS men were not related to these three churches. Most of the objectors who were not from the historic peace churches served in camps operated by the Brethren or the Quakers. There was a camp for Catholic COs, and later in the war there were several government camps operated by Selective Service. Most Amish served in Mennonite camps. By the time CPS ended in 1947, more than 150 camps and detached units had been part of the program.

The Amish were pleased with CPS. As Bishop Eli J. Bontrager put it in 1945, "Taking everything into consideration we believe the present set-up is as nearly ideal as we could reasonably expect." He was less happy with detached service—work in mental hospitals and on dairy farms—and concluded, "We would [have] preferred having our boys remain in the camps" (Wagler and Raber 1945, 6). The camps, usually isolated and rural, seemed a safer environment to Amish leaders than the city-based hospitals and the modernized dairy farms that some Amish CPSers selected.

By World War II, Bishop Bontrager had become one of the foremost Amish bishops, with a reputation as an able mediator in church controversies. At the outset of the CPS program, he joined the governing body of the Mennonite Central Committee. Earlier in the year he had accompanied a delegation of Mennonites that visited the U.S. Attorney General to explain Mennonite and Amish concerns about their young conscientious objectors (Bontrager 1956, 23).

By 1942, a sizable number of Amish youth had been drafted into CPS. Bontrager and Bishop Ira Nissley, of Kalona, Iowa, were appointed by the Mennonite Central Committee to visit, counsel, and minister to Amish boys in CPS. With his usual vigor, the seventy-four-year-old Bishop Bontrager traveled incessantly, visiting every CPS camp that had Amish draftees. In some cases he visited camps twice a year. During one month-long trip in 1944, he traveled seventy-five hundred miles by train, and spent eleven nights on the trip sleeping in his train seat.

CPS Camp Experiences

The experience of Amish CPSers has been wonderfully evoked in several first-person accounts. Henry Swartzentruber, of Oakland, Maryland, received his draft orders on 25 June 1941. Convinced that a deferment was impossible, he responded to his draft orders by traveling via bus and train to a newly opened CPS camp near Grottoes, Virginia. The site was an abandoned Civilian Conservation Corps camp in the western foothills of the Blue Ridge Mountains. Swartzentruber's draft orders called for a one-year stint of service. After Pearl Harbor, the stint expanded "for the duration." The duration for Swartzentruber became four and one-half years. Swartzentruber was a rarity among CPSers—he stayed at the Grottoes camp for his entire term of service. Most CPSers moved many times.

Swartzentruber quickly settled into the routine of the camp, which included other Amish fellows. The work was familiar to an Amish farm boy—digging postholes and helping with soil conservation projects. In September, he was appointed crew foreman. He described the job:

> Today I take on the duty as crew foreman . . . a job I'd much rather not tackle, but someone has to. This involves the ability to understand and fulfill the work orders of the technicians, getting along with the government men, the farmers, and with each person on the crew. Attitudes toward us as COs surfaced at times, especially when farmers had soldier boys in service. Thankfully almost always we could humbly explain our stand by telling them our terms grant us nothing for wages, clothes, and our time. Our churches furnish our food, the government provides this work of national importance, and Selective Service continuously rules over us. (*Mennonite Historical Bulletin*, July 1990, 4)

Swartzentruber liked the Grottoes camp. He had high regard for the camp director, Mennonite John Mosemann. The Amish were always self-conscious about their differences with the Mennonites, and some Amish leaders worried about their young men living and working in such close quarters with them. Bishop Bontrager was quite sanguine about it, however. Reflecting on his visits to CPS camps during the war, he observed, "Many of the Amishmen in the camps scattered throughout the United States lived true to the rules and regulations of the home church and seemed to remember their vows and obligations, letting their light shine and getting much benefit out of their camp life" (Wagler and Raber 1945, 6).

While many Mennonite men complained about the relatively tight discipline at Mennonite camps, most Amishmen felt the controls were often lax. Swartzentruber was upset by some men complaining and breaking the rules. He noted with some acerbity that a group of "unruly" men smuggled radios into the dorms; the radios were then confiscated, and the director canceled all leaves and furloughs. Later he reported:

> Our dorm had a bull session after supper till an all-black-out caused it to stop. One boy wants a warm place to smoke in, another argued that listening to ball games on Sundays on the radio is not harmful. Another tried to tell them the ideal way to keep the Sabbath holy, then about eternal security, different degrees of reward in heaven and hell. We find ourselves so different, yet we're all here for one purpose. We must get along with each other. (*Mennonite Historical Bulletin*, July 1990, 11)

Swartzentruber was a loyal and serious Amishman who found the Grottoes camp stimulating and interesting. He was always appreciative of the religious activities at the camp. For a young Amishman, the energetic preaching and music at Mennonite worship services could be quite seductive. This worried many Amish church leaders and spurred aggressive efforts to visit their young men in the camps.

At Medaryville, Indiana, a Mennonite camp, considerable tension arose between camp administrators and Amish boys over the question of religious services. Several nearby Amish communities sent ministers to the camp every two weeks to conduct Amish services. The camp director insisted that the services be held on Sunday afternoons to avoid conflict with the Mennonite services. The Amish objected. Mediation by Harold Bender, dean of Goshen College, and Bishop Eli Bontrager finally brought peace by allowing

Amish services on Sunday morning alongside the Mennonite services. Medaryville was also unique because it had an "Amish dorm." In comparison to the regular dormitories, it was characterized by a more sedate decorum. The men had group prayer each evening before going to bed, and card playing was strictly forbidden.

THE BOONESBORO UNIT

Problems of this sort led to the creation of the most unusual CPS camp in the program—the Amish unit at Boonesboro, Maryland. The camp emerged out of a plan to create farm units to work at soil conservation in the Cumberland Valley of Washington County, Maryland. The local county agent hoped CPSers could improve conservation practices, but he also believed that soldiers returning from the war might be able to model their own subsistence agricultural efforts after the CPS farms.

The Mennonite Central Committee and the Brethren Service Committee responded to the idea with enthusiasm. Eventually five farm units were established, three under the Mennonites and two under the Brethren. In the fall of 1941, several Amishmen from Lancaster County, Pennsylvania, purchased a farm near Boonesboro, and in the spring of 1942 the unit opened. Although the camp was under Mennonite jurisdiction, it was operated by the Amish, usually with an older Amishman from the Lancaster area as director. Reuben Z. Stoltzfus served for two years as the director, while other persons served for shorter periods of time. The director was assisted by two church committees in the operation of the camp. Three bishops helped in the spiritual oversight of the unit, while another committee of three supervised the business matters of the unit.

Normally the camp had about thirty men from many parts of the country. Typically they were called "easterners" or "westerners"—the latter included anyone from west of Pennsylvania. The men were housed in a large brick farmhouse and in a nearby dormitory constructed for that purpose. Married men got first choice of the farmhouse, which also served as a mess hall and meeting place for the unit. The composition of the unit was somewhat atypical for CPS. Half of the men were married. A third had at least one child; two-thirds of the men were twenty-five years or older; and three-fourths were farmers. Only three men had been factory workers.

Two CPS men operated the 142-acre farm. In 1944 the unit paper, the *Sunbeam*, reported that the farm had 6 horses, 5 cows, 150 chickens, 6 sows, and an assortment of other hogs. Six cats and several dogs completed the animal roster. When market conditions were favorable the farm bought steers in Chicago, which were then fattened and sold on the eastern market to raise cash for its operation (*Sunbeam*, 1 June 1944, 4). The farm provided the basic food and shelter needed by the CPS men working in the conservation program.

The men ate well; in fact, they ate extremely well. David Wagler, newly arrived from the large Mennonite camp at Sideling Hill, remembered his first meal at the farm:

> The meal was simple enough but I can still see the platters heaped with peach dumplings, surrounded by big pitchers of real milk. There was also homemade butter and dishes of preserves placed at convenient intervals. Behind the farmhouse was a large garden which furnished many fresh vegetables and berries for the table. From the henhouse came eggs galore and fresh chicken. The dairy cows furnished milk and cream. . . . We were allowed to help ourselves to the skim milk . . . anytime we wished. (*Ambassador*, June 1966, 16)

Just before Christmas 1944, the unit received seventy-five gallons of apple butter from Lancaster, Pennsylvania, and several bushels of peanuts from Delaware (*Sunbeam*, 15 December 1944, 4). The unit regularly received canned goods, meat, fruits, and vegetables from Pennsylvania Amish communities.

The unit operated like a large Amish family. David Wagler caught the ambience:

> At the head of the table sat the venerable white-bearded camp director, Reuben Z. Stoltzfus, with sufficiently solemn appearance of being the father of the entire group. By his side was his alert little wife, Sarah, with her watchful eye, ever ready to care for the needs of the family under her care. As we bowed our heads in a long and silent prayer of thanksgiving before partaking of the food, we were overcome with awe. We felt here was a touch of home, the kind we dreamed of, filled with love and peace. (*Ambassador*, June 1966, 16)

As in any Amish home, religious activities circumscribed the common life. Wagler describes it thus:

> Every morning after breakfast there was time for a short devotion period. In the evening at a regular time the "family" gathered and listened reverently while the director read a chapter from the Bible and led in prayer. Arrangements were made with the different

Amish congregations to provide ministers on Sundays to conduct church services. Each Sunday evening there was a singing which lasted an hour. (*Ambassador*, June 1966, 17)

The unit had more visitors in one year than any other CPS camp. In fact, they had to renovate a tenant house to lodge visitors. The unit's life and activities were reported in a lively camp paper published twice a month. The editor described the paper's purpose: "Our aim is to put out a plain paper for a plain people written in a way that anyone can understand it" (*Sunbeam*, 1 January 1944, 2). The original subscription, twenty-five cents a year, quickly jumped to seventy-five cents. In January 1945 the paper had 884 regular subscribers, the largest circulation of any camp paper in CPS.

The work of the men in the unit was typical soil conservation work. Area farmers who agreed to improve their pasture fields and take land out of cultivation were eligible to receive CPS labor to help build fences and water diversion ditches and to lay tile to improve drainage. The work was hard, but for the Amish it was similar to farm work at home.

LAYING UP TREASURE IN HEAVEN

The Boonesboro camp involved only a few of the 441 Amishmen in CPS. The rest were scattered throughout the CPS system. In their 1945 book, *The Story of The Amish in Civilian Public Service*, David Wagler and Roman Raber edited the stories of 14 CPS Amishmen. Abraham Graber and Amos Fisher helped to fight flood waters in Iowa and Montana. Leroy Keim led a lonely life on a Forest Service lookout tower. Ed Miller was a subject in a series of human guinea pig experiments at the University of Illinois at Champaign-Urbana. David Yoder cooked for the Smoke Jumper unit at Missoula, Montana. Levi Troyer worked on a dairy farm in Pennsylvania. Alvin Yoder was one of 47 Amish COs who worked in mental hospitals. Harry Weirich, one of the most mobile of all Amish CPSers, transferred to six different camps during his five-year stint. He began his service in Indiana and ended it in Puerto Rico, via California and Montana.

Virtually all Amish who were drafted entered CPS. This compares to 46 percent of the men in the Mennonite church. Clearly, the Amish were less susceptible to the lure of wartime patriotism and the call for civic responsibility than their more assimilated Mennonite cousins. The Amish did have some sense of obligation, however. David Wagler described it this way:

Those who do not share our convictions ought to have no reason to doubt our sincerity. Are we like the man who lays in the shadow and watches his brother work? It is true that we are not on the battlefield fighting but our absence there is excusable only if we are busy working in the Lord's vineyard. If we can live a consistent life and witness for Christ, be it ever so humble, then it will be better than all the vain glory this world has to offer. (*Ambassador*, August 1966, 6)

Wagler's sentiment, shared by most Amish, was not based on a sense of civic obligation. The Amish accepted the government's right to wage war. And they were grateful for the protections offered by the state including, in this case, freedom from military service.

While they valued the opportunity to do humanitarian work, that was not their most important concern. What they really sought was freedom to protect their youth from worldly influences. For example, when service projects detached from camps were approved, they permitted their young men to work on dairy farms. However, they soon learned that dairy farms presented their own special temptations to young men, who lived with the farm families, attended their churches, and operated modern farm machinery. Elders feared that the young men would find it hard to return to Amish ways after their term of service (Wagler and Raber 1945, 6).

Perhaps the Amish position is best illustrated in their strong support for unremunerated CPS service. Many CPS men considered their unpaid labor a form of involuntary servitude. Not so the Amish. The editor of the Boonesboro *Sunbeam* expressed the Amish viewpoint in an editorial: "A large percentage of the Amish church members feel that it is best these men should work without wages." He then noted General Hershey's comment that not paying the CPSers was the "best public relations" advantage the program could have (*Sunbeam*, 1 November 1944, 3). Later the editor said, "Even though we at camp had little chance to gain material wealth, we . . . had plenty of opportunity to 'lay up treasures in Heaven'" (*Sunbeam*, 1 June 1945, 3).

The I-W Program

The last CPS men were released in early 1947, but by then a new military draft loomed on the horizon. Two years earlier, Bishop Eli

Bontrager had accompanied a delegation of Mennonites to Washington to oppose the Universal Military Training Bill pending in Congress. Bontrager visited the office of his congressman and that of Indiana senator George Willis. The senator was absent, but Bontrager left a message about his opposition to the military training bill. The bishop was unimpressed by the senator's response. "In his letter to me in answer to my protest, his position is not clear, as he seemed to avoid the subject" (E. Bontrager 1956, 32).

The draft lapsed in 1947. But with the onset of the cold war, President Harry S Truman called for its reinstatement in early 1948. The new Selective Service bill passed Congress, and in June 1948 Truman signed it into law. The Mennonites and the Amish were dumbfounded to learn that the new law completely deferred all COs. Thus, for the next two years Amish COs simply registered and got automatic deferments. The bill expired in two years. Because of the growing number of casualties in the Korean War, the deferment provision was rescinded in 1950 and replaced with a provision requiring all COs to do "work of national importance under civilian direction." The form of the new alternative service program was finally determined in February 1952. It was often referred to as the I-W program[4]—I-W being the Selective Service classification of COs.

Under the new I-W program, COs worked in government or nonprofit organizations engaged in charitable, health, welfare, education, and scientific work. They could not work in agencies for profit nor remain in their home communities, except in special cases. They could volunteer, choose their service jobs, and serve abroad. In each state, the Selective Service director supervised the program and located jobs for the drafted COs. The term of service was two years. Some agencies such as hospitals paid wages for the work.

The I-W program began operating in July 1952. A wide variety of jobs became available. The Mennonites, Brethren, and Quakers developed and administered relief and welfare projects in many parts of the world. A group of men served as guinea pigs at the National Institutes of Health at Bethesda, Maryland. Most I-Ws took low-level jobs in hospitals. The program was a godsend for the hospitals because it provided reliable labor for low-paying, mundane work—orderlies, janitors, and kitchen helpers. By 1954, 80 percent of all I-Ws held hospital jobs. More than a thousand agencies were accredited as doing "work of national importance," and more than three thousand men had entered the program (*I-W Mirror*, 28 July 1954, 2).

Mennonites and Brethren were delighted with the new program. Their men could now opt for work of genuine significance in settings that offered real opportunities for witness against war. Unlike the CPS program, which had often put the COs in camps in out-of-the-way places, the I-W program promised much more visibility and interaction with the outside world, thus increasing the possibilities for Christian witness.

This was exactly what the Amish feared most. Already in the fall of 1952 David Wagler warned that the new program posed dangers for the Amish. Wagler had served in CPS and now lived in an Amish community in Pike County, Ohio. Young men in his congregation would soon be of draft age. He worried about their future in an article entitled "Is It Balaam's Counsel?" published in the Amish paper *Herold der Wahrheit* (1 December 1952, 726). He began by outlining the attractive features of the new program. The only restriction on the men was that they had to be on hand during working hours. And they were paid wages for their work. "What more could we ask for and how could our government treat us better?" he asked.

But there was also reason for alarm. Invoking the Old Testament story of Balaam, Wagler warned that this unprecedented leniency by the American government represented a subtle but serious danger for young Amishmen who would be inducted into the system. The danger lay in the temptations offered by the city and its environment. "It would seem that it is not God's plan that people should build and live in large cities," Wagler said (727). No Amish youth had yet been drafted, but Wagler's fear of the I-W program became a major theme of Amish concern in the ensuing years.

Ervin Hershberger, editor of the newspaper, highlighted the ironic problems of the I-W program.[5] The provisions for COs could hardly be improved upon. But the draft system forced young men into service, and the churches had little leverage to ensure that it would be a wholesome time of Christian growth. More than two-thirds of all Mennonite men chose earning service, as did nearly all the Amish. These young men, aged nineteen and one-half on the average, were earning money, often for the first time, away from the social controls of their church and family. They were tremendously vulnerable (*Herold*, 15 June 1955, 186).

Rob Schlabach, Amish and a former I-W from Ohio, commented in 1966: "I would enjoy seeing a better program set up for the Amish I-W boys. The thing of having lots of money, no supervision, and long, free evening hours is not good" (*Ambassador*, November 1966, 23). Thus, while the men were earning reputations as reliable workers, the social activities of some of them became a serious problem. Reports of smoking, drinking, and carousing filtered back to the Amish communities. This was a concern for the Mennonites as well, and they responded to the problem by creating a I-W Coordinating Committee in 1954 with Amish representatives. The committee tried to establish closer ties between the I-W units and the churches. By 1960 Ammon Troyer, a minister from Sugarcreek, Ohio, was the Amish member of the committee. Late that year he arranged a meeting between the Amish and John E. Lapp of the Mennonite I-W Coordinating Committee to discuss the problems of the I-W program. The meeting was held near Shipshewana, Indiana, and nearly eight hundred Amish people attended. The Amish were encouraged to appoint regional counselors to help young men find desirable jobs, and ministers were encouraged to visit the COs frequently. Similar organizing meetings were held in Ohio, Indiana, Illinois, and Iowa in 1961. As a result, the Amish developed a much better system of relating to their young men in I-W service.[6]

Dan King, a minister from Bellville, Pennsylvania, represented the Beachy Amish on the Coordinating Board.[7] King organized the country into four districts and appointed a counselor for each district. The counselors were responsible for the welfare of the men in their districts. The Beachy Amish responded to the challenge of I-W by setting up their own Voluntary Service program. They established retirement homes staffed by their I-W men. During the 1960s they began homes in Arkansas, Florida, Michigan, Ohio, and Virginia. When the decade began, 82 percent of their drafted men were in Beachy Amish voluntary service.[8]

Old Order Amish uneasiness with the I-W program heightened as draft calls increased with the onset of the Vietnam War in the mid-1960s. One reflection of the growing concern was the launching of a new Amish periodical in 1966, *Ambassador of Peace*. The original inspiration for the paper came from Sarah M. Weaver, a middle-aged Ohio Amishwoman who was confined to a wheelchair because of muscular dystrophy. She persuaded Joseph Stoll of Aylmer, Ontario—one of the founders of the Amish publishing house, Pathway Publishers—that such a paper was needed. She argued that a periodical could enhance "the spiritual growth and protection [of the young men] while living among the sins and temptations of the world and remind them of a better world to come" (*Ambassador*, February 1966, 3).

Joseph Stoll explained:

The paper is being started because certain people saw a need for it. Many I-W men have said it is the isolation while in service which breaks down resistance to temptation. By this we mean isolation from others of like precious faith. There is far greater probability that the man by himself, away from home, loved ones, and church fellowship, will adjust to his environment and perhaps lose his nonconformity—first in clothes and outward appearance, then in habits and thinking, and finally in his faith. (*Ambassador*, January 1966, 1)

Calvin E. Anderson, of Holmesville, Ohio, became the editor. Atlee E. Miller wrote about I-W regulations, and John J. Yoder offered advice on spiritual matters. The monthly *Ambassador* was designed to strengthen the link between I-W men and their home communities. Amish I-W men received the paper free. In June 1966, 400 free copies were mailed. The cost was covered by another 1,354 paid subscriptions sent to the folks at home. Its circulation eventually passed 5,000.[9]

The paper carried letters from young men describing their I-W work, essays of admonition from ministers, and information about I-W programs. For example, Ora H. Swartz described his work at a Mennonite nursing home near Sturgis, Michigan, where he worked in maintenance. He liked his assignment because it was not in a city and was operated by religious people whose standards were compatible with his own Amish values (*Ambassador*, May 1966, 2).

Thomas Peachey worked at Harrisburg State Hospital in Pennsylvania. He was one of ten I-W men who operated the hospital farm with the help of able-bodied patients. The men lived in a rooming house in the city (*Ambassador*, May 1966, 2).

More typical was Vernon Bontrager's situation at the general hospital in Indianapolis, Indiana, from 1963 to 1965. He lived with five other Amishmen in an apartment. Dozens of Amishmen worked at the hospital in a variety of maintenance and orderly duties. He enjoyed the work and liked the opportunities he had to witness to people on the job about his peace convictions (*Ambassador*, May 1966, 5).

But uneasiness about the program continued to surface. Former I-W man Harold Stoll, of St. Joseph, Arkansas, wrote about his experiences in I-W:

A complaint was brought against the life of the I-W workers by a young woman married to a husband who was overseas in the Army. She had reason to complain. Here were boys who professed to be conscientiously opposed to war living a soft way of life, working only a 40 hour week, receiving regular wages, smoking, drinking, swearing, card playing, driving around in flashy automobiles, attending movies, and other places of worldly sports. Meanwhile her husband was risking his life fighting for his country in Korea. Oh, the shame of it all! (*Ambassador*, March 1966, 1)

Joseph Stoll, of Pathway Publishers, worried about the Amish failure to deal with the problems of I-W service. Mennonites, he observed, were trying to create church projects where their young men could work. "But we Amish have largely neglected these things. . . . We who have perhaps the most to lose . . . are losing it" (*Ambassador*, April 1966, 14).

STEERING COMMITTEE SUPERVISION
The growing ferment about the I-W program led to a historic meeting of Amish bishops and ministers at the Graber schoolhouse in Allen County, Indiana, on 20 October 1966. Those attending agreed that "the present I-W system of so many of our young boys going to the hospitals is unsatisfactory and hurtful to our Amish churches" (Steering 1966–72, 1). Calvin Anderson, editor of the *Ambassador*, reported a conversation he had with Paul Gross, a Hutterite minister. Gross explained that Hutterite elders went to Washington to talk with General Hershey, director of Selective Service, who worked out a special program for them (*Ambassador*, September 1966, 1). Perry Yoder, a minister, reported that many young men did not return to their churches after their term of service.

A group was formed with representatives from large Amish settlements to "see what can be changed without losing what we already have." The group sent a delegation to Washington to see Harold Shirk, executive secretary of the National Service Board for Religious Objectors. The board represented the interests of the historic peace churches to Selective Service. Shirk encouraged the Amish to propose a program to meet their needs. Before leaving Washington the delegation asked Andrew Kinsinger, of Lancaster County, Pennsylvania; David Schwartz, of Allen County, Indiana; and Noah Wengerd, of Adams County, Indiana, to write a plan and present it to other Amish leaders.

Two weeks later, six ministers met in Pittsburgh to study the subcommittee's plan. The plan proposed deferring men to Amish farms in lieu of hospital service. To be deferred the young men would need to be church members. The group named themselves the Old Order Amish Steering Committee. The development and work of this committee is described more fully in Chapter 4.

On 4 January 1967, one hundred Amish leaders met at Bishop Dan Schrock's home in Holmes County, Ohio, to discuss the plan. It was approved. The Steering Committee moved quickly. Two days later, they were in Washington explaining their plan to Harold Shirk. Shirk did not think it would work. He doubted Selective Service would permit I-W men to stay on farms in their own communities. But he agreed to set up a meeting with General Hershey.

Several weeks later, the Steering Committee returned to Washington and met with the general. After exploring many different possibilities, Hershey finally turned to his assistant, Colonel Daniel Omer, and said, "We want to help these people." He then outlined a procedure by which Amish draftees could apply for a farm deferment. If the local draft board denied the request, the Steering Committee could then file an appeal through the National Service Board for Religious Objectors. General Hershey agreed to defer any young man endorsed by the Steering Committee (Steering 1966–72, 9–10).

The Steering Committee, chaired by Andrew Kinsinger, of Lancaster, Pennsylvania, created guidelines to "govern appeals" to the committee for deferments. The applicants must (1) be baptized members, (2) have worked on a farm a year, (3) agree to inform the draft board of all job changes, (4) request a farm deferment before coming to the Steering Committee, (5) channel appeals through the committee, (6) desire farm work and oppose hospital work, (7) have a strong reference from their home church, and (8) behave in ways that would not offend neighbors with sons in the military (Steering 1966–72, 15–16).

To help cover costs, Amish church members were assessed twenty-five cents per year. The new plan worked well, but at the 1969 annual meeting of the Steering Committee, Chairman Kinsinger reported that some men had not received deferments, despite Hershey's intervention. Kinsinger was also disturbed by reports that President Nixon might replace General Hershey. During a visit with Hershey, Kinsinger reported that Hershey encouraged the Amish to establish their own farm system for men who did not get a regular farm deferment.

Kinsinger then presented a plan that the Steering Committee and Hershey had designed for men denied a regular deferment. Under the Farm Plan, the Steering Committee was authorized to lease Amish farms for a period of twenty-six months. The farmers would be paid a wage to manage the farm for the Steering Committee in return for the labor of one or two young men who would work on the farm to fulfill their I-W obligation. The I-W men were paid typical farm wages. They had to work on a farm away from their own home community. Kinsinger was delighted with the plan: "Truly! No Old Order Amish boy . . . opposed to working in Hospitals need do so" (Steering 1966–72, 29).

The Farm Plan was timely, for Kinsinger soon learned that the reach of Hershey's fiat was not absolute; some fifty-seven Amishmen were in various phases of deferment appeal and prosecution. Kinsinger traveled eight thousand miles in a few months trying to resolve the cases with Hershey's help. Furthermore, in the early 1970s, Selective Service eventually denied all farm and dependency deferments. By October 1971, Kinsinger told the Steering Committee that seventy men who had been drafted had been assigned to Steering Committee farms in eight states (Steering 1966–72, 53).

In his comments at the annual meeting of the Steering Committee at the home of Dan E. Miller in Holmes County in 1971, Kinsinger said:

> We have come to the point where the Old Order Amish are recognized and respected by our Federal Government. I regret seriously that the Committee was not formed sooner so that the hospital plan [for I-W men] would not have rooted in so deeply. This has taken many members away from the Old Order Amish churches and caused much grief to some parents. . . . Washington officials were surprised . . . that the Old Order Amish went along with the hospital plan as long as they did, and General Lewis B. Hershey once remarked to me, "It has proved a disgrace to the Old Order Amish name." (Steering 1966–72, 56)

Not all Amish COs accepted the I-W program in its various forms. Over the twenty-year span of the program, approximately one dozen Amishmen served prison terms. John Keim, of Ashland, Ohio, registered for the draft but then decided he could not conscientiously take the easy route of hospital work. He was sentenced to two years in a federal penitentiary, but pressure from his community reduced his sentence to one year. A few years later, a younger brother was also arrested and sentenced for the same reasons (*Family Life*, August 1968, 12).

The Steering Committee was involved peripherally in one prison case—after the fact. Three young men were sentenced to five years in prison and fined two thousand dollars each in the early 1960s. The fines were still unpaid in 1971. Who should pay the fines? The committee decided that the individuals should pay, if they were able, and the church would help as a last resort (Steering 1966–72, 54).

I have traced the Amish experience with American wars from colonial times to the present. The emergence of the Old Order Amish Steering Committee is surely the most significant development in all those years. For the first time in two hundred years, the Amish approached government officials directly to negotiate relief from a draft system that most Amish believed was inimical to their own best interests. The Amish Steering Committee is now a regular feature of Amish life, with its annual meetings attended by hundreds of ministers. If another draft appears, the Amish will be better prepared to represent their concerns to the state than ever before in their history.

In a wide-ranging series of interviews with Amish leaders in 1990, not one person spoke affirmatively about the I-W program, which too often exposed vulnerable Amish youth to social influences. The memories of Amish CPS men, however, were quite positive about their experience in CPS camps during World War II. What has not changed over the last two centuries is the Amish stance toward government and civil society. Their sense of citizenship remains minimal. When they talk of making a sacrifice in the context of a war, they are more concerned about living peacefully with their worldly neighbors than about fulfilling their civic obligation.

An Amishman leaves the corridors of power after meeting with state representatives. Lancaster New Era *photo by Richard K. Reinhold*

CHAPTER FOUR

The National Amish Steering Committee

Marc A. Olshan

The Amish have not developed centralized organizations at either the state or the national level. The difficulties, however, faced by Amish conscientious objectors in alternate service assignments encouraged Amish leaders to organize the National Amish Steering Committee. The Steering Committee functions as a loose, informal federation of Amish representatives who coordinate the Amish response to a variety of church-state issues. Marc A. Olshan chronicles the development and functioning of the committee.

The Old Order Amish are often portrayed as a people apart. A substantial literature celebrates their freedom from the complexities and pressures of modern life. Yet the Amish, like the rest of us, are enmeshed in a pervasive web of laws, standards, codes, regulations, licensing requirements, and programs. Neither their religion nor their indifference to political institutions exempts them from government authority. Such exemptions as exist are, for the most part, the product of negotiation.

At the level of local and state government, specific Amish communities or even individuals might successfully represent themselves, through either reason or resistance. Dealing with the federal government, however, presents a different kind of problem. No formal hierarchy exists within the Amish church beyond the level of the local church district.[1] The highest church official, the local bishop, provides leadership for no more than the thirty to forty families that constitute each district. Community autonomy is central to the Anabaptist tradition from which the Amish originate.

With over nine hundred church districts in twenty-two states, representation of the total Amish population to federal agencies is problematic.[2] The situation is further complicated by the diversity of Old Order Amish groups. Significant differences exist among the various "affiliations," or subgroups, of Amish because they have different church rules, called an *Ordnung*.

These affiliations, or fellowships, differ in their dress, religious practices, level of acceptable technology, and willingness to cooperate with non-Amish authority.[3] An agreement between a bishop of one affiliation and a government official might be rejected by the Amish in other affiliations. Given this situation, a single "Amish response" to federal policies, even those having an impact on all Amish, is unlikely.

The draft for military service has periodically had a significant impact on all Amish communities. As pacifists, the Amish refuse to serve in the armed forces.[4] Each war brings a new confrontation with the state. During the American Revolution and the Civil War, the Amish paid fines or were taxed to hire replacements. By World War I, conscientious objectors (COs) were acknowledged as a distinct category but were still required to wear uniforms and to perform noncombatant work at army camps. Those Amish who refused to cooperate were sometimes ridiculed and beaten.[5] In World War II, COs were assigned to Civilian Public Service camps to perform work of national interest. During the Korean and Vietnam wars, COs were often assigned to hospital work.

Conscientious objector status was eventually formalized and legitimized with its own classification by Selective Service. A classification of I-W was designated for COs "performing civilian work contributing to the maintenance of the national health, safety, or interest" (Shapiro and Striker 1970, 131). Some Amish refused even this degree of cooperation with the government and were sentenced to jail terms ("Behind" 1968). Most, however, accepted alternative civilian service assignments as the U.S. involvement in Vietnam deepened in the mid-1960s.

The Birth of the Steering Committee

The military build-up in Vietnam led to larger draft quotas. These were soon followed by demands for more equitable Selective Service policies. In 1966, an Amishman who had worked with Amish COs was contacted by an official of the National Service Board for Religious Objectors (NSBRO), a private organization that counsels and aids COs. The official advised of possible changes in the draft laws and asked to meet with "some Amish leaders." Amish leadership is traditionally defined in terms of the clergy. Thus, a group of bishops previously involved with draft problems called a meeting in Allen County, Indiana, to discuss a response. Church leaders and laymen from at least four states filled one of the local schoolhouses at the October 1966 meeting. Until then, Amish draftees had routinely been given CO status. Many of these young men were assigned to two years of alternative service in urban hospitals. The result was highly unsatisfactory to the Amish leadership:

> Many boys go with good intentions but by having so much idle time, become involved with amusements, with the nurses, or in other ways are led astray to the extent that when they could return home and become church members there are so many that no longer prefer to, or are in a position where they find they can hardly do so, with maybe a nurse of a different faith for a wife or similar circumstances. (Steering 1966–72, 1)

Only about half of those assigned to hospital work returned home to become members of Amish communities. Of those that did return, many did not join the Amish church (Kinsinger 1988, 130). One Amishman who visited many of the Amish COs reported that only one-third of them were church members (Steering 1966–72, 1).

The devastating consequences of this arrangement, plus Amish awareness that with pending changes in the law they might "lose what we already have," prompted action. At the Indiana schoolhouse meeting, leaders agreed to form a committee to work with the federal government. A month later, in November 1966, a group of ten church leaders and eight lay members met in Washington with the executive secretary of NSBRO. He explained pending changes in draft legislation and suggested that the Amish propose a plan that would be acceptable to their people.

At their hotel that evening, the Amish delegation reaffirmed that "there should be a committee to represent the Old Order Amish from all states as a group to Washington in matters that concern or hinder our Old Order Amish way of life, to counsel with the various groups or states, and see if a unified plan could be found that would be acceptable to the Amish as well as Washington" (Steering 1966–72, 4). After caucusing separately, the bishops announced that they had decided on a three-man committee to represent the Amish in all states (Kinsinger 1988, 130). The three, all laymen, were designated as chairman, secretary, and treasurer of the newly named Old Order Amish Steering Committee.[6] The committee would represent the church districts by having "home community committeemen" appointed locally.

The formation of the committee was endorsed at a meeting in January 1967 in Holmes County, Ohio, attended by over one hundred representatives from Amish settlements in nine states. In February the Steering Committee, in a meeting arranged by the head of the NSBRO, conferred with General Lewis B. Hershey, director of Selective Service. For the first time ever, Amish representatives spoke on behalf of virtually all Amish in the United States. The committee explained Amish objections to hospital work as alternative service. Committee members also offered a plan, already approved at the Ohio meeting, to allow Amish COs who objected to public service to be deferred for farm work. The plan was immediately accepted in principle by General Hershey (Steering 1966–72, 10).

Within a week of the initial meeting with Hershey, church leaders and lay representatives met again, this time in Missouri. They discussed and approved "the form and guidelines for exempting the boys asking for farm deferments through the Steering Committee" (Steering 1966–72, 11). The language is significant. Hershey charged the Steering Committee with the responsibility for setting up and administering the procedures. This mandate soon included evaluating the sincerity of each applicant as well as handling "appeals" for farm deferments from Amish youth who were given wrong classifications or had been refused I-W status by their local draft boards. The Steering Committee had effectively usurped a function of local draft boards. Typically, local boards channeled any appeals for changes of classification to the state appeals board.

Forms titled "Appeal to Old Order Amish Steering Committee" were printed by the committee and distributed to Amish communities. Amish COs who wanted to appeal for farm deferments filled out the form and sent it to the chairman. The chairman then considered the individual's background and forwarded the appeal to Selective Service in Washington. The newly constituted Steering Committee convened for its first scheduled meeting in October 1967 in Lancaster County, Pennsylvania. Representatives from Amish communities in eleven states were told that General Hershey had agreed to accept appeals that were approved by the chairman of the Steering Committee (Steering 1966–72, 19).

The procedure worked remarkably well for the Amish. By the third annual meeting the chairman was able to report that no COs who had appealed through the Steering Committee had been assigned to hospital work. He also announced a formal Farm Plan in 1969, worked out "after about a year of proposals and counter-proposals" between Hershey and the chairman (Kinsinger 1988, 131). Under the plan, privately owned Amish farms would be leased to the local church for a period of twenty-six months to facilitate the placement of COs for their two-year stint of alternative service. For the period of the lease, the former owner would become the "manager" at wages approximating his profits as an owner. Amish COs typically traveled to farms outside their home settlements.

During the negotiations to develop an Amish CO plan, an improbably amicable relationship developed between the chairman of the Steering Committee and Hershey. The pacifist Amishman and the general became "rather closely attached to each other" (Kinsinger 1988, 136). One consequence of Hershey's good will was his readiness to accept the chairman's assessment of cases that were appealed. In one case, the chairman inquired about a young man being prosecuted by an unsympathetic state Selective Service official. General Hershey reassured the chairman that the official's action should not be a cause for concern: "We are busy people, and papers move slowly across our desk" (133). Even after Hershey was no longer actively engaged with Selective Service, he and the chairman met to visit (136). Following the war, the director of Selective Service hand-delivered to the chairman a certificate of appreciation signed by the then-retired Hershey (Steering 1987–89, 4).

The committee was an effective advocate for the Amish. At the fifth annual meeting of the Steering Committee, held in Holmes County, Ohio, in October 1971, the chairman offered "a sample of how the committee works with the national office [i.e. Selective Service] and Senators." He reported that the committee had been asked to comment on changes in legislation affecting the draft, before Selective Service issued its instructions to the state and local boards. The request reflects a sensitivity to Amish interests not evidenced before the committee was established. Summarizing the situation in 1971, the chairman said, "We have come to the point where the Old Order Amish are recognized and respected by our federal government, giving us much authority to take care of our own people and children if we are organized and capable of doing so" (Steering 1966–72, 56).

One indicator of this respect and authority was a request by the Presidential Appeal Office of Selective Service that the chairman personally interview Amish COs being considered for prosecution. These growing demands on one man, uncompensated for his time and attempting to run his own business, became overwhelming.

At the 1971 meeting, the chairman offered a plan to "strengthen and improve" the Steering Committee. The proposed changes further formalized the functions of the committee, transforming it into a rudimentary bureaucracy.

The proposal, approved unanimously at the meeting, included the creation of a "state director" in each state. The state director would function as an intermediary between the Steering Committee and local committee representatives. He would handle minor problems, receive the quarterly reports from church farms in his state, and channel information between the Steering Committee and local committeemen.

Also agreed on were detailed descriptions of the duties of each officeholder, the necessary qualifications for officeholders, and standard procedures to replace state directors and members of the Steering Committee. The legitimate authority of the Steering Committee was formally reiterated in the 1971 meeting: "This Old Order Amish Steering Committee with its state directors shall be considered the voice of the Old Order Amish churches combined, throughout the United States, and no other group or committee shall infringe upon the Old Order Amish churches or the Steering Committee" (Steering 1966–72, 59).

The statement clarified the committee's scope. It did not intend to limit itself to Selective Service issues. The committee's initial mandate was, in fact, to represent the Amish in all matters that concerned or hindered their way of life. With the winding down of the Vietnam War, pressure from Selective Service eased. In 1972, about one hundred COs were working on church farms, the maximum number during the life of the program.

Some Amish youth continued to participate in the government's alternative service programs for COs. Others served jail terms rather than work in any government-sanctioned plan, including the church farm program. Both actions undermined the Steering Committee's position that the government CO programs were objectionable to the Amish and that its own program would not violate religious scruples. Selective Service officials, while not understanding this range of behaviors, according to the chairman did "realize that each person has a right to his own belief and do not hold this against the committee" (Steering 1966–72, 54).

Despite the diverse responses to its program, the Steering Committee was becoming "the voice of the Old Order Amish." It soon began to function as a point of articulation between the Amish and other government agencies as well.

An Expansion of Functions

Following passage of the Occupational Safety and Health Act of 1970, the Amish found themselves at odds with the federal government in another area. The act required employees to use approved head protection in a variety of work situations. Hostetler (1984, 45) reported that hundreds of Amish workers were furloughed from their construction jobs. The chairman of the Steering Committee made several trips to Washington to press for an exemption from the Department of Labor.

He argued that dress was part of religious practice. To wear a standardized hard hat in place of the traditional black felt hat (or presumably the summer straw hat) was considered a breach of principle. In May of 1972 the Department of Labor communicated its decision: "Considering the provisions in the United States Constitution relating to the free exercise of religion . . . the Occupational Safety and Health Administration adopts a policy whereunder no citation will be issued nor civil penalty proposed against employers for failure by men of the Old Order Amish to wear 'hard hats' on construction jobs."[7]

The chairman immediately requested that the exemption be extended to those Amish working in jobs other than construction where the law called for head protection. Two weeks after sending out the initial exemption, the assistant secretary of labor complied with the chairman's request. In a second letter he exempted other categories of jobs where head protection was mandatory: "We understand that the latter jobs, such as work in buggy shops and feed shops are no more hazardous than jobs in the construction industry. Under these circumstances, please consider the policy as so extended upon the basis of the facts and representations which have been heretofore made."[8] Despite the quasi-legalistic language, the rapidity of the expanded exemption suggests a decision almost cavalier in its informality.[9] The Steering Committee had won another concession. In the same year, an agreement between the Steering Committee and the State Department exempted the Amish from submitting photographs of themselves when immigrating from Canada to the United States (Steering 1966–72, 71).

The functions of the Steering Committee continued to expand. In response to a comment at the 1973 annual meeting questioning the continued need for a Steering Committee, "with the draft so quiet," the chairman cited a host of issues being addressed by the committee: changes in the milk cooling laws, conflicts with state and local education officials, the development of an "employer notice" document requesting employers of Amish under the age of twenty-one to make out paychecks in the parents' and child's name, and the Social Security issue, "which has been turned over to the Steering Committee." The message was clear. In the words of the committee minutes: "The Steering Committee is needed as much or more than ever before. After this meeting there should not need again be further counsel as to whether the Steering Committee should be kept in force" (Steering 1973–80, 3).

The proliferating array of issues engaged by the Steering Committee confirms this need. Almost all of these concerns resulted from changes in state or federal laws, altered administrative procedures, or the introduction of new programs. Between 1973 and 1990, the Steering Committee investigated and made rulings concerning an appropriate Amish stance toward workers' compensation, Federal Housing Administration loans, the Internal Revenue Service's earned income credit program, Medicare, and the homestead credit, an income tax deduction offered in several states.

Other issues addressed by the committee included Individual Retirement Accounts, Soil Conservation Service programs, the use of state-subsidized immunization clinics, the Department of Agriculture's herd buy-out program, appropriate highway courtesy for horse-drawn vehicles, and compulsory kindergarten. Even the Immigration Reform and Control Act was briefly considered by the committee: "Possibly it will not give us trouble here in the central states but if it does cause trouble the committee will check into it" (Steering 1987–89, 7). When a new director of Selective Service was appointed, the committee felt that as a matter of course this meant "getting acquainted and working out a new agreement."

Passage of the Asbestos Hazard Emergency Response Act of 1986 created yet another area of contention. The act required that all schools be inspected for asbestos and asbestos-containing materials. Each school was to develop a "management plan" and use only specially trained and accredited inspectors. Noncompliance meant fines up to five thousand dollars per day for any single school building. In April 1989, members of the Steering Committee met with officials of the Environmental Protection Agency "to hammer out a secret, compromise agreement."[10] The parties negotiated an extension of the compliance deadline to the end of the year and worked out other details to the satisfaction of the Amish leadership.[11]

The committee became involved with health care in 1986 when it developed a form to be used by Amish who were having difficulty paying medical bills. The form explains to creditors the Amish opposition "to accepting Public Hospital Insurance, Medicare, Medicaid, or other public assistance." It then lists a schedule of suggested "charitable contributions"—in essence, reduced rates —that the doctor or hospital is asked to deduct from the Amish patient's bill. The proposed reduction of rates, based on a sliding scale adjusted to the amount of the bill, ranged from 10 to 25 percent. The official-looking document bears the signature of the chairman and the heading "Old Order Amish Steering Committee—Voice of the Old Order Amish." Representatives at the 1986 annual meeting reported that the form was being accepted at many hospitals (Steering 1981–86, 77).

Relations with Selective Service once again became vital when U.S. forces were sent to the Persian Gulf in 1990. At the fall 1990 annual meeting, the committee discussed the possibility of the draft's being reinstated as a result of "world occurrences." Representatives were reminded that it is a federal offense for young men not to register. Procedures for registering were reviewed as well as criteria to qualify for CO status (Steering 1990, 5).

Social Security continued to be a troublesome issue for the Steering Committee. Despite an exemption granted in 1965 to self-employed Amish (see Chapter 7) and a broadening of that exemption in 1988, the need to deal with the Social Security Administration continued. The Steering Committee serves both as an intermediary and as a source of expertise. On several occasions the chairman reminded community representatives of the need for Amish adolescents to fill in their Form 4029 Social Security exemption papers when they prepared to join the church. In those cases where the exemption was turned down by local civil authorities, the chairman asked that it be sent to the Steering Committee, since "we should be able to have it approved" (Steering 1981–86, 3).

The committee tracked proposed legislation. In the case of a bill requiring children aged five or more to be assigned a Social Security number, the committee worked with two congressmen to add an amendment excluding those "religiously opposed" (Steering 1981–86, 75). The procedural details for this exclusion were worked out at a joint meeting of representatives from the Treasury Department, the Internal Revenue Service, the Social Security Administration, and the Steering Committee (Steering 1987–89, 6).

Amish schools are a continuing concern of the committee. In 1978 the committee issued a seventy-two-page pamphlet, "Guidelines in Regards to the Old Order Amish or Mennonite Parochial

Schools." It included sections on creed, goals, school administration, duties of school board members, qualifications and duties of teachers, attendance policy, curriculum, and classroom rules. School-related topics are frequently discussed at annual meetings, and the Steering Committee often provides direction as new questions arise.

In 1979, the U.S. Senate requested a statement from the committee during debate on proposed changes in Selective Service guidelines. The same year, the chairman represented the Amish to a committee investigating the accident at the Three Mile Island nuclear power plant.[12] In 1983, local officials in one community, requesting assistance in controlling the rowdiness of some Amish youth, wrote the chairman of the Steering Committee rather than church leaders (Steering 1981–86, 35–36). Contacts between the Steering Committee and members of Congress have become routine.

The Committee Today

At a special meeting in 1989, the Steering Committee and its state directors convened to elect a new chairman. The chairman of the committee since its founding in 1966 was stepping down. His health curtailed regular participation, and he would now continue to contribute his time in the newly created position of "senior chairman." The new chairman had previously served as an adviser to the committee, especially in tax and Social Security matters.

The committee's organization consists of four tiers of responsibility: (1) the chairman, (2) other members of the committee who formally constitute the committee, (3) state directors, and (4) local home community "committeemen." The four-member committee now consists of the chairman, secretary, treasurer, and senior chairman. They are assisted by fourteen state directors.[13] Each spring the state directors meet with the committee members for counsel and a briefing.[14] Although the spring meeting is intended for state directors rather than Amish society at large, members of the host community and other visitors often observe the proceedings. At a recent meeting, attendance exceeded one hundred.[15]

The official annual meeting of the Steering Committee is typically held in September. This meeting is often attended by several hundred people. In addition to the four-man committee, the state directors, and local committeemen from church districts across the country, the meeting is well attended by interested persons in the host community.

The location of the spring and fall meetings rotates among various states. Each of the twelve states represented by its own state director has hosted the annual fall meeting at least once. Several states with larger Amish populations have hosted the fall meeting three or four times. Special meetings are held as necessary to elect new state directors when additional states are represented, or when former directors resign, move to other states, or die. On these occasions the meeting is held in the state in question and is attended by members of the committee. The committee then supervises an election for a new state director from among the local representatives.

Following the fall meeting, the minutes are published in pamphlet form and distributed to state directors. Each state director then holds a state meeting, usually in November.[16] The location of the state meeting rotates among the various Amish settlements within the state. The state director distributes copies of the minutes for the spring and fall national meetings and makes appropriate explanations. The state and national meetings have become an Amish institution.

Each year after the various state meetings are held, the newspaper *Die Botschaft*[17] is studded with references to the travels and visiting associated with the annual gathering. An Indiana writer's report is typical: "The IW state meeting was held at [A.L.'s] last Friday. With a good attendance. And well worthwhile." And from New York: "Last Wednesday spent the day at [C.R.'s], as they opened their house to have the meeting for NY Steering Committee. Believe there were between 80–100 present. Thought it was very interesting."

Following the state meetings, the local committeemen then hold meetings in their own settlements to inform local folks of the committee's position on various issues, changes in the law, and any other subjects discussed at the national meeting. Local committeemen also serve as an ongoing source of information for Amish persons registering with Selective Service or applying for Social Security exemptions for the first time. The local representatives also provide resources for Amish persons who encounter problems with workers' compensation, the Internal Revenue Service, or state school authorities.

The Steering Committee has asked each local church district to designate a "home community committeeman." In practice, however, a committeeman might represent as many as a dozen districts. In some settlements, he reports during a settlement-wide annual school meeting. In others, he may hold a special meeting just for committee business. If he represents a single church district, he may pass on the information informally after church services. The level of participation and interest in the work of the committee varies greatly, even within the same settlement.

Those working on Steering Committee business are not reimbursed for their time. Travel and miscellaneous out-of-pocket expenses are, however, paid for by the committee. Funds for the support of committee business are raised through contributions solicited on a rotating basis among the states. On an average of once every three to four years, each church district in a state is asked to collect one dollar per member for the committee.

Given the range of issues that the Steering Committee has considered to date, it interprets in the broadest possible way its mandate "to represent the Amish in all matters that concern or hinder the Old Order Amish way of life." The committee has explicitly rejected its own involvement in any litigation. Aside from that restriction, it seems prepared to communicate and negotiate with officials of any and all government agencies.

The committee has also become involved in problems not directly related to Amish-state relations. For example, in 1975, it was asked to assist in setting up an Amish-controlled newspaper, *Die Botschaft* (Steering 1987–89, 31). On at least two occasions, differences between churches have been brought to the committee for its opinion.[18] The extensiveness of the committee's concerns is suggested by the chairman's once worrying about the "international monetary situation."

The committee has become a vehicle for dealing with all manner of problems beyond the local community level. In a world where all communities are increasingly buffeted by national and even global forces, the Steering Committee may come to occupy a correspondingly important position in Amish society.

Reasons for Success

The success of the Steering Committee derives in part from the enhanced coordination afforded by its quasi-bureaucratic structure. More importantly, its leaders have become highly adept at dealing with government. They have been characterized, in the words of Kidder and Hostetler (1990, 908), as "Amish lay lawyers who do everything we might expect of professional lawyers—lobbying, negotiating settlements, inventing and successfully selling unique legal 'loopholes,' [and] advocating other members' cases before official bodies." The committee represents an effective adaptation to the highly bureaucratized legal environment in which the Amish, like all other citizens, must operate.[19]

The committee's first chairman proved to be a felicitous choice in terms of his ability to capitalize on the strengths of the new organization. He was initially selected for the job in part because the bishops who met in Washington in 1966 felt that "they wouldn't be able to express themselves in English as well as they wanted to."[20] The chairman's facility in English has since been augmented by other more specialized knowledge. His familiarity with the world of congressional bills, subcommittees, and administrators and his working relationship with members of Congress are advantages that were unlikely to develop as long as the Amish presence in Washington was limited to occasional ad hoc delegations.

The committee's success must also be understood in terms of the deference, even veneration, with which Americans generally treat Amish culture. The Amish adherence to traditional values and technologies, their pacifism, and their self-discipline are seen as admirable, even if impractical, by much of American society.[21] The Amish, suggest Kidder and Hostetler (1990, 915), "receive support for doing what others wish they had the courage or means to do."

For example, officials responsible for enforcing sanctions against Amish who have violated the law often carry out their duty reluctantly or apologetically. Following their seizure of one Amishman's horses for his failure to pay Social Security taxes, Internal Revenue Service officials felt obliged to explain that the case "presents an unpleasant and difficult task. . . . However there is no authority under which Amish farmers may be relieved of liability for this tax. . . . It is incumbent on the Internal Revenue Service to proceed with collection enforcement action as provided by law. We have no other choice under the law."[22]

With regard to the draft, the chairman of the Steering Committee reported at the 1988 annual meeting on possible changes in the law: "Selective Service has said not to worry if the regulations seem tough, they are not aimed at us; they need tough regulations to be able to determine which are sincere COs and which are not" (Steering 1987–89, 26).

The following year, the chairman commented on the recently passed extension of Social Security exemptions to Amish employees: "This should eliminate the need to set up a partnership or other scheme for our workers to be exempt from the Social Security tax. A lot of our so-called partnerships and schemes would not stand up if the IRS were to really check into them. However, the IRS has been sympathetic over the years and did not interfere" (Steering 1987–89, 45).

During the negotiations over Amish compliance with the Asbestos Hazard Emergency Response Act, one government official explained: "We're doing everything we can to get them to cooperate. . . . We don't like to go in there with fines."[23]

This reluctance to prosecute is born of a mélange of nostalgia, admiration, and, perhaps, guilt for the pathologies of the dominant society. The Steering Committee is not responsible for these attitudes. The success of Amish delegations in securing the first Social Security exemptions, for example, predates the committee. But the effectiveness of the Steering Committee has certainly been enhanced by the generally supportive milieu in which it operates.

The Committee and the Churches

The bishops who initiated the meetings that led to the formation of the Steering Committee deliberately selected laymen as the committee's three highest officials.[24] The use of ordained church leaders in these positions would have created a potentially awkward situation. As the chairman later explained: "Some groups are stricter than the committeemen and some not so strict. This could become somewhat difficult for a bishop to work with the various groups" (Steering 1966–72, 64).

Individual laymen are one step removed from the tensions that sometimes exist among Old Order factions. Despite the fact that each is a member of a particular church affiliation, he does not formally represent it. Nonetheless, the task of speaking for the entire spectrum of Amish groups is ticklish. The committee sees its function as working "to uphold the principles, religion, and customs of the Old Order Amish as they are handed down to us in a way that the Oldest [i.e., most conservative] of the Old Order can cooperate and benefit as much as possible" (Steering 1966–72, 63).

In fact, the participation of the most conservative communities is marginal. For example, one ultraconservative group, the Swartzentruber Amish, held back from full cooperation with the committee's church farm system for COs. The group did, however, accept its youths' being "sentenced" to church farms.[25] At least from the Swartzentruber group's point of view, its participation was less than voluntary. Today the Swartzentruber communities continue to distance themselves from the activities of the committee. As one Swartzentruber bishop stated unequivocally, "We don't join groups."

In representing the Amish to the government, the Steering Committee has inevitably been driven to identify some practices as more appropriate than others. If Amish communities were to adopt varying stances toward the law strictly on the basis of local counsel, the committee's claim to speak for all Amish would be significantly undermined.

The committee has no formal authority over church districts or individuals. In discussing Amish-state relations, however, the committee has frequently identified behaviors that are not "fitting for the Old Order Amish." For example, voting, holding public office, serving on a jury, teaching children at home, and participating in the Medicare program have all been discouraged (Steering 1981–86, 16–17).

The committee also becomes involved in the question of whether or not an individual is a church member in good standing. Those individuals who leave the church are no longer Amish and therefore no longer qualify for the various exemptions. The committee has asked that all such individuals be reported to it.[26]

At another annual meeting, the committee was asked whether it was appropriate for Old Order Amish businesses to join the Chamber of Commerce.[27] For Amish individuals, these questions can only be authoritatively answered by their local bishop. Yet there is no way for the committee to avoid discussing and even judging the appropriateness of diverse practices. In the course of negotiating with government officials, the committee must articulate Amish values. Committee members communicate what they think are generally acceptable practices according to Amish religious principles. To throw these questions entirely back to the church districts would ignore the circumstances that led to the creation of the committee in the first place.

Without a continuing consensus, past agreements might also be jeopardized. For example, with regard to school issues, the chairman argued for national standards to be followed by all the communities, regardless of their affiliation: "It is the committee's definite concern that one small group does not upset the general school system appreciated by many and approved by the United States Supreme Court."[28] Several years later, the chairman again exhorted community representatives to adhere to high standards and to "have a school that will not give the states reason to come up with new regulations for the schools that we will have difficulty to abide with. Let's not have one small group make it hard eventually for all the others" (Steering 1981–86, 32).

Such pleas for uniformity are, however, usually tempered by endorsing the principle of local autonomy. The above statements of concern, for example, were bracketed by references to "home rules and regulations" and a discipline "approved by the home community." At a meeting held several years later, the same dilemma is apparent. The chairman introduced his remarks on schools with an acknowledgment of their independent character: "Regarding schools we do not wish to say too much as they should be under home rule" (Steering 1987–89, 7). But he then went on to explain the pivotal role of the schools in perpetuating Amish life and to suggest certain guidelines that all schools should consider.

On several occasions, the chairman has felt it necessary to issue disclaimers, denying any ultimate authority to the committee: "Some people may think that the committee is trying to run the churches but this should not be so. *The committee is only the voice of the churches combined.*"[29] Using a more graphic simile, the chairman later argued that "the committee is like a wheel. The hub is like the various churches. . . . The spokes are like the state directors connecting the hub with the rim, and the committee is the rim holding all together, each useful in its place" (Steering 1973–80, 50).

On another occasion, the chairman again deferred to the religious leadership: "The bishops are our highest human authority and the Steering Committee their servants" (Steering 1973–80, 3). In fact, the clergy continue to play an active role in the functioning of the committee. Both annual meetings are opened and closed with prayers offered by bishops. These men may be members of the community where the meeting is being held. Often they are part of the large number of people, both ordained and laymen, who come from around the country to observe the proceedings.

Before the end of each meeting, all attending bishops are asked to "stand and express themselves." The fall 1990 annual meeting was typical in this regard: "Between 50 and 60 bishops were present and the total group gave their approval in unity" (Steering 1990, 9).

Deference to the authority of the bishops is more than lip service. The fact remains, however, that the bishops represent a variety of Amish affiliations. The differences among them preclude their initiating, as representatives of their various churches, a uniform Amish position. To the extent that the Amish present a unified stance to federal authorities, it comes through the efforts of the Steering Committee. The committee represents a delicate balance between the autonomy of the church districts and the practical need of the Amish to represent themselves effectively in a single voice to government officials. It is a balance charged with paradox.

Innovation in the Defense of Tradition

The paradoxical stance of the Amish toward the state (see Chapter 1) is epitomized by the Steering Committee. In its dealings with the government, the committee consistently expresses respect, submission, friendship, and even gratitude. For example, after receiving a certificate of appreciation from the director of Selective Service, the committee members agreed that they "should have been the ones to appreciate the privilege to be able to work with our United States government or its men in authority" (Steering 1987–89, 4). Yet, at the same time, the Amish leadership makes clear by its opposition to government policies that the values, concerns, and objectives of the state are often antithetical, and at best irrelevant, to Amish culture.

One of the most telling expressions of Amish ambivalence toward government, and of the paradoxical character of the Steering Committee, is found in this admonishment by the chairman: "Each community should have home rule and each community or state its home standards, but all rules and standards should fit within the scope of the green guideline booklet *so as to be protected as well as possible from legal action and the law.*"[30]

The Amish can effectively "protect themselves from the law" only by negotiating with government and then abiding by the agreements born of these negotiations. Yet a national committee with authority to speak for all of Amish society, as well as to issue guidelines to that society, is wholly incompatible with the Amish principle of local autonomy of church districts.[31] Despite this incompatibility, a new strategy of adaptation became necessary. The regulation and standardization of many facets of American life that previously had not fallen under the purview of government prodded some Amish to form a new central authority through which they might effectively defend traditional practices. The Steering Committee has enhanced Amish bargaining power by providing a single point of contact for federal officials otherwise baffled by the amorphous structure of Amish society.

The man who led the Steering Committee for twenty-three

years was straightforward about the value of discussions with government officials: "If you sit down with the right person and you learn to know each other, 90 percent of the time you can find a way to work within the law and can avoid law suits and going to court." He even noted that the practice of submitting Steering Committee recommendations to the bishops for endorsement could prove an advantage in negotiations:

> We are called upon to meet with some of the highest officials as to what we can do or accept and what we can not do and proposals are made and counter-proposals until patience becomes thin and we come to the end of the road for that day. When we do not arrive at a satisfactory solution I can always wind up by saying, "We are only the voice of the various churches and we will now discuss with the bishops to see what their reaction will be so as to decide our next move." When I am requested [to come] back with the bishops' decision, the officials are nearly always ready to accept that and start from there with new interest for a new day. (Steering 1966–72, 64)

So far, the Steering Committee has been able to walk the tightrope of paradox. By repeatedly and explicitly acknowledging the ultimate authority of the bishops and the autonomy of the church districts they represent, the committee has legitimized its own authority to speak for the bulk of Amish society. By negotiating with government, it has obviated the need for more threatening compromises with the law in day-to-day Amish life. If the committee's new leadership can preserve its delicate internal balance with the clergy, and if the larger society maintains its appreciative stance toward Amish culture, the committee should continue to be an effective instrument for insulating the Amish way of life from the state.

Children scamper for cover in an Iowa cornfield in 1965 when authorities try to transport them to public schools. Photo by the *Des Moines Register*

CHAPTER FIVE

Education and Schooling

Thomas J. Meyers

 The consolidation of public schools in the twentieth century brought highly publicized clashes between state officials and Amish parents in many states. After the U.S. Supreme Court exempted Amish youth from attending school beyond the eighth grade, one-room Amish schools flourished as conflicts with state officials subsided. Thomas J. Meyers explains why Amish parents objected to sending their children to public high schools and traces the many conflicts that eventually led to the Supreme Court ruling.

Until the middle of the twentieth century, most Amish youth attended one-room public schools. The impetus for the development of alternative schools came from the consolidation of rural schools.[1] In many communities, the strict enforcement of state laws requiring school attendance until age sixteen also spurred the establishment of Amish schools. The first recorded school conflict between the Amish and the state occurred in 1914 in Geauga County, Ohio. Three Amish fathers were fined when they refused to send their children to high school.[2] The children, all under the age of sixteen, had completed the eighth grade.

The problem worsened with the passage of the Bing Act by the Ohio General Assembly in 1921. This law compelled children to attend school until the age of eighteen. However, upon parental assurance that a child would work, permits were issued for sixteen-year-olds. Amish parents were unhappy with this law. In their opinion, children were already spending too many years in school. They also objected to their children's being exposed to what they considered unnecessary subjects—history, geography, and hygiene.

After telling their children not to study these subjects, five fathers were arrested in 1922 and charged with contributing to the delinquency of minors. On 12 January 1922, eight children from Holmes County, Ohio, were taken from their parents to the Painter Children's Home. The parents were accused of neglect.

The children were released from the home on 28 January after the parents agreed to pay fines and to allow their children to study all subjects.[3]

Tensions in Geauga County eased in 1926 when County Superintendent Frank Schofield met with four bishops and several ministers. They reached the following agreement: "The Amish are to send their children to school every day until they are through the eighth grade or turn sixteen. They are not to keep them home for work or any other illegal reason or excuse. Sickness is the only excuse. This agreement is to hold as long as any Amish children go to any school in the years to come" (Hershberger 1985, 28).

Unfortunately, school officials in other areas of the country were less willing to negotiate this kind of agreement. For the next five decades, the Amish in many communities faced opposition over schooling issues from state and local school authorities. Gradually the Amish developed a separate educational system for their children. The first Amish schools established in various communities are listed in table 5.1.

Delaware and Pennsylvania

The Apple Grove school, established in 1925, was the first Amish-owned and -operated school in the twentieth century.[4] It was located in the small settlement near Dover, Delaware. A proposal to send seventh- and eighth-grade students to large consolidated high schools prodded the school's development. Ironically, an influx of Amish families to the community added pressure for consolidation. Amish parents were troubled by plans to eliminate country elementary schools and bus children to town.[5]

Thirteen years later, in 1938, a second Amish school was built in the Dover community, the same year that the first school opened in Lancaster County, Pennsylvania. The Dover Amish community worked amicably with state authorities, but this was not the case in Pennsylvania.

Difficulties for the Amish in Lancaster County began in 1937 when officials of the East Lampeter school district decided to replace ten one-room schools with a consolidated elementary school. Although the Amish and some of their neighbors successfully halted construction for a brief period of time, the new school opened in the fall of 1937 (Kraybill 1989, 122).

Consolidation was not the only threat that the Amish faced. In July of 1937, the Pennsylvania legislature extended the legal age

TABLE 5.1

The First Amish Schools in the United States and Canada, 1925-1954

Community	School Name	Date of Origin
Dover, Del.	Apple Grove Mennonite[a]	1925
Moyock, N.C.		1925[b]
Lumberton, Miss.		1929
Lancaster, Pa.	Oak Grove	1938
Wayne–Holmes Co., Ohio	Fountain Nook	1944
Lawrence Co., Tenn.	Middle Amish	1945
Hohenwald, Lewis Co., Tenn.		1947
Elkhart–Lagrange Co., Ind.	Plain View	1948
Buchanan Co., Iowa	Amish No. 1	1948
Bowling Green, Mo.	Maple Branch	1948
Lebanon Co., Pa.	Millbach Springs	1949
Pike Co., Ohio		1949
Conewango Valley, N.Y.	Gardner	1949
Crawford Co., Pa.	Atlantic	1950
Mercer Co., Pa.	Hilltop	1950
Pike County, Mo.	Shady Creek	1950
St. Joe, Ark.		1950
Geauga Co., Ohio	Parkman	1951
Nappanee, Ind.	Borkholder	1951
Lawrence Co., Pa.	Little Beaver	1952
Mifflin Co., Pa.	Clearview	1952
Aylmer, Ontario	West	1953
Hardin Co., Ohio	Amish No. 1	1953
New Wilmington, Pa.	No. 8	1953
Tuscarawas Co., Ohio	South Sidling Hill	1954

Sources: Amish community directories, the record of Amish schools published each November by the Blackboard Bulletin, correspondence in the files of Heritage Historical Library (Aylmer, Ontario), personal interviews, and Luthy 1986.
[a]See note 4 for a clarification of the name of this school.
[b]This is undoubtedly the only Amish school that was ever held in a hotel. When the settlement was established in North Carolina, a hotel was built to house the first settlers until their homes could be constructed. In the 1925/26 school year, an Amish school was held in the upstairs of the hotel (Luthy 1986, 300).

from fourteen to fifteen when farm children could obtain work permits. This law also lengthened the school year from eight to nine months.

The Amish organized a formal protest against what they called "depressive" school laws (Shirk 1939). On 14 September 1937, nine ministers and seven deacons—representing the sixteen church districts in Lancaster County—met to chart a course of action.

How should they respond to the new Pennsylvania law? They felt that the school laws violated their right as a religious people to live, according to their deeply held beliefs, separate from the encroaching influences of the modern world. The record of this meeting refers to their rights under the Fourteenth Amendment of the Constitution, the Scriptures, and their *Dordrecht Confession of Faith* (A. E. Beiler 1941).

A committee drafted a petition and circulated it among the citizenry of Lancaster County. It respectfully asked the state to rescind the law of 1937. More than three thousand Amish and non-Amish persons signed the following petition concerning the New School Law of 1937.

> We the undersigned, a religious country folks [sic]. Pertaining to Agriculture, do hereby certify that Conscientiously, we can not send our Children unto the World's nurture, and teachings until they are grown up.
>
> And do hereby petition the Boards of public instruction to be Lenient with a well meaning people. If we are Granted, eight month schooling in a year and the Children are exempt when they get through the low grades, and let us have the one room school houses, and teach the truth, we can with a free conscience send our Children to the Public Schools.
>
> We would be very Thankful if the above would be granted.
> (C. Lapp 1991, 141–67)

The Amish presented their petition to the legislature to no avail. To make matters worse, in December 1937 Amishman Aaron King was sent to prison for keeping his fourteen-year-old daughter from attending high school (*Commonwealth v. King* 1937). The case went to the federal district court in Philadelphia, but the appeal was rejected (Keim 1975, 94). King was one of the first of many Amish to face imprisonment for refusing to cooperate with school officials.

The decision to provide an Amish alternative to public schools arose from this milieu of conflict. By 1938, the doors to the second and third Amish schools had opened. These schools emerged to protect Amish youth from unwanted external influences. The matter of children who had completed eighth grade but were still under the age of fifteen was, however, unresolved. In 1939, the state of Pennsylvania reversed its earlier decision and granted fourteen-year-olds work permits. However, consolidation pressures continued, and in 1949 the state once again raised the age for work permits to fifteen.

Lancaster's Amish school committee persisted in pressuring

state and local officials for special consideration. Under the leadership of a gifted lay leader, Aaron E. Beiler, the committee drafted another petition in 1941 and presented it to the Pennsylvania legislature.

> In order to perform the duties of our calling, we shall "bring them up in the nurture and admonition of the Lord"—Eph. 6:4; also to educate them for farm and domestic work—homemaking—by practical training under Christian supervision in compliance of a general need for the "staff of bread"—spiritual and natural—Psalms 105:16—"that we might not be changeable to any of you"— 2 Thess, 3:8.
>
> We resent the idea of the public teaching a Christian's youth, especially after they have achieved the primary studies in elementary schools. To surpass the equivalence of the 3 Rs as well as wasting priceless time in school under the world's nurture and environment, conflicts with the dictates of our conscience—"for the wisdom of this world is foolishness with God"—1 Cor. 3:18–21; we conscientiously object to any excessive compulsory attendance of the public's instruction—James 4:4. (A. E. Beiler 1941)

This effort and others like it in the ensuing decade were not successful. Many noncompliant parents were arrested in the fifties. The courts occasionally ruled in favor of the Amish, but more frequently found that the right of the state to enforce school attendance laws superseded the rights of the Amish to refuse compliance.

Keim (1975) cites two contradictory examples. In 1949, an Amishman was charged by a justice of the peace with violating the compulsory attendance law by refusing to send his children over the age of fourteen to school. The case, *Commonwealth v. Petersheim*, went to the Somerset County Court on appeal. The Amish argued that "Pennsylvania law did not apply because the children were fifteen years old, were engaged in farm or domestic work for their parents, and were thus entitled to a permit exempting them from the compulsory attendance laws" (Keim 1975, 95–96). The court agreed with this reasoning and ruled in their favor, citing their constitutional rights to liberty and conscience under the Fourteenth Amendment.

Commonwealth v. Beiler (1951), heard in the Pennsylvania Superior Court in Lancaster, had a different outcome. Two Amishmen had kept their children home after the eighth grade. The court recognized the conflict between religious liberty and the state's right to enforce its school attendance law. In its decision the court asked: "In the realm of secular education, which is paramount? The State functioning according to democratic processes and depending for its virility upon enlightened citizens; or parents, whose deep and sincere religious convictions reject advanced education as an encroachment upon their way of life" (Keim 1975, 96)? The court's response was that "parents do not have a constitutional right (state or federal) to deprive their children of education even though their religion apparently commands that formal education be limited. And the parent's religious liberty is not violated when the state demands that children become intelligent members of society" (Boles 1967, 308).

Finally, in 1955 an agreement was ironed out between the Amish and the state of Pennsylvania. The Pennsylvania Department of Public Instruction accepted a plan on 16 January 1956 which allowed children who were fourteen and had completed the eighth grade to attend a special "vocational" school for several hours a week until they turned fifteen. The plan called for these students to study at home and to keep a diary of their daily activities. Teachers in the local Amish school monitored their work. In some cases, a special teacher was hired for this purpose.

One of these vocational schools is described in a letter written by an Amish observer to the Amish School Committee chair, Aaron E. Beiler. A portion of the literal text of this letter describes a vocational school for eight scholars in 1956.

> I was at Aaron Stoltzfus Sat. afternoon. where they had class for the
> 14 yr olds. was well pleased think Aaron has a very nice way of
> handling them. first he read part of Matt. 4 and Our Father prayer.
> then had them write report in their Diaries in Composition book.
> while he looked over their home Arithmetic work. then spelling
> they changed sheets while he spelled them out of book. those that
> had some words wrong wrote them 5 times then he went from one
> to other and had them spell them again. they read and spelled out
> of Matt 4. by memory two verses . . . are to learn two last ones for
> next Sat. and sang about 6 lines [from the] Ausbund. (A. E. Beiler
> 17 January 1956)

The vocational school plan was the last hurdle for Pennsylvania's Amish. The School Committee continued to coordinate school developments. In 1957, Amish communities throughout the state initiated an annual meeting of school leaders to set guidelines and standards for Amish schools (Pennsylvania Amish 1973, 21).

Ohio

The enactment of the Bing Law in 1921 required sixteen-year-olds, even with work permits, to stay in school. This created little difficulty for the Amish, because country schools permitted them to repeat the eighth grade until they reached sixteen years of age (Hershberger 1985, 2). This simple solution ended in the forties, however, when Ohio public schools began to consolidate. Amish parents were pressured to send their youth to high school. Many refused.

In 1942, Wayne County school officials took action. They arrested Ben Raber. He was given a choice between prison or sending his son to high school. Raber spent thirty days in jail. Upon completion of his sentence, Raber's son was permitted to stay out of school. Other cases were not resolved so easily. One young man was forcibly removed from his parents' home and sent to a children's home. While there he attended the Smithville High School against his parents' wishes (Hershberger 1985, 4).

These conflicts led to the formation of the first Amish school in Ohio. In July of 1944, the Amish purchased an abandoned schoolhouse and a store because the scarcity of building materials during World War II prevented them from constructing a new school.[6] The Amish renovated the buildings to comply with state regulations.

When the buildings were ready, a teacher was hired and school materials were secured. A Holmes County attorney arranged a meeting between the Amish school board and the state attorney general regarding their authority to operate the school, called Fountain Nook. He assured them that it was their school and said, "Teach what you want" (Hershberger 1985, 10).

School opened in Wayne County, Ohio, on 25 September 1944. On the same day, a judge refused to recognize attendance at Fountain Nook. He informed Amish parents that they had three weeks to send their children to a public school or face trial.

Thus, the situation in the fall of 1944 became nearly intolerable for many Ohio parents. Two trials were held, and in both instances Amish parents were accused of neglect for not sending their children to school. In the first case, Martin Hochstetler was fined twenty dollars. His daughter had completed eighth grade but no state-approved alternative to high school had been arranged. Hochstetler's daughter had been attending Fountain Nook Amish school, but the judge refused to accept this school as a legitimate alternative to public schools. She was to be removed from home and placed in the care of a "fit woman" (Hershberger 1985, 6).

The second case, however, nullified the Hochstetler outcome. In November 1944, a visiting judge from Ashland, Ohio, ruled against a charge of neglect imposed upon Amishman Abe Weaver for not sending his son to high school. Judge H. E. Culbertson ruled that there was insufficient evidence for convicting the parents under Ohio's neglected child statutes. He declared that the Weavers did not neglect their son's education by sending him to Fountain Nook School.[7] This ruling overturned the decision in the Hochstetler case and ended the controversy for a time (Hershberger 1985, 6). These significant cases tested the viability of Amish schools as legitimate alternatives to public schools in Ohio.

Ohio Amish parents once again were accused of neglect in the 1950s. *State v. Hershberger* (1958) attracted nationwide attention. It began in January 1958 when a Wayne County truant officer notified the local welfare director that Amish children were not attending high school. Following an investigation, Director Paul Kinney and a deputy sheriff visited a number of Amish homes on 15 February, intending to remove the children from their homes. Although no children were apprehended, three of the couples were accused of child neglect. They were ordered to bring their sons to a hearing in Wooster, when the boys would be sent to the Wayne County Children's Home. The parents went to the hearing on 12 March 1958 without their sons. The judge charged them with contempt, fining each couple five hundred dollars. Upon refusal to pay the fine, they were jailed.

A reporter for the local newspaper recorded the following conversation between one of the accused and Judge Dan Young:

> "For what reason are you holding us in contempt?" John Hershberger asked the judge. "You did not surrender the boy," answered Young. "When the court makes an order it has to be obeyed." "According to the church and the Bible I couldn't give my boy up.
> I couldn't give my boy up and send him to someone else." "It says in the Bible that you are to render unto Caesar what is Caesar's," said the judge. "We are dealing with Caesar's law today." "Doesn't religion stand anymore?" "You must understand that your church rules will not stand in this action," said the judge. "The rules of your church cannot prevail against the statutes of the legislature."[8]

While the couples were in jail, a sheriff—sent to accost their sons—was unable to locate them. The Wayne County Court of Appeals reversed the contempt citations of the juvenile court when the judge concluded that the parents honestly did not know the whereabouts of their children (Keim 1975, 97). Thus, Judge Young's prediction of the outcome of the church-state contest was never tested.

The Ohio Amish, seeking an alternative to litigation, sent a delegation to Pennsylvania to learn about the vocational school plan. In the fall of 1958, the vocational plan was implemented in Ohio. In the early days, it was known as the "Lancaster Plan" or the "Pennsylvania Plan." As in Pennsylvania, students met once a week with a teacher to review their vocational work. They participated in the vocational plan after completing eight grades of formal schooling.

The Amish hoped that vocational schools would alleviate the pressure to send children under the age of sixteen to high school. Their hopes were in vain. The state investigated the vocational schools soon after they were implemented. In 1958, State School Superintendent E. E. Holt ruled that Amish vocational schools were substandard. A second investigation, two years later, by the Ohio Department of Education concluded that the nine vocational schools in the study were all substandard according to seventy-seven of ninety-nine criteria for Ohio high schools.[9] Although the state never pursued its case, tensions continued to surface through the 1960s.

A school board in Medina County, Ohio, tried to close an Amish school and force its pupils to attend public schools. In *Chalfin v. Glick* (1961), the court refused to close the Amish school because "the instruction there adequately met state educational requirements" (Boles 1967, 308).

School officials in Medina County did not desist. They requested that a bill be introduced in the 1963–64 session of the Ohio General Assembly to allow an injunction against any school deemed to be substandard (Saros 1968, 73). This bill was defeated and never became law.

Indiana

The first Amish school in Indiana opened its doors in the fall of 1948. The school, located in Elkhart County near the Lagrange County line, welcomed students from both counties. Preparations for the school began at a meeting on 29 July 1948 at Bishop Henry N. Miller's home near Middlebury. This resulted in the selection of a school board. The group discussed concerns about the education of Amish children. The local one-room public school had been closed. Children were being bussed to a consolidated school where, according to one Amishman, "as much or more stress was put on entertainment as on education, where everything was being modernized more and more, and where evolution instead of creation was taught in science classes" (J. M. Bontrager 1967, 106).

At a second meeting, a group of men from Plain City, Ohio, came to Indiana to share experiences about their parochial school. The Indiana group decided to bid on a vacant schoolhouse at a public auction. They purchased the building, its contents, and one-half acre of land for $3,225 (E. Gingerich 1980, 19).

A retired Mennonite teacher was hired, and school began on 11 October 1948. This elderly teacher consented to teach for only one year. Amish ministers of the Middle and West Barrens church districts discussed the matter of teacher qualifications and decided that some college education would be appropriate.

A young Amishman, Eli Gingerich, was asked to teach. After he had consented, church elders decided he should attend Goshen College. Upon visiting the college, the prospective teacher and an Amish minister were informed that parochial schools were not required to have certified teachers. College officials recommended, however, that Gingerich take the High School Equivalency Test, which he passed.

Gingerich planned to attend evening classes at Goshen College in the fall of 1948. A non-Amish person was scheduled to transport the young man to school. On registration night, however, the ride never came because of a terrible storm. Thus, Gingerich never attended college, which set a precedent of not requiring Amish teachers in Indiana to have some higher education.[10]

Although the Amish in northern Indiana struggled with state and local authorities over their school buildings,[11] it was in central Indiana that parents were taken to court in 1948 for refusing to send a fourteen-year-old son to high school. The boy's father, Chester Gingerich, was sentenced to the Indiana State Farm for sixty days and fined two hundred dollars by the circuit court. Governor Ralph Gates pardoned Gingerich, however, before any time was served.

Because the governor had asked Gingerich to send his son to school, he was arrested once again in 1949 for failing to do so. He was convicted and fined a second time. The Indiana Supreme Court eventually threw out the case, suggesting that the law might allow children to leave school at the age of fifteen. Since the Gingerich boy was past age fifteen, charges were dropped (Luthy 1986, 109).

Many public schools were consolidated in the state of Indiana in the mid-1960s. The Amish reacted swiftly by setting up their own schools. For example, in Lagrange County the Westview school system was established in 1967. Within two years, thirteen Amish schools opened in this district. Fortunately, the Amish were able to establish standards for their new schools that were acceptable to state school authorities. In 1967, an Amish executive committee signed a cooperative agreement with the state superintendent of public instruction.[12] This agreement has never been contested.

Iowa

In 1948, the Amish established schools in northeastern Iowa in response to the consolidation of public schools in the Hazelton and Oelwein districts of Buchanan and Fayette counties. Two vacant schools were purchased, and certified non-Amish teachers were hired. Amish parents completely funded their schools.[13] In 1961, however, the Amish welcomed financial support from the state. This entangled them in a political fracas that undoubtedly was linked to later trouble.

A proposal to merge the Oelwein and Hazelton school districts was put on the 8 November 1961 ballot. Bitter antagonism flared between and within these communities. Hazelton was the smaller of the two. Some of its residents feared they would be swallowed up by the merger; others hoped the move would enhance the college preparation of their children.

The Oelwein superintendent learned from the state superintendent of public instruction, Paul Johnson, that the Amish might vote for consolidation if assured they could continue to operate their own schools with the added bonus of possible state subsidy. On 12 October 1961, Johnson wrote: "I would recommend that if the reorganization took place that the Board hire teachers and provide supervision for the two schools which the Amish people are now operating. I think the new Board should provide good facilities and equipment, and good teachers for these schools, but in so doing recognize these people's feeling concerning education" (Erickson 1969, 24).

This letter was published in the Oelwein newspaper on 4 November. The chair of the Amish School Committee, Dan Borntreger, thought the Amish should support the referendum. With some reservation he lobbied his constituency to vote in favor of consolidation, and the measure passed.

According to Erickson (1969, 26), the proposal passed in Hazelton by only forty-nine votes. Forty-four Amish people had voted, helping to determine the outcome. Their vote angered their non-Amish neighbors. They were "branded as hypocrites, motivated by economic greed, wanting only to keep their schooling costs down and hoping to exploit child labor in the fields" (Erickson 1969, 28). Their communities were described by some of their neighbors "as if [they] were a concentration camp—where children are chained to beds, where barefoot women run farms while their husbands loaf and travel, where the young are 'worked to death,' and where aging wives are allowed to die in childbirth as a substitute for divorce" (Erickson 1969, 28).

Within five months, two major obstacles appeared in the path of Amish schools in Iowa. On 7 May 1962, the Oelwein school board declared that Amish schools could only exist temporarily until they were incorporated into the public schools. Furthermore, the Amish curriculum must mirror the public school curriculum.

On 14 May, consultants from the state superintendent's office investigated the Amish schools near Hazelton. The consultants reported that the schools "were impossible . . . and could never be brought up to an acceptable standard. The State Department of Education would permit the Oelwein Board to operate these schools for the first six grades only and for two years at the very most. Before this could be done, furthermore, the Amish must agree to send all seventh- and eighth-grade pupils to Hazelton at once, with the other children to follow within two years" (Erickson 1969, 32).

In the fall of 1962, the Amish schools opened with Amish teachers in the classrooms. The hostile English community reacted quickly. Amish parents learned they were violating a law if they sent their children to schools taught by noncertified teachers. The new district superintendent, J. J. Jorgenson, sought an injunction in the Tenth Judicial District of Iowa to close the Amish schools. Judge Peter Von Metre "refused to issue the injunction on the ground that Iowa law only authorized the closing of a 'public school' that failed to meet state standards" (Rodgers 1969, 25–26). In his remarks, however, the judge suggested that students who attended unapproved schools could be considered truants.

On 24 November 1962, ten Amish parents were brought before a justice of the peace by the Buchanan County attorney. They were charged with failure to send their children to schools with certified teachers. All ten were fined. Eight spent three days in jail for refusing to pay their fines.

The conflict continued in 1963 and 1964. An attorney representing the Amish tried repeatedly to get an exemption from the teacher certification requirement, without success. The school board proposed a compromise—a special classroom for the Amish in the public school. The Amish declined the offer.

The Amish rejected a second conciliatory proposal: the board proposed hiring a certified Amish teacher from a more progressive Amish settlement. But the Amish said this was "not our kind of Amishman" (Erickson 1969, 39).

Further attempts at negotiated settlements also failed. At the beginning of the 1965 school year, antagonism between the Amish and their neighbors flared. Local authorities took their case against the Amish to court. For three weeks in September, a nightly ritual occurred in the home of Justice of the Peace Minnie Wengert. Fourteen Amish fathers would appear and be summarily fined twenty dollars plus four dollars for court costs. Each evening they graciously refused to pay the fine, arguing that to do so would violate their religious principles.

The unpaid fines soon totaled more than ten thousand dollars. Knowing that the Amish were willing to go to jail rather than pay, the court began to place liens against their properties. By early November, "the county sheriff served writs garnisheeing about $165 worth of property per Amish father" (Rodgers 1969, 28).

The drama unfolding near Hazelton received national attention on Friday, 19 November 1965. The day before, county officials had informed the community that they were going to round up Amish children—whom they considered to be truants—and take them by bus to the public school. When the bus pulled into Amish farm lanes on Friday morning, school-age children had vanished. The only children found that morning were at Amish School Number One. These children ran into adjacent cornfields as officials tried to escort them to the bus. Photographs of the episode appeared in newspapers across the country. The scenes of children fleeing in terror from the authorities prompted sympathy for the Amish far beyond Hazelton.

The following Tuesday, Governor Harold Hughes, hoping to ease tensions, intervened in the case. He issued a moratorium against further actions involving Amish children and ordered the Iowa attorney general to investigate other solutions to the problem. If another state had resolved similar problems satisfactorily, Hughes was quoted as saying, "We will go directly to the scene. . . . Somewhere within the confines of a reasonable society, there has to be a reasonable solution" (Rodgers 1969, 31).

A reasonable solution evolved, but it took nearly two years. In February 1966, the governor proposed a temporary solution. He suggested that the public school board lease Amish schools for a nominal fee and that certified teachers be hired but paid by funds from the Danforth Foundation, a private foundation. This compromise was in effect through the spring of 1967.

In the summer of 1967, the Iowa legislature granted an exemption from state school standards to any recognized church or denomination "which professes principles or tenets that differ substantially from the objectives, goals or philosophy of education embodied in the state-standard law" (Rodgers 1969, 35). This act laid the Amish school controversy to rest in the state of Iowa.

Kansas

In another case that received national attention, Leroy Garber, of Hutchinson, Kansas, was fined five dollars and costs for refusing to send his fifteen-year-old daughter to high school. The daughter, who had completed eighth grade, was attending an Amish vocational school. She was also taking correspondence courses from a school in Chicago.

This case, *State v. Garber* (1967), went to the Kansas Supreme Court in 1966. The court ruled that the only legitimate reason for truancy until the age of sixteen was physical or mental incapacity. Since these conditions did not apply, Garber had violated school attendance statutes.

A more basic question than school attendance, however, undergirded this case. Did the compulsory attendance laws violate Garber's constitutionally guaranteed right of religious freedom? The court agreed with the decision of *Commonwealth v. Beiler* (1951): "Religious liberty includes the absolute right to believe but only a limited right to act. . . . The parental right to believe as he chooses remains absolute. But compulsory school attendance is not a religious issue" (Nolte 1967, 27–28). The Supreme Court of the United States refused to hear this case on appeal.

Wisconsin

The final showdown between the Amish and school authorities occurred in Wisconsin. Once again, local antagonism between non-Amish and Amish erupted into a case that received national attention. The legal precedent set by this case informs the curriculum of law schools across the United States.

After settling in New Glarus, Wisconsin, in 1963, the Amish established their first school. This provided an opportunity for people who, according to John A. Hostetler (1975, 100), "were less than enthusiastic about the Amish settling in their community" to set limits on the unwelcome newcomers. Charges were filed against three fathers who refused to send their children to high school.[14] Their children had all completed the eighth grade but were under the age (sixteen) necessary to leave school.

In March 1969, a trial was held in the court of Green County, Wisconsin. Amish fathers were accused of violating the state's compulsory attendance laws and were found guilty. In his ruling, the judge "acknowledged that their religious liberty has been violated but [he added] there was a superior state interest in forcing the children to attend school" (Ball 1975, 120).

Attorney William Ball, with the support of the National Committee for Amish Religious Freedom, unsuccessfully appealed the case in the district court. Undaunted, Ball pressed on to the Supreme Court of Wisconsin, where the lower court's decision was reversed. The state of Wisconsin, in turn, decided to take its case to the Supreme Court of the United States. The Supreme Court had refused to hear the *Garber* case from Kansas but agreed to consider what became known as *Wisconsin v. Yoder* (1972). Arguments began on 8 December 1971.

On 15 May 1972, the U.S. Supreme Court unanimously ruled that the Amish had a right to refuse to send their children to high school. In summarizing the opinion of the court, Chief Justice Warren Berger concluded that "almost 300 years of consistent practice, and strong evidence of a sustained faith pervading and regulating respondents' entire mode of life support the claim that enforcement of the State's requirement of compulsory formal education after the eighth grade would gravely endanger if not destroy the free exercise of respondents' religious beliefs" (Keim 1975, 159).

This historic ruling settled the question of the right of Amish parents to follow the lead of their conscience in educating their children. *Wisconsin v. Yoder* permitted the establishment of Amish schools; however, it did not address issues such as teacher certification. In Pawnee County, Nebraska, the Amish established a small settlement in 1978. After the Amish built a school, local authorities insisted that only certified teachers could teach. Rather than challenge the issue in court, the Amish left Nebraska in 1982.

Amish Objections To Public Schools

Why have the Amish so tenaciously insisted on establishing their own schools, controlling their own curriculum, and—more importantly—appointing their own teachers? Why have they been willing to undergo persecution and at times great financial sacrifice to challenge the state's authority to require attendance until the age of sixteen? The complex answers to these questions have both theological and sociological strands.

A fundamental principle of Amish life is the religious belief in two kingdoms. The Amish inherited a religious understanding of dual kingdoms from their sixteenth-century forebears, the Anabaptists. On the one hand is the kingdom of this world—the dominant culture and social structures of society. On the other is the kingdom of God—an eternal reality without specific time or place, as outlined in the Bible. Members of the kingdom of God must consciously separate themselves from the values and institutions of the kingdoms of this world. The Amish consider themselves to be the peculiar people that the writer of the book of Peter (1 Peter 2:9) mentions. Their life is filled with literal and symbolic dividers, reminders of the clear difference between the people of the heavenly kingdom and those of the earthly realm.

The Amish desire to withdraw their children from the secular realm of public schools flows directly from their two-kingdom theology. According to one Amishman, "We are taking dangerous chances if we expect our children to mix with the world and not be harmed by it. . . . State schools have always prepared the child for his life on earth, and were never intended to prepare him for eternity. For the world, education is training the mind for success in this life. For the Christian, education is training the child to live for others, to use his talents in service to God and man, to live an upright and obedient life, and to prepare for the life to come" (J. Stoll 1965, 26, 31).

The Amish know that schools teach much more than basic skills in arithmetic, reading, and so on. Among the many things that public schools emphasize are competition, individualism, nationalism, scientific modes of thought, hierarchical organization, and the teenage subculture. All of these clash with the Amish way of life.

The Amish realize that large organizations make it difficult for members to know one another as whole persons. Large organizations require an administrative structure and a bureaucratic division of labor. Rational planning replaces tradition, and the anomalous case is lost in the shuffle of paper. This insight, among others, motivated the Amish to resist sending their children to large consolidated schools.

The one-room schoolhouse, common in rural America through the middle of the twentieth century, fit the Amish preference for small-scale organization. Grades were not divided into separate rooms, and the teacher was known by all the children and community members. When these schools were the norm, the Amish supported them, often participating on school boards.

The one-room school typically ended at the eighth grade. The move to the high school marked a transition that the Amish have rarely been willing to make. As Kraybill (1989, 131–32) observes, the Amish have concluded that public high schools

> would separate children from their parents, their traditions, and their values. Education would be decontextualized—separated from the daily context of Amish life. The Amish world, laced together by religious threads of meaning, would be divided into component parts: academic disciplines, courses, classes, grades, and multiple teachers. . . . Professional specialists—educated in worldly universities and separated from the Amish in time, culture, and training—would be entrusted with nurturing their children. Such experts would encourage Amish youth to maximize their potential by pursuing more education to "liberate" themselves from the shackles of parochialism. By stirring aspirations and raising occupational hopes, the experts would steer Amish youth away from farm and family, or certainly lead to their restlessness if they did stay home.

Other objections to public schools include their distance from home, inflexible schedules, the lure of non-Amish peer groups, and the explicit rejection of religious training. Amish parents would prefer to see their children walk or ride a buggy to a school a mile or two away, rather than putting them on a bus to town. The distance factor not only separates home and school but inhibits contact between parents, children, and teachers. In rural areas, buggies pass by Amish schools daily, allowing the community to keep a watchful eye on school activities. Parents are frequent unannounced visitors. This is less likely in public schools.

Amish schools must conform to state laws setting the number of annual school days. Their schools can, however, flex with the rhythm of community life. When a special occasion arises—a wedding or a funeral—school can be dismissed. Amish school years have few vacation days. This makes it possible to complete the required number of school days in time for children to assist with spring farm work.

Peers are important in Amish society, just as they are in the dominant culture. Parents would much prefer, however, that their children's circle of friends be primarily Amish. As Joseph Stoll (1965, 27) observes, the non-Amish child "lives in a different world from the children of our plain groups. How long can we keep this separation, this distinction, under the pressure of society to make us conform to their standards? Is it possible if we continue to select their children as companions for our children?"

While the Amish have a profound respect for the principle of separation of church and state, they are unhappy with the removal of Christianity from public schools. Although they do not believe that a primary function of schools, including their own, is religious instruction, they cannot understand why it is unacceptable to begin the day with meditation. The Amish school day begins with the recitation of the Lord's Prayer and a hymn or two. Many teachers also read a few verses, without comment, from the Bible.[15]

Reactions to Amish Schools

It would appear that Amish schools pose few, if any, threats to citizens of the communities in which they have been established. In fact, since the Amish pay public school taxes, they are subsidizing the education of non-Amish children. As we have seen, however, their initial attempts to form an alternative school system were often greeted with hostility.

The reasons for such negative reactions to Amish schools are varied and complex. It may not be coincidental that many of the major controversies over Amish schools occurred when the United States was at war. From the Geauga County, Ohio, incident in 1914 to the Wisconsin case in the early 1970s, local events were framed by a national context of war. Since the Amish have consistently refused to participate in war, they have been subjected to criticism and at times persecution for their beliefs. School issues were front stage, but refusal to participate in war was probably in the background.

The Amish are a "peculiar people" in appearance, modes of transportation, and language. Such marked differences breed mistrust and suspicion; and reactions to perceived differences tend to be more pronounced in a time of war. Examples from recent history include the incarceration of Japanese-Americans during World War II as well as the systematic investigation of Arab-Americans during the war in the Persian Gulf.

Even within the public school system, cultural differences in a war environment sometimes foster suspicion and discrimination. At the end of World War I, a case involving objections to the military draft reached the Nebraska Supreme Court.[16] The record shows that when opposition to the draft surfaced in a community, it could be "demonstrated that there were local foci of alien enemy sentiment and that . . . the education given by private or parochial schools in that community was usually found to be that which had been given mainly in a foreign language" (Elson 1969, 106).

The Amish have steadfastly refused to enter the American melting pot. They have insisted that progress, critical reasoning, and the scientific and technological advances of the twentieth century are not necessarily good.[17] Furthermore, their two-kingdom theology requires clear boundaries between themselves and the "world." Few non-Amish understand the religious significance of Amish cultural boundary markers such as the horse and buggy.[18] Non-Amish often perceive these cultural dividers as quaint or as nuisances to be grudgingly tolerated. The price that the Amish pay for being different is often anger and resentment. Hostilities directed toward Amish parents, who quietly send their children off to parochial school, may sometimes have little to do with education.

Objections to Amish schools often include concerns for the welfare of Amish children. Is it not a form of societal neglect to limit children to an eighth-grade education with teachers who have completed only eight grades? The Amish, of course, answer that their way of life requires no more than a basic understanding of arithmetic and rudimentary communication skills. Social scientists have demonstrated that Amish children do indeed learn basic skills in their own schools. In fact, John A. Hostetler (1969) and Wayne Miller (1969) have demonstrated that when Amish school children are compared with public school pupils in the same community, Amish students perform better on standardized tests in spelling, word usage, and arithmetic than their non-Amish counterparts.

Other scholars have argued that Amish schools prepare children for life in less tangible ways. On this point Lindholm (1974, 490) writes: "They emphasize what has become characterized as the *wisdom* dimension, as contrasted with the *technos*. Wisdom is devoted to character, honesty, humility and long suffering. They have no interest in landing men on the moon—they seek only to produce good men."

The development and maintenance of Amish schools is essential for the preservation of Amish culture. Operating their own schools allows the Amish to control curricular content and to limit social interaction with the outside world. The Amish understand the critical importance of childhood socialization for the formation of values and the safeguarding of their culture. Although their educational patterns clash with modern values, their educational ventures successfully prepare Amish youth to live meaningful lives within Amish society. Donald A. Erickson (1965, 9) pungently observes:

> If it is permissible to live the life of an Amishman in the United States, it should be equally permissible to prepare to live the life of an Amishman. In fact, it would be more logical to outlaw public schools in most inner-city areas, for here there has been general failure to protect the state from . . . "social dynamite" by preparing the culturally deprive[d] child to live productively. From this standpoint, a "proof-of-the-pudding" test might well identify the Amish educational process as one of the most effective yet devised.

Jonas Yoder, defendant in the famous Wisconsin v. Yoder *(1972) case, at work on his farm.* Ray Barth

CHAPTER SIX

The National Committee for Amish Religious Freedom

William C. Lindholm

The notorious educational conflicts led to the formation of the National Committee for Amish Religious Freedom. Lutheran pastor William C. Lindholm organized the committee and was elected its chairman. Consisting of sympathetic outsiders, the committee has provided legal assistance and counsel to the Amish on a variety of church-state conflicts. The Reverend Lindholm provides a personal account of the committee's origins and offers an assessment of its role.

Beginnings, a Personal Story

The National Committee for Amish Religious Freedom was founded to preserve the religious freedom of the Old Order Amish. Complex laws, designed to control a monolithic technological society, often threaten the very existence of Amish culture. The Amish are disadvantaged in the modern legal milieu because they do not defend themselves, go to court, or hire lobbyists. The National Committee for Amish Religious Freedom was created to be their advocate—to help those who choose not to help themselves.[1]

How did I as a Lutheran pastor became involved with the Amish? Why would an outsider from another religious tradition organize a committee to speak on their behalf? The National Committee for Amish Religious Freedom began in a strange place—behind a house under construction in the Huron National Forest of Michigan's lower peninsula. One morning in November 1965, I was reviewing the construction progress of a new Lutheran conference center situated on 320 acres of white birch forest and lakes. As chairman of the board for the Lutheran Camp, I conferred with the Mennonite contractor.

I walked to the rear of the new house under construction and saw three men painting. They were all bearded, and jokingly I asked them, "Is there a Centennial planned here?" Many towns were celebrating centennials, and townsmen often grew beards for the festivities. The three painters, all quite shy, mumbled, "No, these beards are for religious reasons." Surprised, I walked to the front of the house and asked the contractor why the men wore beards but not mustaches. They were cousins of his from Indiana, I learned, who were visiting and helping to paint. He said they were members of the Old Order Amish.

Events in my home state of Iowa sparked my interest in the Amish I met that day. My uncle Paul F. Johnston, longtime superintendent for public instruction in Iowa, had tried to solve a controversy in that state when the Amish refused to attend consolidated schools or hire their own certified teachers. Bucking consolidation efforts, Amish leaders chose to retain one-room country schools staffed with Amish teachers without college training. The Amish resistance triggered a clash with state authorities.

Each night via radio my wife listened to the news from Iowa, eight hundred miles from Michigan. The Amish there were fined repeatedly for not sending their children to approved schools. A few days before I met the three Amishmen in Michigan, my wife asked, "Do you know what is happening in Iowa? Today [19 November 1965] the sheriff chased a whole bunch of Amish kids from a schoolhouse into a cornfield!" The sheriff was supposed to coax the Amish students onto a school bus to force them to a newly consolidated school. The children would have no part of it, and they scattered into the cornfield. At first, many folks in Iowa were against the "ignorant Amish" for refusing to send their children to schools with certified teachers.

In high school, I had won first place in the American Legion's statewide oratorical contest in Iowa. In the competition we drew an amendment to the U.S. Constitution out of a hat and spoke extemporaneously on its meaning. Since then I have retained the wording of the First Amendment: "Congress shall make no law respecting an establishment of religion, or prohibiting the free exercise thereof." My chance meeting with the three Amishmen gave me an opportunity to probe their educational views. Why, I asked, were they not giving their children a good education? After talking with them a while, I became convinced that they held sincere religious beliefs. Perhaps the authorities in Iowa were curtailing Amish freedom to practice their sincere religious beliefs.

⁓ Iowa was not the first battleground between the Amish and the state: conflicts with state authorities had begun earlier in the eastern United States. As early as 1915 and again in 1922, Amishmen were arrested in Ohio for failing to send their children to school.[2] Another arrest occurred in 1927 in Ohio when an Amish father failed to send his daughter to school beyond the eighth grade (*Byler v. State*). This was followed in 1937 by the arrest in Pennsylvania of an Amish father who was jailed for failing to pay a two-dollar fine for keeping his fourteen-year-old daughter out of school.[3] In 1948, an Amishman was imprisoned for sixty days, and the Indiana Supreme Court upheld the action (*Gingerich v. State*). In Pennsylvania, the Amish were convicted of high school offenses in *Commonwealth v. Beiler* (1951); and in *State v. Hershberger* (1958), Ohio authorities tried to take Amish children away from their parents but failed. Amish fathers were arrested for keeping their children out of public high school and for sending them to improperly licensed schools without certified teachers. Some agreements were negotiated with state authorities, but in many places the truce was uneasy. The arrests spread westward from Pennsylvania, Ohio, and Indiana to Iowa (1962), Michigan (1965), Kansas (1965), Kentucky (1967), Wisconsin (1968), Virginia (1969), and Nebraska (1980). [4]

After returning home that day, I called the National Council of Churches and talked with their executive director for religious liberty, Dean M. Kelley. Would he help the Amish? It would take too long, he said, to get a resolution through the council. Then Kelley asked, "Why don't you do something about it?" I was angry. What the state was doing to the Amish was not right. I *was* going to do something! I fired off a letter to my uncle, Paul F. Johnston, asking him to side with the Amish. The letter was printed on the front page of the *Des Moines Register* on 27 November 1965. I received a phone call at 7:00 that morning from the Iowa state superintendent of public instruction. My uncle resented being asked to take sides against the educational forces of the state.

Newspapers printed story after story about the Amish refusing to send their children to schools not taught by "state certified teachers"—implying that the non-certified Amish teachers were automatically inferior. The press reports neglected to say that Amish schools were essential to preserving their way of life. I believed that if someone told the Amish side of the story before the public became utterly misinformed and polarized, it would greatly aid the Amish cause. If the public understood that the Amish were not acting out of ignorance, but with wisdom to preserve their religious society, the Amish cause could prevail. If others learned that Amish society, as a school in itself, teaches all the necessary skills for success in Amish culture, then Amish ways might be protected by an informed public opinion.

I began writing letters and making phone calls in 1966 seeking members for a committee to speak on behalf of the Amish. Shortly thereafter, Donald A. Erickson, of the University of Chicago, who was also interested in the educational questions the Amish were raising, directed a national conference on state regulation of non-public schools in March 1967.[4] The governor of Iowa, Harold Hughes, was the keynote speaker. He had become sympathetic to the Amish cause—a rarity in Iowa at the time—because the Amish position was distorted by inaccurate press reports.

Organizational Meeting

The March 1967 conference on nonpublic schools provided the impetus for long-term efforts. At a dinner meeting for anyone interested in the Amish school problem, the National Committee for Amish Religious Freedom was officially organized.[5] I was elected chairman. Robert Showalter, a banker from Yoder, Kansas, and Wayne Fisher, a florist from Houston, Texas, were elected treasurer and secretary, respectively.[6] The initial members of the committee included professors, clergy, attorneys, and other citizens of various faiths—all non-Amish. Members of the committee began defending the Amish by telling their story and providing legal defense.

As the committee was organizing, a legal case, State v. Garber (1966), was pending. An Amish girl took a licensed high school correspondence course instead of attending public high school. The trial record consisted of pages of stipulated facts, but no expert witnesses to support Amish practices. The Kansas Supreme Court ruled against the Amish, saying their "religious beliefs are protected, but religious practices are not" (Garber at 389 U.S. 51). Garber was appealed to the United States Supreme Court, which refused to hear it.

In the fall of 1968, three Amish fathers were arrested in Wisconsin for failing to send their children to high school. The committee learned of the incident through a news story (Rockford Register Star 13 October 1968). As chairman, I immediately wrote to the Amish defendants and offered our aid. The Amish school board wrote back to the committee on 12 November 1968.[7] "We want to thank you for offering your assistance in case of need. So far we have had no serious troubles, although a few threats as to what would happen if we don't have our children above eighth grade attending school, but so far nothing has happened, and we hope nothing will happen, but if we should need help we are glad to know that you are willing to help us."

The Amish had moved to Wisconsin in 1963. They had been attracted to the New Glarus area by a real estate agent selling vacant farms. New Glarus, in Green County, was founded by Swiss immigrants; and the Amish, of course, were also of Swiss extraction. The Amish enrolled their children in high school but withdrew them when they were required to wear skimpy clothing in gym classes. Adin Yutzy said his son had been held down and mistreated by other boys in a shower. The Amish found the values of high school foreign and dangerous to their way of life, and they were uncomfortable sending their children there.

After pulling their offspring out of the public high school, the parents also removed thirty-eight of their children from elementary school and started two of their own. The public school system lost several thousand dollars in state aid with the loss of so many students. Moreover, the Amish settlers didn't seem to be pulling their economic weight in other areas, either—they didn't buy automobiles, appliances, or electrical power. And they were different in other ways as well. There was some pressure to arrest them, but overall there was a surprising amount of tolerance compared to the conflicts in Iowa. In fact, the Amish living under the jurisdiction of adjoining Dane County, Wisconsin, were never arrested. Prosecution was limited to the Amish living in Green County.

The Committee's Mission

The committee had four difficult tasks to accomplish in the Wisconsin conflict. It hoped (1) to persuade the Wisconsin Amish to allow a legal defense on their behalf; (2) to inform the public who hold sway over legislative, legal, and moral actions; (3) to persuade the courts to make a constitutional finding of religious freedom in favor of the Amish; and (4) to raise enough funds to carry the case.

When the national committee decided to defend the Wisconsin Amish, it was told that the Amish would never allow court action on their behalf. Although many Amish fathers had been arrested over the years, asserting one's rights in court was viewed as a biblical taboo (Matthew 5:25). The Amish had gotten as far as the courthouse steps, only to get cold feet, many times in the past.

Following biblical precepts, they turned the other cheek and took their punishment. Or they just moved away. The committee, in the opinion of experienced observers, had little chance of getting Amish cooperation.

On 19 December 1968, however, the committee received a letter from Wallace Miller, one of the fathers in the case.[8] He wrote, "Now it looks like they are going to make a court case out of it. We had a hearing on Monday, December 16 and then got an adjournment on it 'till Tuesday, January 7, at 1:30 o'clock. Now we will leave it up to you whether you want to help us. We would appreciate it if we could talk with someone of the committee before January 7th if possible."

As committee chairman, I drove to New Glarus, Wisconsin, to attempt the delicate task of gaining the confidence of the Old Order Amish. I explained that they were charged as criminals in the legal complaint. The committee's attorney would simply tell the judge what the Amish believed, and ask the judge to rule that their actions were protected by the Constitution's guarantee of religious freedom. I further explained that they would not be "suing anyone" or "taking anyone to law"—prohibitions in Amish religious teaching. Further, I said, they would not need to pay anything—an act viewed by them as defending themselves.

I explained that a case like theirs had never been won before, and if legal efforts were successful, it would help many other religious believers in the United States who highly acclaim the principle of religious freedom. But court records, I reminded them, show that the "slender thread of religious freedom" is "not built on a rock."[9] I also told them that Saint Paul appealed his case to Rome (Acts 25:11), in case it was necessary to appeal to a higher court. The Amish agreed to sign a power of attorney called "Understanding and Agreement" on 6 January 1969 stating that they are "not concerned so much about themselves as they are in allowing the committee to defend the principle of religious freedom for others." The agreement stated that the Amish "will not object to these good neighbors who want to intervene to help." Moreover, they permitted their case to be pursued to its fullest conclusion.

After the Wisconsin Amish agreed to accept assistance, however, the Amish patriarch and school leader in Iowa, Dan M. Borntreger, wrote to the committee. He pointed out that his three daughters lived in Wisconsin and said, "I have talked to Bishops and church members, and we don't feel it would help to take the New Glarus school case to court at this time. . . . Remember if you lose, things will be worse" for us. Were the Amish now telling the committee to stop the legal defense? Nevertheless, the Amish fathers who signed the agreement never revoked it.

Public Relations

The committee needed to explain the Amish position to the public because the Amish often refuse newspaper interviews. When they do talk, they often do not articulate their position clearly to outsiders. In Iowa, Amish leader Borntreger told newspaper reporters that the Amish objected to the new consolidated school because "we've got to do this to keep our faith going. It isn't what they teach in the town schools that we object to, it's what they don't teach" (Mather 1966). Although it was a sincere statement by an Amish leader, most people would not understand the complexity of the issue from such a statement.

The Iowa attorney general, Lawrence F. Scalise, said, "To me, this [Amish refusal to employ certified teachers] is not a religious issue, but simply one of economics."[10] The *Des Moines Register* said the same thing: "In our opinion the issue is not religious freedom" (Mather 1966). The Amish said they would reluctantly accept certified teachers, but they wouldn't pay for them. They would acquiesce to a state-paid teacher in their country school, but they would not pay for their own downfall. Non-Amish viewed the Amish as "stingy" rather than acting out of religious convictions. Thus, the situation became prejudiced against the Amish early on as school authorities told newspaper reporters that the dispute rested on economic, not religious, issues. Finally, the Reverend Dean Kelley, of the National Council of Churches, went to Iowa and contended that the controversy was a religious issue. The governor of Iowa, Harold Hughes, also began to define the school clash as a religious issue (Mather 1966).

The Amish were fined daily in court. The *Oelwein Daily Register*, the *Des Moines Register*, the Rotary Club, the Chamber of Commerce, the Iowa State Education Association, and the Iowa Association of School Administrators all supported arresting the Amish for not having their children taught by "state certified" teachers. The critics didn't realize that half of Iowa's secondary schools had teachers that didn't meet certification requirements and that not a single parochial school in the county qualified for full state certification, but these infractions brought no arrests. One Iowa minister, whom one would think would support religious freedom, wrote to me, "The denial of education to children

. . . is indeed an evil."[11] The committee did not find the situation to be a denial of education per se, but rather a denial of education into mainstream values in public schools.

Admittedly, it is not easy even for a group of scholars, attorneys, and clergy to demonstrate specific Amish reasons for rejecting a mainstream education. We could not point to specific tenets or articles in a creed. But nevertheless, all schooling is a process of acculturation that takes place in the context of values of some kind. The Amish were threatened by the values of the dominant culture, as expressed within the public school system. Later, the Wisconsin Supreme Court understood the significance of the issue in its opinion in *State v. Yoder* (1971). "To the Amish, secondary schools not only teach an unacceptable value system but they also seek to integrate ethnic groups into a homogenized society, resulting in psychological alienation of Amish children from their parents and great harm to the child" (*Yoder* 182 N.W. at 542).

One of the Amish defendants in the Wisconsin case had just moved from Iowa, where he had been fined one thousand dollars for school violations, only to be arrested again. The National Committee for Amish Religious Freedom wanted to inform the public about Amish beliefs and show why the Amish were not sending their youths to high school. As the Wisconsin dispute unfolded, the committee hoped to persuade the media to favor the Amish rather than to criticize them as in Iowa.

Thus, as the committee chairman, I visited the *Monroe Evening News*. I explained the Amish side of the controversy to the editor and reporting staff. The paper published verbatim an article that I had written explaining the Amish position against going to high school.[12] Periodic news releases and interviews with the media were arranged by the committee to explain the religious reasons that prevented Amish parents from sending their youth to high school. Thus, in Wisconsin public opinion favored the Amish more than it had in Iowa.

Legal Proceedings

Could the attorneys win the legal argument in *Wisconsin v. Yoder* (1972)? The *Virginia Law Review* stated that "no court seems to have plumbed sufficiently the depth of the Amish problem, not even the one court that found in their favor [*Commonwealth v. Petersheim*]. . . . The court's almost uniform denial of the Amish claim to be exempted from compulsory education laws is consistent with the conclusions reached when other religions have challenged the school laws. . . . [It] is clear that the approach of the courts to the Amish cases thus far has been unsatisfactory" (Ruxin 1967, 945, 948, 950).

Law professor Robert Casad, of the University of Kansas School of Law, had written a commentary on the most recent Amish case at the time, *State v. Garber* (1966). Casad wrote: "The Kansas Courts erred in treating the [Amish case] in accordance with the long discredited 'act-practices' distinction and ignoring Supreme Court decisions in the past two decades. It is hard to say that the [U.S.] Supreme Court erred . . . the conclusion seems inescapable that even the high tribunal misconceived the nature of the case when it refused to hear the case or send it back for reconsideration under the test of *Sherbert v. Verner*" (Casad 1968). Legal scholars felt that the legal analysis of the Amish cases had not been satisfactory. But would another attempt produce any hope of religious liberty for the Amish?

When the Amish agreed that they would not object to our taking their case, the committee needed a lawyer. As chairman of the committee, I called William B. Ball, a constitutional attorney from Harrisburg, Pennsylvania, on Christmas Eve 1967. Since the Amish had won few legal verdicts in the previous forty years, I asked him, "Do you think that you can help them?" Ball answered, "I would like to think that I can."

Ball requested that the Wisconsin state superintendent of public instruction, William C. Kahl, approve Amish schools under a clause in existing Wisconsin law. The Department of Public Instruction gave a tortured reading of the statutes and refused to accommodate the Amish, and thus the case went to trial.[13]

With legal precedent against him, Ball relied on some newer Supreme Court decisions. The attorney went to court hoping, for the first time in history, to gain for the Amish what the Constitution promises—freedom to practice religious beliefs. Assisting Ball was local attorney Thomas Eckerle, of Madison, Wisconsin. Interestingly, at the last moment, the local district attorney was replaced by a senior attorney, Robert D. Martinson, from the Wisconsin Department of Justice. The prosecution did not attempt to prove that there was a necessity to override Amish religious claims or to demonstrate a compelling state interest. The state simply said the Amish were not attending an approved school.

Ball gave a short but intense defense of Amish beliefs and practices in Green County Court in Monroe, Wisconsin, on 2 April 1969. Expert witness John A. Hostetler explained Amish beliefs.

He said it was "a myth that formal education is automatically good. The Amish are actually being harmed by being forced to send their children to high school. They are educated by their community." For the Amish, "book learning and intellectual disciplines interfere with learning the love of hard work and the soil."

Donald A. Erickson, professor of education at the University of Chicago, defended the Amish educational practices. He said, "The public school benefits the majority of the children, but it's a failure in providing for religious or ethnic minorities. The Amish do a better job of educating than the rest of us—judging by the fact that they have little unemployment, delinquency and divorce."

Minnie Weaver, age twenty-four, teacher at the Amish Plainview school, also testified. She taught arithmetic, English, spelling, reading, geography, and social studies for six and one-half hours, five days a week, in the school. High school age students, she explained, took German and English three hours a week, and the rest of the time learned domestic chores around the home and farm. An Amish minister, an Amish father, the local director of the Welfare Department, and the local sheriff also testified. The sheriff said that the Amish had not been arrested for other criminal offenses. The welfare director testified that none of the Amish were receiving welfare, residing in homes for the elderly, or living in homes for unwed mothers. None were a burden to the taxpayers. An Amish student also testified. Fifteen-year-old Frieda Yoder took the stand and said that she wanted to practice the Amish religion and did not want to go to public high school.

When county judge Roger L. Elmer rendered his opinion, the Amish lost, even though Judge Elmer ruled on 18 August 1969 that "Wisconsin Compulsory School Law does interfere with the religious freedom of the defendants to act in accordance with their sincere religious beliefs and would be unconstitutional if it involved only adults." The court waived the costs and imposed a five-dollar symbolic fine. Nevertheless, the decision deprived Amish youth and their parents of the right to practice their faith without state interference and did nothing to stop repeated and daily fining of such "criminals."

The county court said the state was within its legal rights to destroy an ancient faith by immersing Amish into mainstream values in public high schools. Judge Elmer suggested that the court might find the school requirement unconstitutional if it concerned only adults. In essence, the court said that young Amish were physically capable of having children of their own and old enough to be married under Wisconsin law, but they were not yet old enough to have their religious liberty protected in Wisconsin. If they worshipped according to their conscience they would have to pay a fine.

The committee discovered that the county judge reflected the views of many sincere people who believed that the state was somehow benefiting Amish youth by forcing them to attend public school. Popular opinion believes that a good education brings a good job and good pay. Outsiders often cannot understand how Amish persons find meaning and satisfaction living on a farm in a slow-paced, quiet religious community. Nor do they understand why the Amish would suffer anxiety when forced into public high schools.

These dominant cultural assumptions are revealed in Judge Elmer's query, "Do not these individuals have the right to at least the degree of educational preparation offered by high school in case they decide to become veterinarians, physicians. . .?" The court did not explain how two more years of high school would help to make a person a physician. Nor did the court do anything to protect the young woman who testified on the stand that she wanted to practice her Amish faith without being coerced into a foreign environment.

Following the defeat in the county court, the committee then appealed to the Wisconsin Court of Appeals, where the Amish lost again in a perfunctory opinion. Attorney Ball then appealed the case to the Wisconsin Supreme Court.

When Ball appeared for oral argument in the Wisconsin Supreme Court, it was shortly after a tragic bombing by antiwar activists at the University of Wisconsin, which killed a young researcher. Ball pointed out in an emotional moment that he had taken this case because he believed in it, and that he represented a people who never believed in any kind of violence. They wanted the right to be left alone to practice their religious beliefs. This was a very conservative court, but it was unclear if the Amish case would be viewed as a conservative or a liberal cause. Many felt that liberal judges might be more supportive of the Amish. In a surprising decision, the court favored the Amish in a 7-1 verdict (*State v. Yoder* 1971). The dissenting judge was the only liberal on the court.

The state of Wisconsin then appealed to the United States Supreme Court, which agreed to hear the case. Three Amish representatives from Pennsylvania accompanied me to hear the oral arguments in the United States Supreme Court chambers in Washington,

D.C. The occasion gave newspapers a historic and dramatic photograph of Amish ascending the Supreme Court steps—hoping finally to have their religious liberty affirmed. The Wisconsin defendants did not attend. The outcome favored the Amish. I had the pleasure of telling the Amish defendants that the U.S. Supreme Court had decided in their favor.

The committee had sent letters to various individuals and church groups and inserted paid advertising in selected periodicals to raise funds. It took thousands of dollars to carry the case to the U.S. Supreme Court. Nevertheless, it was gratifying to participate in a major effort to preserve religious liberty in the United States. Moreover, it was satisfying to know that for the first time in the nation's history, compulsory school laws were less important than religious and parental rights.

The Preservation of Religious Liberty

The First Amendment to the U.S. Constitution contains a "Free Exercise Clause." New scholarship on the original meaning of the clause shows that legislatures of the founding generation considered exemption from presumably neutral laws to be part of the reason for the Free Exercise Clause (McConnell 1990). The committee believed from the outset that the political, theological, and constitutional basis of the United States offers freedom to "sincere" religious dissenters, unless they are involved in dangerous practices. The Amish came to this land of religious freedom three hundred years ago to avoid religious persecution in Europe. They migrated here for religious freedom only to suffer heavy fines and imprisonment in the twentieth century for refusing to send their children to consolidated public high schools filled with hostile cultural values.

The exercise of religious freedom means more than merely the right to certain beliefs in the privacy of one's own mind or to worship inside a certain church building. "Exercise" is a verb that means to act or practice. It is possible to believe anything in a totalitarian system, but impossible to act on it. Religion is more than worship, it is a way of life. The Amish emphasize behavior over beliefs, practices over ideas. Religious faith for them is not merely a personal belief; it is a corporate practice fleshed out in daily life by the community.

If the Amish cannot teach their own children Amish ways, their religious culture will be destroyed. The Amish do not go to high school or college because higher education would expose them to alien values that would erode Amish teachings. Moreover, the Bible tells them to avoid the "wisdom of the wise" (I Corinthians 1:19). The committee contends that only Amish persons can model and teach children to be Old Order Amish. Further, just as parents cannot do anything they want to do, such as abusing their children, neither can the government do anything it wants to do in the name of educational laws—like employing standards that destroy a peaceful religious group.

In *Yoder*, the state of Wisconsin argued before the U.S. Supreme Court that (1) the state has the right to compel attendance at school; (2) the state has a right to insulate children from the disease of ignorance; (3) the child has a right to know (this could mean a child should be socialized into mainstream values); and (4) the legislature alone controls educational policy, giving privileges and not rights to private educational institutions.[14]

In contrast to Wisconsin's thinking, consider modern Germany. Its constitution emphasizes the rights of parents (*Elternrecht*) rather than the rights of the state. This constitution was written in the aftermath of Hitler and the horrors of his state-controlled schooling (Littell 1966). Thus, the Amish case leads the struggle for religious liberty and parental rights. The committee contends that religious liberty is a preferred liberty, and that religious practice should be allowed unless it presents a clear and grave danger to public health and safety.

Therefore, some practices could be illegal for almost all of society, but permitted for those who can make a valid religious claim, if the practice does not harm others. To infringe on religious practice and coerce people to act contrary to their religious beliefs, the state must identify what legal experts call "a compelling state interest"—a grave or dangerous consequence if the state does not protect the public order and welfare. The committee further believes that before a state can override a religious practice it must demonstrate with logical reasons and actual evidence that grave dangers will result. Contrasted with the committee's views are those who believe that minorities have no rights that are judicially enforceable against majorities, thus nullifying the whole Bill of Rights (Kelley 1989).

Several religious groups shared the committee's views on religious liberty and submitted amicus curiae briefs in support of *Yoder* in the Supreme Court. The National Council of Churches argued that "responsible religious groups have the right in this country to undertake, not just an imitation of conventional education, but a fundamentally different *type* of education from that generally prevailing in a given state . . . if necessary to embody and inculcate their understanding of what the Divine Will requires."[15]

The National Jewish Commission on Law and Public Affairs called the Amish arrests a "disturbing illustration of an attempt by state authorities to compel nonconformists . . . to adhere to norms which may be entirely sound and desireable for most inhabitants of this country, but which are offensive and harmful to the affected religious minority. . . . the Constitution and traditions of this country do not permit this kind of coercion, which endangers all religious and ethnic minorities."[16]

The Synagogue Council of America asserted that "eight years of school is adequate to assure the informed citizenry upon which democracy depends." It noted that the Civil Rights Act of 1964 decreed that completion of six years of education was satisfactory for literacy requirements for voting, and the Voting Rights Act of 1970 abolished all such literacy requirements for citizenship voting.[17]

Chief Justice Warren Burger concluded in *Yoder*, "We accept it as settled, therefore, that however strong a State's interest in universal compulsory education, it is by no means absolute to the exclusion or subordination of all other interests" (*Yoder* at 215). The Supreme Court said that the First and Fourteenth Amendments prevent the state from compelling the Amish to send their children to high school until age sixteen. Those who assert that state bureaucracies should define educational approaches and values clash decidedly with those who assert that progress and truth are achieved when freedom and diversity prevail (Lindholm 1974).

Attorney William Ball in his brief on *Yoder* to the Court said, "The state is insisting that there cannot be different kinds of education. . . . all education must be dictated by the state with values derived from technology or related to consumption and competition and must be imposed upon every child." He asserted that "the state wants to enter the minds of Amish young people, expose them to worldly education, fill up their minds with state-packaged learning, alien to the Amish way of life, threatening the privacy of their psyche, and causing a painful personality restructuring by placing them in a high school which places the stress upon competition, ambition, consumerism, and speed."

The national committee's efforts and the work of its legal counsel have achieved significant victories for minorities in the United States. Attorney Ball and the committee's efforts in *Wisconsin v. Yoder* have been cited in numerous legal proceedings. In 1990, when the U.S. Supreme Court scuttled the Free Exercise of Religion clause by approving the firing of two Indians who had used peyote in their religious services, the court noted that it was not revoking the 1972 *Yoder* case because it was parentally and religiously based (*Employment Div., Department of Human Resources of Oregon v. Smith*). Interest in the legal implications of this decision continues. The committee continues to receive numerous requests from authors, scholars, and students interested in the legal issues surrounding *Yoder.*

Even though the *Yoder* case was the National Committee for Amish Religious Freedom's most notable effort, it has been involved in other legal issues related to Amish life—slow-moving vehicles, environmental problems, milk standards, hospitalization charges, land use, zoning, enforced chemotherapy, superhighway encroachments, midwife licensure, tourism, Hollywood movies, driver's license photos, and farm land preservation.[18] In protecting the Amish from the infringement of the state, the committee has fortified the precious tradition of religious liberty in the United States and in so doing has helped to preserve the freedom for all religious minorities to practice their religious faith.

Amishmen gather in front of the Internal Revenue Service office in Washington, D.C., after discussing Social Security issues with IRS commissioner Mortimer Caplan in 1961. Wide World Photos

CHAPTER SEVEN

Social Security and Taxes

Peter J. Ferrara

Government-sponsored Social Security created special problems for the Amish when its coverage was extended to self-employed farmers in 1955. Peter J. Ferrara, an attorney and economist who has written widely on Social Security matters, explains why the Amish object to participating in the federal Social Security Program and traces the negotiations that eventually exempted them from Social Security.

Government efforts to address social welfare issues have expanded dramatically in recent decades. Massive new programs, heavy taxes, and extensive regulatory requirements have emerged to counter problems of retirement, poverty, health care, worker safety, disability, and even variations in farm income. As the government's role in these areas has grown, so have the resulting conflicts with the religious beliefs and social structure of the Amish community. After discussing how Amish social arrangements address such social concerns, as well as the religious beliefs underlying those arrangements, this chapter examines the conflicts between the Amish and the state arising from the U.S. government's social welfare policies.

The Amish religion is based on faithful obedience to biblical commands as interpreted by the Amish community. Amish efforts to obey biblical instructions infuse virtually all aspects of daily life in extraordinary detail. The Amish interpretation of the Bible is reflected in a few key themes. One of the most important is the rejection of "worldliness," supported by several references to Scripture. The Amish often cite Romans 12:2, "And be not conformed to this world: but be ye transformed by the renewing of your mind, that ye may prove what is the good, and acceptable, and perfect, will of God." Worldliness may be understood as the values, lifestyles, practices, and conduct of the outside world that reflect its predominantly sinful, ungodly nature.

The Amish rejection of worldliness leads to their religious doctrine of separation from the world. They believe that God calls them to be separate from the larger society with all its sin and ungodliness and cite 2 Corinthians 6:14–18:

> Be ye not unequally yoked together with unbelievers. For what fellowship hath righteousness with unrighteousness? And what communion hath light with darkness?. . . . And what agreement hath the temple of God with idols? For ye are the temple of the living God; as God hath said, I will dwell in them, and walk in them; and I will be their God, and they shall be my people. Wherefore come out from among them, and be ye separate, saith the Lord, and touch not the unclean thing; and I will receive you. And will be a Father unto you, and ye shall be my sons and daughters, saith the Lord Almighty.[1]

Another often-quoted passage justifying separation is 1 Peter 2:9, "But ye are a chosen generation, a royal priesthood, an holy nation, a peculiar people; that ye should show forth the praises of him who hath called you out of darkness into his marvelous light."

The Amish interpret this command of separation strictly, seeking to minimize contacts with the non-Amish world and to maximize economic and social self-sufficiency within their community. This leads them to live in tight-knit settlements, with their own webs of social and economic relationships. These enclaves, however, are not communes. The basic building block of Amish life is the family unit, each living on its own farm or other private property and earning its living through hard work and traditional market transactions. Nor does separation lead to isolation. The Amish engage in economic transactions with the non-Amish community, and they maintain friendly social relations with their non-Amish neighbors.

Separation from the world serves at least two important functions. First, it avoids involvement with the worldliness, and the essentially sinful, ungodly nature, of the outside community. Such avoidance is considered religiously desirable in itself. Second, separation helps to reinforce obedience to Amish religious tenets, by avoiding the temptations and the compromising demands of the outside world.[2]

A closely related theme is the concept of *Gelassenheit,* which defines the attitude and manner expected of Amish persons in daily life. The fundamental biblical concept here is submission or yielding of self to God's will and authority. This is reflected most basically in daily life through an attitude of humility rather than pride, again supported by many references to Scripture. Related attitudes include meekness, modesty, self-denial, self-sacrifice, service to others and the community, contentment, calmness, simplicity, and plainness. Kraybill (1989, 29) has written, "In daily life, Gelassenheit means 'giving up' and 'giving in.'"

The embrace of Gelassenheit naturally prevents the Amish from serving in the military or working in law enforcement, as well as holding public office, as discussed in Chapter 2. Lawsuits are also avoided, though defense against a claim brought by others may be permitted. Participation in such activities would not only be worldly, thus breaching separation, but by relying on coercion would belie the humility and meekness of Gelassenheit. As discussed in Chapter 2, however, the Amish believe that they must obey the law and pay their taxes, except when doing so violates their religious beliefs. They do pay income tax, sales tax, real estate tax, school tax, and personal property tax without objection.

Amish Social Welfare

The Amish approach to social welfare flows naturally from their beliefs, practices, and social structure. The structure of their communities minimizes the need for welfare assistance. The Amish have few illegitimate teenage pregnancies or cases of divorce, and virtually no single mothers. Widows are strongly encouraged to remarry. Long-term unemployment does not exist, because Amish belief and culture encourages individuals to find satisfaction working within the community. There are virtually no instances of drug or alcohol abuse, which often leave individuals incapable of providing for themselves or their families.

The Amish way of life is well structured to provide for the elderly. Traditionally, at retirement, an elderly couple moves into a smaller home, known as the *Grossdaadi Haus*. It is adjacent to the main farmhouse, which, along with the administration of the farm, is given to one of the couple's married children. The continued operation of the farm provides food, clothing, and shelter for the elderly couple. Savings accumulated over the years often provide supplemental support, along with possible part-time employment producing crafts or working in a nearby shop. Even in a non-farm context, an elderly, retired couple would live near one of their children. The elderly receive food, clothing, and shelter within the family context, along with support from other children and supplemental income as noted above. The elderly are highly respected in Amish society. They retain social authority and control as revered patriarchs of large, extended families. This pattern ensures their economic security.

When the usual mechanisms fail and in the face of disaster, the Amish have a strong ethic of mutual aid. This ethic applies to extended families, and to other members of the settlement, and even beyond. The Amish again cite Scripture: "If anyone does not provide for his relatives, and especially for his own family, he has disowned the faith and is worse than an unbeliever" (1 Tim. 5:8). Such mutual aid also flows from the spirit of Gelassenheit, with its doctrine of humility, self-sacrifice, self-denial, and service to others. Mutual aid also bolsters the self-sufficiency needed to maintain separation. Separation would surely be breached if those in need had to turn outside the Amish community.

The elderly who end up in need are supported by an extensive network of relatives and neighbors. Those who need long-term care for disability or illness receive it from family members rather than in nursing homes. The existence of large, extended families, with few elderly and a large pool of young workers, means that support and care for the elderly is not an excessive burden. Widows, orphans, the disabled, and those who otherwise might fall into poverty are provided for by extended families, neighbors, and the church. Each Amish congregation has a deacon who is responsible for assisting those in need.

Ready help is available for those who fall into temporary misfortune. Neighbors and relatives will tend the farms and homes of those who become ill or need special assistance. One of the most celebrated of Amish customs is the barn raising. If a barn is damaged or destroyed by fire or storm, neighbors and relatives will gather together and "raise" the barn within a day. The neighbors and relatives may also contribute replacements for items lost in the catastrophe. Many Amish church districts also participate in a cooperative system, Amish Aid, which makes assessments to raise funds for members who fall into such misfortune. These funds may pay for the materials used in the barn raising.

The Amish social welfare system is entirely voluntary, mostly informal, and largely implicit in the Amish way of life. Yet, there is no evidence that it fails to meet the needs of the Amish community.[3]

The Amish Fear of Social Security

Social Security, including Medicare, is our nation's largest social welfare program, spending over 400 billion dollars per year. This amounts to 30 percent of our entire federal budget and almost 60 percent of total federal domestic spending.[4] The payroll tax that finances Social Security now collects over 425 billion dollars each year, or about 40 percent of total federal revenues.

Social Security includes the Old-Age and Survivors Insurance Program, which pays cash benefits to retired workers over age sixty-five (or over sixty-two at a reduced rate), to the worker's survivors over age sixty-five (or over sixty at a reduced rate), and to preretirement survivors if the family has minor children. It also includes the Disability Insurance Program, which pays cash benefits to disabled workers before retirement age. Medicare pays benefits to cover hospital and doctor bills for those who qualify for Social Security retirement benefits, postretirement survivors' benefits, or disability benefits (after two years). The payroll tax is assessed at a rate of 12.4 percent of wage income, up to a maximum taxable income limit of $55,000 (in 1992) to finance the Old-Age and Survivors Insurance and Disability Insurance programs. An additional 2.9 percent of wage income up to a maximum of $130,200 (in 1992) is assessed to finance Medicare. These taxes are putatively split between employer and employee, but a self-employed worker must pay the entire tax him- or herself. The maximum taxable income limits are indexed to increase automatically each year with the rate of growth in wages.

For the Amish, participation in Social Security violates their religious principles. Accepting this state-sponsored system would naturally violate the principle of separation from the non-Amish world; it would also spurn the spirit of Gelassenheit and the biblical commands that members of the church provide for their own families and assist those in the community in need. Participation in Social Security is also seen as lacking trust in God to provide the necessities of life for his people, promised by several biblical passages. The submission to God's will, for good fortune or bad, central to Gelassenheit, is also undermined by Social Security's attempt to ensure against economic adversity.

The Amish also have little need for Social Security, given the effective social welfare system described above. Since elderly Amish generally live with or adjacent to one of their married children, the larger extended family, the church, and supplemental income provide ample economic security. The disabled and widowed are also cared for by family and community. In the Amish world, participation in Social Security would deprive young workers of substantial amounts of cash each year when they are struggling to save to buy a farm, and would provide them income payments in retirement years that they don't need.

Another practical detriment to participation weighs heavily on Amish minds. Their current social welfare structure of mutual reliance among members greatly strengthens Amish communal solidarity. If individuals began receiving income from outside the community through Social Security or other social welfare programs, the Amish fear that community ties would be undermined and the cohesiveness of their culture threatened. They also fear that taking part in Social Security might jeopardize their current religiously-based exemptions from other programs and activities. The Amish worry, for example, that they could lose their exemption from military service. If they are willing to accept benefits from the government through Social Security, they might well be expected to defend and support the government militarily.

Although a few hold commercial insurance policies, most Amish oppose participation in such programs for similar reasons. Where they have felt the need for a more formal system of communal risk sharing, they have established their own cooperative arrangements. Consequently, the Amish Aid system, described above, provides funds through general assessments to purchase the materials to replace a barn or home destroyed by fire or bad weather. The reconstruction is then performed through the "barn-raising" custom. Amish Liability Aid is a similar cooperative system, which assesses members to pay for tort liability awards against Amish farmers and businessmen. Amish Church Aid is yet another cooperative plan, which assesses members for hospitalization costs. Those who do not participate and who suffer large medical costs receive assistance from church funds for the poor.[5]

The Amish encounter with Social Security began in 1955, when the program was extended for the first time to cover self-employed farmers. The Internal Revenue Service (IRS) consequently sought to start collecting the Social Security payroll tax from the Amish. As noted in Chapter 2, the Amish believe that they generally must obey the law and pay their taxes. But for the reasons discussed above, they also believed that participating in Social Security would violate their religious faith. Consequently, the Amish resisted payment of the tax because they viewed it as a form of government insurance.

The government has always proclaimed to the rest of the country that Social Security is an insurance system, with its own trust funds, and that payments into the system were not taxes but "contributions." But, remarkably, the IRS agents seeking to collect from the Amish repeatedly told them that Social Security was not insurance, and that what they were trying to collect was just a tax like any other tax (W. L. Fisher 1993, 133). The Amish pointed to the numerous government proclamations that Social Security was indeed insurance, including the official legal title of the program— Old-Age, Survivors, and Disability Insurance. The Amish might have chosen to pay the Social Security tax but refuse the program's benefits, just as they pay general government taxes but refuse other government social welfare benefits. But the Amish could not accept the close link between Social Security taxes, or "contributions," and the program's benefits, proclaimed over and over again by the government. Amish leaders feared that if their members paid Social Security, future generations would be unable to resist receiving the benefits for which they had already paid. Payment of the taxes would be seen as participation in the system, and if paying in was allowed, then how could receiving benefits be prohibited?[6]

The Clash with IRS

Amish resistance to Social Security took different forms. For some, the resistance was totally passive, not making the payments or assisting the IRS, but also not blocking the IRS from seizing funds from their bank accounts or debtors—or even leaving funds where they knew IRS agents would come to take them. But others refused to allow the IRS to take their funds, closing their bank accounts and otherwise arranging their affairs so no funds were vulnerable to IRS collection procedures.[7]

In late 1958, the IRS began to seize and sell farm animals from the more resistant Amish, in order to satisfy payment of their Social Security taxes. This generated substantial sympathy for the Amish among the general public. Editorial support, public outcry, and voluntary assistance to replace the lost animals began to spring up around the country.[8] But Amish opposition to Social Security gelled with the famous case of Valentine Y. Byler.

Byler was a traditional Amish farmer who lived near the village of New Wilmington, Pennsylvania. In June 1959, the IRS filed a lien against his horses for nonpayment of Social Security taxes. In July 1960, the IRS served Byler with a summons to appear in court. After Byler failed to appear, IRS agents seized him in August 1960 and brought him to the United States District Court in Pittsburgh to answer contempt charges. But the judge released Byler out of respect for the religious basis for his refusal to pay the taxes.[9]

The IRS tried again early on the morning of 18 April 1961. Byler had hitched up three horses to his plow and was diligently pursuing spring plowing. Three IRS agents strode across his field, stopped his work, and demanded payment of his past-due Social Security taxes. When he refused on the grounds that doing so would violate his religion, the agents unhitched his plow horses and took them away in a waiting trailer. They later sold the horses at public auction, using the proceeds to pay Byler's past-due Social Security taxes and the cost of transporting, keeping, and selling the horses. A remaining sum of $37.89 was returned to Byler.[10]

The IRS reeled under the resulting public protest. Many were outraged that the IRS would seize the plow horses of a self-sufficient, independent farmer at the time of the spring planting. The *New York Herald Tribune* in May 1961 asked, "What kind of 'welfare' is it that takes a farmer's horses away at spring plowing time in order to dragoon a whole community into a 'benefit' scheme it neither needs nor wants, and which offends its deeply held religious scruples?"[11] Perhaps most eloquent was editorialist William H. Fitzpatrick, of the Norfolk, Virginia, *Ledger-Star*, who wrote on 2 May 1962:

> Our society now is hardly less regimented than those the Amish and others of their kind sought to escape in Europe. Everyone has a number, now, and the land of the free and the home of the brave is the country of conformity where all the people must walk in lockstep or find themselves in danger of being trod upon in the march of progress.
>
> But when the last Amish buggy has disappeared from the dusty byroad—or has been sold like Valentine Byler's three plow horses —it will mark more than the passing of a sect who were overwhelmed by time and change. It will mark also a milestone in the passing of a freedom—the freedom of people to live their lives undisturbed by their government so long as they lived disturbing no others. It was a freedom the country once thought important.[12]

The IRS also confirmed that the seizure of Byler's horses was being reported by the press in Communist countries as evidence of the lack of freedom in the hypocritical United States.[13]

The harsh public reaction led IRS commissioner Mortimer M. Caplan to agree to meet with Amish bishops in September 1961 in an attempt to settle the matter. Dozens of Amish and church officials from eight states attended the meeting at IRS headquarters in Washington, D.C. The Amish leaders explained the religious grounds for their objection to the tax and read several passages from the Bible to Caplan and his staff. They traced their lineage in America back to William Penn, who invited their forebears to settle in Pennsylvania and promised them a safe haven to practice their religion. But the IRS officials defended their actions against the Amish, arguing that they had no legal basis for granting an exemption.

Then IRS officials proposed a compromise that they felt was within their legal authority. The Amish would pay the taxes required by law, and at retirement the Amish would receive back the taxes they had paid, with interest, in monthly increments equal to the benefit amounts for which they would otherwise be eligible. The benefits would stop, however, when the exact amount of their previously paid taxes had been returned.[14]

The Amish leaders rejected this compromise on the grounds that it still amounted to forced participation in a public insurance scheme that violated their religious principles. The meeting was resolved instead on a procedural rather than on a substantive compromise. The Amish would sue for a determination as to whether they had a constitutional right to exemption from Social Security, and the IRS would adopt a moratorium on the collection of Social Security taxes from the Amish until that question was resolved.[15]

After the meeting, a suit was filed with Byler as the plaintiff in April 1962. But the Amish soon had second thoughts, on the grounds that going to court also violated their religious beliefs, as discussed in Chapter 2. Consequently, in January 1963 the Amish withdrew their suit.[16]

The Dilemma of an Exemption

After dropping the court action, the Amish redoubled their efforts to obtain a legislative exemption from Congress, which they had sought since Social Security was first extended to them in 1955. In that first year, the Amish submitted to Congress the first of many petitions asking for an exemption, this one including fourteen thousand signatures. Rep. Paul B. Dague, of Pennsylvania, also introduced in 1955 the first bill providing an exemption for the Amish or others who objected to participation in Social Security on grounds of conscience.[17]

Amish bishops frequently visited Washington over the next several years to press their case for an exemption, meeting with congressional representatives and other government officials. In addition to Congressman Dague, other congressmen and senators from Pennsylvania, joined by legislators from other states with significant

Amish populations, supported the Amish cause and vigorously pressed for a legislative exemption.[18] Since the Amish vote somewhat irregularly, as explained in Chapter 2, their warm reception among congressional representatives from their states suggests a high regard for the Amish by their neighbors in these states.

The celebrated Byler controversy broadened support for the Amish campaign for an exemption. In the summer of 1961, Amish representatives met with President Kennedy's secretary for Health, Education and Welfare, Abraham Ribicoff. Secretary Ribicoff expressed the Kennedy administration's support for trying to develop a workable exemption for the Amish, though he expressed concern over the practical difficulties in designing an exemption that could be effectively limited to the Amish or others with an equivalent claim.

In September 1962, eighty Amish representatives journeyed to Washington and visited over four hundred congressional offices seeking support for a legislative exemption. They proceeded in this effort under a biblical mandate to go "two by two" in spreading the word, and this, along with their faithful adherence to Amish dress codes and their sincere demeanor, was very effective in establishing the validity of their cause. An exemption thereafter passed the Senate, with the strong support of Senator Barry Goldwater, of Arizona, but it was not brought to a vote in the House.[19]

A staff memorandum prepared for the Department of Health, Education and Welfare (HEW) in 1964 discussed policy concerns of granting an exemption to Social Security for the Amish. The memorandum most prominently argued that if Social Security were voluntary, a problem of adverse selection would develop. The good risks who expected to get less from Social Security would opt out, leaving behind the poor risks who expected to qualify for more. The memorandum argued that "this would increase the cost of the program for all who participate." Consequently, the memorandum concluded, Social Security must be compulsory for all.[20]

˙ This is a common argument for compulsory Social Security, but it is fallacious. Private insurance of all kinds is purely voluntary, yet the private insurers are able to manage potential adverse selection problems and remain viable. If Social Security were to charge actuarially fair rates as private insurers do, there would be no reason why Social Security would lose disproportionately more good risks than the private insurers.

Moreover, workers generally cannot predict if they are going to be good or bad risks for Social Security, because they cannot know how long they will live in retirement. Consequently, they could not beat the system by choosing to opt out of Social Security during their working years. Some very sick individuals may learn that they are unlikely to live very long, and therefore would be unlikely to live to retirement to collect benefits. These individuals might choose to opt out of a voluntary Social Security system to avoid paying further taxes. But individuals this sick are unlikely to be working and paying taxes, in any event; and even if they were, why should we be forcing these very sick individuals to pay for benefits for the rest of us that they can never collect?

Finally, this argument would not apply to an exemption for the Amish, because they would not be opting out based on whether they were good risks or bad risks for Social Security. Amish who were likely to live longer in retirement, live less long in retirement, or not live to retirement, would all be opting out equally.

Interestingly, a more valid and broadly recognized concern over voluntary Social Security was not even mentioned in the HEW staff memorandum. Social Security does not operate by saving and investing each taxpayer's payments for his or her own future benefits. If it did, a voluntary option would be easy to manage, because the system would simply not accumulate the contributions of those who opted out and would save the contributions of those who remained to finance their benefits. But instead, Social Security basically operates on a pay-as-you-go basis, with the tax funds paid by today's workers used to finance the benefits of today's retirees. The future benefits of today's workers will be paid from the taxes of those working when today's workers are retired.

If such a system were made voluntary, those who opted out would stop paying into the system, and insufficient funds would remain to pay benefits to current retirees. Any proposal to allow workers to opt out of Social Security must address this problem. But this issue hardly involves an Amish exemption, because they are such a small part of the total U.S. population. Allowing them out would not sufficiently reduce revenues to endanger benefit payments to current elderly beneficiaries. In the long run, of course, the exemption for the Amish would have a neutral effect on Social Security financing, since the Amish would not be receiving Social Security benefits in their retirement years and therefore would not be drawing out Social Security tax revenues paid in by workers at that time.

The HEW memorandum also argued that if Social Security were voluntary, low-income individuals who need Social Security the most would not participate, because they would use their tax funds for other more immediate needs. But if low-income workers believe they have more urgent uses for their funds, then why is forcing them to pay into Social Security making them better off? In any event, this concern again would not apply to an exemption for the Amish, because they have an effective alternative system of their own.

The memorandum also questioned whether any exemption could be effectively limited to the Amish. It suggested that drafting an exemption that applied only to the Amish would be difficult politically. It also proposed that any such exemption would, in any event, establish a precedent that might have to be expanded to other groups with similar religious claims, or to individuals who objected to participation on grounds of conscience. Over time, more and more individuals might claim such religious or conscientious grounds to avoid Social Security. For the reasons discussed above, however, this would not create an adverse selection problem, as the memorandum claimed, but it would create the previously discussed financing problem for current benefits. Perhaps the best solution to this problem is the current experience, with the exemption that was ultimately granted to the Amish. This exemption was successfully tailored to be limited to the Amish and has not been expanded over time to include others.

The memorandum further questioned what would happen to individuals who left the Amish church after they had opted out of Social Security, a possibility heightened by the Amish practice of shunning those who are excommunicated. But an exemption could allow those who leave the Amish to resume paying into Social Security; and indeed, that is how the exemption that was eventually passed addressed the issue. Those who leave the Amish well into their working years have lost many years of coverage, which significantly reduces their benefits. But few leave the Amish community at this point—and any that do would have fairly exercised their freedom to enter and to leave the Amish faith and would validly bear the consequences of such decisions. The government should not paternalistically deny them the freedom to make such choices, particularly since that would deny the vast majority of the Amish the freedom to exercise their permanent choice of an exemption.

The HEW memorandum concluded by recommending the same option offered by IRS commissioner Mortimer Caplan to the Amish bishops in 1961. The Amish would pay Social Security taxes in full, and during retirement years would receive those taxes back in the form of regular monthly Social Security benefits until the full amount of the worker's taxes plus interest was returned. The Amish rejection of this option is not surprising. It would have amounted to full participation in Social Security, except that benefits might end abruptly at some point in retirement, when past taxes plus interest had been returned. If the Amish could participate in Social Security to this degree, then it would make no sense to discontinue the benefits during remaining retirement years. Moreover, over time, the amount of Social Security taxes plus interest for each worker is getting closer to the total amount of benefits to be paid to the worker, and for future generations will likely exceed the value of benefits. Consequently, under this alternative, the Amish would receive regular benefits for more and more of their retirement, and eventually for all of their retirement, leaving no difference from regular participation in Social Security.

The momentum behind the Amish cause overcame all these objections and finally carried them to victory in 1965. An exemption to Social Security was attached to the Medicare bill and was enacted along with that legislation. Self-employed workers qualified for the exemption if they were members of a recognized religious sect with established tenets opposed to accepting the benefits of any private or public retirement plan or life, disability, or health insurance. Workers must adhere to these established tenets and consequently be conscientiously opposed to receiving such benefits. Each worker must individually file to receive the exemption, which applies to Social Security and Medicare, and must do so before becoming entitled to receive any benefit from these programs. The worker also must waive all rights to future benefits for self and dependents under those programs.

In addition, HEW (today Health and Human Services) must determine that the sect to which the worker belongs has been in existence continually since 1950, holds the established tenets against public or private insurance described above, and for a substantial period of time has provided reasonable support to its dependent members. Upon qualifying for the exemption, the worker no longer pays Social Security taxes and may receive a refund of any past taxes paid. If the worker leaves the sect, or the sect no longer meets the qualifications described above, then the worker must resume payment of Social Security taxes, with benefits calculated only on the years of work and tax payments after that point.[21]

The Department of Health, Education and Welfare quickly made the requirements to qualify the Amish, and the IRS soon distributed forms among them for the exemption (Form 4029). Experience under the exemption has been highly satisfactory for all

parties concerned. For the government, the exemption was narrowly tailored effectively to apply to the Amish alone, and none of
the concerns for wider exemptions have developed. For the Amish,
the great majority who are farmers or otherwise self-employed in
shops or elsewhere can be exempted from Social Security and
Medicare on terms consistent with their religion, through a relatively simple filing procedure. The one remaining and growing
problem, however, was that Amish who were not self-employed
were still forced to pay into Social Security, even though they did
not claim its benefits.

The Legal Battle

Soon after the 1965 exemption was passed, the Amish began trying to expand it to Amish workers who were not self-employed.
Several bills were introduced to enact this expanded provision. But
with the great majority of the Amish already exempt, the public
appeal of the Amish effort for expansion was deflated. Moreover,
an exemption for employed workers raised new ambiguities and
difficulties. Amish working for Amish and non-Amish employers
diverged from traditional Amish ways, and so their claim for an exemption to follow traditional beliefs was weakened. These workers
might also receive less traditional Amish support in their retirement than those who owned farms or even small businesses. Thus,
the means of their retirement support was more questionable. In
addition, how an expanded exemption would relate to non-Amish
employers and their usual obligation to pay half of the Social Security tax for their workers raised new, although not insurmount-
able, complexities and problems. For all of these reasons, Congress
was not responsive to Amish efforts to expand the exemption.

Finally, with no legislative action, the issue was taken to the
courts in 1982 in the case of *United States v. Lee* (1982). Amishman Edwin Lee employed Amish workers on his farm and in his
lumber business. He refused to pay the employer's share of the Social Security tax for these workers because the Amish prohibited
participation in Social Security. In 1978, he sued for an injunction
against IRS collection efforts and for a refund of a small amount of
Social Security tax he had paid for these workers. The suit contended that forcing him to participate in Social Security when his
sincere religious beliefs forbade such participation violated his
right to the free exercise of religion guaranteed in the First
Amendment to the U.S. Constitution.[22]

The federal district court held that requiring Lee to participate in Social Security and pay the employer tax for his workers would be unconstitutional on these grounds, and it exempted him from the program. But on appeal, the U.S. Supreme Court reversed the case in an unanimous decision. The Court accepted that both the payment of taxes into Social Security and the receipt of benefits from the program violated the Amish religion. But the Court held that this infringement on Lee's religious liberty was essential to accommodating an overriding government interest.

The Court argued, without explanation, that "mandatory participation is indispensable to the fiscal vitality of the Social Security system," and that a voluntary system would be "difficult, if not impossible, to administer" (*Lee* 1982, 258). But as Justice Stevens recognized in a concurring opinion, the small number of Amish that would be exempt from Social Security under a ruling for *Lee* would not remotely undermine Social Security financing. Indeed, far more Amish workers had been exempted under the 1965 legislation, and that had not damaged the fiscal foundation of Social Security. Moreover, that exemption already in place showed that administration of such an exemption was not a difficult problem. In fact, extending the already existing exemption to the small additional number of employed Amish would be a simple administrative matter, as Justice Stevens also argued.

These concerns were not, however, the real basis for the Court's conclusion. What the Court feared was that if it held that the Constitution required this exemption for the Amish, it would not be able to draw a reasonable, manageable line against the claims of others. It first focused this concern on Social Security, saying "it would be difficult to accommodate the comprehensive social security system with myriad exceptions flowing from a wide variety of religious beliefs" (*Lee* 1982, 259–60). But the existing legislative exemption again showed, as Justice Stevens also recognized, that a clear line narrowly limiting the exemption from Social Security can be drawn. Indeed, no other religious groups besides the Amish and the Old Order Mennonites have ever qualified under this legislative exemption.

But the Court went a step further, and this is where Justice Stevens joined the others. The Court argued that if it allowed this exemption for the Amish, it could not see how it could reject the claims of others seeking exemptions from the payment of other taxes generally, based on religious objections as to how the tax funds were to be used. The Court feared that constitutionally mandating such wide-ranging tax exemptions would wreak havoc with government policy. The Court said:

There is no principled way, however, for purposes of this case, to distinguish between general taxes and those imposed under the Social Security Act. If, for example, a religious adherent believes war is a sin, and if a certain percentage of the federal budget can be identified as diverted to war-related activities, such individuals would have a similarly valid claim to be exempt from paying that percentage of the income tax. The tax system could not function if denominations were allowed to challenge the tax system because tax payments were spent in a manner that violates their religious belief. (Lee 1982, 260)

The Court concluded that since maintaining a viable tax system is such an overriding public interest, that interest justified the restriction on Lee's religious liberty that would result from denying his claim for an exemption. The Court said, in sweeping terms, "Because the broad public interest in maintaining a sound tax system is of such a high order, religious belief in conflict with the payment of taxes affords no basis for resisting the tax" (Lee 1982, 260).

But this argument is fallacious as well, because Lee's claim for an exemption from Social Security could clearly be distinguished from exemptions from other taxes. The payment of Social Security taxes by the taxpayer is directly tied to the receipt of specific benefits by that taxpayer, as the government continually tells us in treating Social Security as insurance and its payments as contributions. Generally, however, the payment of other taxes is not tied to any specific government expenditure. Clearly, no public interest is undermined if an exemption is allowed on religious grounds from a tax with specific benefits to the taxpayer, and if the taxpayer forgoes the public benefits and attains the needed benefits elsewhere. It is also necessary that the exemption not undermine the viability of the particular program. This was all true of the exemption sought by Lee.

This would be in clear contrast to exemptions from other taxes generally, which would deprive the government of the funds to achieve its policy goals. In rejecting Lee's claim, the Supreme Court implicitly held that Social Security is not actually an insurance program, as the government claims it is, but in reality is just a tax-and-spend program like any other.

Nevertheless, Lee lost. As William Ball suggests in Chapter 13, in violating the traditional Amish prohibition against going to court, Lee's effort backfired and actually established a strong constitutional precedent against exemption from taxes on religious grounds. The case, however, only held that such exemptions were not constitutionally required. It did not restrict in any way Congress's power to grant such exemptions as it chose.

Despite the Supreme Court setback, Amish efforts for a legislatively expanded exemption continued and gained momentum. Though this effort did not gain the national attention that the campaign for the 1965 exemption did, it gained sympathetic supporters through quiet, persistent lobbying by the Amish and their congressional friends. In 1988, the Amish succeeded again. The 1965 exemption was expanded to include Amish employees working for Amish employers, exempting both from the tax. This resolution finally satisfied the Amish in regard to Social Security.[23] The only Amish, under current legislation, who are forced to pay into Social Security are those employed by non-Amish employers. Although relatively small in number, these persons pay into the system but generally do not accept its benefits.

Other Social Welfare Programs

The Amish oppose participation in other social welfare programs for most of the same reasons that they oppose taking part in Social Security. Receiving benefits from government programs violates the principles of separation and service to others, as well as the self-sacrificing spirit and personal responsibility of Gelassenheit. Relying on "worldly" big government programs reveals a failure of the community to follow biblical commands to provide for those in need. Given their industriousness and self-sufficiency and their effective system of mutual aid, the Amish have little need for outside social welfare. Turning to government services for such aid would weaken the bonds of dependency within the Amish community, which are fortified by their system of mutual aid. The Amish justifiably fear that receiving such government assistance would jeopardize their exemptions from other government activities, such as military service.

For most government social welfare programs, financed out of general taxes, the Amish simply refuse to receive any benefits, even though they pay general taxes without objection. Consequently, applying to receive Aid to Families with Dependent Children, food stamps, Medicaid, or other government welfare assistance is unheard-of in the Amish community. If the Amish receive checks for the earned income tax credit, which provides cash for low-income families with children based on their income tax filings, they return the checks to the U.S. Treasury Department. The Amish also refuse, as much as possible, assistance from government farm subsidy programs.[24]

For programs in which the benefits are tied to payment of a specific tax, such as unemployment insurance or workers' compensation, the Amish try to avoid payment of the tax as well as receipt of the benefits, consistent with their position on Social Security. Self-employed workers are automatically exempt from unemployment insurance and workers' compensation taxes, because these taxes are only paid by employers to cover benefits for their employees. This naturally exempts most of the Amish, who tend to be self-employed in farming or cottage industries. For the others, the Amish try to arrange their business operations so that employees will qualify as self-employed to the extent possible. Consequently, Amish businesses with employees are often organized as legal partnerships, with the workers legally qualified as self-employed partners entitled to a share of the company's income. Workers on farms may be given the right to receive the income from a certain number of cows or portion of a crop as their compensation, qualifying them as self-employed as well. Members of some Amish construction crews also seek to be paid individually in order to qualify as self-employed. The Amish have also lobbied state legislatures for an exemption from unemployment insurance and workers' compensation, with limited success. In Pennsylvania, an exemption from workers' compensation applies where Amish employees work for Amish employers.[25]

The Amish at times also refuse to comply with certain social welfare regulations because of their religious beliefs. A rule of the Federal Occupational Safety and Health Administration (OSHA) requiring workers to wear hard hats in construction and carpentry jobs conflicted with the Amish requirement that men wear broad-brimmed hats. Amish lobbying convinced OSHA to grant Amish workers an exemption from the regulation.[26] Slow-moving vehicle regulations, discussed in Chapter 9, are another example of this sort of conflict.

Amish Values and Secular Society

To the rest of us, the Amish approach to social welfare may seem appealing but unworkable in a modern secular society, outside the cocoon of Amish culture. But perhaps that is too easy. For aren't the Amish just practicing the same values that the rest of us also profess? Do we not all believe in providing for the needs of the members of our families, including our elderly parents, and in providing assistance to our neighbors, friends, and others in need? Perhaps in seeking effectively to delegate this responsibility to large, disinterested government bureaucracies, we have not developed an alternative means, but rather an elaborate rationalization for abdicating our personal moral duties. And perhaps in the process, we have left those in need with inadequate, cold, ineffective, and even counterproductive substitutes for true charity and a community of care and understanding.

And perhaps we are all much the worse off because of it. For maybe what the Amish experience teaches us is that reliance on the government's beneficence can become a prison of dependency, where we lose our personal freedom along with our personal moral responsibility, effectively delegating control over our lives and the fruits of our own labor, along with the duty to care for others. Perhaps, in losing sight of the distinction between the responsibility of individuals and the responsibility of government, we have lost sight of our freedom as well.

The slow-moving vehicle sign has been accepted by most of the Amish communities. Dennis L. Hughes

CHAPTER EIGHT

Slow-moving Vehicles

Lee J. Zook

 Amish carriages on modern highways symbolize one of the more colorful clashes between modern and traditional ways in the twentieth century. The pattern of conflict between the Amish and state officials over slow-moving vehicles has varied considerably from state to state. Many Amish groups have not objected to special requirements for slow-moving vehicles, whereas others have objected strenuously. Lee J. Zook describes the reasons for the conflicts and the legal outcomes.

Symbols of Amish Identity

Horse-drawn carriages symbolize the essence of Amish identity and mark Amish separation from the larger world. Public highways provide an obvious intersection for Amish and non-Amish cultures. The use of slow-moving vehicles (SMVs) pulled by horses on public highways, alongside modern vehicles, articulates the clash between modern and traditional ways.

Many religious differences characterize the Amish both within and between their many settlements. Yet, as Donald B. Kraybill (1989, 60-68) notes, the horse and buggy are used by all Old Order Amish groups. This means of transportation separates the Amish community from the non-Amish sector and bonds them together despite their internal differences. Slow-moving vehicles have not always distinguished the Amish from their non-Amish neighbors as well as they do today. The advent of the automobile in the early twentieth century and its subsequent rejection by the Amish increased their cultural distance from the larger society.

In more practical terms, horse and buggy transportation holds the Amish community close together geographically. Members of church districts, even in sparsely populated Amish areas, reside close enough to travel to Sunday services by this means. Further, horse and buggy use diminishes other ties with the outside world.

There is no need to register an automobile, obtain a driver's license, have vehicles inspected, or buy automobile insurance. These automotive requirements represent problematic worldly ties for the Amish.

In all of these ways, the carriage implicitly serves as a sacred symbol in Amish religion. Understanding both the symbolic and the utilitarian importance of the buggy in Amish culture sets the stage for an examination of the Amish response to external regulations imposed by the state on SMV travel.

The most troublesome regulation for the Amish concerns the triangular SMV emblem. Besides these SMV clashes, conflict between the state and the Amish has also been triggered by safety equipment, use of metal for buggy wheels, materials used for horseshoes, registration and licensing of buggies, horse manure on roads or in parking lots, hitching posts for horses, and alternative roadways for horses and buggies.[1] These issues, however, do not parallel the magnitude of the conflicts surrounding the SMV emblem. The smaller controversies are, for the most part, dealt with through local ordinances. They have not created the public safety concerns of the SMV emblem and have not generally been litigated in the courts.

Court cases dealing with Amish objections to SMV signs have occurred since 1970 in Kentucky, Ohio, Michigan, Minnesota, and New York. The pivotal *Minnesota v. Hershberger* case, resolved in 1990, will be examined in more detail than the other cases.[2] Argued with the cumulative knowledge of previous cases, *Hershberger* was the only SMV case reviewed by the United States Supreme Court.

Development of the SMV Emblem

Most Old Order Amish groups place SMV signs on their buggies. In fact, prior to the development of the SMV emblem, some Amish themselves considered creating warning signs. In 1951, an Amish buggy shop manufactured a large-letter sign saying, "Slow Moving Vehicle." The sign was made of crushed glass glued onto the words. With a black background, it reflected the headlights of oncoming cars. Further, in 1954 Indiana Amish discussed using Scotch Lite tape. A local sheriff held demonstrations regarding the tape and encouraged the Amish to use it on their buggies.[3] Reflective tape was manufactured and sold in Lagrange County, Indiana, the nation's third largest Amish settlement.

Research on the SMV sign was conducted at Ohio State University in the early 1960s with support from the Automotive Safety Foundation. The study focused on vehicles with a maximum highway speed of two to twenty miles an hour (Harkness and Stuckey 1963, 1). The research found that 87 percent of SMV accidents occurred in daylight hours and that only 6 percent involved animal-drawn vehicles. The remainder were mostly farm vehicles. Further, over half of the accidents between slow-moving and regular vehicles occurred on open highways. In 62 percent of the cases, the SMV was struck from the rear. The report concluded that a geometric design with appropriate color for day and night would reduce SMV accidents. The researchers proposed a standardized emblem consisting of an equilateral, base-down triangle, combining fluorescent yellow-orange and reflective red (Harkness and Stuckey 1963, 10-24).

Various safety groups, including the Ohio Farm and Home Safety Committee, the National Safety League of Canada, and other farm organizations, began promoting the SMV emblem. By 1965, Ohio and Nebraska had passed legislation requiring the use of the SMV emblem on vehicles operating below twenty-five miles an hour.[4] In the same year, Minnesota recommended that the emblem be used voluntarily.[5] In 1967, however, Minnesota held hearings prior to adopting legislation requiring its use (Minn. Stat. § 159.522). The federal Department of Transportation adopted the SMV sign in 1971 through its Uniform Vehicle Code, thus standardizing it across the United States, even though some states did not require it until later.[6]

Swartzentruber Rejection of SMV Signs

Which Amish communities have clashed with the state over SMV emblems? Identifying the similarities of these communities may increase our understanding of this issue and also help us predict the location of future conflicts. Most, but not all, SMV court cases have involved Amish affiliated with the Swartzentrubers, a subgroup of Amish living in Wayne and Holmes counties, Ohio. The Swartzentrubers broke off from the main body of the Old Order Amish in 1913. The division erupted from a disagreement over the status of members leaving the Amish church for more liberal Anabaptist groups such as the Beachy Amish or the Mennonites.[7]

The Swartzentruber group—named for an early bishop—is one of the most conservative Old Order Amish subgroups. According to Janice Heikes (1985, 40), they are more conservative in dress, the length of men's hair and beards, the use of technology, and stipulating transportation rules. The Swartzentrubers hire private automobiles only in dire emergencies, relying on public transportation for long-distance travel whenever possible. Moreover, they do not haul livestock to market by truck, nor do their buggies have the amenities typical of many Amish buggies. Their farm lanes, basically dirt or mud tracks without added gravel, are not conducive to motor vehicles (Heikes 1985, 41). The SMV cases have typically involved the Swartzentrubers, whose conservative impulses flare when confronted with the requirement to display the SMV emblem.

Most of the Swartzentruber Amish church districts embroiled in conflicts over SMV signs have been established since 1970. New settlements usually remain tethered to the parent settlement by adopting its *Ordnung*—religious rules and discipline—and by retaining the same bishop. By the time the new settlement ordains its own bishop, it has already adopted the conservative practices of the parent group. Consequently, change comes slowly. If the Ordnung of the parent settlement prohibits SMV emblems, this taboo becomes the entrenched practice of the new community as well. Several of the original SMV cases were heard in Ohio in older established communities, but much of the SMV conflict has erupted in relatively new Swartzentruber settlements in other states.

The SMV controversies may sometimes reflect deeper social conflicts. New settlements usually form in communities that have little understanding of the Amish way of life and may therefore feel threatened by it. The Amish settlers may also threaten the economic welfare of the larger community by their self-sufficiency. Tractor and automobile dealers lose sales to former, non-Amish farmers who leave the area; they also cannot sell products to the newcomers, nor perform service work for them. Insurance companies lose clients. Sales of gasoline and many other products may slump when non-Amish sell their land to the Amish. Land values may decrease and Amish children bypass public schools. All things considered, the Amish are less involved in the social fabric of the community. In short, such newcomers are not always viewed as good neighbors. Misunderstanding and rumors about the Amish also increase community suspicion. These threatening shifts in the economic and societal base sometimes find an outlet in an SMV controversy (Zook 1989, 29, 32).

The Swartzentruber Amish base their objections to the SMV emblem on the principle of separation from the world—a religious belief endorsed by all Amish groups. Most Amish, however, see the SMV requirement as a safety feature they are willing to accept for the welfare of the larger community. One Amishman said he was thankful that the horse and buggy could still be used in the modern world and that the SMV signs were a small price to pay to retain this unique mode of transportation.

The convictions of those who object to SMV emblems, however, are genuine. Amish men and women have gone to jail in several states rather than pay fines when the law would not budge and the fines continued. Those who object to SMV signs cite several reasons (*State v. Swartzentruber* [1988]). First, they are worldly symbols. Second, they are too "loud" or bright in color, and finally, using them would mean trusting in the symbols of man rather than in the protection of God. Testifying in a district court, one Amishman stated, "We were always admonished against the use of bright colors on our buggies."[8]

Defense attorneys invariably argue that forced use of the SMV symbol violates the Amish right to free exercise of religion guaranteed by the First Amendment to the United States Constitution: "Congress shall pass no law respecting an establishment of religion, or prohibiting the free exercise thereof; or abridging the freedom of speech, or of the press, or the right of people peaceably to assemble, and to petition the government for a redress of grievances."

In arguing SMV cases, the four-step test, formulated by the U.S. Supreme Court in *Sherbert v. Verner* (1963) and used in *Wisconsin v. Yoder* (1972), is often utilized to determine whether illegal behavior is permissible for religious reasons. The *Sherbert* test includes four questions: (1) Is there a genuine, sincere religious belief? (2) Does the law infringe on the practice of religion? (3) Is the infringement justified by a compelling state-society interest? (4) Does a less restrictive, alternative means satisfy the compelling interest?

Most SMV cases were decided while the test used in *Sherbert* and *Yoder* was still intact, prior to the Supreme Court case of *Employment Div., Dep't of Human Resources of Oregon v. Smith* (1990). *Smith* altered some of the assumptions used in *Sherbert* and *Yoder*. The most recent SMV case, *State v. Hershberger* (1990; hereafter, *Hershberger II*) was decided after the *Smith* case.

SMV Court Cases

The SMV emblem first became a problem in Orange County, Indiana, in 1968 (*Family Life*, July 1970, 10-12). Amish people were given tickets for refusal to use the SMV sign. Little information is available about the court case that occurred there. This settlement is not affiliated with the Swartzentruber Amish of Ohio, but is in fellowship with a settlement in Hardin County, Ohio. The Hardin County settlement's difficulties with safety regulations will be discussed later.

On 7 September 1977, *State v. Weaver*[9] was heard in Holmes County, Ohio—the geographic home of the conservative Swartzentruber group. Weaver was ticketed for not displaying the SMV emblem. Instead, he used reflectorized tape, which the Ohio Department of Highway Safety allowed and which was to be cut in one-inch strips of any length and placed on the rear of horse-drawn vehicles. The strips could outline the vehicle or be used in any other way, so long as seventy-two square inches were used.[10] Several Amish leaders had been negotiating with the Department of Highway Safety to use the material as an alternative to the emblem. The case came to court as the negotiations were drawing to a close. Weaver was not convicted.

After this case, the Department of Highway Safety held a news conference stipulating the use of reflective tape and specifying that at night a buggy must be visible at least five hundred feet from the rear. Additionally, to "conform with the Amish group's wishes," the triangular emblem was not required. The department expected, however, that "animal-drawn vehicles which normally travel or are normally used at a speed of less than twenty miles an hour shall display on the rear thereof devices consisting of reflector materials and a lantern, or a red flashing light, either of which shall be visible from a distance of not less than five hundred feet to the rear during the time and under the circumstances specified in the Revised Code (section 4513.03). The red flashing light or reflector devices and lantern shall be approved by the director of highway safety."[11] The Department of Highway Safety hoped, nevertheless, that all Amish would continue to use the SMV emblem, even if it was not mandatory.

The judge who heard *Weaver* was satisfied that Amish following the new regulation would not be arrested. The new regulation was a negotiated compromise designed to respect the Amish concern about SMV emblems and at the same time to ensure public safety. Thus, *Weaver* was the first case in which the reflectorized tape could be used instead of the SMV emblem, as the Department of Highway Safety was willing to compromise on the issue.

In November 1977 in Hardin County, Ohio, the case of *Fussner v. Smith* (1977) was heard. Smith and others were ticketed for not displaying the SMV emblem on their buggies. They had, however, been using the seventy-two square inches of tape. A group of Amish had resided in Hardin County for nearly twenty years. The judge noted both *Sherbert* and *Yoder* and based the court's findings on these cases. The court ordered the sheriff of Hardin County not to ticket Amish who followed the Department of Highway Safety's ruling of seventy-two square inches of tape. Why *Smith* came to court several months *after* the department made the new tape ruling is not clear.

There were problems with Amish noncompliance with safety regulations in Hardin County prior to this case. As early as 1961, *The New York Times* reported that twelve Amishmen were jailed for refusing to use flashing lights on their buggies.[12] More recently, a judge in Kenton Municipal Court had confiscated an Amishman's buggy when the owner refused to pay fines for rejecting the SMV emblem.[13] Eventually, in 1987, the Ohio legislature passed a law saying the SMV sign was not necessary for the Amish. The new Ohio law concerned only about twelve church districts of twenty to forty families each.[14]

The Ohio alternative to the SMV emblem—reflective tape—provided Amish in new settlements in other states with an option to suggest to local authorities. As we shall see, however, some controversies in other states were not resolved as easily as those in Ohio.

An SMV conflict in St. Lawrence County, New York, emerged in the 1980s. The Amish settlement that formed there in 1974 had ties to the Swartzentruber Amish in Ohio. In 1983, New York passed a law requiring the SMV emblem. The Amish did not use the triangle, but the sheriff in St. Lawrence County chose to avert conflict by not enforcing the regulation.[15]

At dusk on 12 November 1983, a buggy was struck from the rear by a car, seriously injuring an Amish child. The person driving the car was reportedly intoxicated,[16] although neither the newspapers nor local authorities mentioned this as a contributing factor. Nevertheless, as a result of the accident local residents petitioned officials to enforce the SMV law. Five Amishmen and a woman were soon arrested for not using SMV signs. The men were jailed for refusing to pay fines; but the woman, pregnant at the time, was spared from jail. A local lawyer asked the court to release the men and promised to arrange a compromise between the Amish and law enforcement officials. According to Martha Ellen (1984), the promptly negotiated compromise consisted of four points: (1) using tape, as required in Ohio; (2) hanging lanterns higher on the buggies, (3) keeping buggies on the extreme right side of roadways at all times, and (4) prohibiting nighttime driving unless absolutely necessary.

The compromise was apparently negotiated without input from the local residents who had earlier petitioned authorities to enforce the SMV law. Subsequently a town meeting was held and legislatures became involved. The Amish agreed to four new issues. They would (1) hang lanterns on a high bracket at the back of the buggy, (2) use a four-inch lens on the lantern, (3) place seventy-two square inches of reflective tape on the rear of the vehicle, and (4) use similar tape on the left front post of the vehicle. These requirements were sent to the New York Department of Motor Vehicles, where they became a part of the Motor Vehicle Code.[17]

Several items of interest complete the New York story. Damages were paid by the insurance company of the driver to the Amish child in the November crash, who apparently suffered permanent disability.[18] On 6 June 1984, a young Amishman was charged with improperly hanging a lantern on his buggy after a motorcycle collided with it. The Amishman paid restitution of $450 rather than a court fine for improperly hanging his lantern.[19] The resolution of the New York conflicts involved negotiations between the Amish, the public, and law enforcement officials rather than specific court interventions.

In Michigan, *State v. Swartzentruber*[20] began in a district court in 1980. Swartzentruber lived in a Michigan Amish community with ties to the Swartzentruber group in Ohio. He and others refused to use the SMV emblem and were ticketed. When the case went to the district court in 1981, the ruling favored the Amish. The decision, based on *Yoder*, also cited the *Sherbert* test. The Amish had threatened to leave the state if the problem continued. The Michigan Court of Appeals, which later heard the case in 1988, stated that "forced migration of a religious minority is inherently inconsistent with the constitutional freedom of exercise of religion."[21]

The state, however, appealed the district court decision on *Swartzentruber*, and in 1985 the Circuit Court of Gladwin County supported the state's claims.[22] It argued that the state was responsible for ensuring reasonable safety on the roadways with a uniform warning device such as the SMV emblem:

> Common sense compels the conclusion that such a warning to unsuspecting motorists helps to prevent collisions between the Amish . . . and motor vehicles. . . . [The present case] is analogous

to a group having a religious belief against tail lights on motor vehicles after dark. . . . Amish contact with society by their use of public roadways brought about the legal conflict. If they wish to use public highways then they must comply with reasonable statutory safety requirements. . . . [The] state['s] interest justifies the incidental burden that is placed on the [Amish] free exercise of religion. (*Swartzentruber* [1985], at 3-5)

The circuit court in *Swartzentruber* concluded that despite sincere religious belief, "when the practice of one's religion conflicts with the public interest the rights of the few must give way to the rights of the rest of society" (*Swartzentruber* [1985] at 4).

In 1988, *Swartzentruber* moved up to the Michigan Court of Appeals (*State v. Swartzentruber* [1988]). The court supported the Amish on the grounds that the state had not proven that reflective tape presented a public safety hazard. The appellate court did not view the tape alternative as valid, as a matter of law, but contended that the state had not effectively satisfied the compelling interest argument. The appeals court refused to enforce the law on these grounds and in essence supported the Amish in *Swartzentruber:* "We think it is clear in this case that the state requirement . . . is 'at odds with [the] fundamental tenets of their religious beliefs' on the pain of legal penalty." The appeals court argued that no evidence was offered that the requirement had benefited public safety or that the buggy itself was not enough warning during daylight hours. Neither did the state question the effectiveness of the reflector tape or the red lanterns suggested by the Amish as alternatives to the emblem.

Several Amishmen in *Swartzentruber* had testified of their beliefs about the SMV triangle. They asserted that their trust should be in God, not in man-made symbols, that the color was too "loud," and that the standardized symbol was objectionable. These three items—trust in God, bright colors, and worldly symbols—would recur in the *Hershberger* case.

Meanwhile, in Kentucky, *Commonwealth v. Zook* (1985) came before the Barren County District Court. Two Amish settlements begun in this county in the early 1980s also had close ties with the Swartzentruber Amish in Ohio. Zook was arrested for traveling on a public highway without an SMV emblem attached to the rear of his buggy as required by Kentucky law. He had used seventy-two square inches of reflective tape, making the buggy visible from six hundred feet at night. A brief was submitted by the American Civil Liberties Union on his behalf. The court found that Zook did hold a sincere religious belief that forbade him to display any symbols, including the SMV emblem.

Again, the four-step *Sherbert* test was cited by Zook's defense. The court offered that the state did have a legitimate interest in protecting safety on the highway. However, the court reasoned that the state's interest was protected by the reflective tape and lanterns to warn approaching motorists at night. The court in *Zook* agreed with the defendant: "In the daytime . . . a horse and buggy is universally recognized as a slow moving vehicle and no further warning is needed" (*Zook* at 3). The court stated that the First Amendment compels toleration of sincerely held beliefs of minority religious groups and pointed out that the Amish would be respected by the majority of people in the county even if the First Amendment did not exist. Further, the district court said, "[I]f this opinion imposes any additional burden on the majority, it is certainly small. It is because we are a great nation that we can allow diversity which would not be tolerated in repressive societies" (*Zook* at 4).

Minnesota v. Hershberger

The *Hershberger* case will be explored in detail because of its significance.[23] After an Amishman was sentenced to prison by a Minnesota trial court, *Hershberger* came to a Minnesota district court in 1988, which ruled against the Amish. *Hershberger* then moved to the Minnesota Supreme Court, which ruled in favor of the Amish (*State v. Hershberger* [1989], hereafter *Hershberger I*). The state pressed *Hershberger I* to the United States Supreme Court, which returned it once again to the Minnesota Supreme Court for reconsideration (*Minnesota v. Hershberger* [1990]). It was returned because the United States Supreme Court had recently ruled on *Smith*, which carried implications for the Amish. Subsequently, the Minnesota Supreme Court in *Hershberger II* once again ruled in favor of the Amish, in 1990.

In 1974, Amish from Wayne and Holmes counties, Ohio, affiliated with the Swartzentruber group, moved to Fillmore County, Minnesota. Tickets for failure to display the SMV sign were issued in Minnesota as early as 1977. The Amish paid the eleven-dollar fine but did not change their behavior.[24] This continued until 1983, when Sheriff Gudmundson approached the Amish bishop in the area in a serious attempt to resolve the problem. The bishop and several Amish lay leaders discussed the problem with the sheriff, the county attorney, and the Minnesota Department of Public Safety and Transportation. In 1985, the department accepted an SMV emblem with a black (not red) center outlined with gray (not orange) reflective tape. The department believed that keeping a standard shape for the SMV emblem was important for uniformity, and the Amish were satisfied that they had not compromised on the issue of color (Zook 1989, 30).

In August 1986, however, the Fillmore County commissioners passed a resolution urging Minnesota to require all SMVs to use the standard emblem without substituting colors.[25] Subsequently, the Minnesota legislature passed a bill requiring Amish buggies to carry the red-and-orange triangle at night but permitting the black-and-gray one in daytime.[26] The new law was unacceptable to the Amish, who felt their earlier negotiations with the Department of Public Safety had been fruitless.

To complicate matters, the Amish community in Fillmore County disagreed over the use of SMV signs. Three factions emerged. The largest Amish group used the black-and-gray SMV emblem. Of the two smaller factions, one used only reflective tape on the backs of their buggies, and the other accepted the typical red-and-orange triangle as prescribed by law.

The new law requiring the red triangle at night became effective in 1987. Amish were soon arrested. Some were arrested for using the black-and-gray triangle during inappropriate hours or weather conditions. Others were cited for using only reflective tape to outline the backs of their buggies and a red lantern.[27] During eight months in 1988, fourteen people were arrested for noncompliance with Minnesota law.

In 1988, Margaret Johnson, Fillmore County Trial Court judge, heard the cases of several Amishmen with multiple citations. One of them, Gideon Hershberger, refused to pay his fines and was sentenced to jail for seven days. Judge Johnson, quoted by the *Star Tribune* (28 July 1988), said, "Religion is not a defense in this case." This story and ensuing newspaper articles prompted Attorney Philip Villaume to press the case for the Amish.

On 26 October 1988, a hearing was held in Fillmore County District Court. Fifteen defendants appeared at the hearing. The defense argued that the Minnesota law requiring the red triangle at night violated their rights to free exercise of religion as guaranteed by *both* the First Amendment to the United States Constitution and Article I, Section 16, of the Minnesota Constitution. The defense argued that refusal to display the state-required SMV symbol met *Sherbert's* four-step test.

I served as an expert witness to establish the historical and religious context of the issue. In this role I cited three reasons why the Amish object to the SMV emblem: (1) its bright, flashy color, (2) its worldly symbolism, and (3) the fact that it put faith in a human symbol above faith in God.[28] While none of the defendants actually testified in court, several Amishmen who were chosen by Amish leaders did testify.

The district court judge discovered, as noted earlier, that members of the Amish faith in Fillmore County were divided on the use of SMV signs. Some had used the fluorescent triangular sign in the past, but upon examination of conscience stopped using the sign and confessed their sin to the community. Gideon Hershberger, Amishman from Fillmore County, admitted, "I have used it and I confessed for it too."[29]

The district court concluded that the defendants did not have a collective, genuine, sincere religious belief concerning the SMV symbol. Judge Snyder held, "The evidence presented at this trial shows that the matter of religious beliefs reflects the individual choice of Amish persons and is not a sincere belief held by the community as a whole."[30] He also wrote: "[The] evidence suggests that the most substantive objection was to the fact that it was a 'worldly symbol' and such 'worldly symbol' indicates conformity to a requirement dictated by man and not by God. However, such 'worldly symbol' was being used for a considerable period of time before objection by the Amish community and a substantial number of Amish do not object on the basis of a sincere religious belief at this time."[31]

The district court determined that the state statute infringed upon the exercise of the religious belief of *some* members of the Amish community, but did not infringe upon the sincere beliefs of others. The court found that the infringement was warranted by a compelling state-society interest. The protection of the "health, safety, and welfare of the public" was paramount in this case. Although white reflectorized tape makes buggies more visible at night, there are circumstances, the court noted, in which its effectiveness is negated.[32]

Finally, the court found that the SMV emblem is the least restrictive alternative. Judge Snyder contended that the Minnesota legislature had already established an alternative for the Amish: the black-and-white SMV sign for daylight hours. He also wrote: "The SMV [emblem] is almost universally the same in design and recognition throughout the United States. It is included in most Driver's Trainers Manuals so it is easily recognizable in all areas by all users of our highways. In addition, the statute has made it minimally intrusive on the vehicle since it is only required to be on the rearmost part of the slow moving vehicle."³³ Snyder thought that reflectorized tape would only confuse other drivers on the highway.

After this decision, Attorney Philip G. Villaume requested that the matter be certified to the court of appeals and to the Minnesota Supreme Court. Judge Snyder granted this certification on 21 December 1988 and stayed proceedings in the cases consolidated in his decision.³⁴

Summary arguments from the lower court were heard in the Minnesota Supreme Court on 1 June 1989. The Minnesota Supreme Court filed its decision on 18 August 1989 (*Hershberger I*). The court concluded that the Minnesota statute (Section 169.522) requiring the red triangle at night does infringe on the rights guaranteed by the free exercise clause of the First Amendment to the United States Constitution. The trial court's order was lifted, and the charges against the Amish were dismissed.

The Minnesota Supreme Court addressed the free exercise clause with the four-step *Sherbert* test. The court did not find another relevant case that required that a "sincerely held belief" must be shared by the religious community as a *whole*. On the contrary, in *Thomas v. Review Bd. of Ind. Employment Sec. Div.* (1981, 714), the United States Supreme Court specified that "religious beliefs need not be acceptable, logical, consistent, or comprehensible to others in order to merit First Amendment protection." Instead, the United States Supreme Court explained that the focus should be on whether *individual* belief is sincere. It concluded in *Thomas* that "the guarantee of free exercise is not limited to beliefs which are shared by all members of a religious sect. Particularly in this sensitive area, it is not within the judicial function and judicial competence to inquire whether the petitioner or his fellow worker more correctly perceived the commands of their common faith. Courts are not arbiters of scriptural interpretation" (*Thomas* at 715-16).

In *Hershberger*, the district court made an implicit finding in 1988 that the statute infringed upon the sincere religious beliefs of the appellants, but not of the Fillmore County Amish community as a whole. The Minnesota Supreme Court believed that since one Amishman actually went to jail and since others expressed a willingness to do so, rather than follow the statute, this proved the sincerity of their religious belief. Therefore, the Minnesota Supreme Court held that the defendants' sincere religious beliefs protected them from displaying the SMV emblem (*Hershberger I* at 286-87).

Secondly, the Minnesota Supreme Court found that the statute does burden the exercise of Amish religious beliefs. "They face a choice of either adhering to their religious beliefs by refusing to adopt 'worldly symbols,' bearing 'loud colors,' and suffering the consequent criminal sanctions therefore, or rejecting those beliefs in order to comply with the SMV statute" (*Hershberger I* at 287).

The third requirement of the *Sherbert* test asks: Is the infringement justified by a compelling state-society interest? The state interest claimed by the trial court was the public safety of all persons using the public highways. In *Hershberger I*, however, the Supreme Court of Minnesota pointed out that the state presented no evidence that accident rates were related to whether or not vehicles displayed the SMV emblem.

The final issue for consideration was the less restrictive alternative. The state argued that the black-and-gray SMV sign provided a less restrictive alternative. The Minnesota Supreme Court found that this rule "only partially eases the statutory burden on the Free Exercise rights of the appellants" (*Hershberger I* at 288). Further, no recorded evidence demonstrated that displaying the alternative black-and-gray emblem in daylight was more effective than the presence of the black, square, horse-drawn buggy itself, "which, as a matter of common sense, serves as a warning that the vehicle is moving at less than prevalent highway speeds for motorized vehicles" (*Hershberger I* at 289). The court concluded that the state's public safety interest would not significantly diminish if it permitted reflective tape and red lanterns to be used by the appellants and those of similar belief.[35]

Hershberger to the U.S. Supreme Court

The state of Minnesota was not about to concede to the Amish. It petitioned the Supreme Court of the United States for a writ of certiorari on 18 August 1989. In the petition, the state argued two questions. First, the Minnesota statute did not violate the respondents' rights as protected by the First Amendment to the U.S. Constitution. None of the respondents, argued Minnesota, actually testified to personal, sincere religious beliefs. Experts had testified to Amish beliefs, but no proof of personal belief was ever made because none of the defendants had testified in district court. Second, the state argued that the Minnesota Supreme Court decision in essence "established" religion, thus violating the First Amendment. The state contended that the Minnesota Supreme Court was advancing (establishing) religion by allowing the Amish special rights that others could not enjoy.[36]

Surprisingly, the Minnesota Civil Liberties Union presented a brief supporting the state's contention. The MCLU reasoned that the Minnesota Supreme Court decision reduced the state's power to regulate conduct on government highways through commonly recognized signs, thus endangering interstate and local traffic on highways.[37]

The brief of opposition to the U.S. Supreme Court supported the 7-0 decision of the Minnesota Supreme Court. The brief argued that the decision did not conflict with former decisions of the United States Supreme Court or state courts. For this reason, the brief asked that certiorari be denied.[38] On 23 April 1990, the United States Supreme Court granted the state's petition for a writ of certiorari, vacated the Minnesota Supreme Court decision, and sent *Hershberger I* back to the Supreme Court of Minnesota for further consideration in light of *Smith*.[39] Why was *Smith* so pivotal?

Smith, decided by the U.S. Supreme Court just one week earlier on 17 April 1990, altered the "compelling governmental interest" and "the less restrictive alternative" tests from *Sherbert*. *Smith* thus threatened to revise the standard assumptions that had evolved with the application of *Sherbert* and *Yoder*. *Smith* involved a case of two Oregon drug counselors fired for using peyote in religious ceremonies. The U.S. Supreme Court, in a 6-3 decision, upheld the Oregon Employment Division's denial of unemployment benefits to these men. The *Smith* opinion held that the free exercise clause of the First Amendment does not relieve an individual of the obligation to comply with a law that forbids something that his religious belief requires.

Meanwhile, back in Minnesota, the *Smith* decision left the Minnesota Supreme Court with a dilemma. What to do with *Hershberger?* Should it follow the United States Supreme Court's words of wisdom and change its earlier decision in *Hershberger I?* Did the Minnesota Constitution offer guidance? Would a reconsideration of *Hershberger I* set precedents for other Minnesota Supreme Court cases? Might the controversial *Smith* be overturned in the future?

To gain some insight into this quandary, the Minnesota Supreme Court directed the Amish appellants to answer two questions.[40] First, does *Smith* control the Minnesota Supreme Court's application of the free exercise clause of the First Amendment to the United States Constitution? Second, does the Minnesota statute section requiring the red triangle at night violate the free exercise rights of Amish defendants protected by Article 1, Section 16, of the Minnesota Constitution?

During the oral arguments held on 12 September 1990 before the Minnesota Supreme Court, Joseph L. Daly, attorney for the Amish, told the justices to deal only with the freedom of conscience clause of the Minnesota Constitution. In response to one justice's request for a "road map" in writing the decision, Mr. Daly replied, "Forget *Smith* and deal only with the Minnesota Constitution."[41]

Religious liberty is protected more expansively under the Minnesota Constitution than under the federal constitution, as the former refers to "freedom of conscience" and the latter does not. Thus, religious liberty is independent of the provisions of the federal constitution and cases such as *Smith*. Daly urged the Minnesota Supreme Court to interpret the state constitution independent of the federal constitution, offering greater protection for individual liberty. The state court could be freed from the Supreme Court's decision in *Smith*.[42]

The state, on the other hand, argued that the U.S. Supreme Court, upon reviewing *Hershberger*, vacated the judgment of the Supreme Court of Minnesota and remanded it back to the state court. For this reason, the state concluded that *Smith* specifically applies to *Hershberger*, and the Minnesota Supreme Court was bound by the U.S. Supreme Court decision in *Smith*.[43]

The Minnesota Supreme Court once again decided in favor of the Amish on 7 November 1990 in *Hershberger II*, basing its decision solely on the Minnesota Constitution. The court concluded that the state failed to demonstrate that both values—freedom of conscience and public safety—cannot be achieved through the alternative means of using reflective tape and a lighted red lantern (*Hershberger II* at 398).

Thus, the SMV controversy concluded for the Amish in Minnesota, since the decision could not be appealed to the U.S. Supreme Court. It is not conclusive for other states, however, because its outcome rests on the Minnesota Constitution. While it may give guidance to other cases in the future, state constitutions vary, and not all contain the same language as Minnesota's.

Legal conflicts in health care have often involved childbirth and immunization. Wide World Photos

CHAPTER NINE

Health Care

Gertrude Enders Huntington

 Health care conflicts between the Amish and state officials raise significant issues of moral responsibility and appropriate modes of medical care for Amish and non-Amish alike. Anthropologist Gertrude Enders Huntington describes the religious and cultural values that undergird the Amish response to health-related issues and traces some of the major confrontations between the Amish and state officials and health care providers.

In a clemency petition to the governor of Indiana, the children of an imprisoned Amish bishop wrote, "The Amish believe they should assume their own responsibility as much as possible and depend on the state as little as possible."[1] The Amish petitioners were referring to the care of their mentally ill sister. In health care matters, the Amish believe they must accept responsibility for their own actions and not depend on services supplied by the state. They are reluctant to depend exclusively on medical professionals to make decisions involving the health of their families. Neither state officials nor medical personnel take kindly to this apparent challenge of professional authority.

Although this small, well-disciplined minority perceive themselves as a "peculiar people," as "not conforming to this world" and living "separated" from it, they are scrupulously law-abiding.[2] Thus, there are relatively few confrontations with state or medical authorities. With a high literacy rate, excellent genealogical records, consanguinity, and large families, coupled with good nutrition and good general health, the Amish serve as natural laboratories for many medical studies.[3] Many Amish persons have assisted medical researchers by answering detailed questions and giving blood samples for studies of childhood diseases and of patterns of transmission and severity of various contagious diseases.[4]

Misunderstandings in the field of health care often center around the question of responsibility. Who is responsible for the health of an individual? Who is responsible for the health of a community or a specific population? When children or incapacitated adults are involved, differences of opinion often arise about optimal care and treatment. Many of the questions asked by the Amish are also posed by members of the dominant culture. Does an adult, or the parent of a child, have the right to reject available medical technology? Who shall practice what kind of medicine? What degree of choice does a patient or a parent have in selecting the medical care that he or she deems most appropriate? To what extent are the Amish responsible for protecting not only their own community but also the welfare of their non-Amish neighbors? To what extent should the larger society try to control the spread of communicable diseases and insist on universal immunization?

Amish Values

The Amish sense of responsibility is theologically based. As devout Anabaptists, the Amish have always contended that the church and the state are separate entities (see Chapter 2). The practice of voluntary adult baptism underscores the separation of church and state. Those who believe in adult baptism avow that children cannot be born into a church. Therefore the parents, not the church, are responsible for children's souls. Child rearing, not economic competence, is considered the primary task of parents. Since children have neither church membership nor godparents, both their spiritual and their physical care rests squarely with their parents (Huntington 1988, 367–99).

Early Protestant leaders such as Martin Luther and Philipp Melanchthon were suspicious of parents' ability to rear their children without the help and intervention of the state (H. Schwartz 1973, 102–14). In contrast, the Anabaptists never believed that the child or the parent was morally subservient to outside civil or religious authorities. Menno Simons, an early church leader, taught that parents were morally responsible for the condition of their children's souls, should set an unblamable example for them, and should protect them from worldly influences and wrong companions (Simons 1956, 391, 950). Children are viewed as sinless because they cannot distinguish right from wrong. Parents are obligated to teach them such distinctions so that as adults they will choose to become members of the Amish church (Huntington 1988, 367–99).

The hierarchy of responsibility within Amish culture is illustrated by the rank order of commitments: church, family, and state. An Amish individual joins the church as an adult, but before marriage. One's first commitment is to God as manifest in the believing community, and the second is to spouse and family, for marriage is "in the Lord." Commitments to the state are a distant third. If duties conflict, the rules of the church take precedence over family relationships. The laws of the state are obeyed insofar as they do not conflict with the laws of the church or one's duty to family.[5]

The Amish stress personal responsibility, not individual rights. The young adult who joins the community signifies his or her willingness to share responsibility for the group. Following the biblical injunction in Galatians 6:2, the Amish "bear one another's burdens." In the area of health care, this means that the family, assisted by the community, cares for the sick and feeble, utilizing only limited services of state, private, or public institutions. The Amish do not accept Medicare or Medicaid, nor do they subscribe to HMOs or Blue Cross and Blue Shield. When medical expenses loom too large for a single family, the community shares the cost.

On a deeper level, the community accepts responsibility for the health of its members. The suffering of innocent children during the poliomyelitis epidemic that swept the Ohio Amish community in 1952 was interpreted as a chastisement for the whole community.[6] In another instance, an Amish woman writing to a paralyzed Amish youth who had broken his neck, commented, "This is not just for you and your family. It is for all of us." And the boy's father wrote, "We believe that sometimes people must suffer affliction for the sake of those around them" (Wagler 1985, 138, 141). The belief that sickness or accident may be a chastisement for the whole community has frustrated public health officials. The positive side of community responsibility means, however, that when the Amish understand how their actions affect their own health and that of their neighbors, they often modify their behavior to protect the larger community.

The Amish cooperate with high-tech medicine when they understand the usefulness of the procedures (Huntington 1984, 92–118). They will supply blood and stool samples even when they hesitate to accept a vaccine. As grateful recipients of organ transplants, Amish also donate organs to family members and occasionally to outsiders. They receive blood transfusions and are generous in donating blood to the Red Cross. In fact, the Amish are more comfortable in giving to the outside world than in receiving from it. This pattern of behavior parallels their practice of fulfilling obligations and giving necessities to a member who has been excommunicated—

even though members in good standing may accept nothing from the shunned individual.[7]

The Right to Refuse Treatment

Most of the court cases and threatened legal procedures involving Amish health care result from a lack of communication or a difference of opinion over the best care for a sick child. The Amish do not fear death, for death is part of life. The dead person is not to be pitied, because death is the entrance to a better life. On one occasion I sat beside an Amish couple in the hospital. The ill father was preparing to bid his children farewell—a few hours before his death. He was understandably restless and somewhat agitated. His wife said to him, quite sharply, "It's easier for you, you'll be in heaven soon and I'll be left here all alone."[8] The Amish believe that the quality of life is more important than its length, and that a good death is preferable to a few more days or months of pain. An Old Order Mennonite mother, expressing typical Amish sentiments, contrasted the deaths of her two daughters from the same genetic disorder. The older child died in the hospital, the younger died at home. "We have never regretted keeping Regina at home. She seldom cried. Her final illness lasted about thirty days, the same as Cheryl's did, but how very much different! She had no IVs, no oxygen and no blood transfusions. We never had to go away and leave her crying. We believe the tender love and care she got at home was worth more to her than all the medication she could have gotten at the hospital" (Weiler and Weiler 1991, 15–17).

A midwife to the Lancaster County Amish recounts the case of a baby with an incurable invasive brain tumor whose parents took him home because he cried himself hoarse in the hospital. They decided the baby had enough to endure without being put in the hands of strangers where the family could only visit him. When, however, the doctors determined that it was a rare case, and the parents refused to bring their child back to the hospital, the doctors filed suit; the baby eventually died in a Baltimore hospital (Armstrong and Feldman 1986, 145–47).

The Amish family and community are very accepting and solicitous in the care they give their "different" children touched by illness or disability. These children are accepted as they are, and their families enjoy making them as comfortable as possible. The Amish teach disabled persons to be helpful and to contribute economically to their upkeep. But they also believe it is better for the disabled to be loved and to enjoy being cared for than to pressure them toward extreme independence.[9]

Life-support machines are appreciated during surgery or immediately following an accident, but the Amish deem their use inappropriate when they merely prolong the existence of the body. Because the Amish do not believe in going to court, no cases have involved the continued use of life-support machines. The Amish stand is, however, consistent and clear. On one occasion, when it became apparent that doctors in a New Jersey hospital would not permit a life-support machine to be turned off, the family arranged to have their daughter moved to a hospital that would respect their wishes.[10]

An eighteen-year-old Amish carpenter received severe head injuries when he fell while working on a house roof. He was rushed to the hospital and placed on a respirator. Two days later (Friday), the attending doctors pronounced him brain-dead and decided to remove him from the machine. But an Amish correspondent reported that "another health official stepped in before he was released and refused to release his body. This caused undue agony to the already bereaved family. His body could not be released from the machine, while the official claimed he was still breathing, until Monday. . . . You will note that the obituary in a Lancaster news[paper], says that he died on Monday. The time of death and age were announced at the funeral as on Friday."[11] The Amish community did not consider a body kept alive by a machine to be a living person: "The truth was that his soul had fled."[12]

The Amish do not believe that it is the state's responsibility to protect their children. Amish children belong to God even before they belong to their parents and certainly before they belong to the state. The Amish would argue that they and their children should obey the laws of the state, because government is ordained of God, but they would also contend that the Christian does not belong to the state. Therefore, if a conflict arises between the laws of the church and the laws of the state, the church's authority takes precedence.

In the area of health care many concessions have been made, usually willingly, by the Amish. Only a few concessions have been made by the state to the Amish. In some specific cases there have been compromises, of beliefs or accepted practices, between the Amish and the state or the medical establishment. Two well-established legal principles—the state's obligation to protect a child and the parental right to determine how children will be raised—collided in a case involving a thirty-one-year-old Amishman who refused to let his six-year-old son continue chemotherapy treatments for cancer. This confrontation vividly illustrates the unwillingness of the father and the Amish community to concede to the state, and how a compromise was eventually negotiated.[13]

In October 1988, Amos Mast became ill on a bus trip to a wedding. He was diagnosed as having cancer and sent to Kosair Children's Hospital in Louisville. He received two chemotherapy treatments, which made him ill and miserable. When the boy's father questioned the doctor about chemotherapy, the doctor responded by stating that the treatment would continue. "Then the physician beat his hand on a table and cursed." Daniel Mast later explained, "I will not allow a man to treat my son who curses my God." A hospital spokeswoman said the account was not true but declined to give any more information. In any event, Mast refused to bring Amos back to the hospital.

The doctor contacted the Hardin County attorney's office about the possibility of charging Mast with child neglect. The officials petitioned Hardin Juvenile Court to require the resumption of the chemotherapy. At a hearing on 22 December 1988, doctors said that chemotherapy would give Amos Mast a 30 to 40 percent chance for a full recovery. At a second hearing in mid-January, the district judge ordered Mast to bring his son in for chemotherapy, but the father refused. During this period, the Masts took their son to doctors in Indiana and Ohio and consulted a doctor in Texas. Finally, they took him to a clinic in Tijuana, Mexico, where he received a "natural" therapeutic treatment of herbs and vitamins.

On 13 January 1989, temporary custody of the child was given to the state Cabinet for Human Resources so the child could be removed from his family and chemotherapy resumed. But the state officials could not locate Amos, and the father refused to give any information on the child's whereabouts. A sympathetic authority told the parents that the judge could not physically remove the child if he was in a different state. The family quickly hired a driver to take Amos and a relative to a bus station in the next state. Not until the driver had dropped them off did the relative decide where he would take the child.

On 27 January 1989, Daniel Mast was jailed for contempt of court for refusing, from his point of view, to hand over his child to the state. His decision was supported by the local Amish community as well. Community consensus agreed that chemotherapy would negatively affect the quality of the child's short life. If he was not going to recover, he should be able to die in peace rather than in pain. Mast did not request a lawyer, for as his preacher said, "It's not really our way of life to protect ourselves with force." His father-in-law added, "Scripture says if they strike your right cheek, you offer your left." Nevertheless, the court appointed a lawyer for the father and for the son.

There was considerable public support for the father. Both the judge and the hospital received calls from individuals upset by Mast's incarceration. Neighbors started a petition asking for his release. The executive director of a local hospice explained that chemotherapy can be excruciating and that the father may feel the hoped-for outcome of treatment is not worth the pain. The executive director of the American Civil Liberties Union of Kentucky said the court must balance the child's interests with Mast's freedom of religion and right to privacy. She also said the court should not immediately assume that the medical community offers the only effective treatment for cancer.

On 30 January 1989, Mast was released from prison because no one believed that further incarceration would compel him to reveal his son's location. The judge denied a motion to rescind the contempt charges. The assistant county attorney said that the father and members of the Amish community could be indicted on criminal charges if the boy died. How was this impasse negotiated?

Neither the father nor members of the Amish community would cooperate by placing the child in state custody. The chaplain of the county jail acted as a go-between for the Amish and the judge. On 7 February 1989, Mast agreed to take his son for treatment to qualified medical doctors of his own choosing. He selected a doctor in Tennessee who had practiced in an Amish community for twenty-seven years. Mast agreed to abide by the doctor's advice, including chemotherapy, if advised.

The Amish would not negotiate the custody of one of their children, although they would compromise on the treatment when able to maintain control over who determined the treatment. The state acquiesced on the location of the treatment and the demand for a specific treatment, requiring only that the child be cared for by a qualified medical doctor. The Amish community continued to act on their belief that it is pointless to extend life at any cost. When Amos Mast died from complications of chickenpox and pneumonia, his grandmother said, "He's in better hands now than we are. The Lord has promised to take care of the little ones." The state did not press criminal charges against either the parents or other members of the Amish community.

Amish "Doctors"

State officials in the Mast case were uncomfortable with the child not being treated by a qualified doctor—interpreted to mean a state-licensed physician. The Amish, like many other people, make use of alternative and traditional medicine in addition to conventional medicine.[14] The Amish often seek care from individuals, both Amish and non-Amish, who give various treatments involving physical manipulations and who suggest the use of foods, diets, supplements, teas, and herbs. Some treatment givers within various Amish communities are virtually unknown outside of Amish circles and therefore never come to the attention of the state. Occasionally an Amish practitioner will acquire a large following of loyal patients. The heightened visibility can lead state authorities to investigate the practitioner.

In Berne, Indiana, Solomon J. Wickey, the father of twelve children and the owner of a forty-acre farm, supplemented his income by selling herbs. Most of his clientele were Amish, but people came from as far away as California and Germany to solicit his suggestions. He was originally known as an iridologist—one who diagnoses problems by looking at the iris of the eye. After his trial, he was called a nutritionist. The logo on his business card contained the words "Nature's Sunshine," Independent Distributor. His name and address also appeared on his card. In 1980, the Adams County sheriff, responding to a suggestion from the health department, asked Wickey to stop administering medications without a license. Wickey suspended his practice for about ten days.[15]

In September 1983, Wickey was temporarily restrained from selling herbs. Then, on 1 December 1983, a civil case was brought by the state. In a trial heard by a judge, Solomon Wickey was accused of deceptive practices and practicing medicine without a license. But the strong support Wickey enjoyed from his clientele complicated the case for the state (Rodgers 1969, 90–91). Over two hundred people in the courtroom gave Wickey an ovation when he arrived, and the judge had received over four hundred letters from supporters. The judge dismissed the charge of deceptive practices but sustained a charge that Wickey practiced medicine without a license. Wickey and his attorneys argued that he did not pose as a doctor but provided nutritional counseling based on nearly three hundred Bible passages. Wickey maintained that he did not act like a doctor because he did not charge for his services (he accepted donations), and he only *suggested* helpful herbs and did not prescribe them. He was merely helping people, and many believed they found relief using his herbs.

The case was settled out of court when Wickey signed a consent decree with the state of Indiana agreeing to stop diagnosing and treating patients. Wickey was allowed to observe physical characteristics, gather medical background, and make suggestions related to nutritional needs. "'It's practically the same thing we were doing before,' Wickey said about the decree, as he framed a copy to hang on an office wall. He said he will resume formally analyzing clients' nutritional needs by studying their eyes—a method called iridology—when he opens for business today."[16]

The negotiated settlement pleased both the state and Wickey's Amish clientele. Wickey believed he had been vindicated and now was free to practice unhindered by the state. A spokesman for the attorney general's office said, "We think [the decree] stops everything we wanted to stop." In 1991, Solomon Wickey continued to be busy making nutritional suggestions for the many individuals who continued to seek his advice.

In a more recent case, Joseph W. Helmuth, of Goshen, Indiana, who had been "in practice" for about sixteen years and had probably treated more than six thousand persons, was charged in 1989 with practicing chiropractic and physical therapy.[17] Helmuth had learned various manipulative techniques while working earlier in a hospital. Also, when traveling, he would patronize any available chiropractor, especially those recommended by members of the Amish community. Helmuth performed manipulations for back conditions, treated a female patient for infertility "caused by a tipped uterus," and instructed a patient in a massage technique to alleviate an ear problem.

At the injunction hearing, the courtroom was practically filled with Amish people and chiropractors. Following the hearing, the chiropractors issued a press release commending the prosecutor's office for forbidding Helmuth from practicing chiropractic or any other form of medicine. Helmuth did not admit guilt, and his attorney said he would resist a permanent injunction request. In July, however, the state and Helmuth, by mutual consent, signed a permanent injunction order. In October 1989, Helmuth pleaded guilty to a charge of practicing chiropractic treatment without a license in return for dismissal of a charge of unlawful practice of physical therapy. He was fined $250, given a suspended 180-day jail term, and placed on probation for one year. Joseph Helmuth was censured by the church, *not* for practicing medicine without a license, but for hiring a lawyer and going to court. The tone of a letter he wrote in *Die Blatt* (16 February 1989) suggests he found it difficult to be as submissive as expected by his Amish culture. "The hardest thing has been not to defend myself, which has left the other side do & say what they wanted to, but our Lord has taught us not to resist as He will make everything right. We try not to forget that all things work together for the good of those that love Him, and maybe we tend to forget where our talents come from. I'm back in the office with certain restrictions which I will try to accept."

This case involved much less negotiation than the Wickey case, primarily because the charges against Helmuth were more serious than those against Wickey. In addition to replacing qualified medical intervention, Helmuth's aggressive treatments could injure his patients. Furthermore, Helmuth had to contend with a special interest group (the chiropractors) who were pitted against him. Finally, Helmuth was not humble and submissive in responding to the allegations against him. He did not admit guilt and, through his lawyer, said he would resist the state-ordered injunction. Thus, he was censored by the church.

Birthing Centers and Amish Midwives

Of greater importance to the Amish community than the occasional marginal practitioner are the questions of where their babies are born, who will deliver them, and how families pay the costs. The Old Order Amish carry no commercial or government insurance to cover doctor or hospital bills. Pregnancy and childbirth are important events in the life of healthy Amish adults, who have an average of seven living children per married couple. Although the majority of Amish babies are born in hospitals, many Amish parents prefer to have their children born at home. The percentage of home deliveries, however, varies from one community to another. And within the larger communities, location of birth varies from one subgroup of Amish to another, with the most traditional favoring home deliveries.[18] The availability of qualified doctors or midwives to assist in home deliveries is a factor in the decision, as is the cost of a hospital delivery and stay.

An Amish baby "born at home" may actually be born in the parents' home or at the home of a lay midwife. Most Amish midwives are unknown outside the Amish communities. They are found in Amish settlements in Ohio, Pennsylvania, Indiana, Iowa, New York, and Delaware. Amish midwives have families of their own, and some find it more convenient for the laboring mother to come to the midwife's home for delivery. The midwife may have one or more rooms on the first floor of her home specially equipped as a labor room, delivery room, and nursery.[19] Usually the Amish midwife has an informal relationship with a sympathetic doctor who assists in emergencies.

A unique Amish midwife, known as "Bill Barb" Hochstetler (Bill is the first name of her husband), assisted birthing Amish women for over thirty years.[20] She had a birthing center in central Ohio, in a large Amish settlement, and worked closely as a skilled maternity nurse with sympathetic doctors who had many Amish patients. She maintained a strict Amish home without electricity or a telephone, but she had good lighting, powered by battery and gas. A doctor with whom she worked for many years moved a trailer with a telephone onto Hochstetler's farm so he could be called in case of emergency.[21]

Local county health officials recognized that Hochstetler gave her patients good care. They realized that if she did not take mothers into her home, more babies would be born with poorer medical attention. Hochstetler had been assisting deliveries in her home for about twenty years before she came to the attention of the state health department. Someone in the department noticed that a large number of birth certificates had the same rural address. Thinking that the doctors who signed the birth certificates had been illegally delivering babies in their office, the state investigated. The doctors explained that these were home deliveries.

In the early 1970s, two doctors who delivered babies at Hochstetler's birthing center were informed by health authorities from Columbus, Ohio, that state approval was necessary for their maternity center. The senior doctor responded that he did not run a maternity center but merely delivered babies at home if he felt it was appropriate. Some area doctors tried to close the center, but without formal complaints or accusations they could do nothing. Hochstetler's practice fell in a legal gray area. It was permissible to have a baby born at home, but was a delivery a "home birth" if it occurred in someone else's home? Since Hochstetler accepted donations but did not charge any fees, her home was clearly not a hospital. In fact, she frequently was paid nothing and very often received little—perhaps only one hundred dollars for the three-day stay, during which the mother was well fed, had all her laundry done, and received twenty-four-hour nursing care.[22] Interestingly, Hochstetler's birthing center did not reach public notice until she was about to retire in the early 1980s.[23] An Amish contractor,

Jonas D. Yoder, then sought permission to build a birthing center so Amish women could continue to give birth in the security of their own culture.[24]

When word of the proposed Mount Eaton Care Center became public, local hospitals became more attentive to the needs of their Amish patients. Some even instituted birthing rooms within the hospital setting and permitted mothers who brought nursing help with them to pay a smaller fee. Hospital administrators claimed the proposed birthing center would not affect their patient load, even though 40 percent of the maternity cases in one hospital were Amish. Contractor Yoder estimated that the birthing center would save the Amish community seven million dollars in its first ten years. Hospital administrators criticized the proposed facility because no regulations governed a birthing center, since it was not a hospital, nor affiliated with any, and would not accept government or other public funds. About 250 babies had been delivered at Hochstetler's each year. Other babies were born at home, and maternity costs continued to rise, so the need for the center was obvious.

Yoder donated six acres of land, supervised the construction, and formed a board of directors (both Amish and non-Amish). Even before construction, he had raised about $180,000, including $123,000 from Amish churches within a fifty-mile radius of the center. Officials of the center sought state approval. They won support from the Wayne County Board of Health and finally gained reluctant consent from the Ohio Department of Health— which explained it could not prevent the building of the clinic. The Mount Eaton Care Center opened in November 1985. Medical doctors and certified nurses now care for Amish women in a homelike environment at low cost. In 1992, the cost of an average two- or three-day stay at the Mount Eaton Care Center was $305.

Both the Mount Eaton Care Center and Hochstetler's endeavors represent skillfully negotiated compromises that enabled many Amish women to deliver their children safely, in a low-tech, familiar, homelike atmosphere where they and family members feel welcomed. At an affordable price, healthy Amish mothers can have their babies delivered naturally in supportive surroundings while being cared for by qualified physicians or trained midwives.[25]

Some Amish families have consistently refused to abdicate control of the birthing process. When doctors would not cooperate, these women had their babies at home, unattended by trained persons. Within the Amish community, individuals met the need by helping birthing neighbors—sometimes offering them a bed in their own home and assisting in the care of the mother and newborn. With rising hospital costs, impersonal supervision during labor, and the use of machines and drugs, many Amish have been unhappy with hospital deliveries.

The Mount Eaton Care Center, established by the Amish and run jointly by Amish and non-Amish, offers a compromise. The largely Amish-Mennonite staff is interested in and shares the cultural orientation of the patients. Although the environment is low-tech, it includes indoor plumbing, electricity, and telephones. It is only a few blocks from an emergency station staffed with paramedics and ambulances and is also near several hospitals. Supporters of the birth center had to consider local public opinion and negotiate, both formally and informally, with various health departments, doctors, and hospital administrators. Like Amish schools, the care center does not have a strong legal base. These Amish institutions exist on the edge of the legal system, supported primarily by public opinion. Their presence functions to reinforce freedom of choice within contemporary American culture as well as within the Amish subculture.

Non-Amish Midwives

Non-Amish (or "English") midwives also practice in many Amish communities.[26] There are two kinds of midwives, those with degrees in nursing and midwifery and those who trained by apprenticeship but who do not necessarily have a degree in nursing or a graduate degree in midwifery. How these two types of midwives are recognized or licensed, if at all, varies from state to state. In Delaware, for example, both types of midwives can be licensed. Michigan and Pennsylvania grant midwifery licenses only to registered nurses who have both a baccalaureate and an advanced degree in nursing and who have passed a certification exam given by the American College of Nurse-Midwives. According to Sandra Botting, president of the Midwives Alliance of North America, about fifteen states recognize midwives other than nurses. Of the estimated four thousand to five thousand practicing midwives in the United States and Canada, approximately two-thirds are nurses.

Should a family have the right to determine the environment in which their children are born and the right to determine who will help them at the time of birth? Many, Amish and non-Amish alike, consider this issue a basic personal freedom, a constitutional right. Others feel that the perceived safety of the newborn should take precedence over the parents' freedom of choice. These differing perceptions led to the arrest of a Pennsylvania midwife, Grace Lucille Sykes, in 1989 and marked the beginning of a twenty-one-month battle to clarify her legal position.[27] Sykes had been practicing midwifery in northwestern Pennsylvania for about thirteen years and had delivered over six hundred babies, the majority of whom were Amish. She was highly regarded by her patients, respected by certified midwives, and tolerated by area doctors. A doctor explained that physicians had not "turned Sykes in" because they were afraid the Amish would become angry with the medical profession and refuse to seek treatment of any kind. In fact, it was difficult to find anyone who would criticize Sykes or her work.

Lucille Sykes was neither Amish nor a nurse. At the urging of her Amish neighbors, Sykes had trained in Ohio with Amishwoman Barbara Hochstetler. Over a two-year period, she spent four to eight days a month working under Hochstetler. Within ten years she was assisting with more than one hundred births annually. Consistent with midwifery philosophy, Sykes maintains that the mother *delivers* the baby and the midwife *catches* the baby. The birthing parents did not feel like pawns being moved around on a hospital chessboard; instead, they felt empowered as they participated in their own destinies. But because she was working without a nurse-midwife license, Sykes was arrested. She faced criminal charges for the unlawful practice of medicine.

In early March 1989, the director of Children and Youth Services for Mercer County informed Sykes that she must stop practicing midwifery. She had several overdue patients, however, for whom she continued to care. When the director visited an Amish couple and accused them of allowing Sykes to deliver their baby on 23 March 1989, he heard a glowing description of her skill. In order to force the parents to report who assisted at the birth of their child, the director filed a petition of child abuse against them. He told the Amish couple that their children belonged to him until they were eighteen years old and that he could place their nineteen-day-old baby in a foster home.[28]

The director of Children and Youth Services explained that the petition was designed to force the parents to provide information. After the parents complied with the state's request for information, the petition was dropped. The director admitted that the Amish couple was very supportive of Sykes and praised her work.

Four of their six children had been delivered with her help. The first child was born in a hospital. With their fifth child, Sykes advised them of possible complications and urged them to see a physician and to deliver in a hospital, which they did. Their sixth child, born at Sykes's Cradletime Birth Clinic, secured for her parents the petition of child abuse. Typical of the praise from Sykes's patients was the comment by an Amishman that Sykes was ten to fifty times as careful, gentle, and kind as any doctor.

On 18 April 1989, Sykes was arrested on criminal charges. She was freed on condition that she not practice midwifery until her preliminary hearing 22 May 1989. Over 150 Amish stood among some 300 supporters who overflowed the courtroom and heard the district justice dismiss charges against Sykes. The justice said the definitions of midwifery and nurse midwifery in the Medical Practice Act of 1985 were unclear. The Pennsylvania Board of Medicine then sought an injunction prohibiting Sykes from practicing midwifery and filed civil charges alleging that Sykes practiced medicine illegally because she was an unlicensed midwife.

The state Bureau of Professional and Occupational Affairs also filed a suit (5 June 1989) in the Mercer Common Pleas Court against Sykes, asking the court to order her to stop the practice of midwifery and to pay a thousand-dollar fine. A spokeswoman for the state of Pennsylvania explained, "This is the first time we've been able to prosecute a lay midwife. . . . We've never been able to get anyone to testify against them."[29] By threatening to remove the couple's baby under a child abuse provision, the state was able to document that a lay midwife had charged the parents four hundred dollars for care during the birth.

Sykes's lawyer filed responses to both the state Board of Medicine and the Bureau of Professional and Occupational Affairs (21 July 1989). The lawyer argued that a lay midwife does not have to be licensed and is recognized by the Pennsylvania Department of Health as different from a certified nurse-midwife. Midwifery does not constitute the practice of medicine when prescription drugs are not used. Women anticipating childbirth have a basic constitutional right to choose between home birth and hospital birth. Further, the lawyer argued, the Commonwealth of Pennsylvania has asserted no compelling state interest justifying interference with a mother's freedom of choice in this regard. The lawyer continued that there were no allegations that Sykes's services were rendered in a negligent, harmful, or uncaring manner and no basis for saying that the public would be harmed by her continuing to practice as a midwife. The lawyer also noted: "The parents . . . hold the sincere conviction that childbirth should occur in the home setting in the natural way which God intended. The Commonwealth has asserted no compelling state interest justifying interference with the free exercise of such religious beliefs. . . . the U.S. Supreme Court has expressly recognized Old Order Amish beliefs as entitled to First Amendment protection."[30]

Specific Amish families, certain Amish church districts, and some of the most conservative Amish would agree with the lawyer's statement. Many Old Order Amish would contend that home birth fits their way of life better than hospital birth, but they consider place and manner of birth as a cultural preference rather than a religious issue. Home versus hospital delivery is usually decided by the family and the particulars of the pregnancy. The Amish think it should be a personal option—not something dictated by the state.

Amish supporters packed the courtroom at a hearing (4 June 1990) in the Mercer County Court of Common Pleas, where Sykes challenged the attempt by the Pennsylvania Board of Medicine to bar her from practicing midwifery. On 21 December 1990, the judge exonerated Sykes in a detailed nineteen-page statement ruling that a lay midwife does not have to be licensed in the Commonwealth of Pennsylvania, thus dismissing the Board of Medicine's injunction. She was legally freed to assist mothers at the time of birth. Unless reversed in an appellate court, all "midwives in Pennsylvania can now rest comfortably, therefore, that the threat of criminal and/or civil prosecution has been removed."[31]

The Sykes case illustrates an apparent impasse between the Amish and the state. In the eyes of the Amish, children do not belong to the state. They belong first to God, then to their parents, and then to the church through their parents. Amish children do not "belong" to the director of the Mercer County Children and Youth Services, the Cabinet for Human Resources, or any other agency of the state. Therefore, the place of birth and who attends the birth should not be determined by the state. Moreover, the Amish do not understand how the state can permit abortions and then declare it illegal for parents to choose where their baby is born and who assists with the birth.

In Pennsylvania, nurse-midwives were protected by the law, but lay midwives were outside the legal system—or, at best, in an ambiguous situation. In an effort to protect lay practitioners, the Pennsylvania Midwives Association and the Midwife Association of North America pressed for a state law to legalize midwives who did not have nurses' training, thereby recognizing a secondary category of midwives who could register with the state and be eligible for voluntary certification. Pennsylvania Senate Bill 1528, sponsored by Senator Michael Dawida, proposed a Department of Health Advisory Committee to establish criteria for certifying lay midwives or birth attendants. Once certified, hospitals and other medical practitioners would be required to recognize the lay midwives.

A similar House bill was sponsored by Representative David Heckler. Senate Bill 1528 was introduced on 12 March 1990 at a news conference in Harrisburg, the state capital, which was well attended by Amish supporters of lay midwives. On 12 April 1990, over one hundred Amish attended a hearing before the Senate Consumer Protection and Professional Licensure Committee. Two Amishmen spoke in favor of the bill, and two certified nurse-midwives spoke against it, as did several medical groups. The primary objection was that unqualified persons might be able to obtain licenses. How could criteria be determined that would accept skillful Amish midwives with only an eighth-grade education but exclude dubious characters such as the "teaman," an itinerant herb salesman reputed to be willing to deliver babies for a fee? Neither the Senate nor the House bill reached the floor. In 1991 and 1992, new bills were quietly sponsored but not introduced.[32] Some midwives prefer that the bills remain pending; for though the legislation would give them added protection, it would also regulate lay midwives.

A somewhat similar case involving another non-Amish midwife occurred in Missouri. Sheila Nichting, an R.N., had worked in local hospitals and had trained under a doctor for a year and a half before taking patients of her own. In the summer of 1989, she opened her practice about forty miles from Jefferson City, the state capital. The bulk of her patients were conservative Mennonites. She encountered problems when her backup doctors were pressured by the Board of Healing Arts to withdraw support from her. These doctors were informally threatened with the loss of their state licenses. Nichting practiced in a rural area where family incomes were generally about fifteen to twenty thousand dollars, and it was not unusual for a family to have ten children. Hospital deliveries cost at least thirty-five hundred dollars, not including lab fees and various extras. Nichting charged fifteen hundred dollars for prenatal care, delivery assistance, lab fees, and the six-week checkup—unless the family was unable to meet the payment. In her words, she preferred to receive nothing rather than to "take bread off their table." Without the services of a midwife, many women would have delivered with only family members in attendance. Nichting delivered women either in their own homes or in a small birthing clinic.

On 24 January 1991, at 2:15 A.M., Nichting's birthing clinic was raided by seven officials who took everything, including the sheets on which a woman was sleeping, leaving only enough equipment for one delivery. They also confiscated records of thirty-five women whose pregnancies Nichting was monitoring. (Neither the equipment nor the records were returned for eight months.) After six weeks of uncertainty, Nichting was charged with eight felony counts and two misdemeanor counts. She received strong support from her patients. Some thirty thousand dollars was donated toward her legal fees, and about three hundred Mennonites showed up at the hearing in Jefferson City when a bill to legalize midwives was introduced in March 1991.

In September 1991, the case against Nichting was closed with a plea-bargaining settlement in which all charges except one misdemeanor count were dropped. Nichting agreed to abide by her nursing contract for six months, after which time there would be no sentencing and the remaining charge would be dropped. Following a civil suit, the Nursing Board, which had previously given her permission to practice, placed her under probation for five years. One of the terms of the probation was that Nichting give the Nursing Board a letter of support from her backup doctor. To the surprise of the doctor, Nichting, and her lawyer, this letter was rejected by the board, and the Country Cradle Birth Center was closed in October 1991. Nichting was to resubmit the letter of agreement; its acceptance would mean the birthing center could be reopened.[33]

The high cost of hospital deliveries can be prohibitive for young farming couples without any health insurance—especially for those having a baby every other year. Dorothy Kuhns, a Beachy Amish woman, trained in midwifery by the British in Belize, had worked with the United Nations Children's Fund and the World Health Organization. After she married and moved into an Illinois Mennonite and Amish community, neighbor women pleaded with her to help with home deliveries. Without a midwife, some of the Amish women were forced to deliver at home without trained attendants. Kuhns was shocked by the lack of medical care for these rural women. She agreed to do home deliveries with backup assistance from several doctors. A doctor saw the women at least once during their pregnancies and performed the lab tests, while Kuhns handled the prenatal care. Women in labor came to Kuhns's home; when it was time for the delivery, the doctor arrived. After working for about a year in the late 1980s, Kuhns gave birth to twins and stopped working as a midwife. She now teaches prenatal classes but does not assist with deliveries.

Two Old Order Amish women in this Illinois community started a three-year midwifery training program of academic studies and apprenticeship under the direction of lay midwives, but, uncomfortable with the legal ambiguities, they have not completed the training. The status of all midwives in the state continues to be uncertain. A bill passed in 1990–91 forbids diagnosis and/or treatment of any medical condition by anyone other than an allopathic physician, and a bill legalizing midwives was defeated in the House in the 1991–92 session. An exemption that would permit Amish and conservative Mennonites to use midwives is being sought. In the meantime, members of the community learned that the person who cuts the umbilical cord is technically the person who delivers the baby. If the total process takes place within the community, and the father or grandmother cuts the cord, the Amish in this community will have negotiated a comfortable, though legally tenuous, solution to a widespread problem.[34]

When Is Home Care Inadequate?

Whether one considers childbirth or care for the terminally ill, the handicapped, or the mentally ill, valid differences of opinion arise over "adequate care" and under what circumstance home or institutional care is better. Quality of life interpretations and the importance of familiar surroundings versus professional intervention vary by culture and family. The case of the child with a genetic disease, discussed earlier, who was kept at home while she was dying, exemplifies a family that placed a high value on familiar surroundings and personalized, loving care.[35]

Conscientious doctors face dilemmas illustrated by the case of an Amish newborn with cystic fibrosis.[36] A very conservative couple in Ohio brought their newly delivered eighth child into the community hospital. Her parents were informed that she had cystic fibrosis. Her father was familiar with the disease because two of his brother's children were suffering from it. He added, "Had I known that was what it was, I wouldn't have brought her in."

The baby's stay in the intensive care unit was very expensive. The parents worried that they could not pay the bill and wanted to take the baby home. Finally the hospital released the child, telling the parents to bring her back in six weeks. This conservative

Amish home had no electricity, indoor plumbing, or central heating. Nevertheless, the child was carefully and lovingly cared for without special equipment. The parents did not return for the six-week appointment; when the hospital investigated, they learned the baby had died. The doctors then considered bringing child abuse charges against the parents.

Having watched relatives die of the disease, the parents undoubtedly believed that the baby would be better off solicitously cared for with little medical intervention, even though it meant that she might soon be a part of "the family circle in heaven." There was no cure for this degenerative disease; moreover, medical care would be continuous and very expensive. Had the doctors pressed charges, medical care for other babies would have declined because Amish parents, fearing loss of their rights, would hesitate to bring other sick children to the hospital. Even as it was, members of the Amish community and at least one doctor felt the child should have been released to her parents sooner.

A much more complicated case in 1948 involved an Old Order Amish bishop in Indiana who cared for his daughter at home instead of placing her in the state mental hospital.[37] The initial newspaper accounts, sensational and extremely inaccurate, were quoted around the world. The whole episode appeared tainted with anti-Amish sentiment. Bishop Samuel D. Hochstetler, from near Goshen, Indiana, had with the help of his family cared for his mentally ill daughter, Lucy, in their home. As she became older, the daughter developed episodes of violence and became dangerous to herself and others. On one occasion, she knocked her sister unconscious; another time, she threatened a family member with a butcher knife. Once she drank carbolic acid. She would jump out of windows and run away, even when barefooted and the ground was covered with snow. When agitated, she would throw food, rip up books, and tear wallpaper off the wall.

The family had taken her to various doctors, and she had been placed in two different hospitals for diagnosis and treatment. Nothing seemed to cure her. Lucy had had one operation, probably a frontal lobotomy. This operation did not, however, ameliorate her seizures of violence. Finally the family began tying her to her bed when she was unmanageable and freeing her when she was calm. As she became worse, she was tied up more. Amish people who knew the family said that a public health nurse showed Lucy's mother how to tie her so that she could not hurt herself and could easily be released. Family acquaintances and church members knew about Lucy and the dedication it took to care for her.

Following the death of her mother, Lucy's siblings and their father made plans for her long-term care. As an interim measure, children or grandchildren came each day to help. Late Wednesday afternoon, 21 January 1948, a sheriff and a deputy sheriff arrived unannounced, without papers. While the eighteen-year-old granddaughter went to find her grandfather, the officers asked a seven-year-old to show them Lucy. By the time Hochstetler came to the house, the officers had returned to the living room. They identified themselves and asked to see Lucy. Their request was readily granted. Early the next afternoon, the officers returned with two men who photographed Lucy on the bed with the deputy sheriff holding her chains. The seventy-five-year-old bishop was arrested and marched off to jail.

When family members learned of the incarceration, Hochstetler's son and son-in-law hitched up their buggy and drove the seven and one-half miles to the jail to arrange bond. But because their land was owned jointly with their wives, they were not allowed to use it as security. It was too late in the day for their wives to receive a message and come to the courthouse in time to execute the papers. The following day, Hochstetler's son and his wife arrived at the sheriff's office at 9:40 A.M. to sign the papers for the bond. Their father was already in the courtroom, without a lawyer or any family members present. Within a few minutes, Hochstetler had been sentenced to six months at the state penal farm. After Hochstetler freely admitted he was guilty of tying his daughter to the bed "part of the time," Judge Simpson said, "I am sending you down to the State Farm for six months as punishment for doing this inhuman act. A man of your age and intelligence should know better, in a civilized world." Judging by the transcript, the whole proceedings probably took less than fifteen minutes. Hochstetler received the maximum jail time. Three doctors pronounced Lucy to be in good physical condition but definitely insane. She was transferred to a state hospital and remained there for twenty-four years before being moved to a nursing home, where she died in 1978. People who had worked in state hospitals pointed out that violent patients often received worse treatment in the hospitals than Lucy ever received in her home. Indeed, the National Mental Health Foundation stated in 1948 that "standards in the state institutions of Indiana have been notoriously bad."[38]

The family and the church community did not feel that state mental hospitals provided a good environment for Amish individuals, and Hochstetler strongly endorsed the Amish belief that "they should assume their own responsibility as much as possible

and depend on the state as little as possible." In other words, the
major reason for keeping Lucy at home was that her parents reasoned that "as long as they were able to do so it was their Christian duty to care for their own unfortunate daughter."[39] Bishop
Hochstetler's children petitioned the governor for his release, and,
after serving three months, he was freed. Hochstetler died six
years later—never having criticized anyone for his treatment.

The Amish parents believed they were doing the very best they
could for their daughter. Some of the sensationalism surrounding
this case may have resulted from the non-Amish community's desire to discredit the Amish church by portraying a bishop as an
evil, heartless man. In any event, the person who reported Hochstetler to the legal authorities was a former Amishman. His explanation that the daughter had been imprisoned because she wished
to leave the Amish church was certainly without foundation, but
perhaps it struck a responsive chord among ex-members. The in-
formant made his report to the deputy sheriff, who had been raised
in a somewhat dysfunctional Amish family and had subsequently
left the church. Some observers suspect that the deputy sheriff
was largely responsible for the arrest.

The Amish parents' strong sense of individual responsibility,
mild distrust of the state, and profound teachings of humility and
nonresistance made the family reluctant to use the state-run insane asylum or, when accused, to defend themselves. The situation was resolved when the family accepted the court order to
commit Lucy to the mental hospital. The children explained their
father's behavior, his attitude toward individual responsibility, his
attitude toward the state, and his lack of familiarity with the dominant culture to the clemency board and to the governor. Letters
and statements from nonfamily members describing conditions in
mental hospitals questioned the charge of assault and battery against
the bishop.

Although justice appears to have miscarried in Hochstetler's
case, there have been verified instances of child abuse among the
Old Order Amish.[40] In spite of strong moral teachings and close
community surveillance, a population of well over 130,000 living
in diverse communities in twenty-two states can be expected to
have problems. Historically, the Amish have disciplined their own
members; however, they have also stressed obeying the laws of the
state. In cases of abuse, this can raise a dilemma. When is it appropriate for the church to discipline a member, and when is it the legal or moral responsibility of the church to report a transgression
to the state—either to the police or to a social service agency? The

confessor-priest relationship in the Catholic church parallels the individual-community relationship among the Amish. In both situations, the individual makes a religious confession prior to taking communion. What about a case that is suspected, but to which the perpetrator has not confessed in church? Then whose duty is it to report, and to whom? Where there are sympathetic mental health departments and sensitive understanding of Amish ways, the Amish are often appreciative of the help available to them and will voluntarily seek it out.

Immunization

Is immunization safe—spiritually, physically, practically, and morally? Immunizations against diphtheria, pertussis (whooping cough), tetanus (lockjaw), poliomyelitis, rubeola (measles), and rubella (three-day measles) are now required of all children entering school in the United States, unless their parents have a religious conviction against immunization. No court cases have involved Old Order Amish noncompliance with immunization because the federal government and the states exempt individuals who are conscientiously opposed. Because exemptions are obtainable, state medical personnel and private physicians need to use persuasion to obtain compliance. In health matters, the Amish are pragmatists. When approached with facts by individuals whom they trust and when immunization is easy to obtain, most Amish are willing to be immunized. Knowledge of the Amish culture, flexibility, and diligence on the part of health personnel generally lead to high compliance rates.[41] Although pockets of resistance need to be respected and not ignored, their number is decreasing as the advantages of immunization become evident.

The Amish church organization is supremely congregational. Twice a year, before each communion service, the local church district examines itself to determine if the congregation is of one mind and has achieved consensus on important issues. Within a limited range, rules of behavior or even belief vary between church districts. Thus, one church district may leave the question of immunization up to the family, while another district might teach that immunization betrays a lack of faith in God. Both beliefs are compatible with Amish religion. Because the beliefs are inconsistent does not mean that one of them is the "real" Amish belief. The Amish have no centralized authority to determine orthodoxy or to speak for them; ultimately, the local congregation is supreme.

Therefore, caution must be exercised when generalizing about a specific belief or behavior—including attitudes toward immunization.

Old Order Amish and Old Order Mennonite parents of parochial school children in Pennsylvania who seek religious exemption from immunization sign a form that reads in part:

> I do object on religious grounds to have above named child immunized . . . Romans 12:2, Be not conformed to this world; Matthew 6:34, Take therefore no thought for the morrow; Also in Proverbs we are admonished that what we fear shall come upon us, but the desire of the righteous shall be granted. . . . I am most concerned for the well being, Physical as well as Spiritual for the above named child and should the need arise at any time for treatment of *any* disease, it is my aim that the family Doctor be informed and trust that he will treat the child to the best of his knowledge.[42]

The argument that *everyone* accepts immunization does not persuade Old Order Amish individuals and church districts that have religious objections to immunization. Such an argument goes against both biblical teachings on nonconformity to the world (Romans 12:2) and the Amish emphasis on individual and communal responsibility.[43]

Some Amish interpret immunization as putting faith in men rather than in God. "I like to think like David in the second book of Samuel, 24th chapter. 'Let us now fall into the hands of the Lord for His mercies are great and let me not fall into the hands of men.'"[44] Similarly, immunization can be seen as a lack of trust in God: "As for me, I'm not for the shots, as I don't feel it's right. Let's trust in God instead of in shots."[45] An Amish correspondent compared immunization to insurance. "I was taught it is a form of insurance and we don't believe in having insurance in case the future might bring a misfortune or loss. So why vaccinate for a disease that isn't even present in a child's body?"[46] Supporting immunization, another Amish person wrote: "I believe it's our duty to protect our children where we can. But I also believe if God sees fit to take our children from this life He will fulfill His plans."[47] Another said: "I myself, feel we have a responsibility to protect our children's health as well as we know how to. I'd say it's tempting the power above to purposely expose your family. Those same people would surely call a vet if their animals were exposed to a serious disease."[48]

Probably more Amish are concerned about the physical dangers of immunization than the spiritual dangers. Many anti-immunization articles and books circulate among them. Individual Amish are concerned about poisons being introduced into the child's body, the possibility of brain damage, or a link with crib death; and they worry that a child may come down with the disease he or she is being immunized against.[49] Amish favoring immunization counteract such arguments with accounts of people who did not receive the shots and became very ill or even died.[50]

Amish seek sound information on which to make realistic health decisions. This offers an opportunity to health professionals to make such information easily available. The Amish are more likely to consider the information if they have confidence in its source. Thus, midwives, family physicians, chiropractors, nurses, and individuals who are known personally to the Amish are most likely to have an influence.

The practical difficulties Amish face in obtaining immunizations should not be ignored. Nurses in an immunization program in Lancaster County "found that they [the Amish] weren't philosophically opposed to immunizations but it just wasn't convenient for them and so they weren't motivated to do it."[51] Amish farm families lead a full, busy life. Time and money need to be carefully managed. Even if one is not religiously opposed to immunization, the practical person faced with limited resources will ask: Are baby shots worth it? What are the risks and the advantages of having my children vaccinated? Is it worth the monetary expense? Will immunizations involve a long trip in a buggy, or hiring an expensive car and driver? Immunization clinics scheduled conveniently within the community, in an Amish school or home, have improved compliance. Medical personnel must be courteous if they wish the Amish parents to bring their children back for subsequent vaccinations.[52]

The Amish are often viewed as unchanging. Amish responses to modern medicine, however, show a steady acceptance of medical interventions of a corrective and preventive nature. Medical personnel should respect Amish opposition to specific medical practices but also continue to offer services to individual families. An intriguing interpretation of opposition is offered by an Amishman opposed to immunization: "Opposed does not mean we will never do such a thing . . . we feel it is too much of a luxury and not a necessity to take the shots. But now, . . . the illness is worse without shots, so we can say it has become a necessity to take them. We would compare it to a ride in a helicopter. Our parents would have said it's a luxury and they were opposed. But still helicopters are used among the plain people for a medical emergency. Often it's hard to make a line between a luxury and a necessity."[53]

Although only a minority of Amish oppose vaccinations, the topic engenders strong feelings.[54] Immunization also stirs strong sentiments among their neighbors, especially during an epidemic of preventable disease. A public school board member complained of uninoculated Amish children riding on the school bus. "I think that's just wrong, that one family can hold hostage 80 kids, 100 kids."[55] After an Amish school child came down with measles, all the children who rode on the school buses received immunizations, and the whole Amish community responded overwhelmingly to a vaccination clinic.[56] A non-Amish person in Goshen, Indiana, complained, "I have a two-year-old daughter and a wife who is eight months pregnant. I'm afraid to go anywhere where the Amish might be."[57] Some Amish wonder why non-Amish who have received their protective immunizations are afraid.

Since the advent of required immunization, epidemics of poliomyelitis, whooping cough, measles, and rubella have disproportionately affected Amish populations. In Pennsylvania, I was told that measles was "an Amish disease," and during the epidemic of 1979 people referred to "Amish polio."[58] Health officials are concerned about outbreaks of contagious diseases among the Amish because individuals travel extensively to other Amish settlements and gather in large groups at weddings and funerals, quickly spreading the disease from one location to another.[59]

The Amish believe they have a moral responsibility not to bring harm or injury to anyone. They feel a responsibility to non-Amish neighbors as well as to other members of the Amish community. This can be interpreted as an argument in favor of immunization: "For the sake of good relations with our fellowmen it is important that we make an effort to cooperate [with the immunization program.]" In one settlement, when the Amish understood that nonsymptomatic adults could be carriers of polio, they requested vaccination. One grandfather reportedly said, "I'm so old I'm sure I can't get it, but I would feel terrible if I caused a young child to be crippled for life. So I took the vaccine." Another Amishman said, "We're doing this to help protect our English neighbors."[60]

The general acceptance of immunization by the Amish is a happy illustration of successful negotiations between the Amish and representatives of the state. The Amish and state medical personnel have both exhibited flexibility. State officials did not try to legislate or force compliance, which would likely have engendered resistance. Rather, officials worked to find ways to communicate and to present meaningful facts to the Amish. And the Amish were generally willing to listen and to engage in dialogue. State officials brought information and services to the Amish instead of expecting the Amish to come to them. The Amish, in turn, opened their schools and homes as temporary clinics. These negotiations enabled the Amish to maintain a "separation from the world" but at the same time to comply with demands of the larger society. The health departments negotiated the immunization of a significant population and successfully reduced general morbidity. With extra work and effort, both groups profited and both maintained their integrity.

Summary

In the broadest sense, Amish conflicts with the state, even in health issues, are religious conflicts. For the Amish, religious belief shapes not only the details of everyday life (clothing, heating, transportation) but also their view of the world and the individual's place in it. Religious belief structures individual relationships to the supernatural, to nature, and to other persons. Amish religious views, however, are not immutable: they allow for changes in behavior and interpretation. Specific changes are accepted or rejected by group decisions based not on majority rule, nor legislation, but on congregational consensus. Consensus integrates respect for the individual with esteem for the group. Many segments of secular society that are relegated to individual or state jurisdiction are encompassed by the decision making of local Amish church districts. These decisions are seen as *religious* decisions formed under God's leadership by submissive Christians, each of whom is responsible to the church.

The Amish do not automatically accept authority endowed by academic training or institutional membership, but instead contend that individuals are ultimately responsible for their own behavior. This sense of responsibility may lead them to question some health procedures that other citizens take for granted. Amish self-determination is directed and circumscribed by their church—a community in which they actively and continually participate, not only in its rituals, but also in shaping its rules and regulations. Because individual responsibility is so closely tied to social responsibility, the Amish are amenable to programs that protect the health of others. They ask, however, to maintain the right of personal choice and to remain "a peculiar people, separated from the world."

Members of the Amish community gather for a public hearing on a proposed housing development on a farm near the village of Intercourse, Pennsylvania, in 1990. Lancaster New Era photo by Keith Baum

CHAPTER TEN

Land Use

Elizabeth Place

One of the more recent arenas of conflict involves land use, zoning, and pollution. As more Amish enter nonfarm occupations, and as encroaching suburbs encircle some Amish farms, conflicts over land use and zoning are likely to increase. Attorney Elizabeth Place explicates the nature of the growing tensions between Amish and non-Amish over a variety of environmental issues.

Old Order Amish traditions are firmly rooted in the land. According to John A. Hostetler (1987, 5–10), the agricultural life of the Amish fulfills a biblical mandate. Soil, created by God in the Garden of Eden, has spiritual significance, and humankind's first duty is to manage it as good stewards. A rural existence reinforces a basic tenet of the Amish faith: the importance of living in a redemptive community separated from the world. Rural enclaves provide isolation from worldly thinking, strengthen the Amish as an autonomous society, and enable them to resist worldly pressures. Amish land use practices have thus served to strengthen their culture. Labor-intensive farming practices provide family employment. Horse farming on small tracts of land permits conservative financing and ensures economic stability. The subdivision of farms enables a growing number of offspring to continue farming. "Grandpa" houses built next to or adjoining main farmhouses guarantee support for the elderly and maintain strong intergenerational networks of care. Family farming teaches the value of hard work, responsibility, self-discipline, and cooperation.[1]

Historically, rural existence has permitted the Amish to use their land freely with little interference by the state. Recently, however, population growth and development pressure around some Amish settlements—St. Mary's County, Maryland; Geauga County, Ohio; and Lancaster County, Pennsylvania—are increasing government intervention in land use practices. Farming practices, construction, zoning, subdivision, and development, as well as sewage management, are becoming subject to a broad array of government regulations and political considerations. Land use concerns push the Amish into direct contact with government bureaucracy and elected officials, testing their longstanding practice of abstaining from participation in public and political affairs.

Confusion and disagreements inevitably arise as increased governmental oversight and advancing development affect Amish communities. The Amish are equipped with fewer political tools than the non-Amish to deal with these concerns. They do not file lawsuits to advance their claims. Nor do they actively participate in public policy making by holding office or joining lobbying groups. Even more fundamentally, as Thomas M. Foster (1981, 34) has noted, the Amish character traits of humility, modesty, willing obedience, and social conformity make them poor contenders in bureaucratic life. According to Hostetler (1987, 13–15), the Amish response to the hostile outside world is frequently silence, moderation, ineptitude, or resignation: "When confused by a bureaucrat, outwitted by a regulation, or cursed by a worldly man, the Amish response is often silence." In New York, Amish dairy farmers face twenty-one pages of regulations regarding graded milk in cans and over one hundred pages for Grade A milk. As one Amishwoman whose husband left dairy farming explained, "We couldn't cope with the milk inspectors. We'd get one thing right and they'd want something else" (Olshan 1990a, 12).

The Amish settlement in Lancaster County, Pennsylvania, faces acute development and population pressures. For this reason, it provides a useful example of how the Amish have responded to growing state regulation of land use. The Lancaster settlement is the oldest continuously farmed Amish settlement and the second largest in the United States.[2] Lancaster County is developing at a remarkable pace. In the last thirty years, the population has increased by 143,000, and development has claimed 83,000 acres of farmland (*New Era*, 15 October 1990). Observers estimate that 5,000 acres of farmland are being converted to nonagricultural use every year.[3] Increased demands on the land by industrialization, suburbanization, tourism, and farming, as well as the polluting effects of farming on water quality, have increased local and state involvement in land use regulations. The relationship of the Amish to the land is under great pressure. Not only is outside scrutiny increasing, the Amish population itself is burgeoning at a time when affordable farmland for the upcoming generation has become scarce.[4] Amish entanglement in land use issues in Lancaster County has spiraled as they have adapted to a rapidly changing social environment.

Farming Practices

The stability and productivity of their farms has long earned the Amish a reputation as industrious and gifted tillers of the soil. Kollmorgen (1942, 20) reports that the Amish in Europe were among the first to stall-feed their cattle, rotate crops, irrigate meadows, and use natural fertilizers, as well as clover and alfalfa pastures, to restore fertility to the soil. More recently they have also been praised for their energy-conserving practices, relying on human and animal energy instead of advanced technology and fossil fuel as the mainstay of their farming operations.[5] Although the Amish continue to use horses and mules to pull their plows, they have also selectively adopted modern innovations. Amish farmers today in Lancaster County use mechanical milkers, modern seeds, veterinary services, artificial cattle insemination, and pesticides, and also subscribe to major agricultural periodicals. Many types of modern farm implements have been adapted for Amish use by combining gasoline-driven engines with true horse power.[6]

The impetus for change in farming techniques over the years has largely come from within the Amish community, with careful consideration given to the impact of change on Amish lifestyles. Adaptation, however, has occasionally been forced on the Amish by outside forces. For example, in the late 1960s, prompted in part by health concerns, milk inspectors in Lancaster County began to require dairy farmers to store milk in refrigerated bulk milk tanks with automatic agitators—technology forbidden to the Amish. The Amish reluctantly conceded, but only after negotiations with the inspectors in which the Amish agreed to use 12-volt battery-powered (instead of 110-volt electricity) agitators and refrigeration units powered by diesel engines.[7]

In the late 1980s and early 1990s, external pressures once again squeezed the Amish—this time in the environmental domain. In the winter of 1989, the Lancaster Amish community was shaken when two of its farmers were fined, under a state environmental law, for permitting water to run off cattle pastures and barnyards into nearby gullies. In one case, the water was dispersed onto a field across the street from the farm, with the nearest stream at least half a mile away. The water passed through cattle exercise areas as it left the property, and the authorities presumed it carried manure, which might eventually pollute ground water. A few careless Amish farmers had also been fined for isolated incidents in the past. The farmers who were issued these new citations were, however, following customary farming practices, and their citations aroused great uncertainty among the Amish.

State scrutiny of farming practices rose with Pennsylvania's commitment to reduce nutrient pollution of the Chesapeake Bay.[8] The most egregious industrial pollution had been restricted, and attention now turned to Lancaster County, home to 25 percent of Pennsylvania's livestock. Manure runoff from Lancaster County farms, a major cause of the bay's nutrient pollution, also contaminates the local water supply.[9] A U.S. geological survey of well samples near Amish farms found that 67 percent of the wells contained nutrient levels above the safe drinking water standard (*Controlling* 1990, 6).

Amish farmers have long used manure to fertilize their fields and have been rewarded with generous crop yields. In recent years, the subdivision of Amish farms has produced greater concentrations of animals, yielding even more manure per acre. Since most Amish farmers apply manure on the basis of disposal needs rather than crop nutrient needs, the potential for runoff is great.[10] This is particularly true when, according to common practice, manure is spread on frozen ground throughout the winter. Accumulating manure until springtime increases the spreading time—already considerable when using horse-drawn equipment—and interferes with planting.

Nutrient pollution is also caused by Amish agricultural practices, which permit the erosion of manure-enriched soil. Moldboard plowing, preferred by the Amish because it requires less power than other plowing methods, leaves no crop residue on fields, thus increasing the incidence of soil runoff.[11] Other erosion problems stem from decreased farm size and increased concentrations of animals. To maximize land use, many farmers plant all available land, leaving no grass waterways to catch sediment-laden runoff. Animals concentrated in barnyards cause manure to congest in areas that, denuded of vegetation, are particularly susceptible to erosion. Erosion around barns due to horse traffic presents further problems. Since many barns have been built near streams, the danger of water contamination is great.

Although these conditions have existed on Amish farms for years, only recently have government officials threatened to enforce environmental laws. While no statute specifically authorizes the state to control agricultural practices, general authority to regulate water pollution caused by manure runoff is contained in two state statutes that have been applied to farming activities.[12] The farmers mentioned above were cited by the Pennsylvania Fish Commission under the Fish and Boat Code, which contains a broadly worded littering provision making it unlawful to deposit any substance in such a manner that it is carried into the water.[13] The statute is the basis for most enforcement action against farmers in Pennsylvania. This occurs because the Fish Commission is quick to issue citations and also because the statute is the most effective vehicle for citizens seeking redress when dissatisfied with a neighbor's farming practices. In fact, the citations issued in the winter of 1989 were probably initiated by complaints from nonfarming neighbors who, in search of rural serenity, ironically had purchased their building lots from one of the cited farmers.

The Pennsylvania Department of Environmental Resources (DER) is also empowered to control water pollution by virtue of the Clean Streams Law, which prohibits the discharge of any substance that results in pollution[14] and which authorizes DER to regulate activities that create a danger of pollution.[15] The act prohibits the discharge of sewage (defined to include animal waste) unless a permit has been issued.[16] DER, however, waives the permit requirement for the storage or land application of manure if the practices contained in DER's Manure Management Manual are followed.[17]

Government agencies, such as the Lancaster County Conservation District and the USDA Soil Conservation Service, are available to inform farmers of the law and to provide them with technical assistance in its implementation. Most Amish farmers, however, do not solicit government aid, and the agencies do not initiate contact unless complaints have been filed. Many Amish farmers are not acquainted with DER's manure management requirements. One conservation district official estimated that the district has contact with less than 10 percent of Amish farmers. Moreover, since the manure management manual has not been formally issued as legally binding regulations, farmers who do contact the authorities are advised that implementation is discretionary. DER does not have a standard permit procedure for farmers to follow if they do not implement the manual. Since the Amish object to government funding, financial assistance available under government programs provides little incentive for them to follow the manure manual.[18] Amish farmers face significant expense to implement voluntary practices, which they fear will not protect them from prosecution under the broad wording of the environmental statutes.

The erosion problems encountered on Amish farms are regulated by DER's authority to control potential sources of pollution as well.[19] All persons engaged in activities that disturb the earth, including plowing or tilling, must develop and implement an erosion and sediment control plan.[20] The erosion regulations are typically enforced against developers rather than farmers, however, and there is no requirement that plans be reviewed or filed with any government agency. This honor system has compelled neither Amish nor non-Amish farmers to develop erosion control plans. Although the Soil Conservation Service will develop plans without charge, many farmers become aware of the plan requirement only when they request help on a specific erosion problem. Typically this occurs when a municipality requires farmers to implement a soil conservation plan as a condition for expanding farming operations, or when a plan is required for a federal loan. Fewer than half of all farmers have developed plans, and a smaller number implement them (*Controlling* 1990, 16). The numbers are even lower among the Amish. Thus, farms are typically inspected only if a complaint is received.

The citations issued to the Amish farmers in the winter of 1989 alerted others to the state's enforcement powers, which had largely lain dormant. The Amish felt vulnerable. It is impossible to prevent manure runoff completely, yet any discharge constitutes pollution or littering under the law, exposing farmers to fines of one hundred dollars per day as enforced by the Fish Commission.[21] One Amish writer noted, "It has come to the point that the Game Commission and the D.E.R. have clamped down on the dairyman for any wash-off of manure. This can come from exercising lots, spreading of manure, or any possibility of raw manure finding its way directly to ever flowing streams of water" (G. L. Fisher 1989). The writer warned of one non-Amish farmer who was fined one hundred dollars per day until his fine reached ten thousand dollars, at which point his cattle were taken to satisfy the fine. He also wrote of a rumored regulation that would permit only one cow per every two acres of land, effectively putting farmers out of business. He expressed the general bewilderment of the Amish community in his closing comments: "The writer's opinion is, this is only scratching the surface of what is going on today by the law makers. We need help. The problems are greater than we as farmers can handle. . . . This report is true, and we would better get awake before it is too late. Such incidents we sometimes read about from foreign countries, but this is the United States, the land of freedom (Fisher 1989).

The Amish do not generally request information from government officials. In fact, many officials contend that they deliberately avoid learning about regulations that might infringe on their farming practices. While many Amish have consulted with the Cooperative Extension Service of Pennsylvania State University (an organization that provides education and technical advice about a broad array of farming issues) over the years, it has been viewed as a resource for farmers rather than as a government agency.[22] In contrast, both the Lancaster County Conservation District and the Soil Conservation Service have more often been viewed as government enforcement agencies dispensing public funds—and many Amish have kept their distance. The citations by the Fish Commission changed this pattern—at least momentarily. The fines stirred such concern among the Amish about losing their land to unreasonable regulations that some non-Amish friends organized a meeting in a local fire hall to bring the Amish face to face with government officials.

The meeting, well attended by Amish farmers, was a step forward in educating them about their responsibilities under the law and clarifying rumors of impending regulations. It also quelled some of their fears that developers and nonfarming neighbors would contact authorities about the slightest bit of runoff and drive them off their farms. The authorities acknowledged the difficulty of preventing all nutrient runoff. DER and conservation district officials assured farmers that environmental regulations would not be enforced if they implemented soil conservation plans.[23] The Fish Commission made no such promise, but it pledged more lenient treatment to farmers with plans in place.

It would be an overstatement to say that the Amish welcome scrutiny of their farming practices. Farmers in general, and the Amish in particular, are an independent lot wary of government oversight. It is difficult for the Amish to understand that the same farming practices used for generations are no longer acceptable. The impact of an individual farmer's actions on the distant Chesapeake Bay is hard to conceptualize. To some farmers, it seems unjust that authorities scrutinize farming practices when the influx of suburban developments, with their storm water runoff and on-lot septic systems, also tax the land. Nevertheless, word is slowly spreading through the Amish community that manure management and erosion control are important means of protecting water quality and improving soil conditions on farms. A few Amish entrepreneurs, with the encouragement of DER, have even taken the initiative of developing a novel manure composting operation. As much as the prospect of developing government plans goes against their tradition of isolationism, the Amish are a law-abiding people who view their stewardship of the land as a sacred responsibility.

Rather than remaining aloof from the realm of government regulation, there is growing awareness that government regulations can protect the farmer and the land.

It is too early to assess the impact of growing government farming regulations on Amish lifestyles. Proposed manure management legislation might eventually prohibit winter spreading. This could force Amish farmers to abandon exclusive reliance on horse-drawn spreaders and to hire non-Amish farmers to spread manure in the spring. The financial costs of complying with manure management and soil erosion control requirements are also unclear. Farms must be individually evaluated to determine which measures are appropriate. Excessive costs could, however, pressure the Amish to accept government funding in order to comply. Soil Conservation Service officials report an increase in the number of Amish signing up for federally guaranteed loans. This represents a shift in traditional Amish practices and causes concern that their conservative financing—so important to the stability of their farming operations—is being eroded.

Significantly, large numbers of Amish have taken an active role in opposing the state's proposed manure management legislation, attending a series of local meetings at which they signed petitions against the bill and confirming their opposition at a state hearing at which the petitions were presented. The Amish are calling for a voluntary program of manure management, claiming that the environment will be properly served by farmer education rather than government oversight. The Amish remain wary of the long-term impact that regulations will have on their lifestyle. The climate of fear has been partially dissipated through dialogue with authorities, however, and the Amish are showing a new willingness to cooperate with them in protecting the environment.

Agricultural Zoning

Zoning is an important tool in land use management and is increasingly used to protect agricultural land from development. It affects the Amish in a complex way, both protecting the viability of agriculture and restraining Amish ventures into nonfarming enterprises.

In Pennsylvania, local governments have been delegated authority to pass ordinances containing "provisions for the protection and preservation of natural resources and agricultural land and activities."[24] This is accomplished through many different zoning schemes: exclusive agricultural zoning, very low residential density control, subdivision restrictions, and lot frontage restrictions. Municipalities in Pennsylvania have traditionally chosen to impose minimum lot size requirements (Buchanan 1986, 869). Although agricultural zoning substantially reduces the value of property, zoning schemes designed to preserve farmland have received favorable treatment from the courts against challenges that they are exclusionary and confiscatory and therefore unconstitutional.[25] In one recent Pennsylvania decision, a minimum lot requirement of fifty acres was upheld.[26] In another, a two-dwelling maximum on prime farmland, regardless of tract size, was upheld, since the ordinance was an integral part of a larger, comprehensive zoning scheme.[27]

Effective agricultural zoning protects the Amish agricultural lifestyle. By segregating agricultural operations, it reduces conflict between competing land uses and minimizes nuisance complaints against farmers.[28] It makes farmland more affordable and stems the tide of the development of farmland into suburbia. Effective agricultural zoning, limiting residential development to one building lot for each 20 or more acres, exists in thirty-three of forty-one townships in Lancaster County, covering 250,000 acres (Daniels 1990). In the heart of the Amish settlement, however, ordinances permit one house per acre in areas zoned agricultural, providing little protection against development.

The Amish interest in stemming development by effective zoning is tempered somewhat by their own interest in development. Amish farms today are generally small. In 1900, the average Amish farm in Lancaster County was eighty to one hundred acres. By 1970, many farms had been subdivided to forty acres or less (G. L. Fisher 1978, 111). Further subdivision of many farms for the upcoming generation of farmers is not economically feasible, and many young farmers are prevented from buying new land by prohibitive land prices. With a population that has doubled in the past twenty years on a shrinking amount of farmland, the Amish can no longer support themselves in Lancaster County by farming alone.

This places their community in a sensitive relationship with zoning policy. While the Amish wish to preserve agricultural land, they are increasingly using it for nonfarm purposes to make a living.[29] Many Amish have small businesses on their farms or in their homes which supplement farm income or constitute the family's primary earnings. Others work in Amish-owned industries situated off the farms. These businesses include carriage and machine shops, which produce goods and services needed by the local Amish community, and furniture and cabinet shops, which produce goods for the tourist or regional market. These businesses often violate zoning ordinances, either because their owners fail to secure special exceptions from the municipality or because such businesses are prohibited in rural districts (*Intelligencer Journal*, 15 August 1987). Township officials have generally enforced zoning laws against the Amish only upon receiving complaints. Increased enforcement actions are likely, however, as the use of farmland receives greater scrutiny. Complaints by nonfarming neighbors recently closed the business of an Amishman who made barn ventilators on his farm.

Especially where farmland is scarce, cottage industries in rural areas provide necessary employment for the Amish, who prefer to work at or near their homes and within their ethnic group. To protect the cohesion of their community in this manner, the Amish have approached local authorities, seeking accommodation between their lifestyle and zoning ordinances. In Leacock Township, where over 80 percent of the land is owned by the Amish, several Amishmen took the unusual step of hiring an attorney and a planning consultant to obtain zoning changes that would permit the expansion of home businesses. They successfully increased the size of businesses permitted in rural districts.[30] A group of Amish farmers in Eden Township petitioned authorities to allow businesses in agricultural and residential zones. Regulations had permitted only businesses that were located in residences (*New Era*, 16 November 1988). The township agreed to permit certain business uses in the farm support zone and also considered ordinance revisions to permit small businesses in accessory buildings on farms outside of these zones.

Amish farmers in Colerain Township supported zoning revisions that permitted customary home businesses to operate without a special exception from the zoning board. They did, however, protest township requirements that larger family support businesses must exist as a secondary use in agricultural areas. One Amishman in an agricultural area had subdivided his land into two lots—one three-and-a-half acres and the other ten acres. The larger lot was farmed, but regulations prohibited the expansion of a carriage shop on the smaller lot, since it was not secondary to farm use. This man was cited for failing to obtain a building permit when he expanded his business without obtaining a variance or zoning change. Over thirty Amish attended a township supervisors' meeting in his support. Colerain Township is considering permitting businesses in zoned agricultural districts, even where the land is not actively farmed; however, such businesses would be limited in size and use.

Although organized efforts spearheaded by the Amish to change zoning ordinances are still the exception rather than the rule, Lancaster's Amish are more frequently communicating their dissatisfaction with zoning regulations to township officials. It is not unusual for large groups of Amish to appear at public zoning meetings to support those seeking approval for special land uses.

County planning officials are sensitive to the delicate balance that must be struck in zoning policies to maintain the county's economic prosperity. Agriculture is the foundation of the local economy. Virtually all farms are family-owned, with 20 percent owned by Plain Sect families who undergird Lancaster's thriving tourist industry.[31] The Lancaster County Planning Commission states in its model ordinances for farm-based businesses that supplemental income through farm-based businesses is essential to allow Amish families to work together and to ensure the economic viability of the family farm.[32] This policy statement serves as a good reminder of the latent power that the Amish quietly hold. Although outside the political mainstream, their importance to the local economy makes them influential constituents.

Zoning regulations are viewed as a mixed blessing by the Amish. Some are caught in the classic Catch-22 of zoning policy. While they favor farmland protection where the agricultural use of their land has been compromised by encroaching development, they want the right to sell it at its development market value. One Amish farmer is surrounded on three sides by tourist development, rendering his land of little value for agricultural use. Only if he sells his land to developers will he realize sufficient income to purchase another farm. While the Amish have historically refused to sell their land for development, in the early 1990s several Amish farms were sold for this purpose. If this trend continues, the agricultural base of the Amish community could quickly be eroded.

Land Development

Because the Amish have lived in rural separation from the world, they have typically developed their land independently, with little concern for land use regulations or government officials. If an Amish family wished to add a grandpa house to an existing house or to divide land and build a new house for a recently married child, the construction began without concern for zoning ordinances, building permits, land development plans, subdivision plans, hydrogeological studies, land surveys, storm water management plans, or sewage permits. As a rural people, the Amish are unaccustomed to outside control over the use of their land. Moreover, their cultural values and religious beliefs have emphasized self-sufficiency and separation from the world, leading them to eschew government programs, subsidies, and regulations. One farmer, forced to seek a special exception in order to build an Amish schoolhouse on his land, said, "I have difficulty telling my neighbors what to do with their land. If I want to take a little corner of my land and build a school, I used to be able to do that" (*Intelligencer Journal*, 2 February 1989).

As the density of the rural population increases, many local authorities feel they can no longer "look the other way" and make exceptions for the Amish. Increasingly, townships are requiring strict compliance with land use regulations to minimize the impact of land development on their communities. Control over development is necessitated in part because of nitrate pollution caused by on-lot sewage disposal systems and by storm water runoff from land development.

Increased enforcement of the complex body of land use laws compels the Amish to interact with many layers of government bureaucracy to obtain approval for land development. Dealing with the authorities—local planning and zoning boards, sewage enforcement officers, county planning commissions and DER officials, professional surveyors, and engineers—is time-consuming, frustrating, and often expensive. One Amishman prepared a storm water management plan required in order to build a house on his farm for his son. He learned that he would have to spend over ten thousand dollars to change water drainage conditions that had existed on his land for sixty years.

The Amish balk especially when the authorities agree that a landowner's actions do not harm the environment, even though they violate regulations designed to control problems in more dense developments. Though compelled by their faith to be law-abiding citizens, the Amish have difficulty accepting outside rules applied to their unique lifestyle. It is not uncommon for them to throw up their hands in frustration with the bureaucratic maze. One Amish farmer said, "I told them I would just have to start building while they fiddled around with their red tape."

In 1989, the case of one Amishman who failed to comply with

regulations received national attention. Jacob Hershberger bought a tract of land from his father-in-law and built a barn after obtaining a building permit. The permit was rescinded when officials learned that he planned to add a residence for his family of nine in the upper level of the barn. Regulations prohibited building a residence without a sewage permit.[33] Soil tests needed to obtain the sewage permit were not conducted until after the barn's construction. The test results showed that the only sewage system permitted at the building site was a raised sand mound, which would cost several thousand dollars. Hershberger opposed this type of technology on religious and economic grounds. He sought instead to use a privy for "black water" and to run the "gray water" from household cleaning and washing into his garden.[34]

The township refused to issue a sewage permit. It contended that water pumped into the barn constituted "water under pressure," thus preventing the use of a privy under state law. When Hershberger installed a privy and inhabited the residence without the permit, he was fined for violating the Pennsylvania Sewage Facilities Act. Despite great public outcry, he was jailed. Township officials charged with administering the statute acknowledged that Hershberger was not polluting the environment. Nevertheless, they were not willing to make a special exception for an Amishman, particularly since non-Amish also suffered economic hardship when complying with the act.

This incident illustrates the difficulty of applying statutes promulgated for the population at large to the Amish. The septic system required of Hershberger was designed to treat four hundred gallons of waste per day, calculated to accommodate large quantities of water used in modern homes with flush toilets, automatic dishwashers, washing machines, and garbage disposals. The regulations made no allowance for a simple rural lifestyle. They were designed to protect public health in densely populated areas with heavy sewage output.

Similar tension between public regulations and Amish ways are found in other areas of land development. Families in the Lancaster area who want to build a grandpa apartment attached to their main house often have to jump over many regulatory hurdles. They may be required to (1) obtain a land survey, (2) prepare a storm water management plan, (3) submit a land development plan to the planning commission, (4) prepare a sewage planning module for review by the municipality and DER, (5) prepare an erosion and sediment control plan if grading or excavation is involved, (6) obtain a preliminary hydrogeological study if located in an area with a high nitrate level, (7) obtain a sewage permit from a municipal sewage enforcement officer, and (8) obtain a building permit from the township. The building of a one- or two-bedroom grandpa apartment onto an existing home—often considered building a second dwelling rather than an addition to a home— could cost thousands of dollars in planning costs alone. While these planning requirements are meant to protect the environment, the unintended effect is to undermine an important part of Amish culture—caring for aging relatives in the context of the extended family while allowing them to live independently.

Some townships have addressed this problem by permitting elder cottage housing, a policy endorsed by the Lancaster County Planning Commission. This is a small temporary structure for elderly relatives which connects to the existing sewer and water lines of the main residence. It is not considered land development, thereby eliminating many of the planning requirements. The building must be removed, however, when the relative no longer resides in it, rendering this compromise wasteful and unsatisfactory in the eyes of many Amish.[35]

In an effort to address these issues, which were highlighted by the Hershberger jailing, the National Committee for Amish Religious Freedom approached DER to initiate a dialogue between DER and the Amish. The committee was not seeking favors for the Amish but hoped to facilitate discussion and awareness of the negative impact of certain regulations on Amish lifestyles. Meetings with high-level state officials culminated in a "town meeting" between DER officials, political representatives, sewage enforcement officers, and members of the Amish community.

As a result of this effort, DER made several policy revisions. It eliminated the requirement of a planning module component and preliminary hydrogeological study for grandpa apartments where the new sewage flow was less than four hundred gallons. Sewage enforcement officers were given discretionary powers to determine if existing sewage systems were adequate, thus eliminating the need for a sewage permit for a grandpa house. Regarding subdivisions of land with nitrate levels above 5 ppm and less than 10 ppm, hydrogeological studies were no longer required if the municipality had a Sewage Facilities Act base plan and restricted development by nitrate levels, or if landowners of fifty acres implemented a nutrient management plan.

DER agreed to permit a 40 percent reduction in the absorption area of sewage systems using a privy. Most Amish have inside bathrooms with flush toilets, but not automatic clothes washers or dishwashers. DER also authorized an additional 30 percent reduction for dwellings without electrical service, automatic dishwashers, and automatic clothes washers, contingent upon the local municipality's requiring a standard system if a change in use would occur. DER verified that a municipality cannot prohibit a privy on a lot larger than one acre without pressurized water. It stated that hand-pumped water does not constitute water under pressure. DER continued to insist that gray water must be treated. Thus, despite the many concessions, Hershberger still needed to install a system to handle gray water. He chose instead to sell his land and move from Lancaster County.[36]

Land development in Lancaster County is closely tied to agricultural practices. Some Amish are unable to develop their land because nitrate levels exceed 10 ppm. DER prohibits all development in areas with high nitrate levels unless a spray irrigation sewage system is installed—an expense of sixteen thousand dollars. Although an additional residence system contributes little to the overall nitrate problem, in the absence of effective manure management, it is administratively easier to address the problem by withholding sewage permits. High nitrate levels are also causing townships to forbid the installation of privies, traditional on small Amish school plots. As nitrate pollution restricts the Amish in developing their land, they may be more willing to implement effective manure management plans.

Preservation of Farmland

With a growing population and a thriving economy demanding ever more land, it is widely feared that the agrarian base of Lancaster County is in jeopardy. Plain Sect families, who, as noted above, own 20 percent of Lancaster farmland, have historically maintained the agricultural use of their land. But with tremendous population growth in the Amish community and a shortage of affordable farmland,[37] the relationship of the Amish to the land is changing. Their traditional religious tenets hold that they are only stewards, "renting" God's land during their stay on earth. The harsh economic realities of development are forcing them to view the land as a commodity.

Many Amish farmers hold land worth hundreds of thousands of dollars if sold for development. At the same time, their farming practices are increasingly scrutinized by their new nonfarming neighbors and environmental officials. While only a handful of

Plain Sect farms have been sold to developers, the purchase prices have been very tempting: 1.4 million dollars for an 83-acre farm and 2.1 million for a 68-acre farm (*New Era*, 18 October 1990). The land quickly becomes a commodity when Plain Sect people realize that the million dollars gained from selling a 70-acre farm in Lancaster County could be used to purchase four 150-acre farms in many rural areas of the country.

Public policy in Pennsylvania protects agricultural land.[38] The Agricultural Area Security Law provides that a unit of five hundred or more acres of land may be designated an agricultural security area.[39] Municipalities in which agricultural security areas are located may not "unreasonably restrict farm structures or farm practices within the area,"[40] and their ordinances must exclude from the definition of nuisance any agricultural activity in an agricultural security area conducted by "normal farming operations."[41] Limitations are placed on the state's ability to take land located within a security area by the power of eminent domain. Moreover, land within these areas is eligible for conservation easement purchases by county agricultural preserve boards. The goal of the act is to foster agricultural land use by creating pockets of farmland protected from conflicting nonfarm land use.

Amish farms make up a significant amount of the 101,000 acres of land in agricultural security areas in Lancaster County. Half of the land in a 7,700-acre security area recently created in Strasburg Township is Amish-owned.[42] Despite Amish reluctance to seek favors from government, they joined non-Amish neighbors in seeking township approval for the preserve. The desire to be protected from nuisance claims and eminent domain proceedings—particularly with the prospect of a new highway in the midst of Amish farmland—provides a strong incentive for joining.

The most noteworthy feature of the Agricultural Area Security Law, as amended by Act 149, is the creation of a one hundred million-dollar state fund to preserve agricultural land. The money, distributed as grants or matching funds to counties, is used to purchase development rights of farms approved for preservation by county agricultural land preservation boards. Prior to the establishment of the state fund, the Lancaster County Agricultural Preserve Board operated only with general county funding. The availability of state funds significantly improves the board's ability to preserve agricultural land in Lancaster County.

Act 149 is an important step in farmland preservation. Despite efforts to elicit Amish participation, however, the board has had little success in preserving farmland owned by Lancaster's Amish.

There are several reasons for Amish reluctance. The Amish have a centuries-old tradition of self-sufficiency and adamantly refuse government entanglements—including any form of government subsidy or assistance. Although the Amish are deeply concerned about the future of farming in Lancaster County, the terms commonly associated with farmland preservation—"easement" and "restrictive deed"—conjure up negative images of the government inching its way into their lives. One Amish farmer decided not to donate his development rights when he learned he would have to prepare soil conservation plans. This fear of government encroachment is reinforced by the fact that Act 149 is administered by a county agency. More importantly, the financial incentives available under the funding mechanism of Act 149 hold little appeal for a people who are strongly opposed to public assistance. Consequently, in the early 1990s, even though an Amishman sits on the Lancaster County Agricultural Preserve Board, only one Amish family has donated development rights to the board, and none has sold it development rights.

The Lancaster County Agricultural Preserve Board recently entered into an agreement to coordinate its preservation effort with Lancaster Farmland Trust—a private preservation organization. The board hoped the private organization might spearhead efforts to cultivate Amish interest in farmland preservation. Many Amish initially viewed Lancaster Farmland Trust as a government entity and were unreceptive to its overtures. The recent development of a few choice farms and a proposed ninety-home subdivision on a farm owned by a former Amishman in the heart of the Amish settlement, however, awakened Amish sensitivities to the threat of development, piquing their interest in the work of the trust and its educational efforts. Given the exorbitant value of farmland for development, the work of the Lancaster Farmland Trust will be essential for retaining land for future Lancaster County farmers.

The first conservation easements were recently placed on farms that Amish subsequently purchased. In one case, the Lancaster Farmland Trust purchased a 110-acre farm, which it then sold to an Amish farmer with a conservation easement. The trust made a six-figure investment in the property by placing a conservation easement on the farm before selling it to the Amish farmer at its agricultural value.[43] The sale grew out of the trust's Farmland Registry, which matches prospective buyers with sellers. The Amish purchaser was willing to enter into this transaction despite the fact that Lancaster Farmland Trust will eventually be reimbursed by public funds. Since this private organization acted as broker, the specter of government intrusion and the Amish fear of government subsidies faded. Lancaster Farmland Trust recently purchased two additional conservation easements on farms that were then sold to Amish farmers. In March 1991, the trust announced that for the first time in history, an Old Order Amish farmer sold a conservation easement to the trust to preserve his farm.[44]

The involvement of a few Amish farmers in farmland preservation in the early 1990s represents a significant departure from their prior practice. It has spawned interest in preservation programs in the Amish community, since these buyers are well respected by their peers. There are good reasons to expect increased Amish involvement in efforts to buy and sell protected lands in the future. At the same time, many Amish are ambivalent about participating in such programs. Even when funds flow from private sources, the Amish point out that it is not their way to burden others by accepting donations.

Despite much discussion, the Amish community has not embraced the practice of donating restrictive easements to preservation groups. The Amish note that it is rare for them to develop their land. Their tenacity as farmers makes them remarkably effective preservationists without the need for legal documents. Many are reluctant to embrace restrictions contained in the easement agreement, viewed as complicated and as restricting their ability to operate businesses on their land—an increasing necessity if families are to remain working together on the farm.[45] In the face of rapid changes in the rural character of Lancaster County, and with sons coming of age who need farmland, many Amish are reluctant to devalue their land permanently by restricting its use. The sale of their Lancaster County acreage would enable them to purchase far more acres in other parts of the country at lower prices, thus assuring land for future generations of Amish farmers.

Other Instances of Amish Activism

The Amish evidence a determined desire to remain aloof from the regulatory maze and land use policy making. Where economic necessity and lifestyle convictions collide with public policy, however, as in the case of home businesses and sewage regulations, they have approached the state in an effort to negotiate policy changes. There are other instances of activism by Lancaster

County Amish. In Leacock Township, the Amish joined their English neighbors in opposing the expansion of a quarry. They also signed petitions and attended meetings to block a ninety-acre development and joined a write-in campaign to elect antidevelopment township supervisors. In Strasburg Township, Amish voters helped to upset a prodevelopment township supervisor with reputedly anti-Amish sentiments when they voted in significant numbers for a write-in candidate. In 1988, over twelve hundred Amish turned out at a public meeting convened by the Pennsylvania Department of Transportation to review plans for a highway that would cut through the heart of the Amish settlement. Their presence drew international attention and has caused plans to be shelved until the department determines the impact of proposed routes on Plain Sect culture. While the Amish have not initiated organized opposition to controversial developments, they have shown their concern, and often opposition, by attending meetings and/or signing petitions.

Some Amish concerns are met without litigation or overt political pressure. The Amish are indisputably an important economic resource both for their agricultural output and for their contribution to tourism. Efforts are made to accommodate their concerns—for example, in the policy plans of the county Planning Commission. The governor recognized the Amish as an important cultural resource and political force in tabling the highway plans. There is also growing public awareness of the need to preserve farmland and to protect the Amish culture. Non-Amish citizens often lead the opposition to development practices that threaten agrarian culture, and they solicit Amish support along the way.

Recognition of the uniqueness of Amish culture is not reflected, however, in any systematic effort by officials to consider the impact of regulations on the Amish. Nor is there a concerted, ongoing effort by the Amish to monitor legislation or proposed policies that might compromise their lifestyle. Zoning changes that benefit developers often go unnoticed until a subdivision plan is proposed publicly—often after development is beyond prevention. Similarly, plans to extend public sewers into the county, the precursor to land development, are adopted without Amish input. Amish attention tends to focus on crisis oriented problems. Only recently the National Committee for Amish Religious Freedom began monitoring state legislative activities to alert the Amish to proposed legislation that may cause land use problems.

Even where circumstances have pushed the Amish into the public sphere, their priorities are clear: maintenance of their community and Amish ways. For example, while the Amish attended township meetings in opposition to the ninety-home development, they were conspicuously absent from the final meeting—held on an Amish wedding night. Similarly, an Amish farmer gave his regrets for failing to attend a meeting with a high-level government official. He could not make the trip, he said, because he had to fix some machinery on his farm. These priorities serve to perpetuate Amish culture—including, in large part, their avoidance of government affairs.

Amishwomen gather in Harrisburg, Pennsylvania, in 1990 in support of a bill to legitimize lay midwives. Outsiders were instrumental in organizing the Amish demonstration during Senate hearings. Wide World Photos

CHAPTER ELEVEN

The Role of Outsiders

Robert L. Kidder

 In many conflicts with state and local authorities, the Amish have benefited from the aid of sympathetic outsiders. These friends not only have assisted the Amish but also at times have organized and marshaled the Amish response to local, state, and national officials. Sociologist Robert L. Kidder describes the role of outsiders in a variety of conflicts with the state.

Separation from "the world" of all those who are not Amish has, from the very beginning, been a fundamental feature of Amish belief and practice. Donald B. Kraybill (1989, 212–34) has tendered a well-documented argument that the Amish in North America have, paradoxically, become dependent on the outside world for their economic survival even as they have increasingly diverged from mainstream modern culture. Kraybill (1989) and Hostetler (1993) have presented the case for the economic integration of the Amish with modern economic institutions. They have also shown how the cultural gap is sustained by the wary attention of Amish church members and leaders to even the most mundane of new products and services being developed by the outside world. Further, these scholars have described the Amish doctrine of nonresistance, pointing out that Amish pacifism goes beyond mere rejection of military service to complete avoidance of adversarial procedures in law courts.

It is one thing for a family patriarch to say he will not defend his farm against an outsider's treachery or a government's meddling. It is quite another for a whole group to live and even prosper in a postindustrial society that makes many decisions in the context of legal institutions premised on struggles between self-interested

This chapter is based on research supported by the National Science Foundation, Division of Law and Social Science, grant no. SES-8617794. My special thanks to John A. Hostetler for his invaluable assistance and to the many Amish people in Lancaster County, Pennsylvania, whose patience and good will made this research not only possible but enjoyable.

individuals. Hence, the survival and prosperity of the Amish is problematic because they reject fundamental American legal principles and practices. Moreover, Amish separation from the world places them outside the American melting pot, which fosters integration and the acceptance of core American values (Glazer 1975). Not only does Amish ideology make them vulnerable to economic exploitation, it invites charges of exclusivism, which could expose them to aggressive accusations of being un-American.

The growth of the Amish community, its relative immunity from harassment springing from ethnic differences or misguided patriotism, and its continued economic stability each add another paradox to Kraybill's (1989, 212) paradoxes of Amish "public relations." Kraybill identifies the paradoxes of modern Amish life in economic terms, and therefore most of his conclusions are based on economic factors. Yet, in examining Amish ways of handling disputes or conflict with the world, other less clearly economic forces and actions also contribute to the perseverance and growth of Amish communities. We could call these processes political, ideological, or moral, depending on how we slant them in macrosociological analysis. I refer to these processes as *ideological work* in order to emphasize the dynamic, creative, and responsive aspects of actions designed to legitimize change by cloaking it in the language and forms of tradition.

This chapter, based on research conducted between 1987 and 1990 in Lancaster County, Pennsylvania, describes what John A. Hostetler and I have elsewhere (1990) called a social "cocoon."[1] This cocoon around the Amish consists of an intricate web of relationships with outsiders which developed amidst the paradox of separation and dependence described by Kraybill (1989). The outsiders in the protective cocoon include ex-members, neighbors near and far, government authorities, vested interest groups, and the media, among others. The protective buffer emerged from, and continues to be produced by, interactions between Amish leaders and various elements of the non-Amish world as each group supports the other (Kraybill 1989, 212). Mutual interdependence, however, reflects more than the fact that the Amish are "entangled in the economic network of the larger social system" (Kraybill 1989, 213). In addition, the Amish have become an important symbol in the development of broader belief systems in American society. Viewing themselves as a people *apart*, the Amish may be more accurately described as a people *within*. They are a sheltered minority preserved in a cocoon—in a symbiotic relationship with the very social world that they reject. This social cocoon is the deliberate creation of activist leaders both within and without the Amish community.

Managing Relations with the "World"

The Amish do not deny that conflict is inevitable in human relations, both within their community and in dealing with the world. Their mode of dispute management is modeled on pacifist, nonlegalistic practices. Amish pacifism is well known among their neighbors and occasionally attracts widespread attention, as in the Hollywood film *Witness*. Their young men refuse military service of any kind. Amish nonresistance means a commitment to seek peace within the community and with the world outside. Should conflict arise, the Amish person should seek understanding with the other side and strive to settle differences peacefully. If outside forces, such as government bodies, demand behavior incongruent with Amish beliefs, their faith requires submission to whatever punishment or oppression outsiders might inflict. The only acceptable alternative is to abandon their homes and relocate. This doctrine of nonresistance means that they neither employ lawyers nor use litigation or threats of legal action to defend their legal rights against challenges.[2] Amish members rely on the church community to sustain them if they suffer losses as a result of their nonresistance.

Within the community, Amish responses to conflict are a good example of legal pluralism.[3] If conflict arises between Amish members, the community tries to cooperate in finding a peaceful settlement. If the church community takes a position, any member resisting it risks being excommunicated and shunned. Other members are forbidden to socialize, eat, or do business with the violator in the hope that he or she will repent and conform to the church's *Ordnung*.

Beliefs and practices described this way constitute what we usually call *culture*, in this case Amish culture. It is the face that the Amish present to the world, as well as the body of standards by which they evaluate themselves. Public images of the Amish give a slant—a set of expectations which structures what observers expect to see and hear among the Amish. Our research uncovered some important ways in which Amish practice differs from their public image and their professed philosophy. Identifying these discrepancies is important, not to debunk or demythologize the Amish, but to better understand their relationships with the outside "world"

—a significant symbol itself in the Amish world view. Stated briefly, modern Amish society is produced and reproduced not only by practices within Amish communities but by equally important planned and unexpected legal and political interactions with the world. Producing and reproducing Amish society requires constant ideological work, and an important product of that work is the cocoon that has thus far sheltered unique features of Amish life.

Part of the cocoon that surrounds Amish society is composed of two layers of discrepancy between Amish image and practice. Both layers of interaction help to preserve Amish society and sustain its antilaw ideology. Furthermore, the patterns described here put a new twist on the idea of legal pluralism. The legal activity of a special group within a larger heterogeneous society may be so intertwined with the larger legal-political system that the group's uniqueness lies not only in its internal dynamics but, more importantly, in the nature of its interaction with the external system. Instead of reaching a simple functionalist conclusion that Amish legal methods "work" because they fit with other internal elements of a system, I believe that the vitality of Amish legal pluralism is strongly influenced by relations with the larger society. This influence is facilitated by the two layers of protective discrepancy between the Amish image and the reality described below.

MISCONCEPTIONS OF AMISH SIMPLICITY

The first layer of protective discrepancy involves outsiders' misconceptions about the Amish. In addition to the economic integration about which Kraybill (1989) and others have written, Amish society is protected by the tendency of outsiders to project their own values and dreams onto Amish behavior and philosophy. Such misperceptions provide a buffer of tolerance for unconventional Amish behavior because outsiders tend to romanticize the Amish as models of American virtues.

One example concerns Amish rejection of modern technology. Outsiders usually assume that the Amish reject modern comforts in the same way that monastics take vows of silence and poverty and sleep on hard beds. Such monastic asceticism is a way of purging the individual of sinful ways. It is suffering sought for suffering's sake and a means of obtaining individual salvation. The Amish motivation for rejecting modern technology springs from a different source, although the Amish benefit from the moral credit that ascetics gain from their self-denial.

Amish asceticism is oriented toward the sociological and spiritual needs of the community, not the salvation of the individual. Being old-fashioned has value only if it helps the Amish preserve their community as a pure offering of love for God. Technological lags preserve separation from the world and avoid fractious influences within the community from eroding community solidarity. Amish choices are thus based on a practical, worldly assessment resembling social engineering more than asceticism. They do not limit the use of automobiles, electricity, telephones, and tractors to seek suffering and redemption through hardship. Rather, decisions about accepting modern conveniences are based on the anticipated effect that a new product might have on the community. Changes that might create tension within or between families or open the community to excessive dependence on outside institutions are rejected. Does a machine or service create conspicuous differences between "haves" and "have nots," or might it distract members from the community? If so, it should be banned because jealousy and envy tear at a community's roots, as do outside involvements. New technology is not rejected out of hand. The community constantly struggles with the implications of innovations.

Because outsiders usually misinterpret Amish simplicity as asceticism, neighbors sometimes view Amish adaptations as either contradictory or hypocritical. Outsiders, especially those in direct competition with Amish entrepreneurs—real estate developers, small manufacturers, farmers—may see the selective use of technology by the Amish as irrational and incongruent. They sometimes respond with resentment or anger, saying that the Amish pretend to be angels while actually using shrewd tactics along with their false ascetic image to promote their material well-being. What these outsiders really resent is the image Amish people have among more distant outsiders, and particularly distant government officials who feel pressure to make exceptions for the Amish because of the idyllic view of their asceticism.

Amish material success and rejection of suffering for suffering's sake also stir resentment among fundamentalist Christians who see them as too worldly. These Christians believe the Amish need to be evangelized to become more spiritual. This evangelical concern for the spiritual well-being of the Amish stems from the fact that the Amish do not accent *individual* salvation, with its emphasis on being saved by accepting Jesus Christ as lord and master, as heavily as modern evangelicals. The Amish view the claims of born-again Christians that they have been "saved" as expressions of pride, a vice the Amish try to avoid. They prefer to avoid theological discussion, trusting instead that what is required is simply to live a loving life in a pure (contented, happy, and caring) community. Thus, the community, and the land that sustains it, is a trust that, ideally, one generation nurtures and hands on to the next.

Consistent with this philosophy, the Amish place little emphasis on personal evangelism and individual salvation. Paradoxically, this philosophy makes them appear even more robustly worldly than the evangelicals who focus so heavily on individual sinfulness and salvation. Again, outsiders are confused by this apparent religious contradiction. Misinformed bystanders lump the Amish with other "conservative" Christian groups and misunderstand key aspects of Amish faith. To their fundamentalist critics, the Amish seem to be wallowing in the material treasures of agrarian wealth. To themselves, Amish wealth is a divine trust. As in other areas, there is a gap between public assumptions about Amish religious beliefs and the actual convictions of Amish people themselves.

The discrepancy between public images of the Amish and their own beliefs protects them against pressure by outsiders to conform to general American norms. But, as noted, it also at times exposes them to hostility from neighbors. For example, our interviews with Amish leaders and government officials revealed that when state government officials were asked by outsiders for the same special treatment given to the Amish to spare them from unacceptable legal obligations, the officials' answer was: "Well, sure, you can be exempted from [the particular legal obligation] as long as you are willing to live like the Amish." Our own interviews with state education department authorities revealed similar comments, which typically squelched outsiders' demands. The implication was that few outsiders would be willing to endure the material hardships that the Amish impose on themselves. As long as the Amish *appear* to be ascetics, outsiders, including government officials, are more willing to excuse them from inconvenient or culture-compromising legal obligations.

If voluntary poverty were part of the Amish way, it might be less important to preserve the myth of Amish asceticism. One example of the cocoon-like quality of Amish economic relationships with outsiders illustrates the importance of this myth. A drastic increase in land values in Lancaster County makes practically all land-owning Amish families conspicuously wealthy, but this escalation really hampers the ability of Amish parents to pass on farms to all their sons. Moreover, those Amish who do farm also become targets of envy and exploitation by nearby outsiders who seek economic benefits from the sale of Lancaster County land. One important defense mechanism is the empathy of more distant outsiders who harbor no economic ambitions in Amish territory but urge the "preservation of old-fashioned values," which they see in Amish society. Amish society's role as a "living museum" may well depend on a mythology that aligns the Amish with ideals held by outsiders rather than with those held by the Amish themselves.

PRACTICAL DEVIATIONS FROM PURITY
The second layer of protection that serves to protect Amish ways involves a discrepancy between the beliefs endorsed by the Amish and the actual practices they use to protect themselves from the world. While Amish behavior diverges from their own ideals—unlike the first protective discrepancy—this gap may be essential to preserve a system that allows the Amish to believe in the validity of their own ideals. In other words, while the relationships described earlier may protect Amish society by permitting the outside world to believe in the value of protecting Amish society, the next layer of relationships may be necessary to permit the Amish to believe in themselves: that is, to believe in the validity of their collective experiment—the creation of an alternative culture.

This discrepancy relates to two fundamental Amish values: (1) separation from the world—avoiding strife, impurity, and evil temptations; and (2) nonresistance—seeking peaceful solutions to conflict without contesting opposing claims. As noted earlier, these doctrines raise very practical questions. How can the Amish preserve their way of life and protect themselves and their unique communities in the midst of a superpower nation that emulates the values of science, technology, aggressive economic behavior, and military preparedness? How can a passivist preindustrial lifestyle survive in the latter stages of a twentieth-century America rife with conflict, racial and ethnic intolerance, legal confrontation, adversarial use of the law, and melting pot pressures? Does the practice of nonresistance simply mean remaining true to one's values? Is outside romanticism about Amish society sufficient to protect these communities?

Answers to these questions parallel Amish responses to technology. Instead of a slavish obedience to doctrinal discipline, the Amish make ad hoc adjustments to their environment in order to preserve their pure community. Adaptations in the domain of law and external conflict evolved differently, however, than did their adjustments to technological change. In the case of technology, whole congregations discuss and ponder possible responses. Moreover, their decisions are strictly local—each church congregation makes its own decisions about particular new gadgets, and its decisions may differ from those of other congregations. Conflict with the outside world, however, reveals a different pattern of adjustment. It is a pattern that seems to contradict the basic values of nonresistance and separation by importing the "shadow of bureaucracy" (Kraybill 1989, 86).

First, while separation from the world is the ideal, a well-developed but generally unpublicized network of relationships has developed with non-Amish individuals and groups who willingly use legal services and political action to protect the Amish. For their own reasons, these outsiders have provided additional layers to the protective social cocoon around the Amish and other conservative groups.[4] Second, although Amish ideology rejects litigation and political involvement as unacceptably confrontational, a loosely organized but politically astute national leadership group has emerged.

As described in Chapter 4, the National Steering Committee negotiates special relationships that protect the Amish from unacceptable national, state, and local regulations. The efforts of this committee are virtually identical to those of lawyers and politicians in some of America's toughest urban and bureaucratic environments. Amish lay lawyers in effect do everything we might expect of professional lawyers—lobbying, negotiating settlements, inventing and successfully selling unique legal loopholes, and advocating other members' cases before official bodies. The only elements missing from their "practice" are the acceptance of fees for services and arguing cases in court. Leaders who play this role walk a fine line, having to avoid any appearance of "contamination" from their work by conspicuous reaffirmation of their farming roots and their willingness to be inconspicuous about everything else. The efforts of these lay lawyers are, moreover, supplemented by real lawyers hired by non-Amish activists who seek to protect the Amish way of life, or lawyers who have a personal interest in helping the Amish. Decisions about such legal entanglements do not emerge from consensual meetings of congregations. Instead, long-term strategy and day-to-day decisions are guided by lay leaders with specialized abilities and political connections. The results of their work often affect all Amish congregations across North America.

The Amish Cocoon

The Amish are not alone. Legal work done by their leaders is supplemented by, and interacts with, the active intervention of sympathetic outsiders. This cocoon of sympathetic outsiders surrounding Amish society is essential to its preservation.

When the Amish began forming their own schools to avoid the consolidation of public schools in the 1950s, their decision to halt education at age fourteen clashed with state requirements. In several states, confrontations flared when parents refused to send their children to school. Authorities threatened to jail the parents. In the face of such threats, the traditional Amish response would, of course, be nonresistance and passive refusal. How was this confrontation resolved?

The resolution came in a Supreme Court decision (*Wisconsin v. Yoder* [1972]) that upheld the Amish right to terminate formal education at eighth grade, operate their own schools, and make their own educational policies. If the Amish do not hire lawyers or engage in litigation, how did such a case reach the Supreme Court? A committee of non-Amish was formed to lead a nationwide movement in defense of the Amish. The National Committee for Amish Religious Freedom, described in Chapter 6, raises funds, hires lawyers, and, in the school case, mounted an obviously successful defense despite the fact that no Amish participated in the committee or paid for the lawyers it engaged.

In similar fashion, a recent crisis in Pennsylvania led to the formation of a countywide political action committee, the Lancaster Alliance for New Directions (LAND). The state proposed the construction of a four-lane limited access highway through the center of Lancaster County. The committee in its platform and organizing strategy argued that the highway would destroy some of the best Amish farmland in the United States. The road would physically divide Amish church districts in ways that would destroy them, while also increasing traffic, possibly even forcing the Amish out of Lancaster County. Not a single member of LAND was Amish, yet it advocated on behalf of the Amish for protection from the state. The antihighway committee leafleted hundreds of Amish homes, successfully convincing them to attend a mass meeting with state officials at a local high school. Over one thousand Amish men and women attended. According to local experts, it may have been the largest gathering of Amish ever, for a public meeting. The Amish spoke little despite an invitation to participate in question-and-answer dialogue. Their presence was clearly used by the committee to lend moral force to its position against the highway. The issue was temporarily resolved when the state governor announced that the new highway would not go through the heart of the Amish community.

Thus, a vital element of the Amish social cocoon has been produced by several related groups, all with their own reasons for wanting to protect the Amish. One group consists of several elements of the tourist industry. In 1988, tourism around the Lancaster Amish settlement generated over four hundred million dollars of commerce, at least half of it plausibly attributable to the desire of tourists to see the Amish (Kraybill 1989, 228). When government authorities and elected officials accommodate Amish needs, part of their thinking includes the fear that too much pressure might force the Amish to migrate. Thus, even though Amish voting rates are low, their role in the tourist industry gives them political clout in Harrisburg, the state capital.

A second source of support comes from outsiders seeking to preserve traditional lifestyles so they will be able to achieve other goals that may be at odds with Amish values. In Lancaster County, for example, many non-Amish, middle- and upper middle-class residents moved to the area because they enjoy the rural environment. They are not farmers, but they like the social atmosphere and physical beauty of the agricultural region. Thus, when events begin to threaten the Amish way of life, these non-Amish neighbors are sometimes eager to help defend the Amish to protect their own share of the ambience.[5] In the highway controversy, many of those who decried the victimization of the Amish were in fact resident property owners threatened themselves by the proposed highway.

Part of the cocoon protecting the Amish is economically based, as Kraybill (1989) has argued. Economics, however, is only part of the picture. There are, in addition, ideological or moral fibers woven into this protective cocoon. Such strands characterize a variety of groups that have a special relationship with the Amish. This part of the cocoon is composed of more progressive Anabaptist groups, such as the Mennonites, who share many beliefs with the Amish and want to protect their own religious freedom within American society. Mennonites also practice adult baptism and refuse military service, although more progressive Mennonites accept most, if not all, advances in modern technology and are willing to use formal legal procedures to protect their rights.

Amish congregations also create non-Amish buffers around them consisting of young Amish persons who decide not to join the church. Baptized church members are excommunicated and shunned if they transgress major rules of the community; however, church members freely interact with those who, in good conscience, decide not to be baptized and do not join the church. Those who stray frequently live nearby and join more progressive churches, often conservative Mennonite groups, which share the Amish community's historical roots. These nonjoiners sometimes feel protective of the Amish and are free to take direct action on their behalf. Many who are born (but not baptized) Amish go away to college and relocate to large cities and modern jobs. Often, however, they retain close ties with their families and are eager to preserve Amish society even though living another lifestyle.

In addition to these semi-outsiders with a direct affinity to the Amish, other outsiders derive philosophical satisfaction from the survival of Amish society. Amish values satisfy a longing, which many share, for the purity of rural ideals that have been long abandoned. These outsiders may feel "there is still hope for America as long as the Amish survive."

Amish communities are constantly inundated by curious tourists. During the highway crisis, the mass meetings were covered by national television networks and other media heavyweights such as the *New York Times*. Their story angle always focused on the potential damage that state bureaucrats, in cahoots with heartless business and real estate tycoons, might inflict on the innocent, hard working, and defenseless Amish. Media editors sensed that viewers and readers were curious about such threats.

Other evidence of outsider sympathy comes in the form of unsolicited charity. Outsiders, some of whom have never even seen an Amish person, are periodically moved to aid the Amish. Although the Amish have no central office or treasury, congregations maintain a modest "poor fund" to provide emergency medical or other assistance to members in distress. Contributions are solicited from within the church when a specific emergency arises. Occasionally outsiders have given unsolicited donations to the Amish, apparently feeling that they deserve an award for their stalwart defense of human values. Although the donors view the contributions as similar to those given to support the survival of a favorite college, the Amish find such donations problematic. Who should decide how to distribute them? Where should they be kept? The image that the Amish are just trying to mind their own business and preserve basic values esteemed by other Americans attracts support. So the Amish receive support for doing what others wish they had the courage or means to do.

Amish "Lawyering"

In recent years, Amish legal work has grown in response to a variety of challenges posed by the bureaucratized welfare state. The military draft has always been an especially bothersome issue. Consistent with their nonresistance, the Amish have insisted on being classified as conscientious objectors (COs) to avoid military activity. During the Vietnam War, conscription once again threatened Amish ways because local draft boards were given the responsibility of accepting or rejecting individual claims for conscientious objection (Dolbeare and Davis 1968). In some areas, the Amish experienced no problem, since local boards were sympathetic. In other regions, however, board members were angry that Amish boys were "getting out of the draft" while non-Amish boys had to serve. Some draft boards refused to grant CO status, while some of the most conservative Amish churches urged their boys not to register for the draft at all. In the early years of the Vietnam War, as the draft became a national political issue, the Amish were on a collision course with the outside world.

In response to these crises, the National Amish Steering Committee was formed to negotiate with Selective Service officials. Instead of channeling their concerns through the Mennonite Central Committee and the National Service Board for Religious Objectors, the Amish chose to negotiate directly with government officials. The Steering Committee formed quietly, as described in Chapter 4. Because of Amish resistance to participating in politics and their rejection of large-scale organization among themselves, the Steering Committee retained a low profile.[6] Nevertheless, some of the Amish on this committee became quasi-experts in conscription law. More importantly, they established personal relationships with key Selective Service officials—including General Lewis B. Hershey, the national director—senators, state governors, and members of the House of Representatives. On several occasions, such officials visited committee members in Amish homes to discuss draft problems.

Amish committee members also became familiar with the corridors of power in Washington via frequent visits and phone calls to official offices. Relationships like these enabled members of the committee to place telephone calls, visit Washington offices, and hold urgent conferences when draft boards refused to abide by the informal agreements negotiated with Selective Service officials or other political leaders. In some instances, local board decisions were reversed on the same day they were made by quick intervention from national authorities responding to calls from Amish leaders. One leader described several episodes where "a quick call on a public phone to my friend General Hershey," the Selective Service director, produced same-day results.

When Amish boys faced prosecution for refusal to comply with draft board orders, committee members accompanied them to court. As one Amish leader put it:

> We might just take along someone [a lawyer] just to make sure that there isn't something done that shouldn't be done. Just to sit there and watch and be sure that the boy isn't treated unfairly. You know that can happen sometimes. But we aren't there to make a fuss or argue back or defend against the charges. But we do have some friends . . . lawyers . . . who will just go with us to court to make sure things are done the right way. But we never pay him and he always says he'll get around to billing us, but he doesn't seem to. So we just take him some fresh baked bread, or some garden vegetables, and that's how it seems to go. So we don't really hire lawyers or put up defenses or anything.

The alternate service options approved by draft boards for Amish boys also created problems. Amish families did not want their boys shipped off to big cities where they might learn non-Amish ways. The Steering Committee worked out a deal with Selective Service officers which allowed everyone to stay technically within the law. Some Amish farmers leased their farms to the Amish church so that when a draft board assigned an Amish boy to alternative service, he could be sent to a "church farm." From a legal standpoint, the "church farm" was a part of a nonprofit religious organization. The draftee could continue to lead an Amish lifestyle, away from the outside world, while fulfilling alternative service requirements.

Members of the Steering Committee became itinerant troubleshooters, assisting Amish families all over the country. They traveled to local church districts if a crisis developed and entered into sometimes intense and protracted negotiations with local authorities. Their farms were tended by other family members as they became nearly full-time negotiators. Although this ad hoc pattern of negotiating existed earlier, it became more systematized during the Vietnam crisis.

We found numerous other examples of negotiated agreements between Amish "lawyers" and government bureaucrats. We were struck repeatedly by the innovative legal thinking displayed by these lay lawyers, their savvy about government organizations, their knowledge of pragmatic strategies, and their extraordinary ability to think on their feet as they fended off challenges and led their adversaries into acceptable compromises. Although the military draft stimulated the formation of the Steering Committee, its lay lawyers continue to work on a widening circle of issues.

One concern has been Social Security. The Amish reject external forms of social welfare—Social Security, Workers' Compensation, medical insurance, life insurance, liability insurance, and so on—provided by non-Amish organizations on the grounds that the church community is responsible for the care of its members. If members rely on outside insurers, ties will weaken within the community. Amish lawyer-negotiators played a role in crafting the original exemption of self-employed people from Social Security obligations. But this exemption did not cover Amish people working in nonfarm jobs. Amish lay lawyers resolved this problem in a way that would please any lawyer.

An Amish owner of a small factory employing about twenty other Amishmen was required to withhold Social Security payments from his employees' paychecks. Steering Committee members, in consultation with Social Security administrators and key members of Congress, suggested that the employees become shareholders in the company, thus making it a legal partnership. The employees, now self-employed owners, would receive profits instead of wages, thus qualifying for the self-employed Social Security exemption. This solution became a general practice for many Amish businesses. Social Security administrators agreed to abide by the arrangement.

Such arrangements require legalistic creativity. They also hinge on relationships built over years of patient networking. As one Amish negotiator related: "Of course, we had been working on things even ten years before, like Social Security . . . why I remember when I was working with Wilbur Mills—he was chairman of the House Ways and Means Committee at the time, and he and I were pretty good friends. Well I just worked with him on this question of Social Security and got him to understand."

In 1988, Amish leaders were still trying to exempt Amish workers from all Social Security payments, even those working for non-Amish employers. The following quote from an interview with one Amish leader illustrates the scope of their work:

> We have still the problem, with our fellows who may be working in a factory or somewhere for wages, and we have not been able to exempt them from Social Security. But now, with this new legislation

that we are getting through, it should take care of the problem. They have written it into the bill so tight that they would have to drop the whole bill if they wanted to take that part out of it. And now I have notified Senator Heinz that it is coming over [from the House of Representatives where it had just passed] so that he can help it through the Senate.

In another example of creative lawyering, the Amish fended off an attempt by the state of Pennsylvania to require teachers in one-room Amish schools to be certified by the state after three years of high school training. Amish leaders told Pennsylvania's attorney general that such a program would deprive them of their most qualified teachers—young, committed Amishwomen without any high school training. Education authorities proposed supplying the Amish with qualified teachers, but Amish leaders explained that outsiders could teach neither the German language nor Amish songs. Moreover, they said, Amish schools could not pay the high salaries of outside teachers.

Several other state proposals also met with Amish objection. The Amish leaders finally met with Pennsylvania's attorney general and asked, "Does a substitute teacher need to have a diploma or be certified?" "No," replied the attorney general, "a substitute teacher is taken when there is a shortage or when there is no one better qualified to fill the spot, usually on a temporary basis." The Amish spokesman responded, "Our Amish teachers are the best teachers that we have or can find for a one-room Amish school. From now on our Amish teachers will be 'substitute teachers'" (Kinsinger 1988, 126). State authorities, at that point, dropped any further discussion of teacher training. As a precaution, the Amish issue a "diploma" signed by three Amish school board members to any Amish teacher with three years of experience as a teacher or a "substitute."

In another case, the Pennsylvania attorney general threatened to shut down a new Amish school using a woodburning stove in its classroom. The state demanded that a separate room, or a basement with fire walls, be constructed to reduce the fire hazard and conform to state regulations. Amish leaders explained that a stove in the school basement was against their religious beliefs since they would not have such arrangements in their own houses, and the schools were really extensions of their homes. The attorney general issued several threats. The Amish responded with gentle but insistent refusals, saying that they would have to keep their children home if a "closed" sign appeared on the school's door.

Faced with this dilemma, the attorney general confessed, "This is very embarrassing," and asked, "When can you come to Harrisburg?" (Kinsinger 1988, 122). After the meeting, the parties agreed to a compromise: The Amish would put a separate stove in the new school, but the state would cease inspections of all other Amish schools, including new ones built thereafter. State inspectors, according to some Amish leaders, "have been ordered to stay away from Amish schools."

In the course of these activities, Amish "lawyers" have developed their own practical wisdom and effective strategies to deal with their "adversaries." Consider the implications of the following quote from one leader speaking about several different legal problems—the draft, Social Security, and workers' compensation:

> It's not usually the top people in government, but you know how it is—it's the people below them who . . . well if you ask them anything, they have to say "hold on while I check that." And then they have to go running to somebody higher up, and it's very hard to get anything done that way. And so they will, instead of sitting down and talking about something, they will just tell you "this is the rule." So you really have to go to the higher up people to get things done.

Thus, a multitude of legal relationships with the outside world have been handled without litigation or traditional electoral political pressure.[7] It would be wrong to say that the Amish simply accept whatever happens to them without using legal services or political action, as we might expect from their profession of nonresistance. Legal services, provided by well-informed Amishmen, include detailed knowledge of formal law, the willingness and know-how to lobby, and patient skill in negotiating—sometimes on the front porches of their farm homes and other times in the offices of government bureaucrats.

Schism, Defection, and Community

The wariness we found among Amish members with respect to the social cocoon and the lawyerlike activities of Amish leaders raises the question of schisms and defections—activities that have, paradoxically, sometimes contributed to the preservation of Amish life. The deviations from ideological purity described above have sometimes fostered both splits in church communities and the loss of young Amish to the outside world. It may be true that

the social cocoon and the Amish "lawyers" have been vital in preserving Amish culture. But it is also true that schismatic reactions
against these activities bolster the continuity of traditional Amish
culture. This is accomplished in successful examples of what I earlier called "ideological work" or ideological production.

Schism and defection have been such regular features of Anabaptist history that a paradoxical connection is suggested between "inside" Anabaptist groups and "outside" host societies.[8]
Redekop (1989, 268–69) argues that "the existence of a surrounding host society which presents alternatives can contribute to the
schismatic tendencies." Yet the paradox of Mennonite society is
that "in spite of the many migrations and the resulting differentia-
tions—as well as the specific schisms—the historical identity of
Mennonite groups with the original and overall Mennonite tradition remains as strong as ever, or even intensifies" (Redekop 1989,
265). In other words, schismatic activity seems to solidify the tradition, uniqueness, vitality, and separateness of Mennonite identity.

My research on the Amish suggests that Redekop's concept of a
"host society" needs more precise differentiation and specifica-
tion. For the Amish, the Mennonite tradition itself can be seen as
part of the "outside" from which Amish communities not only
isolate themselves but upon which they depend for protection.
Whereas more modern Mennonite groups might be influenced to
split into factions in reaction to non-Mennonite values and beliefs, Amish groups are often surrounded by a spectrum of increasingly liberal Mennonite groups whose ways deviate from current
Amish practices. The external challenge to Amish ways, therefore, comes not just from the host society—government, courts,
lawyers, and an undifferentiated sea of non-Amish Americans. In
addition, Amish identity and solidarity is constantly challenged
by the relatively small steps that Redekop (1989, 38) calls the "escalator" to liberalism out of an Amish church into a relatively
similar but separate Mennonite community.

The "Breach of 1966," described by Kraybill (1989, 182), is a recent example of the schismatic process. It involved the departure
of one hundred families from Lancaster's Old Order Amish community and the formation of several New Order Amish groups.
The new groups reacted against retroactive restrictions ordered by
a conclave of Amish bishops. Though the split began over questions of technology, it spread to basic questions of religious practice and belief. The dynamics of this schism provide a good example of the paradoxical effects of conflict on the preservation of
Amish society.

In one interview, for example, I spoke with a New Order Amish-man and his wife about their experiences since leaving the Old Order church. Because of his move to the New Order splinter group, Eli (pseudonym) and his wife had been excommunicated from their old community. Even his parents would not speak with him. In many respects, his home and farm appeared like so many other Amish farms I visited. The basic architecture and furnishings were the same, and his wife and oldest daughter wore starched white caps. He dressed in black, and his nine children also had a "plain" appearance. But his New Order church preached individual salvation, had a church building, and maintained relations with an evangelical movement. In addition, his house was electrified, although the electrical fixtures were carefully crafted to look like gas or kerosene fixtures in an Old Order home. He had a telephone in the otherwise Amish-looking kitchen, a two-way radio for his work as a volunteer for an emergency squad and fire company, and he drove his own black truck.

Despite excommunication, he and his wife knew the latest gossip in the Old Order Amish community. Their new lifestyle was selectively different from that of the Old Order Church where most of their brothers and sisters still belonged. Although their move was an emotionally wrenching experience, it did not require a radical departure from the Old Order culture. It was a small but significant step on Redekop's escalator.

The social migration of farmers like Eli rids the Amish community of a significant threat to its core identity. Because the escalator is there, it does threaten Amish society with the loss of individual members, but if effective interpretations of those losses can be created and sustained, it also reinforces the core of Amish ideology. It means that outside observers continue to see "unelectrified" Amish, and insiders who remain Amish can continue to validate their own membership, which includes the ideology of separation. The core of the Old Order Amish remains intact and in close, though cautious, contact with the likes of Eli, who may reject aspects of Old Order practice but who also need tolerance from those further up the escalator. Hence, Eli's family, like others, becomes one more part of the cocoon sheltering the core of Amish life.

The process of schism does not offer a panacea for social and cultural preservation. It does not eliminate conflict but, rather, channels it into recurring patterns, which can be interpreted in traditional terms. The interpretation converts the potential damaging energy of conflict into a reaffirmation of conservative purity. This is ideological work or production.

Yet the failure to resolve conflict carries considerable destructive potential. Perhaps the harshest challenge to Amish preservation comes from embittered former members who seek revenge, wish to expose the hypocrisy of Amish ways, or hope to take advantage of Amish naiveté for personal economic advantage. Two recent real estate transactions illustrate this problem. One involved a concealed sale, which took a large farm out of Amish hands in a way that hid the transaction from the community until the deed was done. The new owner discreetly planned to convert the land to residential use. This clandestine move could only be done with the cooperation of the "insider" who owned the farm. The sale sowed seeds of fear and mistrust within a community threatened by a constantly shrinking supply of increasingly expensive farmland. Who might be next to succumb to the lure of big money for the best farmland in the world?

In a second, more highly publicized case, a family excommunicated in 1953 because the father purchased a used car (*Philadelphia Inquirer,* 24 June 1990) decided to cash in on the development value of its farm. The owners proposed using the farm for a high-density housing development (*Philadelphia Inquirer,* 21 June 1990). This move posed two threats: the loss of more farmland and the introduction of a new, non-Amish population. The suburbanite newcomers would alter the social fabric by increasing traffic congestion and adding new tensions between Amish and non-Amish.

Some Amish speculation interpreted the proposed development as more than economic opportunism. Alongside the family's commercial exploitation of its Amish roots with its popular Amish-theme restaurant, the land-development scheme was viewed by some as a subtle snub directed against the family's former church community. Moreover, hints of scandal tinged the development, since a son of the landowner chaired the township's Board of Supervisors—the governing body that decided zoning questions in the case. All of these events created precisely the kind of public conflict that flies in the face of traditional Amish ideology.

These events are too recent to assess fully, but it is clear that the cocoon of sympathetic outsiders tried to halt the proposed development or at least soften its harsher effects. Moreover, this incident has evoked Amish action both consistent with, and deviant from, historic Amish ideals. At township hearings, many non-Amish leaders and residents rallied to protect the "Plain Folk" and their lifestyle and to protest the prospect of increased flooding, worse traffic congestion, and encroaching suburbanization promised by the housing development (*New Era,* 20 June 1990). Mass media attention zeroed in once again. Newspaper reports attacked those who would set a "tract development right in the middle of God's green acres" (*Philadelphia Inquirer,* 24 June 1990). Philadelphia's television stations aired the story, and a national network failed to put the story on prime time news only because neither the Amish participants nor the excommunicated landowner would agree to be interviewed (*New Era,* 8 July 1990). Clearly, national media were interested in the story only because it involved a threat to the Amish.

In this case, Amish values have been sorely tested. More than 150 Amish families signed petitions against the development, appeared at public hearings to "witness" against it silently, and even took the unusual step of speaking publicly in favor of traditional values and, thus, against the development. Subsequently, Amish values were reasserted as Amish leaders recommended compromises to minimize the development's impact (*New Era,* 7 August 1990).

This case threatened the economic viability of Amish society by reducing its life source, the land. By entangling the Amish in a web of public conflict and distrust with both near and more distant outsiders, the case also tainted the purity of their commitment to nonresistance. Such actions threaten further divisions in the community, and therefore create the necessity for ideological work to give actions and the history of events an interpretation that promotes reintegration. If Amish survival rested only on the economic base of preindustrial farming, cases like this would signal the final, fatal blow to Amish society. But ideological production is a central ingredient in the patterns of interdependence between the Amish and the "world" and, thus, important for Amish survival. Therefore, cases such as this hold the potential not only for destruction but also for regeneration of a social pattern, a community, that is recognizably Amish. Amish society, in other words, is not just an economic anachronism. It is, in addition, an ideologically produced social corner of modern North American society.

The Paradoxes of Separateness

The housing controversy just described illustrates all the features of the protective social cocoon surrounding the Amish. As a real estate development, it raises all the economic issues that Kraybill has identified as the paradoxical side of Amish attempts to be separate. There is the threat of reduced economic resources for Amish sons and their families-to-be, and consequently the ever-lurking fear that the Amish will just "pull out" and leave the tourist industry, and therefore the county and state, destitute. In addition, however, we see all the noneconomic paradoxes of separateness. Out comes all the symbolic weaponry of moral and legal rectitude in an inseparably entangled relationship between insiders and outsiders. The dispute becomes complex, with general moral values invoked by outsiders, legal issues also invoked by outsiders, internal Amish morality, and internal Amish "legal" activity, in the sense of legal pluralism. Amish and non-Amish cooperate toward a common goal. Lawyers play a role in pursuit of that goal by representing the case before government bodies. The values of simplicity, continuity, rural lifestyle, community, and good-neighborliness are, in the angry, righteous voices of outsiders, fired in salvos at the invading forces of development. Part of the cocoon thus speaks in anger and threatens legal action. At the same time, leading Amish voices speak softly, and in evident despair, about the loss of values and the possible necessity to leave, thereby reaffirming the rightness and validity of Amish values within the community even as they join the battle swirling around them. And their gentle lament is spread far and wide by the tools of mass media, reinforcing existing elements of the cocoon and perhaps adding new layers to it.

Yet this particular conflict over the issue of encroaching development represents the reemergence of issues left buried like a time bomb by the failure of the internal Amish "legal" processes of excommunication and shunning to resolve conflicts. Excommunication fails to resolve the conflict because of incomplete economic and ideological separation between insiders and former members who become outsiders. This particular dispute owes its existence and its ability to produce pain precisely because of the latent internal-external ties. The outsiders—former members—maintain control over a precious internal Amish resource with symbolic value—precious farm land—because their status as outsiders is only partial. This case involves precisely the kinds of actions and reactions that have in the past produced schisms in Amish society and added steps on the Anabaptist escalator to more liberal lifestyles and beliefs. Yet, as Redekop (1989) has shown, schisms have not destroyed the commitment of large numbers of people to Mennonite values and communities. Rather, they seem to have rearranged these people into revised groupings based on ideological commitments. All of this activity has, thus far, taken place within, and helped to reinforce, a cocoon of protection which allows some to opt for the ideology of Amish ways.

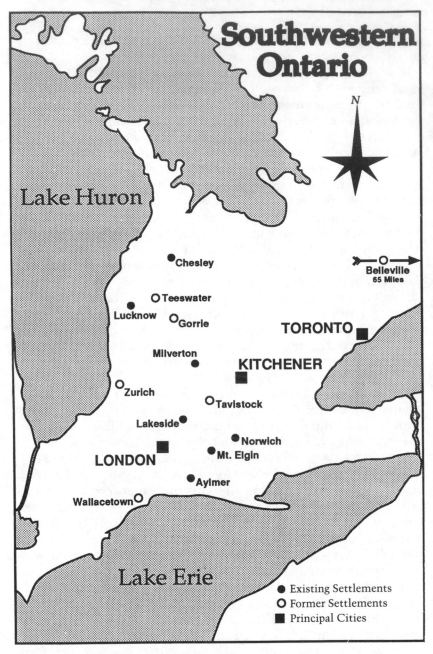

Southwestern Ontario

N

Lake Huron

●Chesley

○ Teeswater

● Lucknow   ○ Gorrie

Milverton ●

○ Zurich

KITCHENER ■

○ Tavistock

Lakeside ●

TORONTO ■

Belleville
65 Miles

■ LONDON

● Norwich
● Mt. Elgin

● Aylmer

Wallacetown ○

Lake Erie

● Existing Settlements
○ Former Settlements
■ Principal Cities

Amish settlements in Ontario, Canada. Kurt Walker

CHAPTER TWELVE

Canadian Government Relations

Dennis L Thomson

 Although the bulk of North American Amish live in the United States, several settlements are located in the Canadian province of Ontario. The Canadian political context provides a contrasting setting for relations between the Amish and the state. Political scientist Dennis L Thomson chronicles the patterns of interaction between the Amish and Canadian officials.

The Amish had settled in Upper Canada by 1824, having come directly from Europe. They were joined by some Amish from Pennsylvania, and together they settled in an area that is today Wilmot Township, Waterloo County, Ontario (Epp 1982, 4). Their fundamental doctrines are similar to those of the Mennonites, who had settled in Waterloo County nearly a quarter of a century earlier. The Mennonites, found over a much wider area, surrounded the Amish in Ontario. The Old Order Amish, or House Amish, are more conservative than most of the Canadian Mennonites.[1]

As in the United States, the Amish have practices and beliefs that bring them into contact and potential conflict with government agencies. In particular, their insistence on a total separation of church and state and their subsequent refusal to use the legal system make it difficult for them or the state to mediate the problems that arise. The Amish fear assimilation and consciously strive to maintain a minority culture through dress, a nonmechanized lifestyle, and use of an old German dialect. They do understand that

The research for this chapter was conducted under a Canadian Studies Program Grant from the Canadian Embassy in the United States. Some additional assistance was provided by a College Research Grant from the Dean of the College of Family, Home, and Social Sciences, at Brigham Young University. The author greatly appreciates having been given access to the documents and records of the Heritage Historical Library, in Aylmer, Ontario, as well as the personal assistance and guidance of David Luthy. For other accounts of the Amish in Canada, see Gingerich 1972 and Huntington 1990. A much abbreviated version of some of this article appeared in the *International Political Science Review*, October 1992, in an article entitled, "Comparative Policy towards Cultural Isolationists in Canada and Norway."

they cannot live in total isolation but must interact with the secular society to some degree. The question is, how much? And to what extent does the Canadian government accommodate Amish efforts to maintain their distinctiveness? In many places, their attempts to maintain isolation have met with mixed success. They often suffer local pressures and restrictive legislation. Thus, at times they have been impelled to move. Yet, it is for neither of these reasons that the Amish left congregations in the United States and settled in southwestern Ontario.

In 1953, there was only one Old Order Amish settlement remaining in Canada, at Milverton, Perth County, Ontario. It had been there for over a century. In March 1953, a group of six families moved to Aylmer, Ontario, from Pike County, Ohio, and Daviess County, Indiana. The culminating reason for moving was the fact that in 1952 the U.S. Atomic Energy Commission had chosen Pike County in southern Ohio as a site for an atomic plant. The plant was to be built five miles east of the Amish settlement. It was not only fear of an atomic plant which caused them to emigrate but also the probable increase in population and traffic, which would endanger Amish buggies traveling on hilly roads. The reasons they chose to move to Canada rather than elsewhere in the United States were four: (1) Canada had cheaper and better land; (2) it did not have conscription; (3) it did not have compulsory social security in 1953; and (4) it had fewer government farm programs in 1953 (e.g. soil bank, subsidies). Although Canada had family supplements and a baby bonus—which would be expected to be attractive to groups with large families, such as the Amish—the Amish did not and have not applied for these benefits.

By 1964, seven additional settlements had formed, all from Amish communities in the United States. Since then, another one has been settled, and several have become large enough to be split into multiple districts (congregations). Seven have disbanded, six since 1964.[2] Thus, there are now seventeen Amish districts in Canada, all in Ontario:

> Five near Milverton, Perth/Waterloo counties (1824)
> Three near Aylmer, Elgin County (1953) (originally from Ohio and Indiana)
> Two near Norwich, Oxford County (1954) (originally from Ohio)
> Two near Chesley, but in Grey County (1954) (originally from Ohio)

One near Lakeside, Oxford County (1958) (originally from Maryland, Delaware, and Ohio)

Two near Mount Elgin, Oxford County (1962) (originally from Iowa)

Two near Lucknow, Bruce County (1973) (from the Norwich districts)

All but one of the present-day settlements were formed by immigrants from the United States. The largest settlement, which consists of five districts near Milverton, had over 149 households in 1985. The smallest, the Lakeside district, has about twenty families. There are approximately twenty-five hundred Old Order Amish in Canada.[3]

In Canada, the Amish have confronted the government on several issues: military service, the Canadian Pension Plan, Social Insurance numbers, cemetery laws, education, jury duty, and milk storage regulations. Military service is mentioned because it is a perpetual concern for Amish wherever they live. In reality, there have been no military-related problems for the Amish since the major migration to Canada in 1953. Canada has not been engaged in a war, and so the issue has not arisen. Nonetheless, the Amish are quick to mention that there have been no military problems, thus in effect addressing the issue and indicating a continuing concern about it.

Education

The Old Order Amish have established schools primarily to avoid outside influences rather than to engage in religious education. They have resisted integrated (Amish and non-Amish) schools and consolidated schools, which would mean that their children would have to ride buses. The Amish schools, however, usually only run through the eighth grade. They teach reading, writing, arithmetic, history, geography, and health. They teach no science except a basic knowledge of plants, animals, and birds. Religion is not explicitly taught in the schools. Potential education-related conflicts with the government have emerged over the requirements that teachers be certified and that students attend school until age sixteen. Probably as a result of a number of new Amish and Old Order Mennonite schools being started up in 1966 (four began in that year alone), the Ontario Department of Education wrote to the Amish leadership in each community. At Aylmer, in

August of 1966, a letter requested the name of the teacher for the coming year, "her address, and what qualifications she has, if any, for a teaching position."[4] The Amish replied that two teachers had been hired, neither with any experience. Their attitude toward the educational requirements imposed by the state is reflected in a letter that one of the Amishmen wrote to an Amish friend in the United States at that time:

> The department of Education here is insisting that we use only teachers who have a grade 12 education. We had a meeting the other day . . . and there were [Amish] representatives there from most of the settlements in Ontario. Everyone seemed to be agreed that we could not meet the requirements and would have to take our stand. It may eventually mean jails and fines, but we hope not, and have notified our department of Education that we are unable to comply. So I guess it[s] up to them to push it or leave it lie.
> . . . Personally, I doubt if the school officials care to come to a showdown. I believe they are plenty scared of public opinion and that the state officials will do anything they can to avoid it. As soon as you start imprisoning anyone for the school then it looks right away like religious persecution for that is what it is, and nobody wants to stir that up.
> As long as the children get a good education which will enable them to make a living and to be honest and useful citizens, and not become a liability of the government, the state has no right to interfere.[5]

There was continuing correspondence between Amishmen responsible for local schools and school officials. Finally, on 25 July 1967, the provincial Department of Education wrote:

> Over a period of time there has been correspondence with the department and discussions with officials regarding the qualifications of teachers in the private schools operated by the Old Order Mennonites and Old Order Amish.
> The purpose of this letter is to indicate that, while it is assumed that the private schools will endeavor to secure teachers with the best possible qualifications, there is no intention to interfere with the operation of these schools if it is not possible to meet the minimum requirement of Grade 12 standing for teachers.[6]

At about the same time, Ontario changed its age requirement for children's school attendance from fourteen to sixteen years of age. The Old Order Mennonites had lobbied the Ministry of Education in Toronto, which told the Amish in the summer of 1968 that the "Minister of Education seemed sympathetic and the officials promised to go slow on the matter."[7] Since 1967 and 1968, the Ontario government has not enforced its regulations with regard to the Amish. Since then, the Ministry of Education has not demanded a certificate of a teacher, nor has the ministry asked for an account of the curriculum taught. The Amish routinely file the enrollments and name the teacher each year in a "Private School September Report."

The Pension Plan

The Amish have not fared so well concerning the Canadian Pension Plan. The Amish do not believe in "public" insurance of any kind. In fact, most of the Ontario districts do not have the traditional fire plans within their communities that are found in many Amish communities in the United States. Only the Canadian districts in Milverton have a private insurance plan for their community. The Amish also object to receiving public assistance. On both grounds, therefore, they have objected to the Canadian Pension Plan as they had to the U.S. Social Security System. In the United States, the Amish objected, refused to pay, and had liens put on their property by the Internal Revenue Service until 1965, when they were exempted from paying Social Security taxes if they were self-employed. In Canada, however, social security has been resolved with less rancor. The issue arose in 1967 in Canada when Revenue Canada seized Amish milk checks and tapped Amish bank accounts for not making annual payments to Canada's Pension Plan. The amount per taxpayer would have been about one hundred dollars.

The Mennonite Central Committee appealed to Parliament; and in December 1971, the minister of National Health and Welfare and the minister of Revenue Canada jointly recommended to Parliament that an exemption be given to the Amish, the Old Order Mennonites, and the Hutterites. It passed on 14 January 1974 and was made retroactive to 1 January 1972 for self-employed persons. Those who seek the exemption must file for it individually. Those who are not self-employed and who work for a non-Amish person are obligated to pay. Amish companies have worked out partnerships in which profits are shared and assigned to the individual. Revenue Canada takes what is due from the individual's account. In the case of a nonprofit corporation such as Pathway Publishers, the Amish publishing house, the government comes in and seizes what is due. This system works well: the Amish do not freely make a payment, yet the government gets what it determines is due.

With regard to the mandatory Social Insurance number, the government has provided the Amish with exemption numbers beginning with zero, which cannot be drawn upon. All other numbers begin with four. This satisfies the Amish because they do not object to having a number—only to its possibly enticing some of their members to draw upon the plan.

Milk Storage

Milk storage regulations have created the most difficult problems for the Amish in their relations with the Ontario government. This became the culminating issue that led the Tavistock settlement to disband and that caused others to shift to other agricultural products. The issues concerning Canadian milk storage regulations were similar to those encountered by the Amish in Lancaster County, Pennsylvania. While the Canadian government's response was different, the Amish accommodation to public policy was similar.

Many Canadian Amish farmers sold milk as a source of cash income. In 1976, the Ontario Milk Marketing Board (OMMB), established by the provincial legislature, mandated a policy that ended the marketing of milk in cans and set a deadline of 31 October 1977. Thereafter, all milk could be marketed on the farms only in cooled bulk tanks. The Amish objected. Bulk tanks would require an electric cooler, and the Amish do not allow electricity on their farms. Additionally, the milk, picked up on a two-day rotation, would require a Sunday pick-up every second week. The Amish initially proposed a community tank. Under this plan, each Amish farmer would transport his cans of milk to a community depot to be picked up by a tank truck. The OMMB asked its staff to investigate this proposal. The staff report said, "It would be technically possible to operate a program of this nature" and still meet the standards that the board had established. Although the board acknowledged the report, it turned the Amish proposal down because "(a) . . . the program could not meet existing or future Grade A quality requirements. . . . [and] (b) On a matter of principle, and legal feasibility, the Board cannot discriminate against all other producers . . . because of religious beliefs."[8]

The Amish then appealed to their member of Parliament, John Wise, who later became minister of agriculture in Joseph Clark's cabinet, and R. K. McNeil, their MPP in the Ontario Provincial Legislative Assembly. They also appealed to the Milk Commission of Ontario and were turned down. Next, the Amish appealed to the Ontario ombudsman in Toronto and the Ontario Human Rights Commission in London. They were supported by the Christian Farmers Federation of Ontario, and their repeated appeals were extensively covered by the press. The Mennonite Central Committee retained lawyers who exerted pressure at all points.

The OMMB eventually agreed to the concept of a community tank, which the Amish had proposed. As it turned out, the Amish in Aylmer and Lakeside have never used community tanks but have instead installed individual ones and used diesel engines to cool the bulk tanks. The other Canadian Amish communities did not allow members to use bulk tanks. Thus, farmers in those settlements who wanted to continue in dairying had to resort to selling cream. As a result, some Amish communities have lost families who have moved to Michigan and Wisconsin because they wished to produce and sell fluid milk. Those who converted to bulk tanks had to pay extra to have a fourth pickup each week rather than every other day, in order to avoid the biweekly Sunday pickup. This affected about ninety Amish and Old Order Mennonite farmers altogether, as well as the Netherlands Reformed congregations, a conservative branch of the Christian Reformed Church.

When representatives of the OMMB first met with the Amish in December 1977 to discuss other than Sunday pickups, they indicated that the extra pickup would be charged at the normal rate of $4 to $6 per pickup after 1980.[9] When the OMMB finally set its policy in September 1981, it charged $40 for each additional pickup. Upon being questioned about this practice in June 1982, the OMMB said the new charge would be $44.80, which reflected a 12 percent increase in "anticipated extra costs." The regular rate that the OMMB calculated per pickup cost for a small producer was $7.30. The price for hauling a rejected tank of milk away was $17.60. Large milk producers who required daily pickups were charged $7.00 per extra pickup fifteen times per month. In contacting milk transport haulers, the Amish found that they were paid approximately $16 per pickup.

Armed with this information, the Amish farmers appealed the rates charged "no-Sunday shippers" to the Farm Products Appeal Tribunal in 1983. The tribunal upheld the OMMB. The OMMB argued that the cost was a pooled cost, shared by all who did not have milk picked up on Sunday. In addition, the OMMB argued that the Amish and other non-Sunday producers should share the cost of the milk hauled on Sunday because a truck was in the area. The Amish felt they were unfairly charged and asked for a breakdown of the fees. In response to their appeal for a review of the fees charged, the OMMB replied that, with one exception, the milk transporters were paid between $6 and $16 per pickup. A separate sheet of calculations showed the cost at between $7.39 and $15.01 per pickup.[10]

The Amish farmers contacted their friends in the national government who replied that the issue was a provincial one and they could be of no help. In their letters, the Amish indicated that they did not want the issue played out in the press as the bulk-tank controversy had been. Some of those to whom they appealed for help noted that their best opportunity to bring pressure on the board was through the press; if they rejected that option, there was little anyone could do.

Furthermore, the Amish complained that they were being charged for fifty-two extra pickups rather than an extra one every other week—or twenty-six. They went to a chartered accountant in London, Ontario, who pressed their complaints with the board. In a reply to the accountant, the board admitted: "In Board documentation, we have sometimes referred to 52 extra pick-ups, with respect to the no-Sunday shipper. This may be somewhat misleading, since as you indicate, the producer receives only 26 additional or extra pick-ups. However, in requiring two unscheduled pickups every other weekend, the producer does receive 52 'special' pick-ups."[11] Indeed, one of the "special" pickups could also be counted as a regular pickup. In further communication, the board denied any savings by not picking up on Sunday.

The Amish farmers and the board were at an impasse. Appeals to the board, politicians, and accountants had brought no relief. Then, however, a member of a Netherlands Reformed congregation, Gilbert Janssen, of Owen Sound near Chesley, filed a complaint with the Ontario Human Rights Commission in September 1990 that he was being discriminated against by the OMMB by the extra charge for no-Sunday pickups. Picking up milk on Sunday, he argued, is against his religion. The OMMB offered to reduce its pick-up surcharge of $44.80 to $35, then to $32. He refused both offers and asked for no more than $7 and a reimbursement of overcharges since 1980. On 10 October 1990, the Ontario Human Rights Commission ruled in Janssen's favor. Once again, the Amish benefited from a concession granted to their co-complainants.

In recent years, the OMMB has established high production quotas, which have forced Amish farmers into other farming activities. Fewer younger Amishmen operate dairies. In one community, twenty of twenty-six Amish farmers who were no longer milking cows sought an alternative. Some families began goat husbandry for milk production, with herds of up to a hundred goats. Others started hog, beef, veal, and chicken production. Some even raise puppies for the pet animal market (Huntington 1990, 4–5). Many have turned to raising vegetables for the fresh garden produce market. The Amish established a marketing co-op to enable Toronto wholesale grocers and supermarket chains to deal with only one large marketing entity rather than several smaller ones.

Other Issues

The confrontation with the Ontario Milk Marketing Board has been described in some detail because it illustrates the way the Amish make political demands. In general, the Amish have difficulty sustaining their position because they do not believe in lawsuits. They resort to persistent correspondence with government officials, even though they generally do not participate in the political process through voting (some do vote in school elections, however), and they never run for office. Therefore, they are at the mercy of the majoritarian society. In the instance described above, they would not hire lawyers to exert pressure. They were, however, aided by the Mennonite Central Committee, which had no compunction in using conventional pressure tactics. The Amish, of course, do not represent any votes for their members of Parliament or of the provincial legislature. They will appeal and petition, in the hope that good will or rationality will win out. They have been successful often enough that their hopes are justified. They don't worry about how politics works so long as they obtain a satisfactory resolution—though one suspects that they are not as naive as they would appear.

Two short case studies serve as examples of the success of their approach. A young woman who was also a dwarf wanted to immigrate to Canada from the United States to work at Pathway Publishers, the Amish printing plant in Aylmer, Ontario. Her application was rejected by the Canadian Consulate. The reason for the rejection is not known, but some Amish suspected that it was because she was a dwarf. The prospective Canadian employer contacted his local member in Parliament, John Wise, who was also a member of the cabinet at the time. He in turn presented Pathway's appeal to the minister of employment and immigration, who resolved the issue satisfactorily. The woman immigrated and lived in Aylmer as a landed immigrant.

In a more recent case, Harvey Wengerd wanted to immigrate to Canada from the United States. He and his wife are Amish. Canada requires that an applicant for immigration have a passport from the country of origin. As Wengerd could not have his picture taken, he could not be granted a U.S. passport. The U.S. State Department would not waive the rule that a photo be submitted in order that a passport be issued, but it would allow a waiver letter to be issued indicating that the person must travel without a passport because of religious principles. That step did not, however, meet the Canadian requirements. Again the Amish contacted John Wise, their highly placed member in Parliament, who again contacted the minister of employment and immigration, who gave Wengerd a "minister's permit," thus waiving the passport rule.

Nevertheless, these successes should not lead one to believe that all cases are resolved to Amish satisfaction upon appeal. Most Amish families engage in some nonagricultural economic endeavor. Some of the ventures, such as blacksmith shops and buggy and stove manufacturing plants, are located on farms. Houses, barns, and sheds are built on some farms and transported elsewhere to be finished. There are also bakeries, woodcrafts, and sewing crafts. A number of Amishmen work away from their farms, particularly as carpenters, and are therefore subject to numerous workplace regulations.

The Amish sent a twelve-man delegation to petition the government to grant them an exemption from workers' compensation because they are self-insured. It was not granted, but nevertheless is often ignored. The Amish also sought an exemption from wearing hard hats on construction projects because of the religious requirement that they wear their black hats out of doors. Canadian rules do not require the wearing of protective headgear on one's own property, but do require it if the work is being performed on someone else's property. The Amish cited an exemption granted by the U.S. assistant secretary of labor to Amishmen in similar circumstances. The Canadian Amish were not successful; however, some Sikhs, who wear turbans, fought the issue in Canadian courts and won.[12]

Two other issues on which the Amish have dealt with the government are cemeteries and jury duty. Meeting government requirements concerning cemeteries is not a uniquely Amish problem: it is difficult for any Canadian group or community to establish a cemetery. The Amish have had to confront that issue as their communities have begun to age; but they have no peculiar requirements, and the government has no peculiar demands. Nonetheless, it has been an irritating problem because the Amish have had to engage in more bureaucratic contacts than they desire.

With respect to jury duty, however, the Amish do appear in court, but they are then excused on grounds of religious convictions. Most first-generation Amish in Canada have not sought Canadian citizenship but remain U.S. citizens, which is a further mitigating factor. But as succeeding generations become indigenous, all Canadian Amish will become eligible for jury duty.[13]

It appears that in contrast to the Amish in the United States, who have delineated their rights through court cases, albeit reluctantly fought, the Canadian Amish have been equally successful, if not more so, by appealing to the bureaucracy of various agencies. More often than not they have been accommodated. Historically they have struggled to maintain their separate existence wherever they have lived, and they continue to struggle in Canada.

The Political Reality of Pluralism

The Amish have not looked to the government to achieve their objectives.[14] In fact, throughout their history they have tried to have as little as possible to do with government. The implication is that they desire a limited government, or at least one with a limited role. Politically, the Amish have been more concerned with liberty than with equality. While some kinds of equality appear to be important within the group, it is not a consideration in their relations with the outside. But in the context of Canadian society, they desire freedom to develop and live as they wish.

In a pluralistic political system the participants demand, posture, bargain, make coalitions, receive benefits, and defer rewards. The involvement is uneven, but the system supposedly operates so that no participating group is left out all the time, however weak and ineffective it may be.

But there are groups like the Amish that prefer to isolate themselves and not to participate in government because they do not wish to be influenced or coopted. For such groups, maintenance of group norms is more important than societal benefits. They do not share in the rewards and resources distributed to others (Pantoja and Blourock 1975, 6). I call them "cultural isolationists." The

most common type of cultural differentiation found among those
who attempt to maintain a distinctive group identity is religion
(Young 1977, 47–65). As Donald Eugene Smith (1970, 172) has
said, "The religious tradition of a society articulates values more
explicitly than any other aspect of the society's general culture."

The national policy in most countries is assimilation rather
than acculturation or real cultural pluralism. The political theory
upon which Canadian government rests does not recognize communities as loci of legitimate political process. Instead, the political reality of pluralism in Canada has centered around interest
groups. They are recognized as legitimate participants, although
viewed as relatively ad hoc and temporary, while groups whose
identity is based on isolation from the political machinery of the
larger society are not.

In Canada, pluralism is incorporated into the political process
and used in political performance—sometimes in support of government, sometimes in lieu of it. Thus, Canadian pluralism is in
effect an extension of governmental processes and is an integral
part of the system. Racial and religious diversity have never been
considered legitimate, while cultural and linguistic diversity have
been. Eventually, biculturalism and bilingualism have become accepted institutionalized policy. But groups such as the Amish,
which are not automatically accredited, may or may not be seen as
performers of public policies. They have to be justified each time
they become involved in the political process. At best, Canadian
pluralism extends to secondary groups only when they do not interfere with the progress and extension of dominant societal values.

As the state has expanded and become more assertive, it has increasingly insisted on a holistic view of "the national interest"
rather than sectional interests. This, of course, conflicts with the
assertive role of the provinces and particularly with that of Que-
bec, which has a linguistic, religious, and cultural base for its particular interests. At the same time, corporations, specialized and
bureaucratized, have emerged as the dominant center of power
outside the state, often replacing the church. Thus, public attention focuses on the needs and problems of business rather than of
religion (Cawson 1978, 179–80).

Not surprisingly, the most significant conflicts have arisen with
the Amish in business ventures. Government assumes that contact or negotiation will take place with interest groups and that
the government will arbitrate competition between groups. Moreover, it assumes that outcomes presume to reflect the public's policy preference (Cawson 1978, 180–83). These assumptions, how-

ever, fail to consider those groups that are not oriented toward the political system or, as with cultural isolationists such as the Amish, those who wish to avoid the political system. They never mount an opposition. They are most successful when someone else engages the system in their behalf. Thus, the Amish benefit from the efforts of their Mennonite brethren, the Netherlands Reformed congregations, or sects such as the Sikhs.

By not competing within the political system, the absent groups tend to be ignored by legislatures and bureaucracies. Thus, legislative and administrative procedures are aimed to sustain interest demands that often run counter to specifically religious concerns. Aggrieved religious groups then play political catch-up through appeals to the legislature, the bureaucracy, or the courts, in reaction to policy applications, rather than trying to carve out an area of protection beforehand.

The Canadian Mosaic

There are numerous reasons why Canada has adopted its particular stand toward religious minorities. Some are basic to the practice of policy; others are the result of tensions in the society caused by the conflict of values. Mainstream societal interests are represented, recognized, and responded to. Groups like the Amish, however, have the disadvantage of small size, isolation, and countersocietal values. Moreover, as a religious group, even if they wished, they would have to struggle to achieve legitimate access to the policy arena. From the government's standpoint, the crucial transformation of an interest group occurs when it changes from a private protective organization to one with regular and mutually supportive relationships with the government (Cawson 1978, 191).

The Amish do not view political relationships as important to their interests. In fact, in many ways Amish values run counter to dominant philosophical views. They have not necessarily been alone—witness the Inuit as political outsiders who have had no other choice than to move assertively onto the political stage. But the aforementioned factors have made isolationists such as the Amish more vulnerable. The cultural isolationists may also face additional pressure because of confusion over public and private sectors as they become more interdependent with society. Those who insist on being distinctive will be suspect.

On a different level of analysis, there has always been a tension in Anglo-American nations, including Canada, between conservatism and liberalism. This conflict arises between those who view national well-being as tied to established institutions and those who welcome change and new structures; between those who emphasize society and thus the state, and those whose primary values center around the individual; and between those who most value freedom and those who emphasize equality. Independent-minded religious groups adhere to conservative values, but not of the mainstream, politically conservative kind. What these groups espouse, in effect, constitutes an attack upon the conservative structure of society. To allow them to pursue their ends would, paradoxically, bring about liberal aims. Yet, liberals readily recognize that isolationist religious groups do not accept the liberal values of the secular society. Such churches are seen as rigid and often totalitarian, even though their internally held values of equality and individualism (regarding salvation) may coincide with dominant liberal beliefs. Thus, liberal activists cannot be counted on to champion isolationist religious groups.

To the Amish, who have suffered persecution throughout their history, freedom to practice religious beliefs is *the* fundamental political right. Yet freedom does not exist universally. In fact, freedom of religious practice is more likely to be offered to dominant interest groups, or at least to those that participate and make demands. And freedom extended to one group of people may mean that other members of the state are deprived of freedom, however trivial the issue and however indirect the loss may be. Thus, while the Amish may feel a duty to follow their individual or collective conscience, the state may see their action as harmful and needing to be restrained (Nicholls 1975, 20–21).

Cultural pluralism, even in Canada, where it is trumpeted, is at best only a stated goal. It is not an unconditional reality; rather, it is dependent upon the political situation. It functions at the behest of the dominant society and of governmental convenience. To get what is desired out of it requires at least occasional participation in the political system.

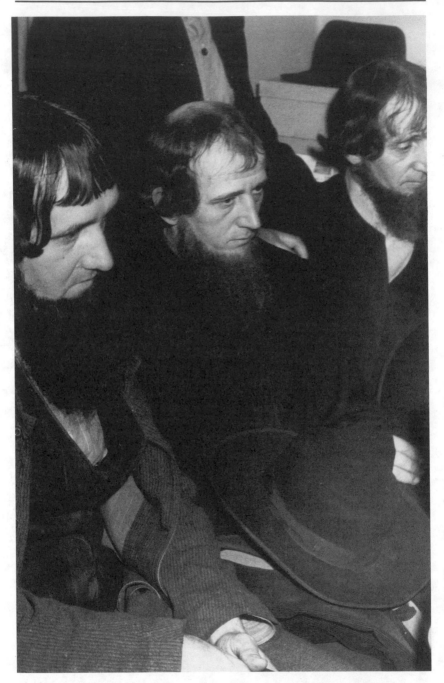

Amish fathers face charges in an alderman's office in 1953 for refusing to send their children to public high school. Richard K. Reinhold

CHAPTER THIRTEEN

First Amendment Issues

William B. Ball

How have the legal issues flowing from Amish-
state conflicts intersected with the First Amendment? Attorney William B. Ball discusses the
significance of notable Amish legal cases for the
preservation of religious freedom for minority
groups in the United States. In reviewing the
cases, he also assesses the legal gains and losses
for religious liberty.

The First Amendment to the United States Constitution protects
a bundle of citizens' rights: free exercise of their religion, their
freedom of speech and of the press, their right peaceably to assemble, and their right to petition government for the redress of grievances.[1] The Amish, who have lived on American soil for the 202
years of the life of the Bill of Rights, have indeed spoken, printed
books and newspapers, and assembled and petitioned, but never,
so far as the records show, have they been in any court of this
country in a case involving any of those liberties. Among the liberties protected by the Bill of Rights, only cases involving their
freedom of religion have found them in litigation.

"Found them in litigation"—the very mention of "litigation" in
connection with the Amish strikes a discordant note. A famous
fact about the Amish is their refusal to "go to the law."[2] It is clear
that the Amish refuse to sue.[3] Upon occasion, however, they have
stood in court in their own defense when sued or have been willing to be represented by attorneys in such a situation (Hostetler
1993, 256).

The uniqueness of the Amish position on litigation is striking.
Almost all religious groups in the nation are frequently found in
court, whether in the role of defendant or plaintiff. Indeed, some
seek to initiate lawsuits or to support cases started by others, for
the purpose of achieving social change that would affect the entire
society.[4] Attorneys who become acquainted with the Amish but
are ignorant of Amish beliefs find it difficult to understand why,
with courts available to render them justice, the Amish refuse to

utilize them. Yet, by avoiding the public role of plaintiffs seeking to vindicate their rights, they manifest a silent fidelity to their ancient teachings. While few in the American society of the 1990s are likely to adopt the Amish habit of refusing to litigate, the presence of their example should give pause to a society that, in the words of former chief justice Warren E. Burger, is drowning in a "litigation explosion" that has "affected us at all levels, including . . . the most sensitive and profound relationships of human life" (Burger 1991).

The Amish, of course, in varying degrees, exercise rights under all of the categories of activity protected by the First Amendment. They publish journals and books and upon occasion will appear in the public forum to speak out on issues of concern to them. More than once, they have petitioned the government for the redress of grievances.[5] While most of these activities have been related in some way to their religion, the collisions with government which some of these have involved raise the broad question of *what* exercise of religion the First Amendment is intended to protect. Or, since the First Amendment protects "the free exercise of religion" but does not define "religion," we can ask whether, in any given case, it is "religion" for which the Amish are claiming protection.

For example, in 1990 a real estate developer moved to create a 107-unit residential and commercial subdivision on an 90-acre tract in the heart of the Amish farmland area in Leacock Township, Pennsylvania.[6] The Amish protested this effort to install a bustling suburbia in their midst because they perceived it as impinging upon their way of life, in which farm life and religion are intimately intertwined. But to the developer and to the township supervisors this was nothing more than the kind of secular problem that has cropped up everywhere in the nation where real estate developers have had to prove to local boards that their projects meet criteria relating to traffic, storm water management, and other technical matters.[7]

Repeatedly, as in all those areas in which the Amish way and secular modernity conflict (education, health matters, land use and zoning, taxation, government social programs, and environmental matters, to name but a few), the constitutional conflict has centered upon opposing claims: that religion is what is really involved; and that the matter is secular, with religion a peripheral matter at most. As we look at the court cases in which Amish religious (First Amendment) rights have been at issue, we find the persistent thread of this conflict. Since 1990, this conflict has come into especially sharp focus in view of the historic decision of the U.S.

Supreme Court in *Employment Division v. Smith* (1990).

Prior to the *Smith* decision, the Supreme Court had displayed a keen (though not always consistent) sensitivity to religious liberty. When someone claimed that government was violating his or her religious liberty or was threatening to, the Supreme Court had always placed an exacting burden upon government. When the matter got into court, the government would have to prove that its action was necessitated by some supreme societal interest (or, in the language of the Court, a "compelling state interest"). That was because the Court had traditionally recognized religious freedom as a fundamental right, a right so important that ordinary public interests could not be deemed to outweigh it.[8] That recognition viewed religious and secular concerns separately, balancing one against the other but never holding that secular interests are the rule and that religious liberty is to be enjoyed only by exception. All that was changed by the *Smith* decision.

In *Smith*, the Court scrapped the "compelling state interest" test, holding that if a law is one of general application and religiously "neutral," it must be enforced irrespective of religious objections *and* irrespective of whether it is proved to represent a compelling state interest. A state law, therefore, requiring distribution of contraceptives to all high school children could be applied, regardless of religious objections, to children in religious schools; a city ordinance placing a tax on all occupations could be placed on clergymen in the exercise of their ministry. In both cases, the law would be one of "general application" (all children, all occupations), and in both cases it would be religiously "neutral" in the Court's eye (in that it did not single out religious schools or clergy as the particular subject of regulation). In the above example of the law on contraceptives, the Court would now hold that if some minimal public interest (e.g., the supposed prevention of teenage pregnancies) could be said to support the statute, the statute must be enforced irrespective of the fact that it would do violence to religiously founded moral requirements of the religious school children.

As can be seen, then, the *Smith* decision marginalizes religion. It puts the secular interest at center stage. That interest will be held to override religious interests without any need to prove its "compelling" importance. We are thus back to the broad question raised at the outset: *what* exercise of religion is the First Amendment intended to protect? The Supreme Court, as interpreter of the Constitution, now answers, in effect: "Virtually *no* exercise of religion." Almost all laws, however, are laws of general application; it is rare that a law is passed that expressly imposes on a specific religious practice. Moreover, restrictive laws naming a particular religion are never adopted: politicians like to avoid appearing to attack religion.

The danger to religion lies, not in obviously antireligious laws, but in laws that, when applied to secular matters, may be innocuous or even salutary. When lumping religious matters into their coverage, however, they may be disastrous to religious liberty. Some years ago, the National Labor Relations Board attempted to extend its jurisdiction to religious schools. The National Labor Relations Act, after all, applied to all "employers"—and, as a law of "general application" having no provisions referring to religion, it would be called "religiously neutral." But application of the law to religious schools would have destroyed their self-governance and the organization of their ministries.[9]

Until 1972, the Supreme Court of the United States, the ultimate interpreter of the Constitution, had not rendered a decision in any case involving Amish claims to freedom of religion. About a dozen such cases had previously been decided by state courts. Some of these involved the claim that a particular government action that had been resisted by the Amish violated the free exercise clause.[10] The first attempt to secure Supreme Court review in such a case was in 1967, in *State v. Garber*. That case lacked a developed trial record. Probably because the Supreme Court felt that it had insufficient facts before it to have a clear sense of what was involved, the *Garber* petition failed to muster the four votes needed (under the Court's informal "Rule of Four") to bring it on for review. Beginning in 1972 with *Wisconsin v. Yoder*, the Supreme Court has dealt with three cases in which Amish have presented First Amendment claims.

Wisconsin v. Yoder

Multum in parvo—much in little. So might one describe the *Yoder* case. The courage of a handful of Amish living in a small county in Wisconsin at the end of the 1960s in holding to their religious beliefs resulted in a Supreme Court decision that affected a nation of more than two hundred million people.

Yoder, whose facts have been well stated in Chapter 6, has proved to be a decision of major significance in American jurisprudence. According to a leading constitutional scholar, Jesse Choper, it established a "high-water mark" in decisions on American religious liberty.[11] That comment contains a double implication—first, that *Yoder* represents the greatest length to which the Supreme Court had ever gone in upholding religious liberty, not only in the practical result of the decision (freeing the Amish of the legal obligation to send their children to high school), but also in the breadth of the Court's reasoning in coming to that decision and in the many ramifications that the decision would have for the religious liberty of others. But the second implication was that Supreme Court decisions after *Yoder* never again maintained this degree of protection.

The *Yoder* opinion, in addition to aiding the Amish, provided a rationale that courts throughout the land would follow in a variety of religious liberty cases. That rationale had initially been stated in 1963 in *Sherbert v. Verner*. In *Sherbert*, a Seventh-Day Adventist woman had been denied state unemployment compensation benefits because she had refused to accept proffered employment on Saturday, her religiously required day of rest. The Supreme Court upheld her claim that to force her to choose between disobeying her religion and giving up her state benefits violated her religious liberty as protected by the free exercise clause.

The Court laid down a four-part test, which summarized its thinking, at that point, on religious liberty. First, the religious claimant would have to show the court a sincere and truly religious claim. Second, the religious party would have to demonstrate that the contemplated government action was really injurious to religious practice. The burden of proof would now shift to the state. Third, the state would have to prove that its action was necessitated in the name of a "compelling state interest." And, finally, the state would have to show that no alternative means existed to its contemplated action which would be less burdensome to religious liberty.

The meaning of the words "show," "prove," and "demonstrate" is that actual evidence would have to be produced, first by the religious party under the first two parts of the test; second, by the government in the last two parts of the test. This matter of requiring proof in court is extremely beneficial, both to the state and to religion. It filters out false religious claims and false claims of injury to religion. Moreover, it forces the state to come up with actual *proof* that its actions are necessitated in the name of a supreme societal interest and that no less restrictive means exist to accomplish that interest. It was this test that the Court employed in *Yoder*. But in *Yoder* it gave the test far greater body and meaning than is to be found in the unemployment compensation case, *Sherbert*.

State and federal courts followed *Sherbert* and *Yoder* in requiring the foregoing test to be applied in cases in which religious liberty was claimed to have been involved. When several states threatened to close fundamentalist Christian schools that could not, on religious grounds, comply with what they saw as excessive state regulatory requirements, the courts relied upon *Yoder* in upholding the rights of the schools and their parents.[12] As noted, when the National Labor Relations Board sought to impose its jurisdiction upon Catholic schools in Philadelphia and Scranton, the courts relied upon *Yoder* in declaring for the freedom of the schools against such government intrusion. An antiwar employee was held entitled to unemployment compensation in spite of his religiously based refusal to accept employment manufacturing armaments (*Thomas v. Review Board* [1981]). Rights of churches, religious rights of parents, and rights of ministry, of worship, and of evangelization were all comprehended within the protective scope of *Yoder*.

But, as noted above, there was a second inference in Choper's noting of *Yoder* as a "high-water mark" in the jurisprudence of religious liberty. *Yoder*, decided in 1972, represented a pinnacle; from 1972 on, decisions of the Supreme Court have descended from that height, producing decisions far less protective of religious freedom. This downward trend began in 1982 with the decision of the Court in *United States v. Lee*.

United States v. Lee

Lee was the second case in which the United States Supreme Court dealt with Amish matters. I have carefully said, "dealt with Amish matters," rather than "dealt with the Amish," because, though the Court treated the case as if, as in *Yoder*, the *sensum fidei* of the Amish faith community was involved, it was not. Edwin Lee, an Amishman from northwest Pennsylvania, was engaged in the profitable business of finishing lumber for builders of residential homes. He employed other Amish in this commercial undertaking.

Unhappy with having to pay the employer's share of Social Security taxes on his employees, Lee brought a suit in the U.S. District Court for the Western District of Pennsylvania seeking a judgment that the imposition of such a tax violated the free exercise clause. Here was an Amishman refusing to obey a general law and starting a lawsuit in order to vindicate his refusal to pay taxes.

Nothing in the record showed that his refusal was pursuant to any judgment of Amish bishops or even represented a consensus of the Amish community to which he belonged. Nevertheless, he claimed in court that fundamental teachings of the Amish faith required his resistance to the tax in question.

The case proceeded without a trial. That is, no witnesses, as in *Yoder*, took the stand in order to elucidate and defend the alleged Amish teachings. The case instead proceeded on the basis of a mere "stipulated record," a short typed-up agreement between Lee's attorneys and the government attorneys reciting Lee's refusal, on religious grounds, to pay the taxes. As fate would have it, the district court, relying on *Yoder*, upheld Lee. The government then appealed to the Supreme Court, which reversed. I have pointed above to *Lee* as the first of a series of decisions marking a downward trend in Supreme Court holdings on religious liberty. *Lee* was, in fact, a disaster in terms of religious freedom. The Court utilized Lee's religious liberty claim to write a frighteningly broad opinion relating to religion and the government's power to collect taxes. At one point in its opinion (now, unhappily, quoted in many subsequent decisions of lower courts throughout the land) the Supreme Court stated: "Because the broad public interest in maintaining a sound tax system is of such a high order, religious belief in conflict with the payment of taxes affords no basis for resisting the tax."[13]

Lee was a case that should never have been brought. No Amish teachings had declared that the Amish religion forbade the payment of the employer's share of Social Security taxes. Indeed, as other chapters in this book have shown, the Amish, when faced with that tax on the self-employed, proceeded not to court but to Congress in order to seek relief. The *Lee* litigation, unfortunately, provided no real factual basis for the Supreme Court's decision. It appears never to have occurred to the justices that it was unusual, to say the least, for an Amishman to be suing. The law profession's ancient adage, that "bad cases make hard law," could not be better exemplified than by *United States v. Lee*.[14]

In *Lee*, the Court duly noted (and distinguished) the *Yoder* decision; but in fact it created a significant limitation on that decision. The Court dealt carelessly with the question of whether part one of the *Sherbert-Yoder* test had been met by Lee, and it all too readily accepted his claim that the Amish religion forbids payment of Social Security taxes. It dealt yet more carelessly with part three of the test (the requirement that the government prove a compelling state interest in imposing the tax). On this point, the Court relied on generalizations instead of evidence to support its new view that the power of government to tax religion is almost without limitation.[15]

The Continued Trend Away from Yoder: The Goldman, Roy, and Lyng Decisions

After the *Lee* decision in 1982, a trend away from the *Yoder* pinnacle became alarmingly evident in Supreme Court decisions. In *Goldman v. Weinberger* (1986), the Court had before it the question of whether an Orthodox Jewish Air Force captain could be barred, under Air Force regulations, from wearing the religiously symbolic yarmulke in pursuing the work of his ministry indoors. Goldman, the officer in question, asserted that wearing the yarmulke was a requirement of his religion. Observers of the litigation expected the four-part *Yoder* test to be applied. In fact, it was ignored, and the Court denied Goldman's religious claim.

Bowen v. Roy (1986) involved the contention of American Indians that obtaining a Social Security number for their two-year-old daughter would violate their Native American religious beliefs. The government conditioned the receipt of Social Security benefits by members of the household on their obtaining a Social Security number for their daughter. Upon trial it had been disclosed that the Indians held the belief that use of the number by the government would "rob the spirit" of their daughter. The Supreme Court held that the Indians' free exercise of religion was not violated by the government's requirement.

What is of interest here is not whether the ruling was correct, but whether the Court dealt at all with the *Yoder* test and, if so, in what way. The Court in *Roy* did pay heed to *Yoder*—but very limited heed. It closely qualified what had been widely believed to be *Yoder*'s very broad ruling in favor of religious freedom. The Court said that "in the enforcement of a facially neutral and uniformly applicable requirement for the administration of welfare programs reaching many millions of people, the government is entitled to wide latitude" (*Roy* at 707). If the legislation was not intended to discriminate against a particular religious group or religion in general, the government need show only that the legislation is a "reasonable means of promoting a legitimate public interest" (*Roy* at 708). While eight justices agreed that the government could not be enjoined for use of the child's Social Security number, three justices believed that *Yoder* should have been applied. They stated that the free exercise clause was "clearly implicated in this case," noting that "this Court has consistently asked the government to demonstrate that unbending application of its regulation to the religious objector 'is essential to accomplish an overriding governmental interest'" (*Roy* at 728).

Here, then, was a most serious departure from *Yoder*. It was the first statement by the Court that if a statute is "neutral" as far as religion is concerned and is designed to be uniformly applied, the fact that, in one or some of its applications, it destroys religious free exercise is immaterial.

Another case, *Lyng v. Northwest Indian Cemetery Protective Ass'n.* (1988), involved Indian religious liberty claims. Here the Supreme Court held that the free exercise clause did not prevent the government from pursuing timber harvesting in, or constructing a road through, a national forest area that had been utilized for at least two centuries as a sacred site for the religious ceremonies of Indian tribes. Those who observed this case while it was in the courts came up with differing opinions as to whether the Indians' free exercise claim should be upheld or whether the government had a superior right to proceed with its logging and road-building operations. But the critical question was how the *Yoder* test would be applied. Unfortunately, that vitally important test was not applied.

The Court stated that "even assuming that the government's actions here will virtually destroy the Indians' ability to practice their religion, the Constitution simply does not provide a principle that could justify upholding the Indians' legal claims" (*Lyng* at 451–52). Here indeed was a dramatic departure from the high religious liberty standard established in *Yoder*. The Court said that so long as the government does not coerce individuals into acting contrary to their religious beliefs, and so long as the government's action is not specifically directed at a particular religion but is, instead, "neutral," the government is not required to come forward and prove a compelling state interest in what it is doing.

The *Lyng* decision represents yet a further departure from *Yoder*. While the Court acknowledged the *Yoder* decision and did not directly overrule it, the Court now, disturbingly, refused to hold the government to the *Yoder* test. Of course, the government's actions in this case did not force the Indians to contradict their religious beliefs; it merely destroyed their opportunity to practice them.

Minnesota v. Hershberger

The facts of this case, the third one in which the Supreme Court dealt with specifically Amish matters, are described in Chapter 8. At both the trial court and intermediate appellate court levels, the question I have earlier noted, "Is it religion that is really involved?" became central. The two lower court judges dealt with that question, but indistinctly. The trial court judge said that, if religion was involved, it could not be held to be a defense against the government's requirement. The intermediate state appellate court held that, since resistance to the requirement did not reflect a religious consensus of the Amish community "as a whole," the free exercise claim could not be sustained.

The Minnesota Supreme Court rejected the view that the religious claim of an individual must be disregarded if it is not shared by at least a majority of the members of the religion to which he says he belongs. That court then specifically followed the *Yoder* test and held that the slow-moving vehicle (SMV) requirement was not justified by a compelling state interest and did not constitute the least restrictive means for protecting the state's interest in traffic safety (*State v. Hershberger* [1989] [*Hershberger I*]). As Wisconsin had surprisingly done in *Yoder*, following its loss before the Wisconsin Supreme Court, so Minnesota now did in *Hershberger*: it sought reversal by the Supreme Court of the United States. Unlike Wisconsin, Minnesota won (*Minnesota v. Hershberger* [1990]).

The State of Minnesota's victory at the U.S. Supreme Court level was not, however, based upon the Court's application of the *Yoder* test but upon its rejection of that test. On 17 April 1990, the Supreme Court had, in effect, changed the rules of the game by its decision in the *Smith* case. While I consider the future implications of *Smith* at the end of this chapter, it suffices for now to say that, with its *Smith* ruling as the basis for doing so, the Supreme Court reversed the Minnesota Supreme Court and accordingly remanded the SMV case to that court. The Minnesota court, now told that the religious freedom protection of the U.S. Constitution was not available to the Amish on the SMV issue, turned to the Minnesota Constitution, Article 1, Section 16 of which provides:

> The enumeration of rights in this constitution shall not deny or impair others retained by and inherent in the people. *The right of every man to worship God according to the dictates of his own conscience shall never be infringed;* nor shall any man be compelled to attend, erect or support any place of worship, or to maintain any

religious or ecclesiastical ministry, against his consent; *nor shall any control of or interference with the rights of conscience be permitted, or any preference be given by law to any religious establishment or mode of worship; but the liberty of conscience hereby secured shall not be so construed as to excuse acts of licentiousness or justify practices inconsistent with the peace or safety of the state,* nor shall any money be drawn from the treasury for the benefit of any religious societies or religious or theological seminaries.[16]

This lengthy constitutional passage actually differed in no way from what the U.S. Supreme Court, in its decisions through 1972, had interpreted the free exercise clause to embrace. Now, however, the Minnesota Supreme Court was faced with the fact that it had already determined that the SMV claim of the Minnesota Amish was a genuine religious claim and that no supreme societal interest dictated overriding that claim. The state court believed that it could at once protect the liberties of the Amish and avoid the limitations of *Smith* by having recourse to the above language of the state constitution. Of course, in doing so, it was well aware of the principle that the Supreme Court of the United States will not review the final interpretation of a state constitutional provision by that state's highest court. The *Hershberger* case thus ended favorably for the Amish.

The Future

It should be clear that the *Smith* decision leaves the exercise of religion largely at the mercy of government. The decision contains some exceptions, but these are narrow indeed. One exception would be a situation in which a statute or regulation expressly singled out a religious practice or a particular religion by name for burden or restriction. But that exception is almost meaningless, since the politicians who make our laws are not about to risk charges of bigotry by making any such proposals. The immense danger posed by *Smith* lies precisely in the fact that almost all laws that threaten religious freedom are religiously neutral laws of general application.

The compulsory attendance law in *Yoder* and the SMV law in *Hershberger* were such laws—that is, they applied generally (in *Yoder*, to all school-age children; in *Hershberger*, to all vehicles). And those laws did not speak of the Amish religion or of any religion and were thus "religiously neutral." As legislation increasingly intersects areas of American life that have been the traditional domain of religion—education, health, the care of children, and morality, for example—it is the "religiously neutral law of general application" which, through hostility, or by ignorance or accident, will limit or destroy religious freedom. That is what all religion in America now faces, and that obviously includes the Amish.

It is true that the Supreme Court, in *Smith*, did not expressly override *Yoder*. It treated *Yoder*, however, as though *Yoder* had not been what it essentially was: a religious liberty case. The Court, to the contrary, treated *Yoder* as a parental rights case and nothing more. The Amish were accorded exemption from high school solely because the rights of parents, as parents, were involved. That, of course, is a totally false picture of *Yoder*—a caricature to be deplored, a representation of that case which the very reading of the superb opinion in *Yoder* contradicts.

Will the sole constitutional recourse of the Amish be in state laws in future cases in which their religious freedom is threatened? Unless and until the Supreme Court of the United States rectifies its *Smith* decision, the answer is twofold. The first answer lies in legislation, at both the federal and the state level—legislation creating specific exemptions where needed. Other chapters in this book have referred to successes, on behalf of the Amish, in securing such exemptions. The second answer is that reliance on state constitutional provisions will doubtless be necessary—for example, when enforcement of religiously unacceptable laws is threatened. But not all state supreme courts, it must be realized, may be as liberty-minded as has been the Supreme Court of Minnesota.

The future must not be regarded as constitutionally dark and forbidding. The Supreme Court has many times overruled its own past decisions, or so nuanced or qualified them as essentially to change them.[17] The Constitution, in all of its integrity, cannot long be distorted in its meaning. The Supreme Court has, at the moment, virtually stricken the free exercise clause from its provisions. But that can, must, and will pass. And there is much public sympathy for the Amish, and that, too, is a factor that can affect the political scene—for example, with respect to needed exemptive legislation. The Amish have endured centuries of oppression and difficulty, and I do not foresee their imminent legal doom. But they, and all their friends, must labor against the forces that would bring that about. In doing so, the religious liberty of all will be secured.

Significant Legal Cases

Elizabeth Place

This annotated listing of legal cases provides a brief description of some of the cases appearing in the text. It is not an exhaustive listing of cases relevant to the Amish, but it contains those of particular legal significance.

Borntrager v. Commissioner, 58 T.C.M. (CCH) 1242 (1990). The United States Tax Court upheld the IRS's finding that an excommunicated Old Order Amish man was not entitled to an exemption from the self-employment tax under the Internal Revenue Code. Congress had granted an exemption from the obligation to pay Social Security tax to members of religious sects whose practice it is to "make provisions for their dependent members." § 1402(g)(1)(D). By virtue of the petitioner's excommunication, he was no longer a member of the Old Order Amish. Even though he shared the Amish view that it is wrong not to provide for oneself and one's family, the court found that he was not in a position to benefit from the group's communal welfare system and therefore fell outside the congressional exemption.

Bowen v. Roy, 476 U.S. 693 (1986). The U.S. Supreme Court rejected a claim that the religious beliefs of American Indians were violated by a government requirement that applicants for social benefits obtain Social Security numbers. The Indians believed that use of the numbers could rob one of one's spirit. Finding no violation of the First Amendment, the Court stated that the free exercise clause prevents government-compelled worship but does not "afford an individual a right to dictate the conduct of the Government's internal procedures." 476 U.S. at 699. The Court held that the government is "entitled to wide latitude" in the "enforcement of a facially neutral and uniformly applicable requirement for the administration of welfare programs reaching millions of people." Id. at 707. The statute was upheld as a reasonable means of promoting the legitimate and important state interest in preventing welfare fraud.

Brown v. Board of Education, 347 U.S. 483 (1954). Overruling the "separate but equal" doctrine announced in *Plessy v. Ferguson,* 163 U.S. 537 (1896), the U.S. Supreme Court held that segregation of children in public schools on the basis of race, even where tangible factors such as building and curriculum are equal, deprives minority groups of the equal protection of the law, guaranteed by the Fourteenth Amendment. The Court found separate educational facilities to be inherently unequal.

Byler v. State, 26 Ohio App. 329, 157 N.E. 421 (1927). The conviction of a parent for a second violation of Ohio's compulsory school attendance laws was reversed. The court found that the charge of a second offense was not adequately stated and that no legal evidence of a prior conviction, a prerequisite to conviction for a second offense, had been presented.

Caulfield v. Hirsch, No. 76-279 Civ. (E.D. Pa. July 7, 1977). Application of the National Labor Relations Act to the employment relationship between Catholic elementary schools and their lay teachers was held to violate the First Amendment. The pervasive authority of the National Labor Relations Board over labor issues interfered with the free exercise of religion: the board could cause division in the faith community in the course of determining bargaining units; mandatory bargaining would include issues relating to the religious mission of the schools; and NLRB investigation of unfair labor practices would cause the board to evaluate ecclesiastical concerns. No compelling state interest justified this burden on the religious liberty of the schools. In addition, the board's broad authority, including the power to investigate various aspects of the employment relationship, if applied to religious schools would constitute excessive entanglement of the government with religion in violation of the establishment clause.

Commonwealth v. Beiler, 168 Pa. Super. 462, 79 A.2d 134 (1951). The court upheld the conviction of two Amish fathers for violating the state's compulsory school attendance laws by refusing to send their children to high school. The court acknowledged that the defendants held sincere religious beliefs rejecting advanced education. Nevertheless, noting the importance of the "enlightened intelligence" of citizens to the democratic way of life, the court found no religious interference in compelling parents to educate children as prescribed by law, stating, "religious liberty includes the absolute right to believe but only a limited right to act." 79 A.2d at 137.

Commonwealth v. Petersheim, 70 Pa. D & C. 432 (Somerset County Ct. 1949) *appeal dismissed*, 166 Pa. Super. 90, 70 A.2d 395 (1951). The convictions of Amish parents for violating Pennsylvania's compulsory attendance laws were overturned. The court held that enforcing the law against defendants with religious objections to compulsory school attendance infringed on their constitutional rights of religious liberty and conscience.

Commonwealth v. Sykes, No. 11 E.Q. 1989 (C.P. Mercer County, Pa., Dec. 21, 1990). The court rejected the efforts of the Pennsylvania State Board of Medicine permanently to enjoin a lay midwife from the alleged unlicensed practice of midwifery. The court held that the Medical Practice Act of 1985, under which the board brought the action, regulated only the practice of midwifery by registered nurses and did not address or proscribe the unlicensed practice of lay midwifery.

Commonwealth v. Zook, No. 85-T-264 (Baron County Dist. Ct., Ky., August 3, 1985). Following *Yoder*, the court held that the sincerely held religious beliefs of a Swartzentruber Old Order Amish man opposed to displaying symbols were violated by enforcement of a state statute requiring buggies to display slow-moving vehicle emblems. The court found Kentucky's compelling interest in safety adequately served by the use of reflective tape and lanterns on buggies.

Employment Div., Dep't of Human Resources of Oregon v. Smith, 494 U.S. 872 (1990). The U.S. Supreme Court upheld Oregon's prohibition of peyote use and denial of unemployment compensation benefits to members of the Native American Church who were discharged from their jobs because of religiously inspired use. The Court held that the free exercise clause of the First Amendment is not violated by a neutral, generally applicable law that incidentally forbids the performance of a religiously required act. The Court stated that prior decisions holding that such laws violate the First Amendment are distinguishable, since they also involved other constitutional rights. For example, the Court noted that *Yoder* involved parental rights along with religious rights. The Court refused to apply the *Sherbert* test, in which government actions that substantially interfere with religious practices must be justified by a compelling state interest, to generally applicable criminal laws. To hold otherwise, the Court stated, would permit every individual to become a law unto himself. The Court also declined to extend the compelling state interest test just to those cases in which the prohibited conduct is "central" to the individual's religion, since it is not appropriate for the judiciary to determine which beliefs are central to a particular faith.

Fussner v. Smith, No. C-76-363 (N.D. Ohio Nov. 28, 1977). Following *Yoder*, the court held that the county could not require plaintiffs to display slow-moving vehicle emblems on their buggies in violation of their religious beliefs, since a less restrictive alternative (reflective tape and lamps) could be used to further the state's interest in highway safety.

Gingerich v. State, 226 Ind. 678, 83 N.E.2d 47 (1948). The conviction of an Amish parent who violated Indiana's compulsory school attendance law by refusing to send his son to school was upheld by the state supreme court. The court did not address the constitutionality of the conviction, since this issue had not been properly presented before the trial court.

Goldman v. Weinberger, 475 U.S. 503 (1986). The U.S. Supreme Court rejected an Orthodox Jewish officer's contention that Air Force regulations violated his free exercise of religion by prohibiting him from wearing his yarmulke, a skullcap that he was required to wear by his religious beliefs. The Court held that the military is not required to accommodate such religious practices in light of its professional judgment that standardized uniforms encourage the subordination of personal preferences in favor of the military's need for unity.

Kentucky State Bd. for Elementary and Secondary Educ. v. Rudasill, 589 S.W.2d 877 (Ky. 1979) *cert. denied*, 446 U.S. 938 (1980). Kentucky's standards for approval of private schools, which required the certification of private school teachers and the use of state-approved textbooks, were held to violate the state constitution, which states: "nor shall any man be compelled to send his child to any school to which he may be conscientiously opposed." While the court recognized the state's interest in educating its citizens to participate intelligently in a democracy, these requirements were not necessary to satisfy the state's interest. The state's use of standardized tests to monitor the work of nonpublic schools was upheld.

Lyng v. Northwest Indian Cemetery Protective Ass'n., 485 U.S. 439 (1988). The U.S. Supreme Court upheld a plan by the U.S. Forest Service to harvest timber and to construct a road through an area of a national forest which for at least two centuries had been used by American Indians as a sacred site for religious worship. The Court found that the government's actions did not violate the free exercise clause of the Constitution, holding that incidental effects of government programs which may interfere with the practice of religion but do not force individuals to violate their beliefs do not require that the state prove a compelling state interest to justify its actions. It was undisputed that the government's activities could have devastating effects on traditional Indian religious practices. Id. at 451.

McCormick v. Hirsch, 460 F. Supp. 1337 (M.D. Pa. 1978). The National Labor Relations Board was preliminarily enjoined from exercising jurisdiction over parochial schools employing lay teachers seeking to unionize. Both the free exercise and establishment clauses of the First Amendment would be violated by application of the National Labor Relations Act to religious schools. The act gives the board power to determine bargaining units and to investigate unfair labor practices, which includes investigation into the financial affairs of the church. It also requires the board to determine if alleged unfair labor practices are based on anti-union sentiment or religious doctrine. It also forces churches to engage in collective bargaining. Applying the *Yoder* analysis, it was held that exercise of these powers would infringe on the religious liberties of religious schools without a sufficiently compelling state interest and, thus, would violate the free exercise clause. It would also conflict with the establishment clause by causing excessive board entanglement with both the institutional and the spiritual affairs of the church.

Minnesota v. Hershberger, 110 U.S. 1918 (1990) (mem.). The U.S. Supreme Court vacated the Minnesota Supreme Court judgment in *State v. Hershberger*, 444 N.W.2d 282 (1989), and remanded the case for consideration in light of *Smith*.

Nebraska Dist. of Evangelical Lutheran Synod v. McKelvie, 104 Neb. 93, 175 N.W. 531 (1919). The Nebraska Supreme Court upheld an education law requiring that subjects in all schools be taught in English and that foreign languages be taught only to students who have passed eighth grade. Parochial schools claimed the act would prevent their foreign language-speaking children from obtaining instruction in religion and morals. The court recognized the government's interest in a citizenship that knows the language of its country and the nature of its government and interpreted the law as requiring only that state-mandated studies be conducted in English while permitting additional instruction in other languages.

Reynolds v. United States, 98 U.S. 145 (1878). A claim by a Mormon that his conviction for polygamy violated his First Amendment rights was rejected by the U.S. Supreme Court. Recognizing marriage as a most important feature of social life and polygamy as a practice that has historically been considered an offense against society, the Court found it within the legitimate scope of civil government to determine whether to permit polygamy as the law of social life under its jurisdiction. The Court found that "laws are made for the government of actions, and while they cannot interfere with mere religious belief and opinions, they may interfere with practice." Id. at 166. To exempt those whose religion mandates polygamy from complying with the prohibition of polygamy would be "to permit every citizen to become a law unto himself." Id. at 166.

Sherbert v. Verner, 374 U.S. 398 (1963). The U.S. Supreme Court found that the denial of unemployment compensation benefits to a Seventh Day Adventist who was discharged for refusing to work on Saturday, her Sabbath, burdened the free exercise of her religion by requiring her either to forgo benefits or to abandon her religious beliefs in order to accept employment. The Court adopted a four-part analysis under which (1) the claimant has to show a sincerely held religious belief (2) burdened by the government's action, (3) which the government cannot prove is justified by a compelling state interest, (4) or which, even if justified by a compelling state interest, cannot be regulated by a less burdensome alternative. The Court found that the state's interest in limiting false claims and in not hindering employers' scheduling of Saturday work was not a compelling interest sufficient to justify the burden on the worker's sincerely held religious beliefs. The Court found that providing benefits does not violate the establishment clause, since it reflects nothing more than the government's obligation to be neutral in the face of religious differences and does not represent involvement of religion with secular institutions.

State v. Garber, 197 Kan. 567, 419 P.2d 896 (1966), *cert. denied*, 389 U.S. 51 (1967). The Kansas Supreme Court rejected the contention by an Amish father that his religious liberties were violated by his conviction under Kansas compulsory school attendance laws for refusing to send his daughter to public high school. Distinguishing between the right to believe and the right to practice, the former being absolute and the latter limited by the state's public welfare interest, the court found that requiring high school attendance does not infringe on the right to worship or believe. It was further held that, no matter how sincere religious beliefs may be, an individual cannot be permitted upon religious grounds to be the judge of his duty to obey laws enacted in the public interest.

State v. Hershberger (*Hershberger I*), 444 N.W.2d 282 (Minn. 1989), *judgment vacated*, 110 U.S. 1918 (1990). In a decision issued prior to *Smith*, the court held that the state's requirement of brightly colored reflective emblems on slow-moving vehicles violated the free exercise rights of the Amish. The statute burdened the sincerely held religious beliefs of the Amish; and, although the state's interest in public safety is compelling, it can be served by alternative means such as placement of red lanterns and silver reflective tape on slow-moving vehicles at night. It did not matter that all Amish did not object to the symbols, since the court was convinced that the sincerely held beliefs of the defendants led to rejection of the emblems.

State v. Hershberger (*Hershberger II*), 462 N.W.2d 393 (Minn. 1990). On remand from the U.S. Supreme Court for consideration in light of *Smith*, the Minnesota Supreme Court relied on the "liberty of conscience" clause of the state constitution to hold that a state statute requiring slow-moving vehicles to display triangular emblems infringed on the religious beliefs of Amish opposed to displaying "worldly symbols." As a result of *Smith*'s limitation on the protection afforded religious freedom under the First Amendment, the court looked to the state constitution's broader prohibition of "infringement" or "interference" with religious freedom to hold that, if a claimant has proved a sincerely held religious belief, the state must demonstrate that the public safely cannot be achieved by reasonable alternative means. The state failed to prove that the alternative of lighted red lanterns and application of silver tape to buggies did not satisfy the state's interest in public safety.

State v. Hershberger, 77 Ohio L. Abs. 487, 150 N.E.2d 671 (Wayne County Juv. Ct. 1958). Amish parents of a boy found to be a neglected child, since his parents had not sent him to school, were found guilty of contempt of court for refusing to turn their child over to the custody of the State Board of Welfare. The board sought custody of the child, since he had been deemed "neglected" under state law. The court rejected the parents' argument that their religious convictions prevented them from complying with the school attendance laws, stating that the First Amendment was not controlling on the state of Ohio and that the parents' rights under the state constitution to freedom of conscience and to worship as they pleased was not infringed by the state's compulsory school laws.

State v. Hochstetler, No. 4726 (Elkhart Cir. Ct., Ind. Jan. 22, 1948). An elderly Amish bishop pleaded guilty to assault and battery charges brought against him for chaining his mentally ill daughter to her bed when she was difficult to control. Sentenced to six months at the state penal farm, the bishop was later pardoned by the governor.

State v. LaBarge, 134 Vt. 276, 357 A.2d 121 (1976). Criminal prosecution of parents for truancy, based on their children's attendance at an "unapproved" school, was dismissed, since the truancy statute required only that children be sent to public schools or be provided an "equivalent education." Equivalent education is not the same as school "approval," and the Department of Education had not determined whether the school in question, which was unapproved, provided an equivalent education.

State v. Swartzentruber, 170 Mich. App. 682, 429 N.W.2d 225 (1988). Applying Thomas and Yoder, the court held that enforcement of a state statute requiring slow-moving vehicles to display brightly colored reflective emblems violated the First Amendment rights of the Amish defendants. In the absence of any evidence from the state concerning traffic hazards caused by horse-drawn vehicles, the state failed to prove a compelling interest sufficient to overcome the burden imposed by the statute on the sincerely held religious beliefs of the Amish.

State v. Whisner, 47 Ohio St. 2d 181, 351 N.E.2d 750 (1976). Ohio's minimum standards for the operation of schools were held to violate the right of parents of nonpublic school children to the free exercise of religion. The court found unreasonable standards such as those requiring all of the activities of a school to conform to the policies of the state Board of Education, requiring a school to cooperate with the community in which it exists, and requiring a determined amount of instruction in areas that do not lend themselves to the teaching of religious principles. The court also held that the standards violate the liberty clause of the Fourteenth Amendment, since they were "so pervasive and all-encompassing that total compliance with each and every standard would effectively eradicate the distinction between public and non-public education, and thereby deprive [the] appellants of their traditional interest as parents to direct the upbringing and education of their children." Id. at 768. No state interest existed that justified the abrogation of these constitutional rights.

State v. Yoder, 49 Wis. 2d 430, 182 N.W.2d 539 (1971), *aff'd,* 406 U.S. 205 (1972). The court found that Wisconsin's compulsory education law infringed on the right of the Amish to the free exercise of religion, constituting a heavy burden by compelling them to perform acts repugnant to their religion—that is, exposing Amish children to a worldly education at a time in their adolescence that is critical to their religious and cultural development. The court found no compelling state interest in two years of compulsory high school education, finding the Amish claim convincing that their education produces as good a product as two additional years of high school education. The state's attempt to regulate children in its capacity of *parens patriae* was rejected, since "in the important matter of freedom of religion, the natural parents should have the right to rear their children in their religion." 182 N.W.2d at 545.

State ex rel. Chalfin v. Glick, 172 Ohio St. 249, 175 N.E.2d 68 (1961). The state sought to enjoin the operation of an Amish school which was staffed by teachers who were not qualified under Ohio law and which did not comply with state regulations concerning the amount or character of instruction. The Ohio Supreme Court, finding no threat to the morals, welfare, or safety of the public or the children attending the school, affirmed the lower court's denial of the injunction.

Thomas v. Review Bd. of the Ind. Employment Sec. Div., 450 U.S. 707 (1981). The denial of unemployment compensation to a Jehovah's Witness, whose religious beliefs compelled him to quit his job when he was required to work on armament production, was held by the U.S. Supreme Court to violate the free exercise clause of the First Amendment. The Court held that it was improper for the lower court to rely on the fact that the worker was struggling with his religion or that other Jehovah's Witnesses did not share his beliefs, stating that courts are not arbiters of scriptural interpretation. The proper inquiry is whether this worker terminated employment because of an honest conviction that the work was forbidden by his religion. It was further held that when the state conditions receipt of an important government benefit upon conduct that violates a religious belief or denies the benefit because of conduct required by religious beliefs, thus pressuring an adherent to violate his beliefs, the government substantially burdens religion. The Court found no compelling state interest sufficient to justify this burden. Payment of benefits would not constitute a violation of the establishment clause, since it would merely reflect the government's obligation to be neutral and would not represent the involvement of religion with secular institutions.

United States v. Lee, 455 U.S. 252 (1982). The U.S. Supreme Court held that the religious beliefs of an Amish employer that forbade both the payment and the receipt of Social Security benefits were burdened by compulsory participation in the Social Security system. The Court found, however, that this burden was not unconstitutional, since the state's overriding interest in maintaining the nationwide Social Security system justified the limitation on religious liberty. This case was distinguished from *Yoder* because of the difficulty of accommodating the Social Security system to the "myriad exceptions flowing from a wide variety of religious beliefs." Id. at 260. Analogizing the Social Security tax to income taxes, the Court stated that the tax system could not function if, for example, an individual opposed to war refused to pay that percentage of his taxes which funded war-related activities. The Court found that Congress had accommodated the religious beliefs of those opposed to participation in the Social Security system to the extent compatible with a comprehensive national program by providing a religious exemption for self-employed persons.

Wisconsin v. Yoder, 406 U.S. 205 (1972). Following the four-part test established in *Sherbert,* the U.S. Supreme Court held that Wisconsin could not compel the Amish to send their children to school beyond eighth grade. While a state has a strong interest in the education of its citizens, "it is not totally free from a balancing process when it impinges on fundamental rights and interests, such as those specifically protected by the Free Exercise Clause of the First Amendment, and the traditional interest of parents with respect to their children." Id. at 214. The Court found that to apply the state's compulsory education laws "would gravely endanger if not destroy the free exercise" of Amish religious beliefs by exposing Amish children to worldly values contrary to their religious beliefs and by interfering with the religious development of Amish children and their integration into the Amish faith community during the critical period of adolescence. The state's strong interest in education could not prevail over the religious practices of the Amish, since the interests advanced by the state in support of compulsory education were adequately addressed by the Amish alternative mode of education. Forgoing one or two years of education would not "impair the physical or mental health of the child, or result in an inability to be self-supporting or to discharge the duties and responsibilities of citizenship, or in any way materially detract from the welfare of society." Id. at 234.

Notes

Chapter 1. Negotiating with Caesar

1. Aaron E. Beiler, letter to Hugo L. Black, 16 March 1938.
2. For recent discussions of Amish conflict with the state, consult Ball 1988, Robb 1990, Ruegger 1991, Sekus 1989, and Tweedy 1991.
3. The settlements and church districts are updated annually by Ben J. Raber in *The New American Almanac*. See the latest (1993) edition. See also Luthy 1992 for an update of the growth of Amish settlements.
4. For an introduction to Anabaptist history, consult Dyck 1981, Weaver 1987, and the five-volume *Mennonite Encyclopedia* (1956). Nolt (1992) provides a readable introduction to Amish history. Harold Bender (1955) discusses the relation of sixteenth-century Anabaptists and religious liberty.
5. Population estimates and the number of districts are based on Raber's (1992) listing of districts, correspondence with David Luthy, and Luthy's recent (1992) update of settlements. The population estimate includes children and adults and is calculated on a projected average of 150 persons per church district. The size of districts varies by settlement and their longevity. The Amish as a people are experiencing sustained growth, with some settlements doubling nearly every twenty years.
6. For extended discussions of Amish culture and social structure, consult Hostetler 1993 and Kraybill 1989, 1990.
7. Petition "To Our Men in Authority," 17 November 1937, by representatives of thirty-seven Old Order Amish and Old Order Mennonite congregations in eastern Pennsylvania. It was written in response to a proposed 1937 school law. Emphasis added.
8. This wording appears in another petition responding to the proposed 1937 school law, "To the Members of the General Assembly of the State of Pennsylvania," undated and unpublished. Emphasis added.
9. "Statement of the Bishops of the Old Order Amish Church of Lancaster County Regarding Attendance in Public Schools," 22 February 1950, unpublished.
10. Kauffman (1991, 144–49) reports numerous times in the nineteenth century when Amish persons held township offices of supervisor, overseer of the poor, assessor, auditor, and school director in the Big Valley of Mifflin County, Pennsylvania. Perhaps one of the reasons for such a high level of political office holding was the large proportion of Amish and Mennonites living in this particular county. Kauffman reports that even the office of constable occasionally fell to Amishmen by default, but they consistently refused to serve.
11. The structural differences between traditional and modern societies have long been studied by social scientists who differentiate between Gemeinschaft and Gesellschaft, mechanical and organic solidarity, folk and contractual societies, etc.

12. "Repeal from 1937 Enactment," unpublished paper summarizing Amish views on education in Eastern Pennsylvania, p. 4.

13. "Bike Trail Plan Is Opposed by Amish," *New Era*, 9 December 1991.

14. A more extensive discussion of the negotiation model for understanding Amish interaction with modern society can be found in Kraybill 1989, 20–21, 235–49.

Chapter 2. The Amish View of the State

1. This quote and several others in this article are based on correspondence with David Luthy.

2. The title *Aus Bundt [Ausbund]* first appeared on the 1583 edition, which is considered the second edition. The first edition appeared in 1564 under the title *Etliche schöne Christliche Geseng* and contained fifty-three hymns, fifty of which were included in the 1583 second edition, which was expanded to about twice the size of the first. Thus, the *Ausbund* in reality was first published in 1564.

3. Many Anabaptist historians would include the *Schleitheim Confession of Faith* (or *Discipline*, as some would call it), published in 1527, among these historic documents. However, its influence on Amish thought is, at best, only indirect—in that the *Schleitheim Confession* may have influenced other writings of importance to the Amish, as indicated by Snyder (1989, 323–44).

4. John Howard Yoder has said that "the very nature of the state is force" (1964, 7, 12, 82). See also Sanders 1964, 72, and Weber 1958, 77–83.

5. A fuller treatment of the Anabaptist movement would recognize that some Anabaptists do not fit this description. Melchior Hoffman and John of Leiden, for example, were ready to establish the kingdom of God by force.

6. Klaassen 1987, 251–61, and Hillerbrand 1958a, 28–47.

7. Luther, for example, spoke of the "worldly regiment as the left hand of the kingdom and the spiritual regiment of God's right hand" (Sanders 1964, 29). This suggests a closer relation between the two kingdoms and a more positive role for the state in God's economy than what the Anabaptists were prepared to concede.

8. The full title in translation deserves attention:

> Thorough Account from God's Word, How to Distinguish Between the Temporal [or worldly] and spiritual Regimes, Each with Its Order, and Concerning the Power of the Temporal [worldly] Sword; Whether the Government Official May, in Accord with the Demand of His Office, Wield the Sword over Evildoers, Take Vengeance with it, Fight against His Enemies; Preserve, Shelter and Protect with Force; and Whether He May at the same Time Be and Remain a Christian in the Peaceful Kingdom of Christ. (Schnell 1710)

According to Anabaptist scholar Leonard Gross, the earliest known version of this treatise is in the form of a codex, written in about 1575. An interpretive essay and translation of Schnell's essay by Gross will appear in a forthcoming issue of the *Mennonite Quarterly Review*. A published version (1710) of Schnell's treatise may be found in the *Sammelband*, located in the Mennonite Historical Library, Goshen College, Goshen, Ind. The first segment consists of a copy of the 1691 edition of the prayer book, the *Christliche Glaubens-*

Bekantnus . . ., Amsterdam, 1691. The pages of Schnell's work are numbered independently of the other parts of the *Sammelband*.

9. The prayer in translation may be found in *Martyrs Mirror* (Braght 1968, 1135). The original appeared in the 1660 *Martyrs Mirror* (first Dutch edition) in book 2, page 888.

10. Mast 1874, 114–17. This article was reprinted as a tract in 1875 and later included in Stutzman 1917, 128–56.

11. Treyer 1898, 8–16. Treyer's tract was reprinted in Treyer 1920, 178–92. The English spelling of his surname is Troyer.

12. See, for example, R. N. Mast 1970, 236–37, and "Reich Gottes" 1971, 150–51.

13. Kraybill 1989, 37. Generalizing for the overall Anabaptist concept of the "world," John Howard Yoder (1964, 9) says that "it is with reference to the rebellious creaturely order that the term seems to be used most frequently and coherently."

14. The Amish concept of the "world" is well illustrated in D. E. Mast 1920, 82–84; 1933, 1958. See also E. D. Mast 1985, 77–78.

15. Treyer 1898, 8, and E. D. Mast 1985, 77.

16. This passage is used frequently by Amish writers to emphasize the spiritual character of Christ's kingdom. See S. D. Mast 1874, 114.

17. Schnell 1710, 9–10. For a twentieth-century statement concerning the ultimate victory of "Christ's Kingdom" or the "Church of God," see "Gemeinde" 1957, 1–2.

18. Treyer 1898, 12, and Stoltzfus 1982, 245.

19. Editorial in *Herold*, October 1972, 226.

20. David Luthy, letter to Donald B. Kraybill, 29 July 1991.

21. See the statement of four persecuted Anabaptists in 1635–36, as recorded in the *Ausbund* (1991, 840).

22. Cronk 1977, 1981, 7–8; Kraybill 1989, 25–37; Hostetler 1993, 306.

23. For examples of the use of *untertänig* and *Untertänigkeit*, see Esch 1918, 108, and "Obrigkeit" 1968, 426. See also a recent statement issued by the Amish of Holmes County, Ohio (*Truth* 1983, 49), and B. F. Lapp 1959, 153–54.

24. See the extended reference to the witness of the martyrs in Stutzman 1917, 34–35.

25. "Mein Reich" 1918, 515. See also D. Bender 1990, 7, and Stutzman 1917, 33–34.

26. "Christian's Relation" 1972, 231. Although this article originated with a conservative Mennonite group, it was selected and printed by the Amish-controlled *Herold der Wahrheit*.

27. For a succinct statement of the difference between the Lutheran and the Anabaptist versions of the two-kingdom doctrine, see Sanders 1964, 225–26.

28. Luther 1962, 95ff.; 1967, 87–137.

29. For an analysis of Luther's views concerning the participation of Christians in government, see Sanders 1964, 26–43.

30. Kauffman (1991, 137–51) provides a detailed survey of the Amish involvement in local office holding and political affairs in Mifflin County, Pennsylvania, in the nineteenth century.

31. Mast 1874, 114–17. Although this article did not appear in the *Herold* until 1874, it had its origin in a letter written to Mast's brother during or at the close of the Civil War.

32. Mast's essay was reprinted in Stutzman 1917, 128–56, and it appeared again in tract form (Mast 1930).

33. Treyer 1898, 13. See also "Patriotic Citizens" 1956, 330, and Beachy Amish 1968, 188.

34. This line of thought was introduced in 1874 by S. D. Mast (1874, 116).

35. Amishman Elmo Stoll (January 1989, 10) was quoting a Beachy Amish minister, William McGrath. Stoll later left the Old Order Amish but was a member when making the statements that are cited in this essay. See also Stoltzfus 1982, 244–45.

36. Personal interview with Harry Stutzman, Old Order Amish bishop, Middlebury, Ind., 13 June 1990, and Hostetler 1993, 257.

37. E. Stoll February 1989, 10–11. For an analysis of this "strategy of withdrawal," see J. H. Yoder 1964, 89.

38. E. Stoll January 1989, 10, and S. D. Mast 1930, 20. The phrase "with a big mouth" was spoken by Bishop Jonathan Yoder at the annual ministers' meeting of 1863 (Verhandlungen 1863, 14).

39. Stutzman 1917, 126–27; Lambright 1983, 16; Steiner 1989, 3.

40. Stutzman 1917, 126–27. See also "Praying" 1989, 5.

41. David Luthy, letter to Donald B. Kraybill, 29 July 1991.

42. Stoltzfus 1982, 245; E. Stoll February 1989, 11; Hostetler 1993, 257; Kraybill 1989, 217; personal interviews with Harry Stutzman, Old Order Amish bishop, Middlebury, Ind., 13 June 1990, and Eli Gingerich, Old Order Amish minister, Middlebury, Ind., 12 June 1990.

43. Hostetler 1993, 257; Kraybill 1989, 217; Kauffman 1991, 137–51.

44. For a careful presentation of the use of the law by the Amish, especially in Lancaster County, see Kraybill 1989, 222.

45. The charge of vandalism is made by Elmo Stoll (1986, 9).

46. Among the several Anabaptist and Amish confessions of faith or disciplines which have separate articles opposing the legal oath are the Dordrecht Confession of Faith (Article 15), the Thirty-Three Articles as they appear in the Martyrs Mirror (Article 27), and the Amish Discipline of 1809 (Article 6).

47. Oyer 1985, 5. See also Hillerbrand 1958b, 107.

48. Beachy Amish minister Ervin N. Hershberger in an editorial in the Herold (1 November 1956, 330).

Chapter 3. Military Service and Conscription

1. Personal interview with David Wagler, 21 July 1990.

2. D. A. Crist to W. J. Swigart, in Sappington notes, 25 October 1917, File 22, Grant Stoltzfus Collection, Menno Simons Historical Library.

3. Herold, 15 August 1918, 349. Loose translation.

4. The I in I-W is not the letter I but roman numeral one. Many Amish called it "eye-W" rather than its correct name, "one-W."

5. Hershberger, a member of the Beachy Amish, was editor of the English portion of Herold der Wahrheit. Both the German and the English sections were under Beachy Amish leadership.

6. Herold, 15 October 1960, 389; 15 April 1961, 149.

7. The Beachy Amish are an Amish subgroup that is more progressive than the Old Order Amish.

8. Personal interview with Dan King, November 1990.

9. Publication of *Ambassador of Peace* ceased with the December 1970 issue, when it was replaced by *Young Companion*, which began publication in January 1971.

Chapter 4. The National Amish Steering Committee

1. Clergy of congregations connected by common church rules do meet to discuss appropriate positions toward new technologies, styles of dress, etc. See, for example, H. Bender 1934 and 1946, and Kraybill 1989, 81, 84–86.
2. The figure is based on a tabulation of the church districts listed in Raber's *New American Almanac* (1992), which is updated each year. Additional Amish settlements exist in Canada, but they have not been formally involved with the Steering Committee. A settlement consists of all the families and church districts in the same contiguous geographic area. A settlement may contain anywhere from one church district to the almost 150 districts in the Holmes County, Ohio, area. In a mature community, each district will typically include thirty to forty families. In newly established settlements, the number of families in a district may be far fewer.
3. For a further discussion of differences among Amish affiliations, see Hostetler 1993, and Scott 1981, 1986.
4. Those few who have chosen military service have been "in most cases . . . young men who wanted either to see the world or to run away from home" (Hostetler 1993, 274).
5. "Amish Army" 1970, 22–26; "Bits and Pieces" 1971, 23; Luthy 1972, 24.
6. The chairman was Andrew S. Kinsinger; the secretary, David Schwartz; the treasurer, Noah Wengerd (Steering 1966–72, 5). To underscore its national scope, we refer to it as the National Amish Steering Committee.
7. Official correspondence from George C. Guenther to Andrew S. Kinsinger, 30 May 1972.
8. Ibid., 14 June 1972.
9. Kraybill (1989, 59) describes one government official handling an Amish hat and remarking, "That hat is pretty stiff by itself, it is no use in us fighting you." Kraybill suggests that the exemption may have been "merely a playful quirk in the halls of bureacracy."
10. Joe Byrne, "136 Local Schools Fail to Obey U.S. Asbestos Rules," *New Era*, 26 April 1989.
11. Personal interview with Christ Blank, 6 June 1990.
12. "Some Amish Missed News of Nuclear Plant Accident," *Ithaca Journal*, 8 August 1979, 2.
13. Twelve states (Pennsylvania, Ohio, Indiana, Wisconsin, Iowa, Missouri, Illinois, Maryland, Delaware, New York, Michigan, and Minnesota) are each represented by one director. Amish settlements in Kentucky and Tennessee are jointly represented by a director. The Amish in Oklahoma and Kansas are also represented by a single director. Other states with an Amish population are not formally represented by a state director. They certainly benefit, however, from the activities of the Steering Committee at the federal level.
14. Until 1990, the spring meeting was held in April. Because of the new chairman's work as a tax accountant, after 1990 spring meetings were moved to May.
15. Personal communication from Ben J. Raber, 12 July 1990.

16. The national and state meetings are often referred to as "IW meetings." The reference is to the early role of the committee in working with COs. "IW" is a misunderstanding of the roman numeral one sometimes used to designate the I-W Selective Service classification for COs.

17. *Die Botschaft* is an Amish-controlled weekly newspaper composed almost entirely of letters from community "scribes" in Old Order settlements who pass on local news to other subscribers.

18. Both cases involved disputes between churches of different affiliations.

19. For a more systematic treatment of this argument, see Olshan 1990b.

20. Personal interview with Andrew S. Kinsinger, 17 July 1989.

21. This admiration is sometimes mitigated by tensions at the local level. As Martin Marty has noted, "People from a distance often like the Amish a lot, but up close they are sometimes resented." (Quoted in Siewers 1988, 6.)

22. Robert Metz, "The Amish and Taxes," *The New York Times*, 22 May 1961.

23. Joe Byrne, "136 Local Schools Fail to Obey U.S. Asbestos Rules," *New Era*, 26 April 1989.

24. State directors and home community committeemen may be ministers or deacons but not bishops. As of 1991, two of the fourteen state directors were ministers and one was a deacon.

25. Personal interview with Andrew S. Kinsinger, 17 July 1989.

26. Steering 1987-89, 8. Entitlement to exemptions granted the Amish is determined by church membership rather than personal conviction. This was made clear in *Borntrager v. Commissioner* (1990) when an excommunicated Amishman who claimed a religious objection to Social Security was required to pay the tax. See "Expelled Amish" 1990.

27. The answer was no (Steering 1987–89, 24).

28. Steering 1973–80, 42. The reference is to *Wisconsin v. Yoder*, which was decided in 1972.

29. Steering 1966–72, 58. Emphasis in the original.

30. Steering 1981–86, 4. Emphasis added.

31. The overwhelmingly negative reaction in some Amish communities to the formation of the Steering Committee, reported just after its formation (Kidder and Hostetler 1990, 917), was most likely due to this incompatibility.

Chapter 5. Education and Schooling

1. There were Amish schools in existence in the nineteenth century. In 1815, the early settlers of Holmes County, Ohio, built a log cabin schoolhouse on a farm owned by a Stutzman family, with classes beginning in 1817 (Glick 1933; S. H. Miller 1908). In the 1890s, a small group (which became known in the twentieth century as the Amish Christian Church) established a school near Berne, Indiana. Since they considered themselves to be the "one true church," it was important that their children not be influenced by foreign values in public school. The first frame schoolhouse was built by this group in 1898 on a farm owned by Dan Mazelin (Mazelin 1941). This building was later replaced by a brick structure. Jacob D. R. Schwartz, son of David Schwartz, the founder of this group, describes the new school as "very modern with a full basement and a good furnace. It was large enough for about sixty-five pupils . . . Since we were not allowed to go to high school everybody quit

school as soon as they reached the age of fourteen. Since most of the parents were farmers, they could not see the need for a higher education than our parochial school provided. At its best our education in this school was limited because our teacher had no training beyond the eighth grade level" (J.D.R. Schwartz N.d.). In some settlements in the late nineteenth century, the Amish also established "German Schools" alongside public schools. The German schools were designed to preserve the German language while students attended public schools.

2. Keim 1975; Hershberger 1985. In an interesting case in 1915, Joe Miller, from Middlefield, Ohio, refused to send his daughter Mary to school because the school taught that the earth is round, which conflicted with his belief that the world was flat. He argued that the teaching of the school conflicted with the biblical reference to the four corners of the earth ("Would Convince" 1915).

3. David Luthy (1978) describes this incident in more detail in a *Family Life* article. In a more recent publication, Luthy (1986) also describes the development of a settlement in Mexico by Amish parents who wanted to rid themselves of school problems in Ohio.

4. Although all of the children that attended this school were Amish, the school was called Apple Grove Mennonite School. *Mennonite* was the term used by non-Amish to refer to all of the plain people in this community. As this practice changed, the name also changed to Apple Grove Private School, and later to Apple Grove Amish Parochial School (Troyer and Stoll 1965).

5. Troyer and Stoll 1965; Clark 1988.

6. See Hershberger 1985, 9, for a fascinating discussion of the movement of these buildings to their new location. The second story of the store, known as Eshelman Store, had been removed to avoid problems with power lines, but the move attracted attention when it took two days to move the building to its destination. Among the unintended consequences of this protracted move was the drafting of a young Amishman, who was driving a borrowed tractor, into alternative service. This occurred because he was away from the farm he was required to work on as stipulated by his farm deferment.

7. Judge Culbertson's declaration is reported in an undated and unidentified newspaper article in the "School Problems, Wayne Co." file of the Heritage Historical Library, Aylmer, Ontario.

8. "Amish Sent to Jail Here for Contempt of Court," *The Daily Record*, 12 March 1958.

9. John Beaber, "Will the Amish Go Modern?" *The Plain Dealer*, 11 March 1961.

10. Personal interview with Eli Gingerich, 4 October 1980.

11. In 1957, when the second school was built in northern Indiana, a building inspector objected to windows on both sides of the schoolhouse and to the use of lanterns for light. Citing precedence in another case, however, his superior in Fort Wayne granted a variance allowing construction to begin.

12. This 1967 document is entitled "Articles of Agreement Regarding the Indiana Amish Parochial Schools and the Department of Public Instruction."

13. Two of the best scholarly accounts of the origins and difficulties of the Amish school movement in Iowa are Erickson 1969 and Rodgers 1969.

14. Two were Old Order Amish and the third, Wallace Miller, was a conservative Mennonite.

15. See Hostetler and Huntington 1992 and Fisher and Stahl 1986 for descriptions of the daily schedule of a typical Amish school.

16. *Nebraska District of Evangelical Lutheran Synod v. McKelvie* (1919).

17. This does not necessarily mean that the Amish have not had to face social change. In my research and writing (Meyers 1983, 1991), I have described some of the changes with which the Amish are grappling that are directly related to the dramatic increase in their population.

18. See Kraybill 1989 for a more complete discussion of the symbols of separation between the Amish and non-Amish worlds.

Chapter 6. *The National Committee for Amish Religious Freedom*

1. From "Do We Believe in Religious Liberty for the Amish?" a pamphlet published by the National Committee for Amish Religious Freedom.

2. A 17 December 1915 arrest is reported in the *Geauga County Record*, and the 1922 Holmes County, Ohio, case is described by Luthy (1978).

3. *Commonwealth v. King*, Chester County District Court, Pennsylvania, 1937.

4. The National Invitational Conference on State Regulation of Non-Public Schools, held 28–29 March 1967, was directed by Erickson and financed by a grant from the Danforth Foundation.

5. Those attending the meeting and joining the committee included Rev. William C. Lindholm; Wayne L. Fisher; E. Dexter Galloway, Esq.; Dr. John A. Hostetler; Rev. Dean M. Kelley; Elder Roland Hegstad; Prof. Robert Casad; Father Casimir F. Gierut; Leo Pfeffer, Esq.; Dr. Franklin H. Littell; Father Robert F. Drinan; W. W. Sindlinger, Esq.; T. Raber Taylor, Esq.; Dr. Gertrude E. Huntington; Leanore Goodenow; and James E. Landing. Amish guests who attended the meeting but did not join the committee included Joseph Stoll, Aylmer, Ontario; Elmo Stoll, Wellesley, Ontario; Amos Yoder, Kalona, Iowa; Dan Borntreger, Hazelton, Iowa; Menno Hershberger, Independence, Iowa; Henry Hershberger, Apple Creek, Ohio; Henry J. Miller, Millersburg, Ohio; and Dan Weaver, Millersburg, Ohio. Others joining the committee at the very beginning but not attending the initial meeting included Dr. Joe Wittmer; Bernhard H. Olsen; Prof. James E. Wood, Jr.; Prof. Paul Carlsten; Dr. William Keeney; Dr. John H. Yoder; Prof. Paul G. Kauper; Prof. Edward L. Ericson; Edwin J. Lukas, Esq.; Dr. Fred S. Buchanan; and Dr. J. Winfield Fretz.

6. Since 1970, the office of the committee has been located at 30650 Six Mile Road, Livonia, MI 48152.

7. Board members included Roman M. Miller, clerk; Jonas A. Yoder, chairman; Wallace Miller; Henry D. Miller; and William H. Miller.

8. Wallace Miller was a conservative Mennonite. The two Amishmen in the Wisconsin case were Jonas A. Yoder and Adin Yutzy.

9. Lutheran Council USA News Release on Religious Liberty Conference, 19 September 1984, 30. Two conferences (1982, 1984) on religious liberty were held. For a discussion of the first conference, see Kelley 1982.

10. Personal correspondence from Lawrence F. Scalise, attorney general, Iowa Department of Justice, Des Moines, Iowa, 23 December 1965.

11. Personal correspondence from Rev. P. Boyd Mather, First Methodist Church, Tama, Iowa, 11 March 1966.

12. "Briefs Tell the Story of Case for Amish," *The Monroe Evening News,* 10 June 1969.

13. Letter to Attorney William B. Ball from William C. Kahl, superintendent of Wisconsin Department of Public Instruction. The letter was filed as an Exhibit to the Courts, 3 February 1969.

14. *Yoder,* Appellant's Brief to the United States Supreme Court.

15. *Yoder,* brief amicus curiae, National Council of Churches to the U.S. Supreme Court, 15.

16. *Yoder,* brief amicus curiae, National Jewish Commission on Law and Public Affairs to the United States Supreme Court, 15.

17. *Yoder,* brief amicus curiae, Synagogue Council of America to the United States Supreme Court.

18. The committee has functioned as an informal network in recent years. Some of its work has been assumed by the National Amish Steering Committee, described in Chapter 4.

Chapter 7. Social Security and Taxes

1. Though this passage commands a follower not to be "*unequally* yoked," effectively the passage has been interpreted to prohibit binding ties with the outside world regardless of whether the ties may be "equal" in some sense. This is consistent with other Christian interpretations of this passage. Indeed, the New American Standard version of the Bible translates this passage as "Do not be bound together with unbelievers" (2 Corinthians 6:14).

2. For discussions of the Amish view of separation, see Hostetler 1993, 75–77, 111–13; and Kraybill 1989, 16, 18–19, 37–38.

3. See Cline 1968, 123–24, 127 n. 18, 128–29; W. L. Fisher 1993, 128–30; Hostetler 1993, 167–70, 270–73; and Kraybill 1989, 70–71, 86, 216–17, 219, for discussions of these social welfare issues.

4. Domestic spending includes all federal spending except defense, foreign aid and embassies, and federal debt interest.

5. Discussions of the Amish opposition to participation in Social Security and private insurance plans are found in Cline 1968, 122–37; W. L. Fisher 1993, 128–30; Hostetler 1993, 270, 272–73; Kraybill 1989, 86–87, 89, 219; and Robb 1990, 76–77.

6. W. L. Fisher 1993, 133; Kraybill 1989, 220; Robb 1990, 77.

7. Cline 1968, 145–46; W. L. Fisher 1993, 132–34; Hostetler 1993, 270.

8. Cline 1968, 145–48; Kraybill 1989, 220.

9. Cline 1968, 148–50; W. L. Fisher 1993, 132–34.

10. Cline 1968, 150; W. L. Fisher 1993, 133–35; Hostetler 1993, 271; Robb 1990, 81.

11. "Welfarism Gone Mad," *New York Herald Tribune,* 14 May 1961.

12. Fitzpatrick editorial cited in W. L. Fisher, "The Amish in Court," 291, manuscript, n.d.

13. W. L. Fisher 1993, 136; Robb 1990, 81.

14. Cline 1968, 151–52; W. L. Fisher 1993, 138–42; Robb 1990, 79–80.

15. Cline 1968, 152–53; W. L. Fisher 1993, 141–43; Robb 1990, 80.

16. Cline 1968, 150–51, 153–54; W. L. Fisher 1993, 142–43; Robb 1990, 81.

17. Cline 1968, 143–44; Kraybill 1989, 220; Robb 1990, 77–78.

18. Cline 1968, 145, 157–59; Robb 1990, 78–79.

19. Cline 1968, 154, 157–59; W. L. Fisher 1993, 138, 143–44; Robb 1990, 78–79, 82–83.

20. Request of the Old Order Amish for exemption from the Social Security Self-employment Tax, Staff Memorandum, Department of Health, Education and Welfare, 1964.

21. The exemption is codified at 26 U.S.C. § 1402(g). See also Cline 1968, 162–64; W. L. Fisher 1993, 144; Hostetler 1993, 270–73; Kraybill 1989, 220–21; and Robb 1990, 85–86.

22. For additional discussions of the legal consequences of *Lee* for religious liberty, see Brady 1983; Ossian 1983; Stevens and Tulio 1984; and Wiles 1983.

23. Robb 1990, 88–94; Steering 1987–89, 3, 4, 26–27, 42, 45.

24. Cline 1968, 136; Hostetler 1993, 130–32, 270; Kraybill 1989, 216–17, 221–23; Steering 1987–89, 6–7, 28–29, 47, and 1990, 7–8.

25. Cline 1968, 140–41, 242; Kraybill 1989, 206, 222; Steering 1987–89, 3, 8, 29. Other exemptions from unemployment insurance for domestic or farm workers or very small businesses may apply to many of the Amish as well.

26. Hostetler 1993, 273; Kraybill 1989, 58–59; Steering 1987–89, 29.

Chapter 8. Slow-moving Vehicles

1. For examples of these conflicts, see *Die Botschaft,* 11 March 1987; *The Budget,* 1 October 1986; *Intelligencer Journal,* "In Western Pa. the Amish Metal Wheels Banned," 20 December 1980; *Des Moines Register,* "Amish to Get Highway Twenty-Two Buggy Paths," 17 April 1974, and "Amishman Jailed over Steel Wheels," 2 November 1991; and *Watertown Daily Times,* "What Horses Leave Behind Is the Concern of This Article," 27 September 1984.

2. The *Hershberger* case evolved through several phases. It began in the fall of 1988 in the Fillmore County District Court. The author served as an expert witness in the court, thus increasing access to the details surrounding this case. *Hershberger* then proceeded to the Supreme Court of Minnesota in 1989. The decision of the state supreme court in 1989 is referred to throughout the text as *Hershberger I.* A summary of this decision appears in the Appendix as *State v. Hershberger* 1989 (*Hershberger I*). Then in 1990 the case proceeded to the U.S. Supreme Court, which sent it back to the Minnesota Supreme Court for reconsideration in light of the recently decided *Smith* case. The action of the U.S. Supreme Court is summarized in the Appendix under *Minnesota v. Hershberger* 1990. Throughout the text, *Hershberger II* refers to the opinion of the Minnesota Supreme Court when it reconsidered *Hershberger* in 1990 in light of *Smith.* This second opinion of the Minnesota Supreme Court is summarized in the Appendix under *State v. Hershberger* 1990 (*Hershberger II*).

3. These incidents are described on three occasions in the Amish newspaper *The Budget:* 28 June 1951, 11; 22 April 1954, 5; and 27 May 1954, 5.

4. E. M. Larimer to John Jamison, Minnesota Commissioner of Highways, 5 November 1965.

5. John Jamison, Minnesota Commissioner of Highways, 5 November 1967. Memo: Notice of hearing.

6. Testimony of Jack Anderson in *State v. Hershberger,* No. 13834 (Dist. Ct., Fillmore County, Minn., 19 Dec. 1988). Transcript of proceedings: 125.84.

7. Amish ministers from outside the community suggested in 1913 that if Amish members joined a liberal church they should be allowed to do so and should be dealt with by the new church and the Lord. If members left under the ban and the receiving church took them out of it, the home church should follow suit. Bishop Sam Yoder rejected this procedure because he felt it was too liberal to placate the conservative element in the church. This led to the Swartzentruber division. (Personal interview with David Luthy, 30 July 1990.)

8. Testimony of Emory Miller in *Hershberger* (1988), Fillmore County District Court. Transcript of proceedings, 170.

9. No. 77-TR-D-634 (Holmes County Ct., Ohio, 7 Sept. 1977).

10. Ohio Department of Highway Safety press release, September 1977.

11. This decision rested on the Ohio Rev. Code § 513.11 (F).

12. "Twelve Amish Men Go to Jail," *The New York Times*, 13 October 1961.

13. "Court Order to Confiscate Amish Man's Buggy," *The Journal*, 27 February 1976, 19.

14. "Slow Moving Vehicle Emblem Not Necessary for Amish," *The Plain Dealer*, 24 January 1988, Sunday edition.

15. "Five Amish Men Jailed," *Advance-News*, 11 December 1983.

16. Personal interview with Esther Katz, 4 August 1990.

17. "Amish Win Buggy Tiff," *Watertown Daily Times*, 9 May 1984.

18. "Damages Paid in Accident," *Watertown Daily Times*, 23 November 1984.

19. "Amish Man Charged," *Watertown Daily Times*, 26 June 1984.

20. No. 17542 Au. (80th Dist. Ct., Gladwin County, Mich., 29 Jan 1981).

21. *Swartzentruber*, Decision of Court of Appeals.

22. *State v. Swartzentruber*, No. 81-006429-AV (Cir. Ct. Gladwin County, Mich., 14 Jan. 1985).

23. Cara Noreland (1990) gathered and compiled much of the information regarding this case for her senior thesis at Luther College. See note 2 above for an overview of *Hershberger*.

24. Personal interview with Sheriff Don Gudmundson, 13 October 1988.

25. "New Law Changes Slow Moving Vehicle Signage Regulations," *Fillmore County Journal*, 1 June 1982.

26. Minn. Stat. § 169.522 (1) required the red symbol at night.

27. Appellants' Brief at 5–9, *Hershberger I*.

28. *Hershberger* (1988). Transcript of proceedings, 32–35.

29. Ibid., 229.

30. *Hershberger* (1988) at 10.

31. Ibid., 10–11.

32. Ibid., 12–13.

33. Ibid., 14–15.

34. *Hershberger*, 21 December 1988. Order of Certification by Trial Judge Pursuant to Rule 28.03 of the Rules of the Criminal Procedure. The Minnesota Court of Appeals found the request for the appeal to be moot because the matter was simultaneously certified to the Minnesota Supreme Court and denied appeal on 5 January 1989. The Minnesota Supreme Court approved this certification transferring the matter on 19 January 1989.

35. After concluding that Minn. Stat. § 169.522 violated the free exercise clause of the First Amendment to the United States Constitution as applied to the appellants, the court found it unnecessary to address whether Minn. Stat.

§ 169.522 violated Article 1, Section 16, of the Minnesota Constitution. The trial court decision was vacated, and all charges against the appellants were dismissed (*Hershberger I* at 289–90).

36. Petition for writ of certiorari at 14–23 (*Hershberger* 1990).

37. Brief of Minnesota Civil Liberties Union as amicus at 1 (*Hershberger* 1990).

38. Respondents' Brief in Opposition to Petition for Writ of Certiorari at 20–22 (*Hershberger* 1990).

39. The action of the United States Supreme Court is summarized in the appendix under *Minnesota v. Hershberger* (1990).

40. Appellants' and Respondent's Briefs per Remand of the Case by the United States Supreme Court to the Supreme Court of Minnesota (*Hershberger II*).

41. Personal notes from oral arguments, 12 September 1990.

42. Ibid.

43. Respondent's Brief per Remand of the Case by the United States Supreme Court to the Supreme Court of Minnesota at 12–13 (*Hershberger II*).

Chapter 9. Health Care

1. "Amish Bishop Granted Pardon by Governor," *Goshen Democrat*, 16 April 1948.

2. For the scriptural bases for these views, see Titus 2:14, Romans 12:12, and Philippians 2:15.

3. "Genetics" 1964; "Usefulness" 1987. The Amish are an especially valuable population for the study of recessive genetic disorders such as cystic fibrosis (Klinger 1983; Miller and Schwartz 1992), glutaric aciduria ("How a Physician Solved Riddle of Rare Disease in Children of Amish," *Wall Street Journal*, 20 September 1989, A1, A16; Morton et al. 1989; Wolkomir and Wolkomir 1991), phenylketonuria (PKU) (Grossman et al. 1989; Martin 1968; Martin et al. 1963), hemophilia (Wingard 1990; Yoder and Monson 1991), adenosine deaminase (ADA) deficiency ("A Deadly Illness, a Choice for Amish," *The Philadelphia Inquirer*, 24 February 1991, 1A, 4A), and various types of dwarfism and neurological disorders (McKusick 1978). The Amish cooperate with those researching diseases such as cancer (Lynch 1976), arthritis ("Update" 1981), dental caries (Bagramian et al. 1988), and haemophilus influenzae (Granoff et al. 1986).

4. "Johns Hopkins" 1980; Sutter et al. 1991. For other discussions of the Amish and health care, see Wenger 1988 and Yoder 1984.

5. For a more extensive discussion of the Amish family, see Huntington 1988 and Hostetler and Huntington 1992, 19–35.

6. *The Budget*, 17 July 1952, 6. Another correspondent to *The Budget* wrote, "You hear of many different opinions as to the cause of this polio, but after seeing the innocent children going through all this suffering, who can say it is not part of the pestilence promised us. . . . Who can say God is satisfied with conditions as they are today. I feel this polio is just a reminder to us to better ourselves or it might come seven times worse" (*The Budget*, 24 July 1952, 4; Huntington 1957, 305–7).

7. An extreme case is described by Hostetler (1984, 37–38), in which two large chicken houses belonging to an Amishman burned to the ground under suspicious circumstances. In spite of the fact that the member was under the

ban, the church came to his aid and contributed $245,000 toward the restoration of the buildings.

8. University of Michigan Hospital, 1982. A similar sentiment was expressed by another Amish person: "Since a Christian . . . will have it so much nicer after death than in this life, he will be making a gain by dying" (*Die Botschaft*, 22 January 1986).

9. A doctor explained to an Amish father that his son would "need a vehicle that's specially equipped for a person that's handicapped like he is. . . . He really needs this to make him fully independent!" Later the father wrote, "I wished later that I would have pointed out to the doctor that in our way of living, none of us is fully independent. We all need each other and try to help each other to get through this life" (Wagler 1985, 34).

10. *Die Botschaft*, 29 June 1983, 1.

11. "Community Notes," *The Diary*, December 1979, 2.

12. Memorial poem in *The Budget* (1980). The poem also listed his death as 14 December (Friday), not 17 December (Monday).

13. See Kraybill 1989, 244–47, for a theoretical discussion of negotiation between the Amish culture and the dominant culture. The following account is based on a telephone conversation, on 4 February 1989, with Larry Bleiber, reporter for *The Courier-Journal*; correspondence with Bleiber, 2 March and 10 March 1989; and a telephone conversation with Don Pratt, of Louisville, 6 February 1989. The following articles were written by Bleiber in *The Courier-Journal*; "Amish Man Who Ended Son's Chemotherapy Faces Jail," 27 January 1989; "Amish Man Jailed over Ailing Son," 28 January 1989; "Amishman Sent to Jail over Son, Is Released," 31 January 1989; "In Whose Hands? Dispute on Amish Boy's Cancer Treatment Shows Conflicts over Parental Control," 6 February 1989; "Compromise to Let Amish Boy See Doctor, Return to Family," 8 February 1989; "Amish Boy Dies, Ending Ordeal Pitting Parents against Doctors," 1 March 1989. Other news articles related to this case include "Amish Man Freed; Sick Son in Hiding," *Herald-Leader*, 31 January 1989; "Cancer-stricken Amish Boy Now Back with Family," *Herald-Leader*, 8 February 1989; "Haven, KS," *Die Botschaft*, 22 February 1989; "Mt. Victory, OH," *Die Botschaft*, 8 March 1989; "Upton, Kentucky," and "Mt. Hope, Ohio," *The Budget*, 8 March 1989.

14. I only discuss those areas of Amish health care that have been involved in negotiation with the state. Many interesting health adaptations are ignored such as *Brauche*, which secular society would classify as psychological or psychosomatic healing. For a discussion of *Brauche*, see Hostetler 1993, 336–42; and L. Miller 1981, 155–71.

15. The colorful story was reported in newspapers across the country: "Amish Treatment Ordered Stopped," *The News-Sentinel*, 11 July 1980; "Iridologist Draws Customers from across the Country," *The Elkhart Truth*, 10 September 1981; "An Amish Herb-seller of Berne, Ind.," *Mennonite Weekly Review*, 24 September 1981; and "Amish Herbalist 'Cures' Are in High Demand," *The New York Times*, 29 November 1981. For some six weeks, the Associated Press story that appeared in *The New York Times* was reprinted all over the country with slight modifications and a variety of photographs: "Amish Farmer Told to Stop Herb Practice," *Intelligencer Journal*, 13 September 1983; "Trial for Amish Herb Dispenser Opens in Indiana," *Mennonite Weekly Review*, 8 December 1983, 2; "Herbalist Testifies in Defense of Practice," *The Journal-Gazette*, 14 December 1983; "Amish Herb Salesman in Indiana Says

He Doesn't Practice Medicine," *Intelligencer Journal*, 15 December 1983; "Indiana Judge Drops One Charge in Case of Amish Herb-Seller," *Mennonite Weekly Review*, 22 December 1983; "Judge Lets Nutritionist Reopen His Business," *The Journal-Gazette*, 13 January 1984; "Amishman Settles with State," *Mennonite Weekly Review*, 26 January 1984, 5; "Amish Herbalist Told Not to Treat Sick," *Gospel Herald*, 28 February 1984, 163; and *Die Blatt*, 28 June 1984, 1 November 1984, and 16 October 1986.

16. "Judge Lets Nutritionist Reopen His Business," *The Journal-Gazette*, 13 January 1984.

17. *State v. Helmuth*, No. 20D03-8901-CP-10 (Elkhart Sup. Ct. No. 3, Ind., 26 January 1989), Temporary Injunction. This case was featured in many press reports: "Man Faces Charge for Practicing without License," *The Goshen News*, 12 January 1989; "Chiropractor Not Licensed, Say Police," *The Elkhart Truth*, 13 January 1989; "Amish Healer Ordered to Cease Practicing," *The Elkhart Truth*, 17 January 1989; "No Admission of Guilt Here in Helmuth Case," *The Goshen News*, 21 January 1989; "Helmuth Must Stop His Practice of 'Medicine,'" *The Goshen News*, 27 January 1989; "Clarification," *The Elkhart Truth*, 6 February 1989; "Helmuth Helped a Lot of People," *the Paper*, 7 February 1989; "Joe Needs Friends, Support," *the Paper*, 14 February 1989; "Take a Stand on What Is Right," *the Paper*, 21 February 1989; "Helmuth Banned from Playing Doctor," *The Elkhart Truth*, 27 July 1989; "Therapist Must Stop," *The Elkhart Truth*, 13 October 1989.

18. Heikes 1985.

19. In one midwife's home, the cribs were designed to fit next to the mother's bed with no barrier between mother and baby, providing the baby its own space without crowding the mother. The side of the crib could be raised to separate it from the mother's bed.

20. "Amish Woman Greets 250 Babies Each Year," *Akron Beacon Journal*, 8 January 1984.

21. For a description of the birthing center, see Sutter 1980.

22. Based on conversations with women who had their babies at Hochstetler's, with Hochstetler, with a midwife who apprenticed with Hochstetler, and with doctors with whom Hochstetler worked, as well as a visit to Hochstetler's center, and "Longtime Birthing Home Operator to Call It Quits in October," *The Budget*, 14 August 1985, local edition.

23. She was mentioned in an article about the Jacob Ammann Hospital (which never was built): "Plans Snarled for Plain Amish Hospital," *The Cleveland Press*, 27 August 1981.

24. The following account is based on conversations in August 1984 with Jonas D. Yoder, Dr. Elton Lehman, and Dr. Roy Miller, with interested community members and other concerned individuals, and on various press reports: "Jonas Yoder Doesn't Fit Amish Mold," *Akron Beacon Journal*, 8 January 1984; "Amishman to Build 10-unit Maternity Center," *Times-Reporter*, 7 August 1984; "Work Progressing at Mount Eaton on Birthing Center," *The Budget*, 7 August 1985, 14, local edition; "Tradition with a New Twist," *Akron Beacon Journal*, 20 January 1986; and miscellaneous clippings without source or date.

25. Amish mothers complaining to me about hospital deliveries have made such comments as "I do better if I walk during labor. They wouldn't let me get out of bed." "They gave me gas. Gas makes me sick. Having a baby never made me sick." "They wouldn't let me wear my head covering. I need to pray."

I figured God knew it wasn't my fault my head wasn't covered so I prayed anyway, but I'd have felt better with my covering on—at least a scarf."

26. For accounts of non-Amish midwives and physicians who deliver Amish babies at home, see Armstrong and Feldman 1986 and Kaiser 1986.

27. "State Delivers a Legal Battle to Midwife for Amish," *Sunday News*, 30 July 1989, B1, B2.

28. "State/Amish Tradition at Odds over Midwife Case," *Times-News*, 21 May 1989, weekend edition, 1A, 4A, and telephone interview with Sykes, 25 September 1991.

29. "A legislator delivers a bill to allow more midwives in Pa," *Sunday News*, 11 March 1990, A-1, A-4. Contrast this with the readiness of some patients to testify against certain obstetricians.

30. "Midwife Draws Support in Battle," *The Derrick*, 22 July 1989, 1, 10.

31. Letter from P. Raymond Bartholomew, attorney, to Salena Walter, president of the Pennsylvania Midwives Association, 31 December 1990. The account of Lucille Sykes was compiled from a telephone interview with Lucille Sykes, 25 September 1991; telephone interviews with Salena Walter, 3 September 1991 and 24 September 1991; and Judge J. Fornelli's opinion in *Commonwealth v. Sykes* (1989). There was widespread but erratic coverage of the Sykes case, with sections of the same article appearing in many papers. The following references are the most helpful: "State Law vs. Amish Tradition: Unlicensed Midwife Prosecuted," *The Pittsburgh Press*, 30 April 1989, A1, A18; "State/Amish Tradition at Odds over Midwife Case," *Times-News*, 21 May 1989, weekend edition, 1A, 4A; "Accused Midwife Cleared by Court," *The Derrick*, 23 May 1989, 1, 18; "Charge Dismissed against Woman Who Delivered Babies for 10 Years," *New Era*, 23 May 1989; "Charges against Midwife Dismissed," *Mennonite Weekly Review*, 8 June 1989, 11; letter from Lucille Sykes to the editor, *The Budget*, 7 June 1989, 20; "Midwife Draws Support in Battle," *The Derrick*, 22 July 1989, 1, 10; "Mercer Midwife Fights Malpractice Charges," *Sunday News*, 23 July 1989; "State Delivers a Legal Battle to Midwife for Amish," *Sunday News*, 30 July 1989, B-1, B-2; "Amish Pack Courtroom for Midwife's Hearing," *Intelligencer Journal*, 5 June 1990. The following articles appeared in *The Budget*: "Editor's Corner," 10 May 1989, 2; "Cassadaga, New York," 17 May 1989, 13; "Cassadaga, New York," 31 May 1989, 20; "Cassadaga, New York," 20 September 1989, 16; "Cassadaga, New York," 30 May 1990, 5; "Cassadaga, New York," 13 June 1990, 19; and "Cassadaga, New York," 23 January 1991, 11. For a short article and good photos of the Cradletime Birthing Clinic, see Smolan et al. 1990, 72–77.

32. Telephone conversations with Salena Walter, former president of the Pennsylvania Midwives Association, 3 September 1991 and 24 September 1991. Letters from Salena Walter appeared in *The Budget*, "Letters to the Editor," 28 March 1990, and in *Die Botschaft*, "Thanks from the Midwives," 28 March 1990, 11. See also "A Legislator Delivers a Bill to Allow More Midwives in Pa," *Sunday News*, 11 March 1990, A-1, A-4; "Countians to Deliver Opinions on Midwife Bill," *Sunday News*, 6 April 1990, A-1, A-6; response to Salena Walter from Jane L. Ziegenfus-Martin, "For Your Information," *Die Botschaft*, 11 April 1990, 16; "Amish Back, Other Countians Oppose Pa. Midwife Rules," *New Era*, 12 April 1990, A-1, A-6; "New Rules for Midwives Receive Support from Some Area Amish," *Intelligencer Journal*, 13 April 1990, A-1, A-4; "Midwifery Legislation. Please, Understand," *Country Notes and Quotes*, Spring 1990 (xeroxed insert), newsletter from Gordonville, Pa.; "Midwifery

Legislation Update," *Country Notes and Quotes*, Summer 1990. Telephone interviews with Lucille Sykes, 25 September 1991 and 13 June 1992. Midwives from as far away as Canada apprentice with her.

33. Telephone interviews with Sheila Nichting, 27 September 1991 and 13 June 1992. Missouri House Bill 684, legalizing midwives, passed the House 114 to 40 in the 1991–92 session but died in the Senate after a threatened filibuster. A bill to legalize lay midwives was expected to pass in 1993; the Birth Center could then reopen. As of this writing, however, the center remained closed and Nichting was not working as a nurse or midwife. Until suitable legislation is passed, no doctor can afford the increased insurance premiums nor withstand the criticism from conventional practitioners that would result from working as a backup doctor for a midwife.

34. Telephone interviews with Dorothy Kuhns, 27 September 1991, 13 June 1992, and 16 June 1992; personal interview with Dr. Karen Yoder, 26 and 27 September 1991.

35. Weiler and Weiler 1991. As the possibility of high-tech medical interventions increases and medical costs escalate, conflicts between Amish values and medical professionals may also rise. Two recent cases illustrate the conflict. A critically ill Ohio Amish infant was taken to a hospital at the directive of a county prosecutor over the protests of the parents, who, press reports said, "were refusing treatment because they didn't want to incur the medical bills." See "Amish Baby Is Treated but Parents Objected," *Akron Beacon Journal*, 20 August 1991. In another highly publicized case, a central Pennsylvania Amish family refused treatment for an eight-month-old son with a special genetic defect called adenosine deaminase deficiency. A new drug therapy, costing some $190,000 a year for a lifetime, would have enabled the child to live. The parents, after consulting with church leaders for nine days, decided to refuse treatment and keep the child at home, where he died. Medical personnel called the decision "outrageous," and "sad and tragic . . . because an effective therapy is available." Reported in "A Deadly Illness, a Choice for Amish," *The Philadelphia Inquirer*, 24 February 1991, 1-A, 4-A, and "Amish Boy Dies; Had Rare Illness," *The Philadelphia Inquirer*, 20 March 1991.

36. Conversation with doctors involved, Wooster, Ohio, and Millersburg, Ohio, 24 and 25 August 1984.

37. This account was compiled from conversations in 1951 with members of the Ohio Amish community; from letters and manuscripts in the Heritage Historical Library, Aylmer, Ontario; from a transcript of the court proceedings in *State v. Hochstetler* (1948); and from various newspaper articles—of these, some are incomplete, some are typescripts, and others do not have deadlines or titles. The following references are grouped by source: *South Bend Tribune:* "Amish Bishop Sentenced to Six-Month Term for Keeping Daughter, 41, Chained to Bed," 23 January 1948; *The Elkhart Truth:* "Deny Church Objection in Insanity Case," 24 January 1948; "Children's Plea Gets Pardon for Man Who Chained Daughter," 16 April 1948, 1–2; *The Middlebury Independent:* "Amish Bishop Gives Background Account of Hochstetler Case," 29 January 1948, 1; *Goshen Democrat:* "Amish Bishop Granted Pardon by Governor," 16 April 1948; *The Budget:* "The Editor's Corner" and "Berlin, Ohio," 29 January 1948; "Is It Justice?" 5 February 1948; "The Editor's Corner" and "Berlin, Ohio," 12 February 1948; "Milverton, Ontario, Canada," 6 May 1948; *Intelligencer Journal:* "Ind. Man Jailed, Chained Daughter," 23 January 1948; *The*

Berne Witness: "Forum," 27 February 1948; *Die Botschaft:* "Gleaning From Yesterday," 13 November 1985, 7. See also *Gospel Herald,* "'Justice' Fails Again," 3 February 1948, 98; Wenger 1980a, 1980b; Hostetler et al. 1973, 148–51; and Luthy 1972.

38. Letter from National Mental Health Foundation, 21 April 1948, to Guy F. Hershberger.

39. "Amish Bishop Granted Pardon by Governor," *Goshen Democrat,* 16 April 1948.

40. Two Amishmen have been convicted of child abuse: *State v. Schwartz* (Adams County, Indiana, September 1949) and *State v. Yoder,* no. 8598 (Erath County District Court, Texas, 17 December 1987). Both of these cases involved incest, and both families were marginal to the community. *Abandoned Prayers,* a popularized book by Gregg Olsen (1990), tells the story of the only known case of a former Amishman charged with murder. Eli Stutzman, raised in a conservative Amish household, defected from the church and later was sentenced to prison on the charges of abandoning a human body and concealing a death after he left the body of his six-year-old son in a Nebraska cornfield. After his release he was convicted of murdering one of his homosexual roommates. Many other serious but unconfirmed allegations surround Stutzman, who is serving a forty-year prison sentence.

41. During the polio epidemic of 1979, more than 75 percent of the Amish in the United States received one or more doses of oral vaccine ("Another" 1980). The Johns Hopkins University study of childhood diseases in the Amish found 90 percent of the sample Amish families in Pennsylvania protected against polio and measles, as reported in *The Diary,* November 1980, 15. In Wayne County, Ohio, the Health Department services most utilized by the Amish were immunizations, as reported by Carol Jorgensen and Tim Dutton (1984).

42. The form is printed and distributed by the Gordonville Print Shop, Gordonville, PA 17529.

43. For a discussion of factors influencing Amish health choices, see Wenger 1988, 143–49.

44. "Speak Out," *the Paper,* 13 March 1990.

45. "Letters to the Editor," *Family Life,* January 1989, 3.

46. "What Do You Think?" *Family Life,* May 1981, 32.

47. Ibid.

48. "Speak Out," *the Paper,* 27 February 1990.

49. Amish correspondents writing to Amish newspapers sometimes warn of the dangers of immunization. For example, see *Die Botschaft:* "Shipshewana, Indiana," 6 February 1980, 4; "Hazelton, Iowa," 16 April 1980, 14; "Stockport, Ohio," 28 February 1990, 2; *Die Blatt:* "Vaccination Linked to Brain Damage," 17 October 1985, 6; *The Budget:* "Bloomfield, Iowa," 11 January 1989, 16. Complications do occasionally arise from vaccinations. In 1989, all five confirmed polio cases in the United States were due to vaccinations ("Polio" 1991).

50. "Charlotte Hall, MD," *Die Botschaft,* 24 April 1991, 38. An Amish correspondent to an Amish paper wrote: "If I am not mistaken, four Amish persons died of complications from measles during 1989, making the mortality rate several hundred times higher than for the general public. I am not aware that any died from taking the shots or were seriously ill as a result although

probably more took the shots than had the measles" ("Bloomfield, Iowa," *The Budget*, 21 March 1990, 3).

51. "Amish Immunization Program Expected to Grow," *New Era*, 2 December 1987, 1, 3.

52. "Importance of Vaccinating Amish Is Stressed at Indiana Conference," *The Budget*, 8 May 1985, 3. See also K. K. Yoder 1984, 71–81.

53. "Letters to the Editor," *Family Life*, January 1989, 3.

54. "There seems to be a lot of difference of opinion on the subject of vaccines and vaccinations. In most of our communities these vaccines are routinely accepted and used. However, judging from some of the letters that have appeared in *The Budget* and *Die Botschaft*, some people are strongly opposed" (Staff Notes, *Family Life*, October 1990, 6).

55. "Two Clymer School Board Members Upset over Cause of Measles Inoculations," *Corry Journal*, 16 March 1990.

56. An Amish writer said, "I think 90 percent of the children in this area had the MMR or are in the process of getting them . . . sometimes the Amish get the blame for spreading it [measles] being not all take the shots." "Clymer, NY," *Die Botschaft*, 3 January 1990, 3.

57. "Speak Out," *the Paper*, 20 February 1990.

58. For discussions of the 1979 polio outbreak, see *Morbidity and Mortality Weekly Report*, 9 February 1979, 49–50; 11 May 1979, 207–8; 25 May 1979, 229–30; 1 June 1979, 250–51; 8 June 1979, 255; 15 June 1979, 275; 6 July 1979, 309; 27 July 1979, 345–46. The absence of new cases of polio in July 1979 reflects, in part, the success of the multistate immunization campaigns for the Amish. Of the 22 paralytic polio cases reported in the United States in 1979, however, 13 cases involved Amish persons ("Another Good Year" 1980). See also "The Myth of the Obstinate Amish," *The New York Times*, 20 June 1979; "Medical Detective Story: A Polio Virus Tracked Down," *The New York Times*, 28 August 1979; and "What Is Truth?" *Die Botschaft*, 25 April 1979, 14.

An outbreak of whooping cough affected about 200 children in a New York (Conewango) Amish community in 1982. One baby died from whooping cough in the same settlement in 1988. "More Cases Reported of Whooping Cough," *Intelligencer Journal*, 4 November 1988.

Measles outbreaks occurred 1988–90 in most Amish settlements. There was an especially high incidence in Ohio and Indiana, and many Amish schools were closed. In Indiana, the students could receive free measles vaccine or stay out of school until two weeks after the last confirmed case of measles was reported. In Adams County, Indiana, 1,100 Amish school children were vaccinated (*The Diary*, February 1990, 23). A measles outbreak was averted in Pennsylvania in 1988 when about 1,700 Amish received vaccinations in state-sponsored clinics held in their schools and homes ("Fear from Measles Outbreak Spreads to County," *Sunday News*, 24 February 1991, A-1, A-7). Four cases of measles (rubella) were confirmed in the Lancaster settlement in the spring of 1991. By the fall of 1991, health officials estimated as many as 200 cases of rubella in the Amish community. Federal health officials from the Centers for Disease Control, in Atlanta, Georgia, worked with local physicians and midwives in the fall of 1991 to identify babies born to women who contracted the disease early in their pregnancies ("U.S. Probes Local Impact of Rubella," *New Era*, 28 October 1991). See also *Morbidity and Mortality Weekly Report*: "Increase in Rubella and Congenital Rubella Syndrome—United States, 1988–1990," 1 February 1991, 94–99, and "Outbreaks of

Rubella among the Amish—United States, 1991," 26 April 1991, 264–65. Of the 1,253 rubella cases reported by the end of September 1991, nearly a third occurred among unvaccinated children and young adults in Amish communities in Pennsylvania, Michigan, New York, Ohio, and Tennessee, according to the Centers for Disease Control as reported in "Rubella Cases Soar across U.S.," *The Oregonian*, 11 October 1991.

59. Measles spread across the Michigan-Indiana state line when the son of a deceased lady exposed approximately 600 Amish people attending her funeral, resulting in the closure of 35 Amish schools ("Amish Get Measles Vaccine; 30 Schools Open," *The Elkhart Truth*, 31 January 1990, B3).

60. "Ronks, PA," *The Budget*, 6 June 1979, 10. The Amish response was reported in "The Myth of the Obstinate Amish," *The New York Times*, 20 June 1979, and "Polio Buffer for Old Order Amish Indicated," *Patriot-News*, 27 January 1990, A6. A correspondent from Ronks, Pennsylvania, wrote in *The Budget*, 6 June 1979, 10: "My feeling was that an adult was not susceptible and that since the children had their vaccinations before entering school, we would not need to bother. However, we were informed that an unvaccinated adult could be a carrier even if he never contracted the disease himself."

Chapter 10. Land Use

1. For a discussion of the role of the farm as the "seedbed" of Amish families, see Kraybill 1989, 189–90.

2. Hostetler 1988, 8; 1993, 4.

3. Lancaster County Planning Commission, "Farm-based Business Model Ordinance Provisions for Lancaster County," April 1990, Introduction; Hostetler 1989.

4. The Amish population in Lancaster County, nearly seventeen thousand, represents a 100 percent increase in the past twenty years. *New Era*, 15 October 1990, citing Donald B. Kraybill. Completed Amish families average 6.6 children (Kraybill 1989, 74). For an extended discussion of Amish population growth, see Ericksen et al. 1980.

5. See Foster 1980 and Johnson et al. 1977.

6. For a discussion of "farm machinery riddles" in Amish agriculture, see Kraybill 1989, 171–87.

7. Kraybill (1989, 155–57) discusses the "milk tank bargain."

8. See Chesapeake Bay Commission Agreement, Pa. Stat. Ann. tit. 32, §§ 820.11–820.12 (Purdon Supp. 1990). Pennsylvania has committed itself to reducing by 40 percent the nutrients reaching the Chesapeake Bay by the year 2000. The Governor's Select Committee on Nonpoint Source Nutrient Management found that agriculture is the largest source of nonpoint nutrients in Pennsylvania due to the large amount of acreage in agricultural use and the concentration of livestock and poultry (*Controlling* 1990, 1).

9. The Lancaster County Conservation District estimates that Lancaster County produces more than five million tons of manure per year. If applied at an agronomically sound rate, 344,000 acres of farmland would be needed. However, only 274,000 acres of cropland are available (*Controlling* 1990, 10).

10. This is especially a problem for concentrated hog and chicken operations, where farmers often have little land available for spreading. Dairy farms, which are more common among the Amish, generally have a better ratio of

acreage to manure, since they often have sufficient land to grow feed for cattle.
11. For years the Amish used straight row planting, dismissing planting in contoured terraces as "book farming" (Hostetler 1993, 127). Terracing is now much more frequently used and reduces soil runoff.

12. In addition to the Fish and Boating Code and Clean Streams Law discussed below, other applicable statutes include the Dam Safety and Encroachments Act, Pa. Stat. Ann. tit. 32, §§ 693.1–693.27 (Purdon Supp. 1990); the Solid Waste Management Act, Pa. Stat. Ann. tit. 35, §§ 6018.101–6018.1003 (Purdon Supp. 1990); the Pennsylvania Safe Drinking Water Act, Pa. Stat. Ann. tit. 35, §§ 721.1–722.1 (Purdon Supp. 1990); the Pennsylvania Sewage Facilities Act, Pa. Stat. Ann. tit. 35, §§ 750.1–750.20a (Purdon 1977 & Supp. 1990); the Air Pollution Control Act, Pa. Stat. Ann. tit. 35, §§ 4001–4106 (Purdon 1977 & Supp. 1990); the Pennsylvania Fertilizer, Soil Conditioner and Plant Growth Substance Law, Pa. Stat. Ann. tit. 3, §§ 68.1–68.19 (Purdon Supp. 1990); the Pennsylvania Right to Farm Act, Pa. Stat. Ann. tit. 3, §§ 951–957 (Purdon 1990); and the Federal Clean Water Act, 33 U.S.C.A. §§ 1251–1387 (West 1986 & Supp. 1990).

13. 30 Pa. Cons. Stat. Ann. § 2503(a) (Purdon Supp. 1990).

14. Pa. Stat. Ann. tit. 35, § 691.401 (Purdon Supp. 1990). Pollution is "construed to mean contamination of any waters of the Commonwealth such as will create or is likely to create a nuisance or to render such waters harmful, detrimental or injurious to public health, safety or welfare"; "waters of the Commonwealth" include surface as well as underground water. Pa. Stat. Ann. tit. 35, § 691.1 (Purdon Supp. 1990).

15. Pa. Stat. Ann. tit. 35, § 691.402(a) (Purdon Supp. 1990).

16. Pa. Stat. Ann. tit. 35, §§ 691.1, 691.201–691.202 (Purdon 1977 & Supp. 1990).

17. 25 Pa. Code § 101.8 (1990). Compliance with the manual is enforced by DER's Bureau of Water Quality Management. DER policies regarding manure management are presented in its 1986 manual, *Manure Management for Environmental Protection*, and its supplements, which include *Field Application of Manure* and *Dairy Manure Management*.

18. The Pennsylvania Chesapeake Bay Program is a voluntary program of financial and technical assistance to farmers in the Chesapeake Bay Watershed administered by DER's Bureau of Soil and Water Conservation through the conservation districts. Under the program, a farmer who agrees to implement best management practices to control nonpoint source pollution is entitled to 75 percent cost share for erosion control practices and 50 percent cost share for manure storage facilities, up to thirty thousand dollars. 33 U.S.C.A. § 1267 (West 1986 and Supp. 1990). Among other funding programs, up to thirty-five hundred dollars per year is available through the U.S. Department of Agriculture Conservation and Stabilization Service to farmers who implement soil conservation plans.

19. DER's erosion control regulations, 25 Pa. Code § 102 *et seq.*, are issued under the grant of authority contained in the Clean Streams Law, Pa. Stat. Ann. tit. 35, §§ 691.5 and 691.402 (Purdon Supp. 1990).

20. 25 Pa. Code § 102.4 (1989). The plans typically incorporate features such as diversion terraces to control water flow. A soil conservation plan prepared by the U.S. Department of Agriculture Soil Conservation Districts qualifies as an erosion and sediment control plan. The county conservation districts have been delegated the authority by DER to enforce the regulations.

21. Pursuant to § 2503(c) of the Fish and Boat Code, depositing substances in violation of the littering provision constitutes a summary offense of the first degree and is subject to a fine of one hundred dollars. 30 Pa. Con. Stat. Ann. §§ 923, 2503(c) (Purdon Supp. 1990). The Clean Streams Law authorizes a broad spectrum of enforcement actions which could also be taken against farmers, including civil penalties of up to ten thousand dollars per day for each violation, which can be assessed regardless of whether violations are willful. Pa. Stat. Ann. tit. 35, § 691.605 (Purdon Supp. 1990). The Fish Commission does not always or even often issue fines, but offenders could also be fined by DER.

22. The local meeting format used by the agency has been effective in reaching the Amish. Technical assistance on farm production is of interest to farmers, since it increases farm output.

23. The Clean Streams Law states: "If the department finds that the pollution or danger of pollution results from an act of God in the form of sediment for land for which a complete conservation plan has been developed by the local soil and water conservation district and the Soil Conservation Service, U.S.D.A., and the plan has been fully implemented and maintained, the landowner shall be excluded from the penalties of this act." Pa. Stat. Ann. tit. 35, § 691.316 (Purdon Supp. 1990).

24. The Pennsylvania Municipalities Planning Code, Pa. Stat. Ann. tit. 53, § 10603(b)(5) (Purdon Supp. 1990). Ordinances to preserve farmland must take into consideration topography, soil type and classification, and current use. Pa. Stat. Ann. tit. 53, § 10604(3) (Purdon Supp. 1990).

25. In *Codorus Township v. Rogers*, 89 Pa. Commw. 79, 85–86, 492 A. 2d. 73 (1985), the court cited the example of agricultural zoning that diminished the value of land from almost 1.5 million dollars as land for residential development to approximately five hundred thousand dollars as farmland (citing to *Wilson v. County of McHenry*, 92 Ill. App. 3d. 997, 416 N.E. 2d. 426, 1981).

Government interference with the right to enjoy private property is circumscribed by due process considerations. To withstand judicial scrutiny, a zoning ordinance must promote the public health, safety, or welfare; its regulations must be substantially related to the purposes it serves. *Euclid v. Ambler Realty Co.*, 272 U.S. 365 (1926). Under a substantive due process analysis, the public interest served by the ordinance is balanced against the confiscatory or exclusionary impact of the regulation on individual rights. A regulation will be invalidated if it is arbitrary, unreasonable, and unrelated to the public health, safety, morals, or general welfare. *Boundary Drive Associates v. Shrewsbury Township*, 507 Pa. 481, 489, 491 A. 2d. 86 (1985).

26. In *Codorus, supra* (1985), a fifty-acre minimum lot size was held to be rationally related to the goal of agricultural preservation. Minimum lot sizes may be upheld where there is "extraordinary justification." *Appeal of Kit-Mar Builders, Inc.*, 439 Pa. 466, 268 A. 2d. 765 (1970). The *Codorus* decision indicates that agricultural preservation constitutes such extraordinary justification (Buchanan 1986, 871).

27. In *Boundary Drive, supra* (1985), the Pennsylvania Supreme Court upheld the constitutionality of a local zoning ordinance that limited the development of land in agricultural districts based on soil classification. A two-dwelling maximum was established on the highest quality farmland, regardless of tract size. Less productive farmland was subject to a sliding scale that permitted an increased number of homes on the land as tract size increased.

The two-dwelling maximum, regardless of tract size, was similar to the fixed scale zoning turned down in *Hopewell Township Board of Supervisors v. Golla*, 499 Pa. 246, 452 A. 2d. 1337 (1982) (a five-lot maximum in an agricultural district, regardless of tract size, was found constitutionally infirm). The two-dwelling lot maximum in *Boundary Drive* was upheld as part of a larger, comprehensive zoning scheme substantially related to the goal of farmland preservation.

28. Farmers are also protected by the Right to Farm Law, Pa. Stat. Ann. tit. 3, §§ 951–957 (Purdon Supp. 1990), which protects certain agricultural operations from nuisance suits and ordinances.

29. For a discussion of the transformation of Amish work, see Kraybill 1989, 188–211.

30. The Zoning Ordinance of Leacock Township permits "home-related businesses" in rural districts, businesses conducted in the home area or an accessory building which utilize no more than 25 percent of the residence or accessory building and which employ no more than two workers who do not reside on the premises (§ 1713). By special exception, the ordinance permits "farm-related" businesses (§ 1712). A farm-related business between four thousand and six thousand feet in size must be located on a lot that is at least two acres, only 50 percent of which may be covered by the building or by storage or paved areas. The owner must live on the premises. In addition to certain enumerated permitted shops (printing, hatters, blacksmiths, etc.), home- or farm-related businesses include shops "from which supplies are sold strictly and solely related to the carrying on of agricultural pursuits" (Art. V). The ordinance also establishes an agricultural support district for agriculturally related commercial uses (§ 801).

The Leacock Township Planning Commission recently proposed zoning changes that would introduce effective agricultural zoning in the township. Among other things, only one residential dwelling would be permitted per twenty-five acres, and grandparent houses would be permitted to be attached to farm dwellings. The Amish have been studying the proposal and attending public hearings to assess its impact on their lifestyle.

31. Lancaster County Board of Commissioners and Lancaster County Planning Commission, "Policy Plan of the Lancaster County Comprehensive Plan," 16 January 1991, 9. The sensitivity of county officials to Plain Sect (Amish and Old Order Mennonites) land use is reflected in the Lancaster County Planning Commission's *Comprehensive Plan Updates* 1–6, July 1989–May 1991 and in the Planning Commission's *Comprehensive Policy Plan*, issued January 1991.

32. Lancaster County Planning Commission, "Farm-Based Business Model Ordinance Provisions for Lancaster County," April 1990: introduction. The Planning Commission advocates township adoption of a three-tier farm-based business ordinance. "Farm occupations" would consist of businesses permitted as a secondary use on active farms. A wide variety of uses would be permitted but their size would be restricted, for example, in terms of square feet and number of non-resident employees, to prevent interference with the primary agricultural use of the land. "Farm-related businesses" would not need to be located on an active farm but would provide direct goods or services to local farmers. They would also be limited in size but would allow more intensive land use than the farm occupation category. The model ordinance also

contemplates special "agricultural support districts" for similar uses taking place on a more intensive scale.

33. Pennsylvania Sewage Facilities Act, Pa. Stat. Ann. tit. 35, § 750.7 (Purdon Supp. 1990).

34. A privy is defined in DER regulations as a "tank designed to receive sewage where water under pressure is not available." 25 Pa. Code § 71.1 (1989). In this instance, the privy was a rented portable toilet of the type seen at construction sites. Black water is waste from toilets. Gray water consists of waste water from sinks, laundry, and bathing.

35. Elder cottage housing in Leacock Township is permitted by special exception pursuant to the legislative declaration that "the increasing numbers of elderly persons in the township are in need of suitable forms of housing which would allow for the elderly to remain as independent as possible, while maintaining a close connection to the members of their family" (§ 1714[1]).

36. When Hershberger was refused a sewage permit because he had no gray water treatment system, he removed the privy and began disposing of bathroom wastes by burying them in the woods and disposing of all other wastes in his garden. Represented by a self-proclaimed common law attorney, Mr. Hershberger claimed he was not covered by the Sewage Facilities Act since he was using no pipes. The Hershberger case is an unusual one of two extremes: Hershberger's eccentric position and the township's strict interpretation of regulations.

37. In 1900, an acre of land sold for $120; in 1960, it sold for $600; the same land in 1990 sold for $4,800 (*New Era*, 15 October 1990).

38. Pa. Stat. Ann. tit. 3, § 902 (Purdon Supp. 1990). In *Boundary Drive, supra*, the Pennsylvania Supreme Court noted the variety of measures taken by the federal and state governments to protect farmland and the agricultural industry. See, e.g., the Farmland Protection Policy Act, 7 U.S.C.A. §§ 4201–4209 (West 1988) (establishing protection for maximizing the extent to which federal programs contribute to farmland conversion and for assuring that such programs are compatible with state, local, and private efforts to protect such land); I.R.C. §§ 126, 175, 2032A, 6166 (1989) (collectively providing tax incentives to inhibit conversion of farmland and to encourage soil conservation); the Agricultural Area Security Law, Pa. Stat. Ann. tit. 3, §§ 901–915 (Purdon Supp. 1990) (declaring the Commonwealth's policy to conserve, protect, and improve its agricultural land and providing various measures to implement that policy); the Right to Farm Law, Pa. Stat. Ann. tit. 3, §§ 951–957 (Purdon Supp. 1990) (limiting the circumstances under which a farmer may be subjected to local nuisance regulations); Act 515, Pa. Stat. Ann. tit. 16, §§ 11941–11947 (Purdon Supp. 1990) and 72 Pa. Con. Stat. Ann. § 5490.3 (Purdon 1990) (authorizing assessment of eligible farmland at current use value for purposes of local property taxation); 72 Pa. Con. Stat. Ann. § 1722 (Purdon 1990) (providing for the valuation of farmland at its current use value for state death tax purposes); and the Tax Reform Code of 1971, 72 Pa. Con. Stat. Ann. § 7602.2 (Purdon 1990) (exempting family farm corporations from the ten-mill state capital stock franchise tax).

39. Pa. Stat. Ann. tit. 3, §§ 901–957 (Purdon Supp. 1990).

40. Pa. Stat. Ann. tit. 3, § 911(a) (Purdon Supp. 1990).

41. Pa. Stat. Ann. tit. 3, § 911(b) (Purdon Supp. 1990).

42. Telephone conversation with Thomas Daniels, director, Lancaster County Agricultural Preserve Board, 1991.

43. *Lancaster Farmland Trust News* 6, no. 3 (November–December 1990).
44. *Lancaster Farmland Trust News* 7, no. 1 (March 1991).
45. Easement language can be negotiated, although the standard language of the Lancaster Farmland Trust's easement agreement restricts land use to "agricultural and directly associated uses." Directly associated uses are limited to the direct sale to the public of agricultural products produced on the land; structures for processing, marketing, and storing agricultural products produced on the farm; the provision of incidental agricultural services, supplies, and repair by persons in residence; and the conduct of traditional trades and production of home occupation goods as long as the uses remain incidental to the agricultural use and are limited to occupying residential and/or principally agricultural structures. Limited residential development of the land for family members, not to exceed one dwelling per twenty-five acres, is permitted.

Chapter 11. The Role of Outsiders

1. John A. Hostetler and I used ethnographic methods including interviews with various Amish members and leaders, people living as neighbors to Amish farms, and government officials who dealt with policy issues relating to the Amish. We attended public meetings involving issues affecting the Amish, which in some cases were attended by large numbers of Amish. We also kept close watch on mass media coverage of the Amish during this period. Of course, this research was augmented by John A. Hostetler's many previous years of contact with, and research concerning, the Amish in North America.
2. Lawyers may be used for routine actions such as filing wills, forming business partnerships, and conducting real estate transactions (Kraybill 1989, 223). Some businessmen have even begun to employ lawyers to help resolve disputes so long as litigation is avoided.
3. See, for example, Abel 1982; Galanter 1983; Harrington 1985; Hofrichter 1987; and Harrington and Merry 1988. Legal pluralism, as used here, means the simultaneous operation of multiple systems of social control, varying widely along dimensions of formality and rationalization (what Weber would call bureaucratization), within a single nation-state.
4. Redekop (1989, 36) points out, for example, that a similar pattern of protection has formed around the Hutterites.
5. Proximity to farms, however, sometimes also generates friction with the Amish. A current problem arose when new non-Amish residents began complaining about the odor of cow manure, which Amish farmers regularly use to fertilize their fields. Intense negotiations began between the Amish and state and county agencies, which have insisted on new procedures for handling and use of manure.
6. The Amish do not build separate church structures, because worship is held in members' homes, barns, or shops. As many as 150 to 200 people are seated in several rooms of a home or in a barn or shop. Kraybill (1989, 86–90) mentions the National Amish Steering Committee, along with five other organizations, as casting a "shadow of bureaucracy" over the Amish landscape. It is a shadow precisely because organization is so highly suspect within Amish culture.
7. Since many Amish do not vote in elections ("The problem is, if you vote

for one chap, you have to vote against the other, don't you, and then he will feel bad"), they usually don't pose a serious bloc vote threat, even to local politicians in most areas.

8. Redekop 1989, 261–76; Graber 1979, 1982.

Chapter 12. *Canadian Government Relations*

1. There is a congregation of horse-and-buggy Mennonites at Gorrie, Ontario, which is of similar strictness.

2. Six of the seven that no longer exist were located near the following areas: Tavistock, in Oxford County; Gorrie, in Huron County; Wallacetown, in Elgin County; Teeswater, in Bruce County; Belleville, in Hastings County; and Zurich, in Huron County (which had been founded in 1848). The seventh, known as the Milverton Amish settlement, was actually located near Chesley in Grey County.

3. This estimate, supplied by Canadian Amish leaders, includes children and baptized adults.

4. Letter from H. A. Griffith, assistant to the area superintendent, Western Ontario Area, Ontario Department of Education, to Joseph Stoll, Aylmer, Ontario, August 1966.

5. Letter from David Wagler, Aylmer, Ontario, to John Bontrager, Shipshewana, Indiana, 8 November 1966.

6. Letter from J. R. McCarthy, deputy minister of education, Toronto, Ontario, to Joseph Stoll, Aylmer, Ontario, 25 July 1967.

7. Letter from Joseph Stoll to all Amish settlements in Ontario, 30 August 1968, Aylmer, Ontario.

8. Letter from H. Parker, secretary of the Ontario Milk Marketing Board, to the Amish Milk Committee, Aylmer, Ontario, 18 January 1977.

9. As understood by those present and as recorded in a summary of the discussion written by Erwin Wiens, executive director of the Mennonite Central Committee, in a letter to John Laskin, a lawyer, of Toronto, on 14 December 1977. Grant Smith, vice-chairman of the Ontario Milk Marketing Board, and two of his staff were present.

10. Letter from Kenneth B. McKinnon, chairman of the Ontario Milk Marketing Board, Mississauga, Ontario, to Elmo Stoll, Aylmer, Ontario, 26 November 1984. The rate per hectoliter was raised to $1.78 on 31 December 1984.

11. Letter from Kenneth B. McKinnon, chairman of the Ontario Milk Marketing Board, Mississauga, Ontario, to Clarkson Gordon, chartered accountant, London, Ontario, 4 July 1986.

12. Re *Binder and Canadian Nat'l. R.R. Co.*, 23 D.L.R. 4th (1986).

13. Their reluctance to apply for citizenship is primarily a manifestation of their desire to have as little involvement with government as possible, but it also keeps their options open.

14. I draw similar conclusions in part of an earlier article (Thomson 1988, 171–90). In some instances, I use the same wording that I employ in this section.

Chapter 13. First Amendment Issues

1. The First Amendment to the Constitution of the United States states: "Congress shall make no law respecting an establishment of religion, or prohibiting the free exercise thereof; or abridging the freedom of speech, or of the press; or the right of people peaceably to assemble, and to petition the government for a redress of grievances." For a brief discussion of the constitutional freedom to be Anabaptist and some First Amendment cases involving several Anabaptist groups, see Ball 1988.

2. For the delineation of that phrase, see Paton Yoder's discussion in Chapter 2 of this book.

3. But see the discussion below of the case of *United States v. Lee* (1982).

4. See, for example, American Jewish Committee, Litigation Report—AJC in the Courts (as of January 1980).

5. A famous example was their appearance before congressional committees in 1955 to protest the extension of Social Security coverage to self-employed persons (Hostetler 1993, 270).

6. See, for example, "Development Causes Amish to Speak Out," *Intelligencer Journal*, 20 June 1990.

7. Elizabeth Place, in Chapter 10 of this book, details the bewildering environmental problems now faced by Amish farmers in Pennsylvania.

8. The Supreme Court never held religious liberty to be absolute. For example, more than a century ago it had said that if a religion called for human sacrifice, its claim to carry out that mandate would be outweighed by the societal interest in the preservation of innocent human life (*Reynolds v. United States* [1879]).

9. Following pre-*Smith* standards, two federal courts held that the application of the NLRA violated the free exercise clause (*Caulfield v. Hirsch* [1977]; *McCormick v. Hirsch* [1978]).

10. See, for example, *Commonwealth v. Beiler* (1951).

11. J. Choper, in "The Supreme Court, 1988 Term," 57 U.S.L.W. 2227, 18 October 1988.

12. *State v. Whisner* (1976); *State of Vermont v. LaBarge* (1976); *Kentucky State Bd. for Elementary and Secondary Educ. v. Rudasill* (1979), *cert. denied* (1980).

13. *Lee*, at 258.

14. For additional discussions of the legal consequences of *Lee* for religious liberty, see Brady 1983, Ossian 1983, Stevens and Tulio 1984, and Wiles 1983.

15. See part C of the opinion.

16. Emphasis supplied by the court, *State v. Hershberger* 1990 (*Hershberger II*), 397.

17. A famous example is *Brown v. Board of Education* (1954), wherein the Court overruled its 1896 decision that "separate but equal" public accommodations met the requirement of the Fourteenth Amendment's equal protection clause.

References

Abel, Richard, et al.
1982   Ed. *The Politics of Informal Justice*. New York: Academic Press.

Advance-News
1857–   Ogdensburg, N.Y.: Roy H. Park.

Akron Beacon Journal
1839–   Akron, Ohio: Beacon Journal Publishing Co.

Ambassador of Peace
1966–   Aylmer, Ont.: Pathway Publishers. A monthly publication de-
1970   voted to the needs of Amish I-W men during the Vietnam War era.

"Amish Army Camp Experiences—1918"
1970   *Family Life* (December): 22–26.

Ann Arbor News, The
1835–   Ann Arbor, Mich.: Booth Newspapers.

"Another Good Year for Epidemiology"
1980   *Journal of the American Medical Association* 24 (1): 11.

Armstrong, Penny, and Sheryl Feldman
1986   *A Midwife's Story*. New York: Arbor House.

Ausbund, das ist: Etliche schöne Christliche Lieder
1991   Lancaster, Pa.: Lancaster Press. First edition 1564.

Bagramian, Robert A., Sena Narendran, and A. Mahyer Khavari
1988   "Oral Health Status, Knowledge, and Practices in an Amish Population." *Journal of Public Health Dentistry* 48, no. 3 (Summer): 147–51.

Ball, William B.
1975   "Building a Landmark Case: Wisconsin v. Yoder." In *Compulsory Education and the Amish*, edited by Albert N. Keim. Boston: Beacon Press.
1988   "An External Perspective: The Constitutional Freedom to Be Anabaptist." *Brethren Life and Thought* 33, no. 3 (Summer): 200–204.

[Beachy] Amish Mennonite Churches
  1968   "War, Peace, and Social Issues." *Herold der Wahrheit* 57 (May): 188–89.

Beaver, Daniel R.
  1966   *Newton D. Baker and the American War Effort, 1917–1919.* Lincoln: University of Nebraska Press.

"Behind Prison Walls"
  1968   *Family Life* (August–September): 12–14, 16–19.

Beiler, Aaron E.
  1941–   *Aaron E. Beiler Papers.* Archives of the Mennonite Church,
  1954   Goshen College, Goshen, Ind.

Beiler, David
  1888   *Das Wahre Christenthum: Eine Christliche Betrachtung nach den Lehren der Heiligen Schrift.* Lancaster, Pa.: Johann Baers and Son.
  [1928]   *Eine Vermahnung oder Andenken.* N.p., 29 pp. Completed in 1862 but published posthumously in 1928.

Bender, David
  1990   "Fighting for Freedom." *Family Life* (February): 7.

Bender, Harold S.
  1934   "Some Early American Amish Mennonite Disciplines." *Mennonite Quarterly Review* 8 (April): 90–97.
  1946   "An Amish Bishop's Conference Epistle of 1865." *Mennonite Quarterly Review* 20 (July): 222–29.
  1955   "The Anabaptists and Religious Liberty in the Sixteenth Century." *Mennonite Quarterly Review* 29 (April): 83–100.

Berne Witness, The
  1932–   Berne, Ind.: Berne Witness Co. (1992: *Berne Tri Weekly News*, pub. Berne Tri Weekly News Publishing Co.).

"Bits and Pieces"
  1971   *Family Life* (November): 22–23.

Blackboard Bulletin
  1957–   Aylmer, Ont.: Pathway Publishers. Monthly periodical published for Old Order Amish teachers.

Blatt, Die
  1977–   Shipshewana, Ind.: Pleasant Ridge Printers. Biweekly paper published by and serving the Amish of northern Indiana and southern Michigan.

Boles, Donald E.
  1967   *The Two Swords: Commentaries and Cases in Religion and Education.* Ames: Iowa State University Press.

Bontrager, Eli J.
1956   *My Life Story*. N.p. Vivid first-person account by one of the best-known Amish bishops of the twentieth century.

Bontrager, John M.
1967   "Plain View and Pleasant Ridge Amish Church Schools: Middlebury, Indiana." In *The Challenge of the Child*, edited by Joseph Stoll. Aylmer, Ont.: Pathway Publishers.

Botschaft, Die
1975–   Lancaster, Pa.: Brookshire Publications and Printing. Described on its masthead as "a weekly newspaper serving Old Order Amish Communities everywhere."

Brady, P.
1983   "Government's Interest in Taxation Outweighs Amish Free Exercise Rights: *United States v. Lee*." *Tax Lawyer* 36, no. 2 (Winter): 450–59.

Braght, Thieleman J. van
1968   Comp. *The Bloody Theatre; or, Martyrs Mirror*. 8th ed. Scottdale, Pa.: Mennonite Publishing House. Originally published in Dutch (Dordrecht, 1660).

Buchanan, Thomas G.
1986   "Innovative Zoning for the Preservation of Agricultural Land —*Boundary Drive Associates v. Shrewsbury Township of Supervisors*." *Temple Law Quarterly* 59: 861–77.

Budget, The
1890–   Sugarcreek, Ohio. A weekly newspaper serving the Amish and Mennonite communities.

Burger, Warren E.
1991   Review of *The Litigation Explosion*, by Walter K. Olson. *New York Times Book Review*, 12 May.

Casad, Robert C.
1968   "Compulsory High School Attendance and the Old Order Amish, A Commentary on *State v. Garber*." *Kansas Law Review* 16, no. 3 (April): 423–35.

Cawson, Alan
1978   "Pluralism, Corporatism, and the Role of the State." *Governmental Opposition* (13): 179–80.

"Christian's Relation to the Nation, The"
1972   *Herold der Wahrheit* 61 (July): 229–32.

Christliche Glaubens-Bekantnus der Waffenlosen und fürnehmlich in den Niederländern (unter dem Nahmen der Mennonisten) wohlbekannten Christen . . .
1691   Amsterdam. First printed in 1664.

Clark, Allen B.
1988   *This Is a Good Country: A History of the Amish of Delaware, 1915–1988.* Gordonville, Pa.: Gordonville Print Shop.

Cleveland Press, The
1963–   Cleveland, Ohio: Scripps-Howard.
1982

Cline, Paul Charles
1968   "Relations between the 'Plain People' and Government in the United States." Ph.D. diss., American University, Washington, D.C.

Controlling Nutrient Pollution from Nonpoint Sources in Pennsylvania
1990   Harrisburg: Governor Robert P. Casey's Select Committee on Nonpoint Source Nutrient Management, 20 December.

Corry Journal
1912–   Corry, Pa.: George R. Sample.

Courier-Journal, The
1868–   Louisville, Ky.: Courier-Journal Co.

Cronk, Sandra L.
1977   *"Gelassenheit:* The Rites of the Redemptive Process in Old Order Amish and Old Order Mennonite Communities." Ph.D. diss., University of Chicago.
1981   Excerpts under the above title appear in *Mennonite Quarterly Review* 55 (January): 5–44.

Daily Record, The
1889–   Wooster, Ohio: Wooster Republican Printing Co.

Daniels, Tom
1990   "The Challenge of Preserving Agricultural Land." *Lancaster County's New Comprehensive Plan Update* 3(January–February): 4.

Derrick, The
1871–   Oil City, Pa.: E. B. Cowart.

Des Moines Register
1849–   Des Moines, Iowa: Gannett Co.

Diary, The
1969–   Gordonville, Pa.: Pequea Publishers. A monthly periodical devoted to Amish history and genealogy.

Dolbeare, Kenneth, and James Davis
1968   *Little Groups of Neighbors: The Selective Service System.*
        Chicago: Markham.

Dyck, Cornelius J.
1962   Trans. "The Middleburg Confession of Hans de Ries." *Mennonite Quarterly Review* 36 (April): 147–54.
1981   Ed. *An Introduction to Mennonite History.* 2d ed. Scottdale, Pa.: Herald Press.

Elkhart Truth, The
1889–   Elkhart, Ind.: Truth Publishing Co.

Ellen, Martha
1984   "Town Meeting with Amish." *Waterman Daily Times* (24 January): 3.

Elson, John
1969   "State Regulation of Non-public Schools: The Legal Framework." In *Public Controls for Non-public Schools,* edited by Donald A. Erickson. Chicago: University of Chicago Press.

Epp, Frank H.
1982   *Mennonites in Canada, 1920–1940.* Scottdale, Pa.: Herald Press.

Ericksen, Eugene P., J. A. Ericksen, and J. A. Hostetler
1980   "The Cultivation of the Soil as a Moral Directive: Population Growth, Family Ties, and the Maintenance of Community among the Old Order Amish." *Rural Sociology* 45 (Spring): 49–68.

Erickson, Donald A.
1965   "The Amish and the State School Statutes: A Position Paper." Manuscript.
1969   Ed. *Public Controls for Non-public Schools.* Chicago: University of Chicago Press.

Esch, S. S.
1918   "Warum sollten wir uns wehrlos erklären vor der Obrigkeit." *Herold der Wahrheit* 7 (March): 108.

"Expelled Amish Owes Social Security Tax"
1990   *Insight* (26 February): 45.

Family Life
1968–   Aylmer, Ont.: Pathway Publishers. A monthly Amish periodical.

Fillmore County Journal
1982–   Preston, Minn.: Fillmore County News.
1986

Fisher, Gideon L.
  1978   *Farm Life and Its Changes.* Gordonville, Pa.: Pequea Publishers.
  1989   "Are We Awake?" *The Diary* (February): 37.

Fisher, Sara E., and Rachel K. Stahl
  1986   *The Amish School.* Lancaster, Pa.: Good Books.

Fisher, Wayne L.
  1993   *The Amish in Court.* New York: AMS Press.

Foster, Thomas M.
  1980   "The Amish and the Ethos of Ecology." *Ecologist* 10 (December): 331–35.
  1981   "Amish Society: A Relic of the Past Could Become a Model for the Future." *Futurist* (December): 33–40.

Galanter, Marc
  1983   "Reading the Landscape of Disputes: What We Know and Don't Know (and Think We Know) about Our Allegedly Contentious and Litigious Society." *U.C.L.A. Law Review* 31 (October): 4–71.

Garber, Eli
  1960   "What Kingdom Do We Represent?" *Herold der Wahrheit* 49 (November): 412–13.

Geauga County Record
  1905–   Chardon, Ohio: Record Publishing Co.
  1921

"Gemeinde, Gibt es nur eine wahre?"
  1957   *Herold der Wahrheit* 46 (August): 1–2.

"Genetics and the Amish"
  1964   *Journal of the American Medical Association* 189, no. 11 (14 September): 156–57.

Gingerich, Eli
  1980   *Indiana Amish Directory.* Middlebury, Ind.: N.p.

Gingerich, Orland
  1972   *The Amish of Canada.* Scottdale, Pa.: Herald Press.

Glazer, Daniel
  1975   *Affirmative Discrimination: Ethnic Inequality and Public Policy.* New York: Basic Books.

Glick, Nettie
  1933   *Historical Sketch of the Walnut Creek, Ohio, Amish Mennonite Church.* Scottdale, Pa.: Mennonite Publishing House.

Goshen Democrat
  1837–   Goshen, Ind.: News Printing Co.

Goshen News, The
1837–   Goshen, Ind.: News Printing Co.

Gospel Herald
1908–   Scottdale, Pa.: Mennonite Publishing House.

"Government, Our Duties to the"
1972   *Herold der Wahrheit* 61 (October): 226–27.

Graber, Robert
1979   "The Socio-Cultural Differentiation of a Religious Sect: Schism among the Pennsylvania German Mennonites." Ph.D. diss., University of Wisconsin, Madison.
1982   "The Socio-Cultural Differentiation of a Religious Sect: Schism among the Pennsylvania German Mennonites." *Mennonite Quarterly Review* 56 (April): 196–99.

Granoff, Dan M., Thomas McKinney, Eyla Boies, Norman P. Steele, John Oldfather, Janardan P. Pandey, and Brian K. Suarez
1986   "Haemophilus Influenzae Type b Disease in an Amish Population: Studies of the Effects of Genetic Factors, Immunization, and Rifampin Prophylaxis on the Course of an Outbreak." *Pediatrics* 77, no. 3 (March): 289–95.

Grossman, M. H., J. Garner, R. Weinstein, and W. Grover
1989   "Identification of a New Mutation at a Single Hind III Site in an Amish Family with Phenylketonuria (PKU)." Paper presented at the 40th annual meeting of the American Society of Human Genetics, Baltimore, 11–15 November.

Harkness, K. A., and W. E. Stuckey
1963   "Effective Approaches to Reducing Accidents Involving Slow Moving Vehicles on Highways." Interim Report, Ohio State University, 1 May.

Harrington, Christine
1985   *Shadow Justice: The Ideology and Institutionalization of Alternatives to Court.* Westport, Conn.: Greenwood Press.

Harrington, Christine, and Sally E. Merry
1988   "Ideological Production: The Making of Community Mediation." *Law and Society Review* 22 (4): 709–36.

Hartzler, J. S.
1921   *Mennonites in the World War.* Scottdale, Pa.: Herald Press.

Heikes, Janice
1985   "Differences among the Old Order Amish of Wayne County, Ohio, and Their Use of Health Care Services." Master's thesis, Department of Agricultural Economics and Rural Sociology, Ohio State University, Columbus.

Herald-Leader, Lexington
1983–   Lexington, Ky.: Lexington Herald-Leader Co.

Herold der Wahrheit
1864–   The German edition of the *Herald of Truth,* published at times
1901   semimonthly and monthly. In 1901 it merged with *Mennonitische Rundschau.* Elkhart, Ind.: John F. Funk.

Herold der Wahrheit
1912–   A monthly periodical with both English and German articles. Published jointly by Old Order Amish and Conservative Amish Mennonites beginning in 1912. Since 1956 it has been published by Old Order Amish personnel, although not exclusively.

Hershberger, Noah
1985   *A Struggle to Be Separate.* Self-published.

Hillerbrand, Hans J.
1958a   "An Early Anabaptist Treatise on the Christian and the State." *Mennonite Quarterly Review* 32 (January): 28–47.
1958b   "The Anabaptist View of the State." *Mennonite Quarterly Review* 32 (April): 83–110.

Hochstetler, Monroe D.
1972   "Whom Do We Trust: God or Insurance?" *Family Life* (June): 13–16.

Hofrichter, Richard
1987   *Neighborhood Justice in Capitalist Society: The Expansion of the Informal State.* Westport, Conn.: Greenwood Press.

Horst, Irvin B.
1988   Ed. and trans. *Mennonite Confession of Faith* (Dordrecht). Lancaster, Pa.: Lancaster Mennonite Historical Society. Adopted by the Mennonites at a peace convention held in Dordrecht, Holland, 21 April 1632.

Hostetler, Mrs. Amos, David Hostetler, and Jerry Yoder
1973   *Descendants of David J. Hostetler.* Nappanee, Ind.: Evangel Press.

Hostetler, John A.
1969   *Educational Achievements and Life Styles in a Traditional Society: The Old Order Amish.* U.S. Office of Education, Washington, D.C.
1975   "The Cultural Context of the Wisconsin Case." In *Compulsory Education and the Amish,* edited by Albert N. Keim. Boston: Beacon Press.
1980   *Amish Society.* 3d ed. Baltimore: Johns Hopkins University Press.

1984   "The Amish and the Law: A Religious Minority and Its Legal Encounters." Tensions between Religious or Ethnic Communities and the Larger Society: A Frances Lewis Law Center Colloquium. *Washington and Lee Law Review* 41, no. 1 (Winter): 33–47.

1987   "A New Look at the Old Order Amish." M. E. John Lecture, 1987. University Park, Pa.: Pennsylvania State University, Department of Agricultural Economics and Rural Sociology.

1988   "Land Use, Ethics, and Agriculture in Lancaster County." Report to the Pennsylvania Department of Transportation.

1989   "Toward Responsible Growth and Stewardship of Lancaster County's Landscape." *Pennsylvania Mennonite Heritage* 12, no. 3 (July): 2–10.

1993   *Amish Society.* 4th ed. Baltimore: Johns Hopkins University Press.

Hostetler, John A., and Gertrude E. Huntington
1992   *Amish Children: Education in the Family, School, and Community.* 2d ed. New York: Harcourt Brace Jovanovich.

Huntington, Gertrude Enders
1957   "Dove at the Window: A Study of an Old Order Amish Community in Ohio." Ph.D. diss., Yale University.

1984   "Cultural Interaction during Time of Crisis: Boundary Maintenance and Amish Boundary Definition." In *Internal and External Perspectives on Amish and Mennonite Life,* edited by Werner Enninger. Essen, Germany: Unipress.

1988   "The Amish Family." In *Ethnic Families in America: Patterns and Variations,* 3d ed., edited by Charles H. Mindel, Robert W. Habenstein, and Roosevelt Wright, Jr. New York: Elsevier.

1990   "A United States Amish Immigrant Community in Canada: Articulating Values and Behavior." Paper presented at the 89th Annual Meeting of the American Anthropological Association, New Orleans, La., 28 November.

Intelligencer Journal
1794–   Lancaster, Pa.: Lancaster Newspapers.

Ithaca Journal
1815–   Ithaca, N.Y.: Pam M. Johnson.

I-W Mirror
1953–   Akron, Pa. Published by Mennonite Central Committee for I-W
1967   conscientious objectors during the cold war.

"Johns Hopkins' Study of Disease in the Amish"
1980   *The Diary* (November): 335.

Johnson, Warren A., Victor Stoltzfus, and Peter Craumer
1977   "Energy Conservation in Amish Agriculture." *Science* 198 (28 October): 373–79.

Jorgensen, Carol, and Tim Dutton
1984   *Amish Health Care Needs Assessment.* Ohio Department of Health, Bureau of Maternal and Child Health, and Wayne County Health Department.

Journal, The
1879–   Lorain, Ohio: Lorain Journal Co.

Journal-Gazette, The
1863–   Fort Wayne, Ind.: Fort Wayne Newspapers.

Juhnke, James C.
1989   *Vision, Doctrine, War: Mennonite Identity and Organization in America, 1890–1930.* Scottdale, Pa.: Herald Press.

Kaiser, Grace H.
1986   *Dr. Frau: A Woman Doctor among the Amish.* Intercourse, Pa.: Good Books.

Kauffman, S. Duane
1991   *Mifflin County Amish and Mennonite Story: 1791–1991.* Belleville, Pa.: Mifflin County Mennonite Historical Society.

Keim, Albert N.
1975   Ed. *Compulsory Education and the Amish: The Right Not to Be Modern.* Boston: Beacon Press.
1990   *The CPS Story: An Illustrated History of Civilian Public Service.* Intercourse, Pa.: Good Books.

Kelley, Dean M.
1982   Ed. *Government Intervention in Religious Affairs,* National Council of Churches. New York: Pilgrim Press.
1989   "Statism, Not Separation, Is the Problem." *Christian Century* (18 January): 48–51.

Kidder, Robert L., and John A. Hostetler
1990   "Managing Ideologies: Harmony as Ideology in Amish and Japanese Societies." *Law and Society Review* 24(4): 895–922.

Kinsinger, Susan
1988   Comp. *Family and History of Lydia Beachy's Descendants, 1889–1989.* Gordonville, Pa.: Gordonville Print Shop.

Klaassen, Walter
1987   "Investigation into the Authorship and the Historical Background of the Anabaptist Tract *Aufdeckung der Babylonischen Hurn.*" *Mennonite Quarterly Review* 61 (July): 251–61.

Klinger, Katherine Wood
1983   "Cystic Fibrosis in the Ohio Amish: Gene Frequency and Founder Effect." *Human Genetics* 65 (2): 94–98.

Kollmorgen, Walter M.
1942   *Culture of a Contemporary Rural Community: The Old Order Amish of Lancaster County, Pennsylvania.* Rural Life Studies, no. 4. Washington, D.C.: U.S. Department of Agriculture.

Kraybill, Donald B.
1989   *The Riddle of Amish Culture.* Baltimore: Johns Hopkins University Press.
1990   *The Puzzles of Amish Life.* Intercourse, Pa.: Good Books.

Lambright, Harley
1983   "In Whose Steps?" *Family Life* (March): 16.

Lapp, Benjamin F.
1959   "Respect for Those in Authority." *Herold der Wahrheit* 44 (August): 153–54.

Lapp, Christ S.
1991   Ed. *Pennsylvania School History, 1690–1990.* Gordonville, Pa.: Privately published.

Ledger-Star, The
1876–   Norfolk, Va.: Landmark Publications.

Lindholm, William C.
1974   "The Amish Case, A Struggle for the Control of Values." In *Controversies in Education,* edited by Dwight W. Allen and Jeffrey Hecht. Philadelphia: W. B. Saunders.

Littell, Franklin H.
1966   "The State of Iowa vs. the Amish." *Christian Century* (23 February): 234–35.

Luther, Martin
1962   "Temporal Authority: To What Extent It Should Be Obeyed." In *Luther's Works,* edited by Walter Brandt, vol. 45. Philadelphia: Muhlenberg Press.
1967   "Whether Soldiers, Too Can Be Saved." In *Luther's Works,* edited by Robert C. Shultz, vol. 46. Philadelphia: Fortress Press.

Luthy, David
1972   "The Arrest of an Amish Bishop—1918." *Family Life* (March): 23–27.
1978   "An Early Ohio Amish School Problem." *Family Life* (December): 17–19.
1986   *The Amish in America: Settlements That Failed, 1840–1960.* Aylmer, Ont.: Pathway Publishers.
1992   "Amish Settlements across America: 1991." *Family Life* (April): 19–24.

Lynch, Henry T.
1976   "Cancer Screening and Education Amongst the Mennonites: Epidemiologic Correlation." Typescript. Omaha, Nebr.: Creighton University.

McConnell, M.
1990   "The Origins and Historical Understanding of Free Exercise of Religion." *Harvard Law Review* 103 (May): 1409.

McKusick, Victor A.
1978   *Medical Genetic Studies of the Amish.* Baltimore: Johns Hopkins University Press.

MacMaster, Richard K.
1985   *Land, Piety, and Peoplehood: The Establishment of Mennonite Communities in America, 1683–1790.* Scottdale, Pa.: Herald Press.

Martin, Paul
1968   "Six Years of Newborn PKU Screening." *Journal of the Indiana State Medical Association* 61 (August): 1107–8.

Martin, Paul H., Louise Davis, and Dorothy Askew
1963   "High Incidence of Phenylketonuria in an Isolated Indiana Community." *Journal of the Indiana State Medical Association* 56 (August): 997–99.

Mast, Daniel E.
1920   "Trachtet am ersten nach dem Reich Gottes." *Herold der Wahrheit* 8 (February): 82–84.
[1933]   *Anweisungen zur Seligkeit.* Baltic, Ohio: J. A. Raber.
1958   *Salvation Full and Free.* Hutchinson, Kans.: D. and I. Gospel Bookstore.

Mast, Eli D.
1985   "Obrigkeit und das Reich Christi." *Herold der Wahrheit* 79 (April): 77–78.

Mast, R. N.
1970   "Das Reich Gottes." *Herold der Wahrheit* 59 (November): 236–37.

Mast, S. D.
1874   "Das Christenthum und der Stimmkasten, oder die Ursache vorum ich nicht an die weltliche Wahl gehe." *Herold der Wahrheit* 11 (July): 114–17.
1930   Reprinted in pamphlet form. Steinbach, Manitoba: P. P. Reimer.

Mather, P. Boyd
1966   "That Amish Thing." *Christian Century* (23 February): 246.

Mazelin, D. D.
1941   *The Mazelins in America*. Berne, Ind.: Self-published.

"Mein Reich ist nicht von der Welt"
1918   *Herold der Wahrheit* 7 (November): 515–17.

Mennonite Encyclopedia, The
1956–   5 vols. Scottdale, Pa.: Mennonite Publishing House; Hillsboro,
1990   Kans.: Mennonite Brethren Publishing House; Newton, Kans.:
        Mennonite Publication Office. Vol. 5 published 1990.

Mennonite Historical Bulletin
1940–   Goshen, Ind. Published quarterly by the Historical Committee
        of the Mennonite Church.

Mennonite Weekly Review
1923–   Newton, Kans.: Herald Publishing Co.

Meyers, Thomas J.
1983   "Stress and the Amish Community in Transition." Ph.D. diss.,
        Boston University.
1991   "Population Growth and Its Consequences in the Elkhart-La-
        grange Old Order Amish Settlement." *Mennonite Quarterly
        Review* 65 (3): 308–21.

Middlebury Independent, The
1887–   Middlebury, Ind.: Lagrange Publishing Co.

Miller, Levi
1981   "The Role of a *Braucher*-Chiropracter in an Amish Commu-
        nity." *Mennonite Quarterly Review* 55 (April): 157–71.

Miller, Shelly R., and Robert W. Schwartz
1992   "Attitudes toward Genetic Testing of Amish, Mennonite, and
        Hutterite Families with Cystic Fibrosis." *American Journal of
        Public Health* 82 (February): 236–42.

Miller, S. H.
1908   "The Amish in Holmes Co., Ohio." In *Mennonite Yearbook
        and Directory*. Scottdale, Pa.: Mennonite Book and Tract Society.

Miller, Wayne
1969   "A Study of Amish Academic Achievement." Ph.D. diss., Uni-
        versity of Michigan.

Monroe Evening News, The
1825–   Monroe, Mich.: Monroe Publishing Co.

Morbidity and Mortality Weekly Report
1951–   Atlanta: Centers for Disease Control.

Morton, H., M. Bennett, C. Nichter, and R. I. Kelley
　1989　"Glutaric Aciduria Type I of the Amish." Paper presented at the 40th annual meeting of the American Society of Human Genetics, Baltimore, Md., 11–15 November.

New Era, Lancaster
　1877–　Lancaster, Pa.: Lancaster Newspapers.

New York Herald Tribune
　1926–　New York: New York Tribune.
　1966

New York Times, The
　1851–　New York: New York Times Co.

News-Sentinel, The
　1833–　Fort Wayne, Ind.: Knight-Ridder Newspapers.

Nicholls, David
　1975　*The Pluralist State.* London: Macmillan and Co.

Nolt, Steven M.
　1992　*A History of the Amish.* Intercourse, Pa.: Good Books.

Nolte, Chester
　1967　"Religious Freedom—Within Limits." *American School Board Journal* 155 (November): 27–28.

Noreland, Cara
　1990　"A Review of *State of Minnesota v. Eli A. Hershberger, et. al.*: Slow Moving Vehicle Emblems and the Amish." Senior thesis, Luther College.

"Obituary: Isaac Kaufman"
　1886　*Daily Tribune—Johnstown* (18 October): 1.

"Obrigkeit, Gehorsam gegen die"
　1968　*Herold der Wahrheit* 57 (November): 426.

Olsen, Gregg
　1990　*Abandoned Prayers.* New York: Warner Books.

Olshan, Marc A.
　1990a　"Affinities and Antipathies: The Old Order Amish in New York State." American Anthropological Association Meetings, 28 November–2 December. New Orleans, La.
　1990b　"The Old Order Amish Steering Committee: A Case Study in Organizational Evolution." *Social Forces* 69 (December): 603–16.

Oregonian, The
　1850–　Portland, Oreg.: Advance Publications.

Ossian, Kathryn L.
1983   "No Tax Exemptions Courtesy of the Lord: *United States v. Lee." Detroit College of Law Review* no. 1 (Spring): 235–52.

Oyer, John
1985   *Anabaptists, the Law, and the State: Some Reflections Apropos North American Mennonites in 1985.* Washington, D.C.: Marpeck Academy.

Pantoja, Antonia, and Barbara Blourock
1975   "Cultural Pluralism Redefined," in *Badges and Indicia of Slavery: Cultural Pluralism Redefined,* edited by Antonia Pantoja et al. Lincoln: Cultural Pluralism Committee, University of Nebraska.

Paper, the
1972–   Goshen, Ind.: the Paper.

"Patriotic Citizens or Loyal Pilgrims"
1956   *Herold der Wahrheit* 45 (November): 330.

Patriot-News, Sunday
1854–   Harrisburg, Pa.: Patriot-News Co.

Pennsylvania Amish Directory of Lancaster and Chester County Districts
1973   Gordonville, Pa.: Pequea Publishers.

Philadelphia Inquirer, The
1829–   Philadelphia, Pa.: Philadelphia Newspapers, Inc.

Pickett, Clarence E.
1953   *For More Than Bread.* Boston: Little, Brown and Co.

Pittsburgh Press, The
1884–   Pittsburgh, Pa.: Pittsburgh Press.

Plain Dealer, The
1842–   Cleveland: Thomas Vail.

"Polio in the Americas"
1991   *Harvard Health Letter* (September): 7.

"Praying Instead of Voting"
1989   *Family Life* (March): 5.

"President Is Dead, The"
1963   *Herold der Wahrheit* 52 (December): 470–71.

Raber, Ben J.
1970–   Comp. *The New American Almanac.* Gordonville, Pa.: Gordonville Print Shop.

Redekop, Calvin
    1989   *Mennonite Society*. Baltimore: Johns Hopkins University Press.

"Reich Gottes, Das"
    1971   *Herold der Wahrheit* 60 (July): 150–51.

Robb, William Oliver
    1990   "Twentieth Century Conflicts between the Amish and the United States Government." Manuscript. Department of History, Princeton University.

Rockford Register Star (Morning)
    1855–   Rockford, Ill.: Gannett Newspapers.

Rodgers, Harrell R., Jr.
    1969   *Community Conflict, Public Opinion and the Law: The Amish Dispute in Iowa*. Columbus, Ohio: Charles Merrill Publishing Co.

Ruegger, MaryAnn S.
    1991   "An Audience for the Amish: A Communication Based Approach to the Development of Law." *Indiana Law Journal* 66, no. 3 (Summer): 801–23.

Ruxin, Paul T.
    1967   "The Right Not to Be Modern Men: The Amish and Compulsory Education." *Virginia Law Review* 53 (4): 925–52.

Sanders, Thomas G.
    1964   *Protestant Concepts of Church and State: Historical Backgrounds and Approaches for the Future*. New York: Holt, Rinehart and Winston.

Saros, John
    1968   "A Study of Compulsory Education." M.A. thesis, University of Akron.

Schlabach, Theron F.
    1988   *Peace, Faith, Nation: Mennonites and Amish in Nineteenth-Century America*. Scottdale, Pa.: Herald Press.

Schnell, Hans
    1710   "Grundlicher Bericht aus Gottes Wort wie man das weltliche und geistliche Regiment, ein jedes mit seiner Ordnung unterscheiden soll . . ." N.p. Found in the *Sammelband*, located in the Mennonite Historical Library, Goshen College, Goshen, Ind.

Schwartz, Hillel
    1973   "Early Anabaptist Ideas About the Nature of Children." *Mennonite Quarterly Review* 47 (April): 102–14.

Schwartz, Jacob D. R.
N.d.   "The Liberalization of the Church." Manuscript.

Scott, Stephen
1981   *Plain Buggies: Amish, Mennonite, and Brethren Horse-drawn Transportation.* Intercourse, Pa.: Good Books.
1986   *Why Do They Dress That Way?* Intercourse, Pa.: Good Books.

Sekus, Perry
1989   "Dispute Resolution among the Old Order Amish." *Ohio State Journal on Dispute Resolution* 4, no. 2 (Spring): 315–25.

Shapiro, Andrew, and John M. Striker
1970   *Mastering the Draft.* Boston: Little, Brown and Co.

Shirk, Eli M.
1939   Comp. *Report of Committee of Plain People Making Pleas for Leniency from Depressive School Laws.* Ephrata, Pa.

Siewers, Alf
1988   "For the Amish, No Life in the Fast Lane." *Christian Science Monitor* 80 (26 October): 6–7.

Simons, Menno
1956   *The Complete Writings of Menno Simons.* Translated by Leonard Verduin and edited by John C. Wenger. Scottdale, Pa.: Herald Press.

Smith, Donald Eugene
1970   *Religion and Political Development.* Boston: Little, Brown and Co.

Smolan, Rick, Phillip Moffitt, and Matthew Naythons
1990   "Photo Essay—Portrait of a Healer." In *The Power to Heal: Ancient Arts and Modern Medicine.* New York: Prentice Hall.

Snyder, Arnold
1989   "The Influence of the Schleitheim Articles on the Anabaptist Movement: An Historical Evaluation." *Mennonite Quarterly Review* 63 (October): 323–44.

South Bend Tribune
1872–   South Bend, Ind.: John J. McGann.

Star Tribune
1920–   Minneapolis, Minn.: Nixon Newspapers.

Steering Committee
1966–   *Minutes of Old Order Amish Steering Committee.* Vols. 1–5.
1990   Gordonville, Pa.: Gordonville Print Shop.

Steiner, Gerald
1989   "The Two Kingdoms." *Family Life* (April): 3.

Stevens, John V., Sr., and John G. Tulio
1984   "Casenote: *United States v. Lee*, a Second Look." *Journal of Church and State* 26 (Autumn): 455–72.

Stoll, Elmo
1984   "Is Insurance Right or Wrong?" *Family Life* (April): 8–11.
1986   "When the House Is Falling Apart." *Family Life* (August–September): 8–10.
1988   "Politicians or Christians." *Family Life* (June): 7–9.
1989   "Voting, Politics, and Propaganda." *Family Life* (January–February): 9–11, 10–12.

Stoll, Joseph
1965   *Who Shall Educate Our Children?* Aylmer, Ont.: Pathway Publishers.

Stoltzfus, N.
1982   "Das Stimmen für die Obrigkeit." *Herold der Wahrheit* 71 (November): 244–45.

Stutzman, D[avid]
1917   *Der schmale Verleugnungsweg: Eine kurze christliche Vermahnung an meine Kinder.* Millersburg, Ohio: D. Stutzman.

Sunbeam
1944–   Boonsboro, Md. Published by Amish CPS men at Unit 3, a spe-
1945   cial camp for Amish COs.

Sunday News
1922–   Lancaster, Pa.: Lancaster Newspapers.

Sutter, Roland W., L. E. Markowitz, J. M. Bennetch, W. Morris, E. R. Zell, and S. R. Preblud
1991   "Measles among the Amish: A Comprehensive Study of Measles Severity in Primary and Secondary Cases in Households." *Journal of Infectious Diseases* 163 (January): 12–16.

Sutter, Thomas L.
1980   "Home Deliveries: A Changing Amish Pattern." *Journal of the American Medical Association* 244, no. 20 (21 November): 2262–63, Letters.

Thomson, Dennis L
1988   "The Political Reality of Religious Pluralism in the United States." *Brethren Life and Thought* 33 (Summer): 171–90.

Times-News (Weekend Edition)
1969–   Erie, Pa.: Times Publishing Company.

Times-Reporter
1872–   New Philadelphia, Ohio: William Stein.

Treyer, David A.
[1898]   "Eine Erklärung in Bezug auf die weltliche Obrigkeit." Appended (pp. 8–16) to a pamphlet entitled "Eine unparteiischer Bericht den Hauptstanden, welche sich ereigneten in den sogenannten Alt-Amischen Gemeinden in Ohio vom Jahr 1850 bis ungefar 1861." This essay was reprinted posthumously in David A. Treyer [Troyer], 1920, *Hinterlassene Schriften von David A Treyer von Holmes County, Ohio, unter welchem sind auch mehrere Erbauliche und Geistreiche Gedichte.* Elkhart, Ind.: Mennonite Publishing Co.

Troyer, Effie Mast, and Joseph Stoll
1965   "Apple Grove Mennonite School First of Its Kind." *Blackboard Bulletin* 9 (October): 37–39.

Troyer, Levi R.
1977   "Die Obrigkeit der Finsternis." *Herold der Wahrheit* 66 (December): 267–68.
1978   "Besetz in das Reich Seines Lieben Sohns." *Herold der Wahrheit* 67 (January): 3.

Truth in Word and Work, The
1983   *A Statement of Faith by Ministers and Brethren of Amish Churches of Holmes Co., Ohio, and Related Areas.* Baltic, Ohio: Amish Brotherhood Publications.

Tweedy, Ann
1991   "The Amish Community and *Employment Division v. Smith:* Changing Notions of Religious Liberty." Senior thesis, Harvard Law School.

"Update for Johns Hopkins Medical School"
1981   *The Diary* (July): 223.

"Usefulness of Sects, The"
1987   *Economist* 304 (25 July): 74, 76.

Verhandlungen der Diener Versammlungen der Deutschen Täufer oder Amischen Mennoniten . . .
1862–   The minutes of the annual Amish ministers' meetings, 1862–76
1878   and 1878, appear under slightly different titles for some years.

Wagler, David L.
1985   *Through Deep Waters.* Bloomfield, Iowa: Titus Wagler.

Wagler, David, and Roman Raber
1945   *The Story of the Amish in Civilian Public Service.* North Newton, Kans.: Bethel Press.

Wall Street Journal
1889–   New York: Dow Jones and Co.

Watertown Daily Times
1861–   Watertown, N.Y.: Johnson Newspaper Corp.

Weaver, J. Denny
1987   *Becoming Anabaptist: The Origin and Significance of Sixteenth-Century Anabaptism.* Scottdale, Pa.: Herald Press.

Weber, Max
1958   "Politics as a Vocation." In *From Max Weber: Essays in Sociology,* edited and translated by H. H. Gerth and C. Wright Mills. New York: Oxford University Press.

Weiler, Roland, and Mary Weiler
1991   "To Love and to Lose." *Family Life* (June): 15–17.

Wenger, Anna Frances Z.
1988   "The Phenomenon of Care in a High Context Culture: The Old Order Amish." Ph.D. diss., Wayne State University, Detroit.

Wenger, J. C.
1980a   "Anecdotes from Mennonite History: A Modern Amish Tragedy." *Mennonite Reporter* (1 September): 3.
1980b   "Mennonite History: Joy in Tribulation." *Mennonite Reporter* (15 September): 3.

Wiles, John J.
1983   "*United States v. Lee:* Has the Retreat Been Sounded for Free Exercise?" *Stetson Law Review* 12 (Spring): 852–64.

Wingard, Raymond
1990   "Help for Hemophilia." *Family Life* (March): 15–16.

Wolkomir, Richard, and Joyce Wolkomir
1991   "The Doctor Who Conquered a Killer." *Readers Digest* 139 (July): 161–66.

"Would Convince World Is Round"
1915   *Geauga County Record,* 17 December.

Yoder, John H.
1964   *The Christian Witness to the State.* Institute of Mennonite Studies Series, no. 93. Newton, Kans.: Faith and Life Press.

Yoder, Karen Kay
1984   "Influence of Cognitive Style in an American Subculture's Health Seeking Behavior and View of Nurses." Ph.D. diss., University of Michigan.

Yoder, Patricia, and Shelly Monson
1991   "Increasing Understanding and Compliance within the Amish Hemophilia Community of Indiana." National Hemophilia Foundation, 43rd annual meeting, Tampa, Florida, 8–12 October.

Yoder, Sam D.
1977   "Non-Resistance under Test." *Herold der Wahrheit* 66 (December): 280–81.

Young, Crawford
1977   *The Politics of Cultural Pluralism.* Madison: University of Wisconsin Press.

Zook, Lee
1989   "The Amish in America: Conflicts between Cultures." *Journal of American Culture* 12 (4): 29–33.

Contributors

WILLIAM B. BALL argued the landmark case *Wisconsin v. Yoder* before the U.S. Supreme Court. A longtime friend of religious liberty, he has served as counsel to the National Committee for Amish Religious Freedom on a wide variety of First Amendment issues. He is a member of the law firm Ball, Skelly, Murren & Connell (Harrisburg, Pa.).

PETER J. FERRARA, a graduate of Harvard College and Harvard Law School, has written numerous books and articles on Social Security, including *Social Security: The Inherent Contradiction* (1980) and *Social Security: Prospects for Real Reform* (1983). From 1982 to 1983, he was a senior staff member at the White House Office of Policy Development, and from 1987 to 1990 was associate professor of law at the George Mason University School of Law. He currently practices law at the Washington, D.C., law firm of Shaw, Pittman, Potts & Trowbridge.

GERTRUDE ENDERS HUNTINGTON received her Ph.D. degree in social science from Yale. Her three-volume dissertation on the Amish of Ohio has received wide acclaim. Co-author of *Amish Children* (Harcourt Brace Jovanovich, 1992) she has conducted fieldwork and written widely on many Amish communities in addition to teaching at the University of Michigan.

ALBERT N. KEIM grew up in an Amish family in Ohio, where he attended an Amish school. He received his Ph.D. degree in American history from Ohio State University and currently is professor of history at Eastern Mennonite College (Va.). He is the editor of *Compulsory Education and the Amish: The Right Not to Be Modern* (Beacon, 1975), as well as books and scholarly articles that deal with conscientious objection to war.

ROBERT L. KIDDER received his Ph.D. degree in sociology from Northwestern University. He is professor of sociology at Temple University; and his research, focusing on the interface of law and society, includes work in India, Japan, and the United States. Author of *Connecting Law and Society,* he has conducted research on dispute resolution among the Amish and has served as editor of the *Law and Society Review.*

DONALD B. KRAYBILL received his Ph.D. degree from Temple University. Author of *The Riddle of Amish Culture* (Johns Hopkins University Press, 1989), as well as many other books and articles on Anabaptist groups, he is professor of sociology at Elizabethtown College (Pa.). Kraybill also directs the Young Center for the Study of Anabaptist and Pietist Groups at Elizabethtown College.

WILLIAM C. LINDHOLM has chaired the National Committee for Amish Religious Freedom since its inception in 1967. He has been an active spokesman for a variety of religious liberty issues involving the Amish. He is a graduate of the Lutheran School of Theology, Chicago and is pastor of the Holy Cross Evangelical Lutheran Church in Livonia, Michigan.

THOMAS J. MEYERS taught in an Amish school in Indiana before receiving his Ph.D. degree in sociology at Boston University. His dissertation, as well as a variety of journal articles, deals with social change among the Amish. He is professor of sociology at Goshen College (Ind.).

MARC A. OLSHAN received his Ph.D. degree in the sociology of development from Cornell University, where he wrote his dissertation on the Old Order Amish. He is associate professor of sociology at Alfred University (N.Y.) and has published widely on the Amish in journals such as *Rural Sociology, Human Organization,* and *Social Forces.*

ELIZABETH PLACE received a B.A. degree from Swarthmore College and graduated from the Dickinson School of Law. She is an associate with the law firm of Ball, Skelly, Murren & Connell (Harrisburg, Pa.). Attorney Place has been involved in a variety of environmental legal issues involving Amish communities.

DENNIS L THOMSON received his Ph.D. degree in political science from the University of California, Santa Barbara. He has published widely on public policy and church-state issues. He teaches political science at Brigham Young University (Utah), where he also served as associate academic vice-president.

PATON YODER, whose forebears were nineteenth-century Amish, received his Ph.D. degree from Indiana University. He served as dean of Hesston College (Kans.) and taught history at Taylor University (Ind.) and Malone College (Ohio). In addition to two other books on the Amish, Yoder is author of *Tradition and Transition: Amish Mennonites and Old Order Amish, 1800-1900* (Herald Press, 1991).

LEE J. ZOOK grew up in a Pennsylvania Amish community. He earned a B.A. degree from Eastern Mennonite College and a Ph.D. degree from Case Western Reserve University and serves as associate professor of social work at Luther College (Iowa). An expert witness in court for the Amish, he is currently investigating their patterns of mutual aid.

Index